BOYD'S COMMENTARY

for the

Sunday School

2013–2014

VOLUME ONE HUNDRED NINE
STRICTLY ORTHODOX AND
PURELY BAPTISTIC

These commentaries are based on the International Uniform Sunday School Lesson Outlines, copyrighted by the Division of Christian Education, the National Council of the Churches of Christ in the U.S.A., and used by permission.

Entered according to Act of Congress in the Office of Librarian of Congress in the year 1903 at Washington, D.C. by R.H. Boyd, D.D., LL.D.

R. H. Boyd, D.D., LL.D., Founder (1896-1922)

H. A. Boyd, D.D. (1922-1959)

T. B. Boyd, Jr., D.D. (1959-1979)

T. B. Boyd III, D.D., LL.D.,
President/CEO (1979-Present)

A GLOBAL NAME IN PUBLISHING FOR OVER 100 YEARS

An R.H.Boyd Company

www.rhboydpublishing.com

T. B. Boyd III, D.D., LL.D.
President/CEO

David Groves, D.Min., Ph.D.
Director of Publications

Clifford Thomas
Director of Operations

Tiffany Dobson
Director of Marketing

Neil Cumming
Director of Finance

EDITORIAL STAFF:
Jennifer Moorman, B.A., B.S.
(Coordinator)
Christina Zimmerman, D.Ed.Min.
(Associate Editor)
Jared Austin, B.A., M.A.
Christopher R. Cotten, B.A., M.A.
Tia Ferrell, B.A.
Jane Ann Kenney, B.A.
Joshua McArthur, B.S., M.Div.
Aaron Johnson, B.A.
Vanessa Lewis, B.A.
Freida Crawley, B.S.
Carla Davis, B.A.
Frank DiLella

Dr. Tony F. Drayton
Dr. Peter Dare
Dr. Robert J. Holmes
Writers

Melissa Phillips
Cover Design

R.H. Boyd Publishing Corporation
6717 Centennial Blvd.
Nashville, Tennessee 37209-1017

• •

**For Customer Service
and Toll-Free Ordering, Call
1-877-4RHBOYD (474-2693)
Monday - Friday
8 a.m. - 5 p.m. Central Time or
Fax Toll-Free (800) 615-1815**

A WORD FROM THE PUBLISHER

Welcome to the *2013–2014 Boyd's Commentary for the Sunday School*.

Within these pages, pastors, deacons, Sunday school teachers, and laypersons will find strong scholarly insight and interpretation to enhance their ministry and personal relationship with God. Using only the most academically qualified and gifted writers, we at R.H. Boyd Publishing Company believe this commentary offers great readability and accessibility without compromising its level of scholarly excellence. Also, the writers chosen for this commentary have extensive ministerial backgrounds, so they are able to incorporate their experience and expertise into their work for this commentary.

R.H. Boyd Publishing Corporation is also proud to have an accomplished team of editors who takes great pride in its ability to polish and refine the already stellar work submitted by the writers. Together, both the writers and editors have produced a final product that is worthy to bear the R.H. Boyd Publishing Corporation name and one that seeks to bring glory and honor to God.

Our earnest expectation is that this edition of the *Boyd's Commentary for the Sunday School* will continue the tradition of excellence of commentaries past. We also hope that this book will be a useful tool for developing better disciples for the Kingdom of God.

Grace and peace to you,

Dr. T. B. Boyd III
President/CEO

A WORD FROM THE DIRECTOR

It is a privilege for me to present to you the 2013-2014 edition of *Boyd's Commentary for the Sunday School*. Now in its 109th year, *Boyd's Commentary* has a solid reputation for providing biblical commentary that is committed to the truth of God's Word and to the enduring value of that Word in addressing the problems of humanity. As in previous years, each lesson seeks to strike a balance between detailed exposition of the Scripture for the week and concern for how to better embody the teachings of Scripture in everyday life. Moreover, thoughtful attention is given to the manifold ways in which Scripture intersects with the social and ethical concerns that characterize the increasingly diverse and globalized society in which we live.

Designed especially for the needs of busy pastors, deacons, Sunday school teachers, and lay Bible students, *Boyd's Commentary* guides the reader to probe beneath the surface of the biblical text, uncovering truths of exegetical and theological insight. Indeed, it has been designed to be a one-stop resource for help with sermon and class preparation. *Boyd's Commentary* includes extensive bibliographies and supplementary Hebrew and Greek terms that complement the edifying lessons themselves. It is my hope, as we place this resource in your hands, that it will do much good for the Kingdom of God. May your ministry be blessed as you "proclaim the message…whether the time is favorable or unfavorable" (2 Tim. 4:2, NRSV).

Rev. David Groves, D.Min., Ph.D.

NOTE FROM THE EDITOR

The layout of the *2013–2014 Commentary* has been formatted for easy use in the classroom. In keeping with our rich history of publishing quality Christian literature, the Unifying Principle is one helpful feature that enhances our commentary. Listed below is an explanation of all features and their intended use.

Lesson Setting: Gives the basic timeline and place for the events in the lesson.

Lesson Outline: Provides the topics used in the exposition of the lesson.

Unifying Principle: States the main idea for the lesson across age groups. This feature allows the teacher to understand exactly what each lesson is about.

Introduction: Gives the thesis and also any background information that will be useful in the study of the lesson.

Exposition: Provides the exegetical study done by the writer, breaking down the text for discussion.

The Lesson Applied: Provides possible life applications of the biblical text for today's learners.

Let's Talk About It: Highlights ideas from within the text in a question-and-answer format.

Home Daily Devotional Readings: Located at the end of each lesson, the topics are designed to lead into the following lesson.

Know Your Writers

Dr. Tony F. Drayton

Dr. Tony F. Drayton resides in West Palm Beach, Florida. He earned his B.A. in Psychology from Pfeiffer University, Misenheimer, North Carolina; M. Div. from Florida Center for Theological Studies, Miami, Florida; D.Min. from Colgate Rochester Crozer Divinity School, Rochester, New York; and completed a two-year internship in clinical pastoral education at Good Samaritan Medical Center, West Palm Beach, Florida.

Dr. Drayton is the pastor of St. James Church in Riviera Beach, Florida. He is an adjunct professor for Moody Bible Institute and works with numerous local and national groups to serve and promote positive transformation. Dr. Drayton authored *Transformation and the Church: A Push Toward Acceptance Within the HIV/AIDS Pandemic*.

Rev. Dr. Peter Dare

The son of West African immigrants, Rev. Dr. Peter Dare was born and raised in Montreal. After graduating from McGill University in Montreal with a degree in philosophy, Rev. Dare completed studies in theology at Emmanuel College, University of Toronto, which awarded him the M.T.S. with honors. He then went on to complete the M.Phil. and Ph.D. degrees at Durham University in the United Kingdom. His dissertation compared rival understandings of the virtues in Stoic philosophy and the letters of the Apostle Peter. While at Durham, he was blessed to participate in joint Anglican-Baptist dialogue. After graduation, Rev. Dare returned to Canada, where he was ordained by the United Church of Canada. Presently, he serves as the pastor of a congregation in the Malvern neighborhood of Toronto, where he lives with his wife Marie and their son, Thomas. Rev. Dare also enjoys the work he does on the board of a local rescue mission.

Dr. Robert J. Holmes

Dr. Robert J. Holmes is a native of Detroit, Michigan, but he currently resides in Hempstead, New York. Dr. Holmes attended Western Michigan University and earned a bachelor's degree in History. For his post-graduate work, he attended Southeastern Baptist Theological Seminary in Wake Forest, North Carolina, where he earned Master of Theology and Doctor of Ministry degrees. Dr. Holmes is a member of several ministry outreach programs that seek to help the homeless and destitute. He believes strongly in reaching out to the disenfranchised, which is evident in the active role he plays in his church's homeless missions. Among his many interests are kayaking, hiking, golfing, and educating others on the ways of Jesus Christ.

2013-2014 LESSON OVERVIEW

Four major themes are explored in this year's commentary. The first theme is "First Things" (September—November 2013), which examines the story of creation from Psalm 104 and the earliest chapters of Genesis. The patriarchs are also studied as well as some of the events surrounding the Exodus. The second theme for the commentary is "Jesus and the Just Reign of God" (December 2013—February 2014). For this theme, the events immediately preceding and following Jesus' birth are explored. Also, several lessons follow that cover the just treatment of men and women to one another in the Kingdom of God. "Jesus' Fulfillment of Scripture" (March—May 2014) is the third theme of the commentary. This quarter involves a look at some of the prophecies Christ brought to pass during His ministry on earth. Finally, the fourth theme is "The People of God Set Priorities" (June—August 2014). This quarter includes an in-depth analysis of the book of Haggai as well as Zechariah 4. A study of the two letters Paul wrote to the church at Corinth will conclude the commentary.

• •

Boyd's Commentary for the Sunday School 2013–2014

Copyright © 2013 by R.H. Boyd Publishing Corporation
6717 Centennial Blvd.
Nashville, TN 37209-1017

Scripture passages marked KJV are taken from the Holy Bible, *King James Version*. Scripture passages marked NIV are taken from the Holy Bible, *New International Version*. Copyright © 1984 by International Bible Society. Scripture passages marked ASV are taken from the Holy Bible, *American Standard Version*. Used by permission of Zondervan Publishing House. All rights reserved.

Scriptures taken from the *New Revised Standard Version of the Bible* © 1989 by the Division of Christian Education of the National Council of Churches of Christ in the United States of America. Used by permission. All rights reserved.

The "NIV" and "New Revised Standard Version" trademarks are registered in the United States Patent and Trademark Office by International Bible Society. Use of either trademark requires the permission of the International Bible Society.

Printed in the United States of America.

PREFACE

The *2013–2014 Boyd's Commentary* has been formatted and written with you in mind. This format is to help you further your preparation and study of the Sunday school lessons.

We have presented a parallel Scripture lesson passage with the *New Revised Standard Version* alongside the *King James Version*. This allows you to have a clearer and more contemporary approach to the Scripture. This version is very reliable and reputable. It will bless you as you "rightly [divide] the word of truth" (2 Tim. 2:15, KJV).

These lessons have a new look, but they still have the same accurate interpretation, concise Christian doctrine, and competent, skilled scholarship.

The abbreviations used throughout the commentary are as follows:

KJV — King James Version
NIV — New International Version
NRSV — New Revised Standard Version
RSV — Revised Standard Version

To the pastor: It is our hope that this commentary will provide context and insight for your sermons. Also, we hope this commentary will serve as a preparatory aid for the message of God.

To the Bible teacher: This commentary also has you in mind. It can be used as a ready reference to the background of the text and difficult terms that are used in the Bible. To be sure, this commentary will provide your lesson study with the historical context that will enable you to better interpret the text for your students.

Lastly, this text is for anyone who wants to get a glimpse at the glory of God. This commentary seeks to highlight and lift the workings of God with His people and to make God's history with humanity ever present.

We hope and pray that God will bless you and keep you as you diligently study His mighty and majestic Word. Remain ever steadfast to our one eternal God. Keep the faith and pray always.

CONTENTS

FIRST QUARTER

UNIT THEME: FIRST DAYS

UNIT THEME: FIRST NATION

UNIT THEME: FIRST FREEDOM

CONTENTS

SECOND QUARTER

UNIT THEME: GOD SENDS JESUS

UNIT THEME: JESUS USHERS IN THE REIGN OF GOD

UNIT THEME: LIVE JUSTLY IN THE REIGN OF GOD

CONTENTS

CONTENTS

FOURTH QUARTER

UNIT THEME: HOPE AND CONFIDENCE COME FROM GOD

UNIT THEME: LIVING AS A COMMUNITY OF BELIEVERS

UNIT THEME: BEARING ONE ANOTHER'S BURDENS

*For a full bibliography of sources used, please consult the accompanying CD.

First Quarter

Lesson material is based on International Sunday School Lessons and International Bible Lessons for Christian Teaching. Copyrighted by the International Council of Religious Education and is used by its permission.

SEPTEMBER, OCTOBER, NOVEMBER 2013

WRITER: DR. TONY F. DRAYTON

Suggested Opening Exercises

1. **Usual Signal for Beginning**
2. **Prayer:**
   (Closing with the Lord's Prayer)
3. **Singing:**
   (Song to Be Selected)
4. **Scripture Reading:**
   Psalm 104:1-9 (KJV)

Director: Bless the LORD, O my soul, O LORD my God, thou art very great; thou art clothed with honour and majesty. Who coverest thyself with light as with a garment: who stretchest out the heavens like a curtain:

School: Who layeth the beams of his chambers in the waters: who maketh the clouds his chariot: who walketh upon the wings of the wind:

Director: Who maketh his angels spirits; his ministers a flaming fire:

School: Who laid the foundations of the earth, that it should not be removed for ever.

Director: Thou coveredst it with the deep as with a garment: the waters stood above the mountains.

School: At thy rebuke they fled; at the voice of thy thunder they hasted away.

Director: They go up by the mountains; they go down by the valleys unto the place which thou hast founded for them.

All: Thou hast set a bound that they may not pass over; that they turn not again to cover the earth.

Recitation in Concert:
Colossians 1:15-18 (KJV)

15 [Jesus Christ] is the image of the invisible God, the firstborn of every creature:

16 For by him were all things created, that are in heaven, and that are in earth, visible and invisible, whether they be thrones, or dominions, or principalities, or powers: all things were created by him, and for him:

17 And he is before all things, and by him all things consist.

18 And he is the head of the body, the church: who is the beginning, the firstborn from the dead; that in all things he might have the preeminence.

Closing Work

1. **Singing**
2. **Sentences:**
   Genesis 1:31—2:3 (KJV)

31 And God saw everything that he had made, and, behold, it was very good. And the evening and the morning were the sixth day.

1 Thus the heavens and the earth were finished, and all the host of them.

2 And on the seventh day God ended his work which he had made; and he rested on the seventh day from all his work which he had made.

3 And God blessed the seventh day, and sanctified it: because that in it he had rested from all his work which God created and made.

3. **Dismissal with Prayer**

GOD CREATES

ADULT TOPIC:	BACKGROUND SCRIPTURE:
EVERYTHING WE NEED	PSALM 104

PSALM 104:5-9, 24-30

King James Version

Who laid the foundations of the earth, that it should not be removed for ever.

6 Thou coveredst it with the deep as with a garment: the waters stood above the mountains.

7 At thy rebuke they fled; at the voice of thy thunder they hasted away.

8 They go up by the mountains; they go down by the valleys unto the place which thou hast founded for them.

9 Thou hast set a bound that they may not pass over; that they turn not again to cover the earth.

. . . . . .

24 O LORD, how manifold are thy works! in wisdom hast thou made them all: the earth is full of thy riches.

25 So is this great and wide sea, wherein are things creeping innumerable, both small and great beasts.

26 There go the ships: there is that leviathan, whom thou hast made to play therein.

27 These wait all upon thee; that thou mayest give them their meat in due season.

28 That thou givest them they gather: thou openest thine hand, they are filled with good.

29 Thou hidest thy face, they are troubled: thou takest away their breath, they die, and return to their dust.

30 Thou sendest forth thy spirit, they are created: and thou renewest the face of the earth.

New Revised Standard Version

YOU set the earth on its foundations, so that it shall never be shaken.

6 You cover it with the deep as with a garment; the waters stood above the mountains.

7 At your rebuke they flee; at the sound of your thunder they take to flight.

8 They rose up to the mountains, ran down to the valleys to the place that you appointed for them.

9 You set a boundary that they may not pass, so that they might not again cover the earth.

. . . . . .

24 O LORD, how manifold are your works! In wisdom you have made them all; the earth is full of your creatures.

25 Yonder is the sea, great and wide, creeping things innumerable are there, living things both small and great.

26 There go the ships, and Leviathan that you formed to sport in it.

27 These all look to you to give them their food in due season;

28 when you give to them, they gather it up; when you open your hand, they are filled with good things.

29 When you hide your face, they are dismayed; when you take away their breath, they die and return to their dust.

30 When you send forth your spirit, they are created; and you renew the face of the ground.

MAIN THOUGHT: O LORD, how manifold are thy works! in wisdom hast thou made them all: the earth is full of thy riches. (Psalm 104:24, KJV)

LESSON SETTING
    Time: Unknown
    Place: Unknown

LESSON OUTLINE
  I. **God Created the Earth (Psalm 104:5-9)**
  II. **God's Manifold Works (Psalm 104:24-26)**
  III. **God Sustains His Creation (Psalm 104:27-30)**

UNIFYING PRINCIPLE

All humans have some basic needs that must be supplied in order to sustain their daily lives. Where can Christians find a reliable source to assist them in acquiring what is needed? The psalmist tells the reader that God's hands are full to overflowing with the resources needed by everything God created.

INTRODUCTION

Our study for this quarter is a study of beginnings, of firsts, in the Bible. Through a series of lessons from Genesis and Exodus, we will emphasize God's role as Creator of the world and of humanity, certainly, but we will also see Him as the Creator of a new nation, a people for His own possession. Before we get there, though, we will open this quarter with a study of Psalm 104. This might seem odd at first glance. After all, if we are going to be studying texts from the book of Genesis, why not begin with the creation account found in Genesis 1? We could certainly do that. But we want to draw on other texts that affirm God's creation and that display the power and grandeur of it. This text, in particular, will show us how later generations of Israelites remembered and praised God's creative work.

Very little is known about the origins and sources of Psalm 104. It is immediately apparent, even to the casual reader, that the language of this psalm is reminiscent of the language of Genesis 1. But we should not press this connection too far. Others have noticed similarities between the language of this psalm and the hymn to Aten composed by Egyptian pharaoh Amenhotep IV (or Akhenaten; reigned ca. 1379-1362 B.C.). Influence in either direction between these two works cannot be proven, though.

Perhaps more fruitful for the purposes of this commentary is a canonical reading of Psalm 104. In particular, there are important connections that can be made when Psalms 103 and 104 are read together. Both psalms—the only two in the corpus—begin with an exhortation to "bless the LORD" (Pss. 103:1, 22; 104:1, 35, KJV). With regard to content, Psalm 104 expands upon the proclamation of God's reign found in Psalm 103, especially verses 19-22. God, according to Psalm 103, "rules over all" (v. 19, NRSV); Psalm 104 elaborates on this point (see vv. 24, 27). Both psalms focus on God's "works" (Pss. 103:22; 104:24, NRSV). All of these similarities between the two psalms also help us to see more clearly the difference in emphasis between the two. Psalm 104, as we will see, focuses primarily on God's creative work; Psalm 103 on His saving work, most especially His mercy and love (see vv. 4, 8, 11, 13, 17); (J. C. McCann Jr., "The Book of Psalms" in *The New Interpreter's Bible*, Vol. 4 [Nashville: Abingdon Press, 1998], 1096).

All of this has led to the suggestion that these two psalms may have been written as a pair by the same person. That is possible, but we cannot be certain. Likewise, the theory that these two psalms were composed for use in temple worship (perhaps during the celebration of the New Year's Festival) is attractive, but cannot be proven. At any rate, let us now turn to the text.

EXPOSITION

I. GOD CREATED THE EARTH (PSALM 104:5-9)

Psalm 104 opens with a resounding affirmation of God's power and sovereignty over the entire earth. What the psalm affirms is probably best understood against the background in which it was written. In the ancient Near East, especially in the agrarian societies of Israel and Syria, the worship of the storm god, Baal, was a prominent part of daily life. People depended upon rain for the sustenance of their crops, and Baal was understood to be the bringer of storms. In Canaanite and Babylonian mythology, creation was explained in terms of a conflict among the gods. El, the supreme deity, intended to appoint Yamm (the god of the sea, with the sea understood to be a chaotic and threatening force) to be the king of the earth. Yamm, seeking to press his advantage, sent messengers to El demanding that Baal be delivered over to him as a captive. This, of course, angered Baal. So Baal went to battle with Yamm and defeated him, in the process becoming the king of the earth himself.

With that story in mind, we can now see how Psalm 104 responds to the myth of Baal. First, God Himself is the Creator of the entire world: "He set the earth on its foundations; it can never be moved" (v. 5, NIV). That is to say, it cannot be shaken by rivalries among the gods. The psalmist continues, "You covered [the earth] with the deep [Heb. *tehom*] as with a garment; the waters stood above the mountains" (v. 6, NIV). There is probably an intentional play on words in this verse: The Hebrew word translated *deep* is also the name of a Babylonian deity. In other words, the psalmist wants us to know that the deep is not a rival god to Yahweh. Yahweh treats the deep as something of little consequence. It is no threat whatsoever to His sovereignty and control over creation.

What comes next emphasizes the point: "But at your rebuke the waters fled, at the sound of your thunder they took to flight; they flowed over the mountains, they went down into the valleys, to the place you assigned for them" (vv. 7-8, NIV). God, unlike Baal, does not answer to any other deity (recall that Baal is subordinate to El in the Canaanite myth). His Word alone arrested the power of the water, the power of chaos. It was not necessary for the God of Israel to fight as Baal had done; He had only to "rebuke" (ibid.) the waters and they fled like a defeated warrior (cf. Isa. 50:2; Nah. 1:4). Moreover, they "flowed … to the place [God] assigned for them" (ibid.). A key marker of God's creation over the creation stories told about Baal is its sheer orderliness. Needless to say, this is a far cry from the violence and brutality of the Canaanite and Babylonian creation accounts.

The first portion of today's Scripture passage closes with a reference to a different point in time: "You set a boundary they cannot cross; never again will they cover the earth" (v. 9, NIV). The ancient Israelites were not a seagoing people. They viewed the sea as a chaotic and terrifying thing. (For one very prominent example, consider the story of Jonah.) On only one occasion did God loosen His tight control on the chaotic waters. In the time of Noah, He sent a flood to destroy the inhabitants of the earth because of their wickedness. This would have been a terrible memory for the people of Israel. The psalmist calls to their minds God's promise, symbolized by the rainbow, never to destroy the earth by water again (see Gen. 9:8-17). As in the earlier portions of this psalm, there is a great concern for order and stability.

II. GOD'S MANIFOLD WORKS (PSALM 104:24-26)

After going on at great length and with vivid descriptions of God's mighty works, the psalmist exclaims, "How many are your works, O LORD! In wisdom you made them all; the earth is full of your creatures" (v. 24, NIV). As to the function of this verse in the psalm as a whole, Clinton McCann notes, "[Verse] 24 is an exclamatory summary of vv. 1-23. *Everything* derives from God. The heavens, the earth, plants, animals, people—God made them all, and the whole creation is a witness to God's wisdom (see Prov. 3:19; 8:22-31; Jer. 10:21)" (1098; emphasis in original). McCann rightly calls our attention to Proverbs 8, where Wisdom is personified as a woman who was present with God at the creation. The emphasis here is on the sheer richness of God's creation, as well as its unity and order.

The next two verses bring us back to the sea: "There is the sea, vast and spacious, teeming with creatures beyond number— living things both large and small. There the ships go to and fro, and the leviathan, which you formed to frolic there" (vv. 25-26, NIV). Writing about these verses, Brueggemann observes, "God is known to be confident, serene, and at ease. The metaphor for this is 'the sea' (v. 25). Conventionally the sea is [an] expression of dread and intense threat.

Here the sea is God's plaything in which the great sea monster serves only for God's peculiar amusement.… Elsewhere the sea monster is an embodiment of evil" (Walter Brueggemann, *The Message of the Psalms* [Minneapolis: Augsburg, 1984], 32). The "sea monster" of which Brueggemann speaks is, of course, Leviathan. Leviathan is well represented in extant ancient Near Eastern texts. John McLaughlin notes that Leviathan appears in the Ugaritic texts from Ras-Shamra as *Lītānū*. These texts, dating to the fourteenth century B.C., describe how Baal struck down Lītānū, "the twisting serpent, the tyrant with seven heads" ("Leviathan" in *Eerdmans Dictionary of the Bible* [Grand Rapids: Eerdmans, 2000], 803). The psalmist draws on those terrifying images to make an even greater claim about the God of Israel. For God, this terrifying monster is no more than a plaything, perhaps a bit like the rubber ducky that one might have in his or her bathtub. God is sovereign over all of His creation; Leviathan is no threat to Him.

III. GOD SUSTAINS HIS CREATION (PSALM 104:27-30)

The final verses of today's text remind the reader that God sustains His creation. He does not simply create and then step away from His creation. As Bernard W. Anderson has argued, "Creation is not just an event that occurred in the beginning, at the foundation of the earth, but is God's continuing activity of sustaining creatures and holding everything in being" (cited in Terence E. Fretheim, *God and World in the Old Testament: A Relational Theology of Creation* [Nashville: Abingdon Press, 2005], 7). To say that He sustains His creation is to say that creation is an ongoing work. It is not a one-time occurrence; it is part of who God is.

Every creature depends on God for food and every other kind of sustenance: "These all look to you to give them their food at the proper time. When you give it to them, they gather it up; when you open your hand, they are satisfied with good things" (vv. 27-28, NIV). There are allusions to Israel's wilderness experience here, especially the gathering of manna. Conversely, the psalmist acknowledges what happens when God withdraws His sustaining hand: "When you hide your face, they are terrified; when you take away their breath, they die and return to the dust" (v. 29, NIV).

The final verse of today's text may perhaps be a bit confusing. It should be noted here that the words *breath* (v. 29) and *Spirit* (v. 30) translate the same Hebrew word, *ruach*. As McCann notes, "The words 'breath' and 'spirit' (the capitalization in the NIV should be avoided) are the same Hebrew word.... The vocabulary—'breath'/'spirit,' 'dust,' 'created,' 'ground'—recalls Genesis 1—2. The breath of the creatures is not identical to God's breath, but God is responsible for giving life to the creatures" (1099).

THE LESSON APPLIED

Today's text invites us to join in its praise to God for His creation. It demonstrates that God cares for us and that He has ordered the creation to His glory. It shows us, further, that God cares for the totality of His creation, creatures both great and small, even as He has placed humanity at the pinnacle of that creation. We are created in His image, and we are called to be stewards of His good creation.

LET'S TALK ABOUT IT

1. How can we acknowledge God's creation in our worship?

We are called, of course, to be good stewards of God's creation, to care for and protect, to refrain from abusing it. Have you ever considered, though, how we acknowledge God's continuing work of creation in our worship? Naturally, in our reading of Scripture and in our prayers, we thank Him for the beauty of His creation and for the fact that He gives us life: good food to eat, sunshine and rain, shelter, etc. But there are other aspects of worship that point to God's creative work. Consider how, in baptism, water (a symbol of chaos in Genesis 1 and Psalm 104) becomes a symbol of new life, sanctified by the Spirit. Think also about how we are blessed to draw near to Christ through the simple means of bread and the fruit of the vine in the Lord's Supper. In the Supper, we offer up to God these good things that He has created for a greater purpose.

HOME DAILY DEVOTIONAL READINGS
SEPTEMBER 2–8, 2013

MONDAY	TUESDAY	WEDNESDAY	THURSDAY	FRIDAY	SATURDAY	SUNDAY
Living Creatures of Every Kind	Made in the Image of God	Formed from the Dust	In the Likeness of God	Made a Little Lower than God	Created in the Likeness of God	Created Male and Female
Genesis 1:20-25	Genesis 1:26-31	Genesis 2:1-9	Genesis 5:1-5	Psalm 8	Ephesians 4:17-24	Genesis 2:18-25

GOD'S IMAGE: MALE AND FEMALE

ADULT TOPIC:	BACKGROUND SCRIPTURES:
LOVE AND MARRIAGE	GENESIS 1—2; 5:1–2

GENESIS 2:18-25

King James Version

And the LORD God said, It is not good that the man should be alone; I will make him an help meet for him.

19 And out of the ground the LORD God formed every beast of the field, and every fowl of the air; and brought them unto Adam to see what he would call them: and whatsoever Adam called every living creature, that was the name thereof.

20 And Adam gave names to all cattle, and to the fowl of the air, and to every beast of the field; but for Adam there was not found an help meet for him.

21 And the LORD God caused a deep sleep to fall upon Adam, and he slept: and he took one of his ribs, and closed up the flesh instead thereof;

22 And the rib, which the LORD God had taken from man, made he a woman, and brought her unto the man.

23 And Adam said, This is now bone of my bones, and flesh of my flesh: she shall be called Woman, because she was taken out of Man.

24 Therefore shall a man leave his father and his mother, and shall cleave unto his wife: and they shall be one flesh.

25 And they were both naked, the man and his wife, and were not ashamed.

New Revised Standard Version

THEN the LORD God said, "It is not good that the man should be alone; I will make him a helper as his partner."

19 So out of the ground the LORD God formed every animal of the field and every bird of the air, and brought them to the man to see what he would call them; and whatever the man called every living creature, that was its name.

20 The man gave names to all cattle, and to the birds of the air, and to every animal of the field; but for the man there was not found a helper as his partner.

21 So the LORD God caused a deep sleep to fall upon the man, and he slept; then he took one of his ribs and closed up its place with flesh.

22 And the rib that the LORD God had taken from the man he made into a woman and brought her to the man.

23 Then the man said, "This at last is bone of my bones and flesh of my flesh; this one shall be called Woman, for out of Man this one was taken."

24 Therefore a man leaves his father and his mother and clings to his wife, and they become one flesh.

25 And the man and his wife were both naked, and were not ashamed.

MAIN THOUGHT: And the LORD God said, It is not good that the man should be alone; I will make him an help meet for him. (Genesis 2:18, KJV)

LESSON SETTING
    Time: Unknown
    Place: Garden of Eden

LESSON OUTLINE
    I. Man's Lack of Companionship
       (Genesis 2:18)
    II. The Naming of the Animals
       (Genesis 2:19-20)
    III. One Flesh
       (Genesis 2:21-25)

UNIFYING PRINCIPLE

Finding a suitable companion with whom one can share life can be a struggle, but it can also bring great joy. How does one find a suitable partner? According to Genesis 2, God created Eve as a partner for Adam.

INTRODUCTION

As was pointed out last week, we are focusing in this quarter on a series of firsts found in the books of Genesis and Exodus. We will encounter a series of firsts over the next three months. Today's lesson will focus on the first man, his loneliness and need for a helper, God's creation of woman, and His intent for male-female relationships.

Before we turn to today's text, however, we need to address some introductory matters concerning the book of Genesis as a whole: the book's title, author, date, and so on. Speaking to the book's title, Mathews writes the following: "The English title 'Genesis' is derived from Jerome's Vulgate, *Liber Genesis*. This Latin name followed the Greek (Septuagint) title, which probably was taken from [Genesis] 2:4a where a form (genitive plural) of *genesis* ('source, birth, generation') renders Hebrew [*tolĕdot*]" (Kenneth A. Mathews, *Genesis 1—11:26* [Nashville: Broadman & Holman, 1996], 41). For the purposes of our study in Genesis, we should also point out that it was common practice among the ancient Hebrews to call a book by its opening words. Thus, they referred to the first book of the Torah as *bereshit* (Eng. "in the beginning"). This is how it appears in modern Hebrew Bibles.

Among the more hotly contested matters in Old Testament scholarship over the past two centuries has been the authorship of the Torah. These five books have traditionally been attributed to Moses. The books themselves, of course, do not name an author; they are, *sensu stricto*, anonymous. Moreover, there are parts of the books—most notably, the account of Moses' death—that simply could not have been written by Moses himself. Considerations such as these led European scholars during the eighteenth century, especially in Germany, to question Mosaic authorship *in toto*. The nineteenth century witnessed the rise of *Formgeschichte* (i.e., Form Criticism) and what is commonly referred to as the documentary hypothesis. In brief, the documentary hypothesis posited that the Torah was made up of at least four separate documents composed by different authors at different points in Israel's history. These documents, furthermore, embodied sometimes rival theologies of creation and of the place of the Law in Israelite society. This view held sway in Old Testament scholarship for much of the twentieth century.

There have always been dissenters from this position, to be sure. For a long time, conservative commentators focused their efforts on mounting a defense of Mosaic authorship. More recently, with the rise of the narrative and canonical modes of criticism, attention has shifted to the canonical form of the text (i.e., the text as we find it in our Bibles). This makes good sense, of course. After all, what we have received is the final form of the text. While it might be interesting to speculate about how that text came together, such speculation is ultimately irrelevant to the task at hand. Kenneth A. Mathews puts it well: We must not allow ourselves, he writes, to "be distracted by incessant attention to actual or putative literary sources as commentaries on Genesis often do.... We are satisfied that Genesis in its present, final form is a cohesive unit that shows thoughtful order and a self-consistent theology" (24). With that, we turn to today's text.

EXPOSITION

I. MAN'S LACK OF COMPANIONSHIP (GENESIS 2:18)

The Genesis account of creation reveals a God who is our Provider and Sustainer. We see this readily in the first chapter of Genesis. God, with the sound of His voice, made everything that humanity had need of for life: the light and warmth of the sun, the division of day and night, the division of the sea from the dry land, the fruit-bearing trees and plants for food, the birds, fish, and the creatures that dwell on land. Finally, He created us in His own image. All of this, He declared to be good, even "very good" (Gen. 1:31, NRSV).

Chapter two opens by looking at the creation from a different angle. As Brueggemann notes, "After the cosmic assertion of [Genesis] 1:1—2:4a, this text focuses on human persons as the glory and central problem of creation.... Delightful creation is finished ... Now human destiny in that world must be faced" (Walter Brueggemann, *Genesis*, Paperback Ed. [Louisville, KY: Westminster John Knox Press, 2010], 40). Human destiny, he argues, is to live in God's world, to rule over and care for God's other creatures, and to do so on God's own terms (ibid.). In Genesis 2, God calls the man to "till [the garden] and keep it" (Gen. 2:15, NRSV),

giving him the freedom to live out that calling (see v. 16). At the same time, He also hands down a simple prohibition: "You must not eat from the tree of the knowledge of good and evil, for when you eat of it you will surely die" (v. 17, NIV).

That brings us to today's text, in which we encounter an unexpected problem: "Then the LORD God said, 'It is not good that the man should be alone; I will make him a helper as his partner'" (v. 18, NRSV). Heretofore, everything about creation has been good and has had a sense of completeness about it. Now we see that something is wrong. As Wenham notes, "Against the sevenfold refrain of 'and God saw that it was (very) good' in chap. 1, the divine observation that something was not right with man's situation is startling" (Gordon Wenham, *Genesis 1—15* [Nashville: Thomas Nelson, 1987], 68). The writer's language and syntax serve to emphasize the seriousness of the situation: The Hebrew text places the words *not good* at the very beginning of the verse (Mathews, 213).

Likewise, the structure of this passage serves to emphasize the place of this helper in creation. As Mathews notes, Genesis 2's "full description of the woman's creation is unique to the cosmogonies of the ancient Near East. The Hebrews' lofty estimation of womanhood and its place in creation was not widely held by ancient civilizations" (212). The Genesis account is structured to highlight this "lofty estimation." After observing the man's need, God immediately declares His intent to make "a helper as his partner" (NRSV) or "a helper suitable for him" (NIV). Both of these translations are preferable, for contemporary ears, to the KJV's "an help meet for him." (Notice that *help meet* is two words, not one. Furthermore, because *meet* as an adjective is a word that is increasingly falling out of use in American English, many students are likely to miss the point that the text is trying to make.) The word *helper* (Heb. *ezer*) implies no subordinate or inferior status. What, then, does it mean? According to Mathews, "The term means 'help' in the sense of aid or support and is used of the Lord's aiding his people in the face of enemies (Pss. 20:2[3]; 121:1-2; 124:8).... 'Helper'... means the woman will play an integral part, in this case, in human survival and success. What the man lacks, the woman accomplishes" (214).

Mathews further points out that calling the woman "suitable" (NIV; Heb. *kenegdo*) "indicates a *correspondence* between the man and the woman. The focus [of the word] is on the equality of the two in terms of their essential constitution" (213). A suitable helper would help the man in every way: "Of such a help the man stood in need, in order that he might fulfill his calling, not only to perpetuate and multiply his race, but to cultivate and govern the earth" (C. F. Keil and Franz Delitzsch, *The Pentateuch*, Reprint Ed. [Peabody, MA: Hendrickson, 1996], 54). This means that the woman's given role as a helper would not be limited, for example, simply to childbearing or to tending the garden. It would be far more expansive than that. Together, the man and woman would serve as stewards and cultivators of God's good creation. Together, Adam and Eve would serve as regents over His creation.

II. THE NAMING OF THE ANIMALS (GENESIS 2:19-20)

But all of that is anticipation. We are not told at this point what form the helper will take, only that the man was in need of a helper. God's initial response to this need might seem odd to us. He does not just rush in to fix the problem. There is a delay. From a literary perspective, this delay serves to heighten our sense of the man's loneliness and the obviousness of his need. In a way that is perhaps analogous to the delay of Jesus after He heard the news of Lazarus' death (see John 11), the delay in this instance was also "for God's glory" (John 11:4, NIV).

The text reminds us that "the LORD God had formed out of the ground all the beasts of the field and all the birds of the air" (Gen. 2:19, NIV). Now, in light of man's need, God "brought them to the man to see what he would name them" (ibid.). In one sense, these creatures were like the man: they were "living creatures" (Heb. *khayyah*) that were, like him, "formed out of the ground" (ibid.). But what is the purpose of doing this? Why the delay in the story? Is it merely an interpolation into the narrative of the creation of woman? While some scholars have suggested that, it is not an adequate explanation for the function of this narrative. The naming of the animals seems to serve two purposes. First, it highlights the man's freedom and his responsibility for creation. He has been created, as we discussed above, to tend the garden and to keep it. Moreover, he has been given "dominion" (1:28, KJV) or "rule" (NIV) over every living creature. This dominion is not tyrannical in nature; it does not involve the rampant misuse and abuse of the creation. Creation, instead, is given to the man in trust.

Secondly, as Kenneth A. Mathews points out, "The animal world is a foil for the creation of the woman to distinguish her from the animals; her source is traced to the man himself and not to the 'ground.' She is the first of creation to come from a living being. God creates the man first and derives the woman from the man to insure that she is his equal in substance and to maintain the unity of the human family" (215). In other words, the account of the naming of the animals helps to magnify God's work in creating the woman. It calls attention to how special this act truly is. It emphasizes that the kind of helper that the man needed could not be found among the animals.

III. ONE FLESH
(GENESIS 2:21-25)

The final portion of today's text brings us to the climactic moment of Genesis 2 and sets the stage for what follows in Genesis 3. God's creation of the woman is special. As Walter Brueggemann has written, "None of the known elements [i.e., the animals] will suffice. There must be a newness. The good news of the episode is that the well-being of the man requires a fresh creative act of God. The emergence of woman is as stunning and unpredicted as the previous surprising emergence of the man" (47).

After the naming of the animals, man is still without a "suitable helper" (v. 20, NIV). So God acts. He "caused the man to fall into a deep sleep [Heb. *tardemah*]; and while he was sleeping, he took one of the man's ribs and closed up the place with flesh" (v. 21, NIV). How should we understand this story? Why did the man need to be asleep as the act of creation was occurring? What is the significance of the rib? In answering these questions, we must remember that this account is poetic in nature: "It is certainly mistaken to read it as an account of a clinical operation or as an attempt to explain some feature of man's anatomy" (Wenham, 69). We are not meant, in other words, to press the biological details of this account. The man's sleep serves to preserve the mystery of the event for the man (and, indeed, the mystery that still characterizes male-female relations to this day) (Mathews, 216). Moreover, "just as the rib is found at the side of the man and is attached to him, even so the good wife, the *rib* of her husband, stands at his side to be his helper-counterpart, and her soul is bound up with his" (Gordon Wenham, 69, citing Umberto Cassuto, *A Commentary on the Book of Genesis 1-11* [Jerusalem: Magnes, 1961, 1964], 134).

The next verse describes the act of creation: "Then the LORD God made a woman from the rib he had taken out of the man, and he brought her to the man" (v. 22, NIV). Of interest here is the language of the final phrase: "he brought her to the man" (ibid.). This phrasing is very similar to that found in verse nineteen in the description of God's creation of the animals. There we see that God "formed [the animals] out of the ground" and then He "brought them to the man" so that the man could name them (NIV). Just so in this account: God "made a woman from the rib … of the man" and He "brought her to the man" and the man named her (NIV). Superficially, these accounts are very similar. But, as Kenneth A. Mathews points out, this language "reinforces what the man discovers: the woman is Adam's *human* partner. A significant difference between the two passages is that the first has a stated purpose, the naming of the animals. Here, however, there is no utilitarian purpose prescribed" (218). As we hinted at earlier, the creation of the woman is about the creation of a relationship. She is not the man's servant; she is his helper. She is of the same substance he is: Adam exclaims, "'This is now bone of my bones and flesh of my flesh'" (v. 23, NIV). The story closes by stressing the unity between the two and by pointing out the unity is a defining mark of human community as God intended it. Our next lesson will address the rupture of that unity and the community built upon it.

THE LESSON APPLIED

We live in a time of great confusion and upheaval in society and in the Church over the issues discussed in today's lesson. As pastors and teachers, we undoubtedly have seen this play out in our churches, homes, and daily interactions. How do we live out God's design for male-female relationships in our churches, and—just as importantly—in our own lives? How do shifting notions of marriage and sexual morality influence us and our congregants and students? Today's text calls us to deeper

reflection on these issues. As pastors and teachers—shepherds of God's flock—it is our responsibility to Him and to them to faithfully proclaim the divine intent for human relationships.

LET'S TALK ABOUT IT

1. What does today's text say about the place of women in God's creation?

As we noted earlier, the structure of today's text places great emphasis on the creation of woman and the union of man and woman in marriage. As we noted earlier, the notion that the woman is created to be the man's "helper" (Heb. *ezer*) is not meant to imply inferiority or lesser worth on her part. Rather, the emphasis of the text is on the creation of community and the unity ("one flesh") that should characterize that community. Both man and woman contribute to that unity and its stability. The relationship between man and woman described here is the foundational form of human community, out of which all other forms grow and develop. As we will see later, in the aftermath of the Fall, that unity was destroyed (see Gen. 3:16). Both man and woman, as we will see, contributed to the destruction of unity. How do we faithfully live out God's call to unity in our relationships in a world that is severely fragmented?

HOME DAILY DEVOTIONAL READINGS
SEPTEMBER 9–15, 2013

MONDAY	TUESDAY	WEDNESDAY	THURSDAY	FRIDAY	SATURDAY	SUNDAY
Obeying God's Voice	The Blessing in Obedience	Choosing the Life of Obedience	Obeying God Above All	The Enticement to Disobey	The Punishment for Disobedience	The Consequences of Disobedience
Exodus 19:3-8	Deuteronomy 11:26-32	Deuteronomy 30:11-20	Acts 5:27-42	Genesis 3:1-7	Genesis 3:20-24	Genesis 3:8-17

KNOWLEDGE OF GOOD AND EVIL

ADULT TOPIC: CHOICES AND CONSEQUENCES	BACKGROUND SCRIPTURE: GENESIS 3

GENESIS 3:8-17

King James Version

AND they heard the voice of the LORD God walking in the garden in the cool of the day: and Adam and his wife hid themselves from the presence of the LORD God amongst the trees of the garden.

9 And the LORD God called unto Adam, and said unto him, Where art thou?

10 And he said, I heard thy voice in the garden, and I was afraid, because I was naked; and I hid myself.

11 And he said, Who told thee that thou wast naked? Hast thou eaten of the tree, whereof I commanded thee that thou shouldest not eat?

12 And the man said, The woman whom thou gavest to be with me, she gave me of the tree, and I did eat.

13 And the LORD God said unto the woman, What is this that thou hast done? And the woman said, The serpent beguiled me, and I did eat.

14 And the LORD God said unto the serpent, Because thou hast done this, thou art cursed above all cattle, and above every beast of the field; upon thy belly shalt thou go, and dust shalt thou eat all the days of thy life:

15 And I will put enmity between thee and the woman, and between thy seed and her seed; it shall bruise thy head, and thou shalt bruise his heel.

16 Unto the woman he said, I will greatly multiply thy sorrow and thy conception; in sorrow

New Revised Standard Version

THEY heard the sound of the LORD God walking in the garden at the time of the evening breeze, and the man and his wife hid themselves from the presence of the LORD God among the trees of the garden.

9 But the LORD God called to the man, and said to him, "Where are you?"

10 He said, "I heard the sound of you in the garden, and I was afraid, because I was naked; and I hid myself."

11 He said, "Who told you that you were naked? Have you eaten from the tree of which I commanded you not to eat?"

12 The man said, "The woman whom you gave to be with me, she gave me fruit from the tree, and I ate."

13 Then the LORD God said to the woman, "What is this that you have done?" The woman said, "The serpent tricked me, and I ate."

14 The LORD God said to the serpent, "Because you have done this, cursed are you among all animals and among all wild creatures; upon your belly you shall go, and dust you shall eat all the days of your life.

15 I will put enmity between you and the woman, and between your offspring and hers; he will strike your head, and you will strike his heel."

16 To the woman he said, "I will greatly increase your pangs in childbearing; in pain

MAIN THOUGHT: And the LORD God said, Behold, the man is become as one of us, to know good and evil: and now, lest he put forth his hand, and take also of the tree of life, and eat, and live for ever: Therefore the LORD God sent him forth from the garden of Eden, to till the ground from whence he was taken. (Genesis 3:22-23, KJV)

GENESIS 3:8-17

King James Version	*New Revised Standard Version*
thou shalt bring forth children; and thy desire shall be to thy husband, and he shall rule over thee. 17 And unto Adam he said, Because thou hast hearkened unto the voice of thy wife, and hast eaten of the tree, of which I commanded thee, saying, Thou shalt not eat of it: cursed is the ground for thy sake; in sorrow shalt thou eat of it all the days of thy life.	you shall bring forth children, yet your desire shall be for your husband, and he shall rule over you." 17 And to the man he said, "Because you have listened to the voice of your wife, and have eaten of the tree about which I commanded you, 'You shall not eat of it,' cursed is the ground because of you; in toil you shall eat of it all the days of your life."

LESSON SETTING
    Time: Unknown
    Place: Garden of Eden

LESSON OUTLINE
  **I. Naked and Ashamed
    (Genesis 3:8-13)**
 **II. Consequences for the Serpent
    (Genesis 3:14-15)**
**III. Consequences for the Woman and the Man
    (Genesis 3:16-17)**

UNIFYING PRINCIPLE

Everyone at times has given in to lust or greed instead of making a right choice. Why do humans make poor choices? Genesis 3 informs readers that when temptation confronts them, God gives them the freedom to make choices.

INTRODUCTION

Genesis, as we pointed out last week, is a book of beginnings. Last week's lesson focused on the details of God's creation of woman, the helper who was made of the same substance as man, and was suitable for him. Today's lesson picks up from the statement found in last week's text: "The man and his wife were both naked, and they felt no shame" (Gen. 2:25, NIV). As difficult as this is for us to believe, it was God's intent for His creation. He meant for the man and the woman to know and to be known by one another fully. He meant for them to be in His presence unashamed. His desire was to commune with His creation.

But that is not how things turned out. The backdrop for our lesson is found in the opening verses of chapter three. There, a new player in the narrative is introduced. The serpent, we are told, "was more crafty than any of the wild animals the LORD God had made" (v. 1, NIV). There is an interesting play on words here. The previous chapter closed by telling us that the man and the woman were "naked" (v. 25, NIV; Heb. *arummim*). This new chapter opens by emphasizing that the serpent was "crafty" (v. 1, NIV; Heb. *arum*). What is meant by that? How is he crafty? Brueggemann puts it best: "The prohibition [against eating the fruit of the tree] which seemed a *given* is now scrutinized as though it were not a given but an *option*. The serpent engages in a bit of sociology of law in order to relativize even the rule of God. Theological-ethical talk here is not to serve but to avoid the claims of God" (Walter Brueggemann,

Genesis, Paperback Ed. [Louisville, KY: Westminster John Knox Press, 2010], 47-48). He goes on to point out that in Eve's conversation with the serpent, "God is treated as a third person. God is not a party to the discussion but is the involved object of the discussion. This is not speech *to* God or *with* God, but *about* God. God has been objectified. The serpent is the first in the Bible to seem knowing and critical about God and to practice *theology* in the place of *obedience*" (48).

The remainder of the story is straightforwardly told. We know it well: the woman took the fruit, ate of it, and gave it to her husband, who was with her. He also ate. Then their eyes were opened. Before, they had been naked and not ashamed. Now, with opened eyes, they realized they were naked. In a futile attempt to cover their nakedness, they sewed fig leaves together and made coverings for themselves. The temptation of the serpent had been successful.

EXPOSITION

I. NAKED AND ASHAMED (GENESIS 3:8-13)

Adam and Eve listened to the serpent and disobeyed God. Today's text deals with the aftermath of that decision. Verse eight sets the scene: "Then the man and his wife heard the sound of the LORD God as he was walking in the garden in the cool of the day, and they hid from the LORD God among the trees of the garden" (NIV). In order to understand this passage, we have to recognize that quite often we approach it from a fallen perspective. That is to say that we have a difficult time understanding God here because our thinking is clouded with the same guilt and shame that Adam and Eve were suffering. Perhaps it is impossible for us to see it any other way, but let us at least notice a few things about what is said here.

The story highlights God's desire to commune with His creation. The anthropomorphic overtones of "walking" (Heb. *mithallek*) should not be pressed too far. As Mathews points out, the emphasis here is on "the enjoyment of fellowship" between God and His creatures (Kenneth A. Mathews, *Genesis 1—11:26* [Nashville: Broadman & Holman, 1996], 239). Up to this point, they have enjoyed a direct relationship with their Creator. The story also emphasizes God's care for His creation. The Gardener tends to His garden. He takes note of every threat to its peace and security. This also entails that He sees everything in the garden.

Now, however, something has happened. When Adam and Eve hear God, they do not run to His presence. Instead, they hide from Him. In this way, long before God hands down the curses (see Gen. 3:14-17, which we will discuss below), they feel the effects of their sin. Their sin brings its own consequences, even before God addresses the sin directly. Adam and Eve have gained a certain knowledge as a result their act, of course. But it is a knowledge they are not equipped to handle. Recall that oft-quoted assertion of Francis Bacon, "Knowledge is power." In this narrative, knowledge is far from empowering or liberating for Adam and Eve. Rather, it is a burden that turns out to be their undoing. Some lines from Dietrich Bonhoeffer's unfinished *Ethics* capture this well: Man "has become like God, but against God. Herein lies the serpent's deceit. Man knows good and evil, but because he is not [God] …

he acquires this knowledge only at the price of estrangement from [God]" (*Ethics*, Neville Horton Smith, trans. [New York: Touchstone, 1995], 23). This estrangement shows in their pathetic attempts to cover themselves with fig leaves.

This also brings us to another powerful consequence of sin: shame. What is shame? Bonhoeffer can help us here as well. A bit further on he writes, "Instead of seeing God man sees himself.... Man perceives himself in his disunion with God and with men. He perceives that he is naked. Lacking the protection, the covering, which God and his fellowman afforded him, he finds himself laid bare. Hence there arises shame" (24). So shame comes about as a result of our awareness that we are separated from God and that our very selves are laid bare before Him and before others. So, according to Bonhoeffer, shame can be defined as "man's ineffaceable recollection of his estrangement from the origin [i.e., God the Creator]; it is grief for this estrangement, and the powerless longing to return to unity with the origin. Man is ashamed because he has lost something which is essential to his original character, to himself as a whole; he is ashamed of his nakedness" (ibid.).

That is the context of the conversation that follows. God calls out to Adam, "'Where are you?'" (v. 9, NIV). God, of course, knows the answer to this question. The question is important, though, because it seeks to draw out the couple. In this regard, it achieved its purpose. One simple question evokes a stream of awkward blame-shifting (from the man to the woman, and from the woman to the serpent), charges and countercharges,

depressing in their pettiness. No longer is the woman the man's suitable helper. Now she is the albatross around his neck. If it had not been for her, he sputters, he never would have succumbed to temptation. That is ridiculous, of course. It reveals, though, how self-centered their thinking has become.

II. CONSEQUENCES FOR THE SERPENT (GENESIS 3:14-15)

Although we have not alluded to it heretofore, what we are witnessing in today's text is, essentially, a trial. The serpent, the woman, and the man are brought before the bar for judgment. As noted above, they have been questioned. Now comes the sentencing. All three of the main players in this drama are punished in some way, but only the serpent and the ground are "cursed" (vv. 14, 17, NIV).

This text is poetic in nature. Because we are dealing with poetry, we must exercise great care not to trample the language in favor of rigidly literal interpretations of these lines. We should first point out that everything that God says to the serpent is rooted in what the serpent has "done" (v. 14, NIV). God says to the serpent: "'Cursed are you above all the livestock and all the wild animals! You will crawl on your belly and you will eat dust all the days of your life'" (ibid.). "Cursed" (Heb. *arur*), as Mathews points out, "is another wordplay on the earlier 'crafty' (*arum*; cf. 3:1). Both verses describe the serpent's distinction within the animal world. Ill-use of his shrewdness resulted in divine censure" (244). By saying that he is cursed "more than" or "above all" (Heb. *min*) the other animals, God is not saying that the other animals are cursed and the serpent is simply cursed more. Moreover, God's statement that the serpent "'will crawl on [his] belly'" (v. 14, NIV) should not necessarily be taken to mean that the serpent was originally a four-legged creature. More likely, it is a general statement of the serpent's cursed condition, as is the statement that he "'will eat dust all the days of [his] life'" (ibid.). As Herman Gunkel has argued, in this text "the narrator … contemplates the present behavior of the snake and sees in it a divine curse" (Wenham, 79, citing *Genesis*, 9th Ed. [Göttingen: Vandenhoeck, 1977], 20).

Of greater significance for us is the second half of the curse. God tells the serpent, "'And I will put enmity between you and the woman, and between your offspring and hers; he will crush your head, and you will strike his heel'" (v. 15, NIV). Much has been written on this text. There is simply not sufficient space in this lesson to summarize the textual and interpretive debates that surround this text. For our purposes, let us notice just a few things. As we said above, this story is much more than simply an explanation for why the serpent does not walk on four legs. There is significant symbolism in these lines of poetry. Gordon Wenham perhaps says it best: "Once admitted that the serpent symbolizes sin, death, and the power of evil, it becomes much more likely that the curse envisages a long struggle between good and evil, with mankind eventually triumphing. Such an interpretation fits well with 4:7 where Cain is warned of sin lurking to catch him, but is promised victory if he resists" (80). In light of this, it should not surprise us that first-century Jews and Christians read this passage messianically.

They disagreed, of course, about whom it was speaking, but there was no disagreement in the time of Jesus that it spoke of the coming Messiah. For us, the "long struggle between good and evil" culminated with Satan's apparent victory at the moment of Jesus' death on the cross. In the resurrection, however, the strongest weapon in Satan's arsenal—death—was defeated. Jesus, the "offspring" (v. 15, NIV) of the woman, crushed his head, just as God had said.

III. Consequences for the Woman and the Man (Genesis 3:16-17)

God says to the woman, "'I will greatly increase your pains in childbearing'" (v. 16, NIV). The punishment is related to her children and husband, whom she will "'desire'" and who will "'rule over'" her (ibid.). But we must not read these words too harshly. Brueggemann's comments are instructive here: "Perhaps the sentence of 3:8-19 is heavy. But it is less than promised, less than legitimate. The miracle is not that they are punished, but that they live. Graciousness in this narrative is not just in verse 21, after the sentence. God's grace is given in the very sentence itself. Perhaps 'by one man came death' (Rom. 5:12). But the news is that life comes by this one God (cf. John 6:68-69). The sentence is life apart from the goodness of the garden, life in conflict filled with pain, with sweat, and most interestingly, with the distortion of desire (3:16). But it is nonetheless life when death is clearly indicated. This is not a simple story of human disobedience and divine displeasure.… When the facts warrant death, God insists on life for his creatures" (49-50).

Both childbirth and marriage have been touched by sin. The persistent pain of childbirth is to be a reminder of Eve's rebellion against God's Word. From the moment of creation, God instructed His creatures to be fruitful and to fill the earth (see Gen. 1:28). But now, childbearing will entail excruciating pain, pain that is trumped only by the joy and anticipation of new life. Fortunately, mixed with the pain of childbearing is the ultimate hope and promise of God.

In verse seventeen, the final word is in reference to Adam. Adam was to cultivate the ground, but the ground was now under God's curse. Due to Adam's rebellion, he was sentenced to strenuous labor and, eventually, death. As Mathews notes, "Although the woman will die too (2:17), the death oracle is not pronounced against her since she is the source of life and therefore living hope for the human couple" (252). It is Adam who was the primary perpetrator in the story; therefore, he is to shoulder the lion's share of responsibility.

God emphasizes Adam's responsibility by reiterating His original command: "'You must not eat of it'" (2:17, NIV). This verbatim restatement of 2:17 reminds the reader of the severity of the act. The reminder does not allow Adam to evade responsibility. "'All the days of your life'" was a phrase that had been uttered to the serpent. It is now spoken to Adam. Man is to feel the pain of working the ground that had originally been designed to serve him. Through the struggle of work, rebellious man would taste the dust of the ground all of his life.

THE LESSON APPLIED

Today's lesson highlights the consequences of humanity's rebellion against God in the garden of Eden. Nobody likes to focus on negative consequences, of course. They are still there, though. Having said that, there are also the seeds of redemption and renewal here. With judgment comes hope. In light of this, let us focus on the promise that comes out of the Fall: the Offspring of the woman who will crush the serpent's head.

LET'S TALK ABOUT IT

1. **What does today's lesson teach us about decision-making?**

This lesson should cause us to give serious consideration to the choices we make and to how we make them. The Church is the best setting for us to think through the consequences of our choices. We can foster better fellowship in our interactions with God and with each other as we engage in this process together in submission to the Word of God. In this setting, questions of choice, free will, and consequences take on a deeper meaning.

HOME DAILY DEVOTIONAL READINGS
SEPTEMBER 16–22, 2013

MONDAY	TUESDAY	WEDNESDAY	THURSDAY	FRIDAY	SATURDAY	SUNDAY
An Invitation to Covenant with God	Doing All the Lord Commands	Preserved in the Ark	Waiting for the Waters to Subside	A Sacrifice Pleasing to God	God's Covenant with All Humanity	Remembering the Everlasting Covenant
Genesis 6:11-22	Genesis 7:1-10	Genesis 7:11-24	Genesis 8:1-12	Genesis 8:13-22	Genesis 9:1-7	Genesis 9:8-17

AN EVERLASTING COVENANT

ADULT TOPIC:	BACKGROUND SCRIPTURES:
NEVER AGAIN	GENESIS 6:9—9:28

GENESIS 9:8-17

King James Version

AND God spake unto Noah, and to his sons with him, saying,

9 And I, behold, I establish my covenant with you, and with your seed after you;

10 And with every living creature that is with you, of the fowl, of the cattle, and of every beast of the earth with you; from all that go out of the ark, to every beast of the earth.

11 And I will establish my covenant with you, neither shall all flesh be cut off any more by the waters of a flood; neither shall there any more be a flood to destroy the earth.

12 And God said, This is the token of the covenant which I make between me and you and every living creature that is with you, for perpetual generations:

13 I do set my bow in the cloud, and it shall be for a token of a covenant between me and the earth.

14 And it shall come to pass, when I bring a cloud over the earth, that the bow shall be seen in the cloud:

15 And I will remember my covenant, which is between me and you and every living creature of all flesh; and the waters shall no more become a flood to destroy all flesh.

16 And the bow shall be in the cloud; and I will look upon it, that I may remember the everlasting covenant between God and every living creature of all flesh that is upon the earth.

17 And God said unto Noah, This is the token of the covenant, which I have established between me and all flesh that is upon the earth.

New Revised Standard Version

THEN God said to Noah and to his sons with him,

9 "As for me, I am establishing my covenant with you and your descendants after you,

10 and with every living creature that is with you, the birds, the domestic animals, and every animal of the earth with you, as many as came out of the ark.

11 I establish my covenant with you, that never again shall all flesh be cut off by the waters of a flood, and never again shall there be a flood to destroy the earth."

12 God said, "This is the sign of the covenant that I make between me and you and every living creature that is with you, for all future generations:

13 I have set my bow in the clouds, and it shall be a sign of the covenant between me and the earth.

14 When I bring clouds over the earth and the bow is seen in the clouds,

15 I will remember my covenant that is between me and you and every living creature of all flesh; and the waters shall never again become a flood to destroy all flesh.

16 When the bow is in the clouds, I will see it and remember the everlasting covenant between God and every living creature of all flesh that is on the earth."

17 God said to Noah, "This is the sign of the covenant that I have established between me and all flesh that is on the earth."

MAIN THOUGHT: And I will establish my covenant with you, neither shall all flesh be cut off any more by the waters of a flood; neither shall there any more be a flood to destroy the earth. (Genesis 9:11, KJV)

LESSON SETTING
   Time: Unknown
   Place: Probably atop Mount Ararat

LESSON OUTLINE
   I. God's Promise
   (Genesis 9:8-11)
   II. The Sign of the Covenant
   (Genesis 9:12-17)

UNIFYING PRINCIPLE

A natural disaster can cause great anxiety over the safety and welfare of loved ones. How can loved ones be assured of God's protection in the future? God said that the rainbow would remind Him of the covenant to protect all living creatures.

INTRODUCTION

In today's lesson, we move from the aftermath of events in the garden to the aftermath of the Flood. Even after God hands down consequences for disobedience, humanity continues to spiral down deeper into sin and degradation, straying far from God's intent for His creation. Conflict arises between Adam and Eve's two sons, Cain and Abel, resulting in the murder of Abel by his brother (see Gen. 4:1-16). Five generations later, Lamech could boast of not one, but seventy-seven murders (see Gen. 4:17-24). Conditions continued to worsen; humanity grew more and more distant from God. Finally, "the LORD saw how great man's wickedness on the earth had become, and that every inclination of the thoughts of his heart was only evil all the time" (Gen. 6:5, NIV).

This is the point at which the story of Noah and the Flood begins, a story that extends to the end of today's text (see 6:5—9:17). The story has been subdivided

in a number of ways, but most contemporary commentators are agreed in seeing the narrative in dramatic terms. Brueggemann is typical of this, emphasizing "how the text is set into discrete frames and scenes which make dramatic storytelling effective. There is a deliberate pace and structure to the account which means to carry the listener" (Walter Brueggemann, *Genesis*, Paperback Ed. [Louisville, KY: Westminster John Knox Press, 2010], 75). However we might divide up the rest of the story, most commentators have seen 9:1-17 as the final scene. God's thoughts, recorded in 8:21-22, give rise to a renewal of the commission given to humanity at creation (see 9:1-7) and a promise that "'never again will all life be cut off by the waters of a flood'" (9:11, NIV).

In God's thoughts (see 8:21-22), Brueggemann highlights two conclusions. First, even after the Flood, "humankind is hopeless. Creation has not changed. It is deeply set against God's purposes" (80). We see this explicitly in verse twenty-one, where God says that He will "'never again ... curse the ground because of man, *even though* every inclination of his heart is evil from childhood'" (NIV; emphasis added). Second, Brueggemann argues, "God resolves that he will stay with, endure, and sustain his world, notwithstanding the sorry state of humankind. He will not let the rebellion of humankind sway him from his grand dream for creation" (81). It is in full knowledge of humanity's sinfulness that He renews the calling He gave to them at creation (see Gen. 1:28), to "'be fruitful and increase in number and fill the earth'" (9:1, NIV). He does this in spite of human wickedness. Brueggemann puts it this way:

"The one [made] in God's image (9:1-6) is the same one who troubles God's heart (8:20-22). The one whose imagination is evil is the one who is, nonetheless, created in God's image, formed in order to preside over creation" (83). With that, we come to today's text. Here God gives hopeless humanity a sign of hope, hope that is given by God out of His sovereignty and His love for His creation.

EXPOSITION

I. GOD'S PROMISE (GENESIS 9:8-11)

Today's text opens with God speaking to Noah and his sons. Key terms in our lesson are "establish" (vv. 9, 11, NIV) and "sign" (v. 12, NIV). Both terms are used repeatedly, demonstrating their significance. According to Mathews, "Particularly instructive are the variant tenses for the verb 'establish,' showing the divine initiative and realization of the covenant: 'I now establish' (imminent future, v. 9); 'establish' (present perfect, v. 11); and 'I have established' (present perfect, v. 17)" (Kenneth A. Mathews, *Genesis 1—11:26* [Nashville: Broadman and Holman Publishers, 1996], 408). God is behind the covenant. He "initiates, sustains, and completes the covenant" (ibid.). The sign is significant as a reminder to both God and humanity of God's promise not to destroy the entire earth with a great flood as before.

Much of today's text deals with the fulfillment of the promises God gave to Noah and his family at the outset of the Flood narrative. We can see this in the similarities in language between Genesis 6 and 9. For example, recall that God had promised to sustain those in the ark during the Flood (see 6:18). The Hebrew text of Genesis 9:11 is identical to that of 6:18. As Mathews writes, "In the first case it is for those who 'enter the ark' (6:18), whereas here it is addressed to the party that 'comes out of the ark' (v. 10)" (408). Thirdly, both texts use inclusive language for man and all life. "Never again" (v. 11, NIV) echoes God's divine promise announced after the Flood and Noah's exit from the ark (see 8:21-22). Finally, Mathews also points out that the word "destroy" (v. 11, NIV) is the same word used earlier (see 6:17). All of this demonstrates that today's text "is a clarification and amplification of the covenant anticipated before" (ibid.).

We should also highlight the text's emphasis on God as the Initiator of the covenant. Mathews points out that "God's declaration is emphatic in the Hebrew construction: 'Now I—behold—I am establishing my covenant' (v. 9). The covenant obligation rests with the Lord alone, who has determined not to devastate repeatedly the earth's inhabitants ('all life') with floodwaters, despite man's continued sinfulness (cf. 8:21). Both the covenant and its sign have their origins in the Lord: they are 'my covenant' (6:18; 9:9, 11, 15) and 'my bow' (9:13)" (ibid.). Because this is God's own act, it is utterly reliable and irreversible. As we will see with future covenants, humanity's end of the deal is never reliable. Here, though, we see a covenant-keeping God who commits to His creation despite their rebellion and despite their always-fickle commitment to Him.

We should also note that the covenant is universal in scope. God promises "'never again … to destroy the earth'" with water (v. 11, NIV). The language here leaves no doubt that the covenant is universal in scope and extends to all posterity, including the sons of Noah and all those born thereafter. Brueggemann argues that "what has changed is not anything about humankind or creation or waters or floods. What has changed is God. God has made a decision about the grief and trouble of his own heart" (83). Earlier in the narrative, there was "a simple structure of indictment-sentence in which God resolves to punish the guilty…. [Now] the one-to-one connection of guilt and punishment is broken" (84). God decides from henceforth, to deal with creation with "unqualified grace" (ibid.). The "never again" of the flood narrative is similar to the "never again" God later spoke to Israel (see 2 Sam. 7:15-16).

II. THE SIGN OF THE COVENANT (GENESIS 9:12-17)

The second speech deals with the "sign of the covenant" (v. 12, NIV). This concrete connection between the two words *covenant* and *sign* is interesting. The "giving of the sign guarantees the parties of its perpetual validity" (Mathews, 409). The chief significance of the bow is as a demonstrative display of God's mercy, grace, and commitment to peace. There will be no more judgment upon creation by a flood ever again. The sign in the sky is God's self-revelation and promise. Outside of Genesis, the rainbow is also understood as a sign of God's presence (see Ezek. 1:28; Rev. 4:3).

As Mathews points out, "Three things are said of 'sign' and 'covenant' in v. 12. First, the 'sign' is attached to the 'covenant' promise; its purpose is to confirm 'ritually' what has been committed by word. Second, this is the Lord's doing, 'I am making.' Third, the 'sign' marks a universal covenant 'between me and you [pl.]' and for 'every living creature with you [pl.]'" (409). Earlier God had sworn to destroy the earth (see 6:13, 17), but now He is in covenant with it. The choice of image may perhaps be confusing. The "bow" (v. 13) could be understood in two ways. It is, of course, a weapon of war or hunting. The bow in the hands of a man was an instrument of battle (see Gen. 48:22; Ps. 7:12; Prov. 6:2; Zech. 9:10), but the bow bent by the hand of God has become a symbol of peace. Whether the bow is reminiscent of war or peace, God's promise is firm. Significantly, George Mendenhall regards the bow "not only … as a weapon, but as an *undrawn* bow, that is, the creator has won his victory, over the chaos and perhaps also over his inclination to punish" (Mendenhall, cited in Brueggemann, 84).

One should be conscious, as Mathews points out, that a sign always points to some concept beyond itself that requires interpretation. There is no ultimate meaning in the sign itself, rather its importance lies in what it communicates and evokes. Verse fourteen connects the sign's appearance with the forbidding clouds. The word *remember* (Heb. *zakar*) (v. 15) is also central to this text. It is the language of covenant promise. We see this in other places: God remembered His oath to Abraham in behalf of Lot (see Gen. 19:29); He remembered Israel (see Exod. 6:5; Ps. 106:45). Now God remembers Noah. In sum, when God sees the sign of the bow, He repudiates destruction in favor of salvation.

Verse fifteen reiterates the preceding verses' reversal of the threat to destroy all life. In verse sixteen, God now "refers to himself in the third person, 'between God [*Elohim*] and all living creatures' thus indicating a formal declaration of his unilateral obligation" (Mathews, 412). Note the central place of remembering in these verses. God's remembering, according to Brueggemann, asserts that "God is not preoccupied with himself but with his covenant partner, creation. It is the remembering of God, and only that, which gives hope and makes new life possible" (85). The fact that God remembers changes the structure of the world from hostility to commitment. In exile, Israel had complained of being forgotten. Likewise, the Flood might have led some to suggest that God had forgotten or abandoned. Ultimately, both of these events remind us that "the commitment of God to Israel is more reliable than creation itself (Isa. 54:9-17)" (87).

In verse seventeen, "God concludes the formal establishment of the agreement" (Mathews, 412). Certain phrases are essential here: "sign of the covenant" demonstrates God's promise; "I have established" shows that God is responsible for the covenant and bringing it to fruition; "all flesh" highlights the inclusiveness of the agreement.

THE LESSON APPLIED

Today's lesson speaks to the steadfastness of God's love in spite of humanity's sin. God established the covenant sign as a reminder to Himself and evidence to us of His promise never again to destroy all flesh. We learn from today's text that God is still moving creation toward its intended destination. That God continues to give such opportunities to creation reminds us of how we should treat each other. We can be certain that our failures, faults, and insecurities do not lead to being abandoned by God. God's everlasting covenant confirms that He has not abandoned humanity. Let us extend this same grace to one another.

LET'S TALK ABOUT IT

1. Where do we see Christ in today's lesson text?

Even in the aftermath of the destruction of the Flood, God seeks to bless humanity. In this, we see a foreshadowing of the incarnation. When His people had nearly lost hope—oppressed by an imperial power and by unscrupulous religious leaders—He sent His Son to form a new people for His name, a people who would faithfully carry forth His redemptive plan for all of His creation. The sign of the rainbow and the coming of God's Son are both hope-filled promises.

HOME DAILY DEVOTIONAL READINGS
SEPTEMBER 23–29, 2013

MONDAY	TUESDAY	WEDNESDAY	THURSDAY	FRIDAY	SATURDAY	SUNDAY
Dark Counsel Lacking Knowledge	Limited Knowledge and Influence	The Expanse Beyond Human Control	Overshadowed by God's Greatness	The Wrath of the Lord	A Humble and Penitent Heart	Human Achievement Without God
Job 38:1-7	Job 38:12-18	Job 38:28-38	Job 40:6-14	2 Chronicles 34:14-21	2 Chronicles 34:22-28	Genesis 11:1-9

GOD SCATTERS THE NATIONS

ADULT TOPIC:	BACKGROUND SCRIPTURE:
THE PROUD BROUGHT LOW	GENESIS 11:1-9

GENESIS 11:1-9

King James Version

AND the whole earth was of one language, and of one speech.

2 And it came to pass, as they journeyed from the east, that they found a plain in the land of Shinar; and they dwelt there.

3 And they said one to another, Go to, let us make brick, and burn them thoroughly. And they had brick for stone, and slime had they for morter.

4 And they said, Go to, let us build us a city and a tower, whose top may reach unto heaven; and let us make us a name, lest we be scattered abroad upon the face of the whole earth.

5 And the LORD came down to see the city and the tower, which the children of men builded.

6 And the LORD said, Behold, the people is one, and they have all one language; and this they begin to do: and now nothing will be restrained from them, which they have imagined to do.

7 Go to, let us go down, and there confound their language, that they may not understand one another's speech.

8 So the LORD scattered them abroad from thence upon the face of all the earth: and they left off to build the city.

9 Therefore is the name of it called Babel; because the LORD did there confound the language of all the earth: and from thence did the LORD scatter them abroad upon the face of all the earth.

New Revised Standard Version

NOW the whole earth had one language and the same words.

2 And as they migrated from the east, they came upon a plain in the land of Shinar and settled there.

3 And they said to one another, "Come, let us make bricks, and burn them thoroughly." And they had brick for stone, and bitumen for mortar.

4 Then they said, "Come, let us build ourselves a city, and a tower with its top in the heavens, and let us make a name for ourselves; otherwise we shall be scattered abroad upon the face of the whole earth."

5 The LORD came down to see the city and the tower, which mortals had built.

6 And the LORD said, "Look, they are one people, and they have all one language; and this is only the beginning of what they will do; nothing that they propose to do will now be impossible for them.

7 Come, let us go down, and confuse their language there, so that they will not understand one another's speech."

8 So the LORD scattered them abroad from there over the face of all the earth, and they left off building the city.

9 Therefore it was called Babel, because there the LORD confused the language of all the earth; and from there the LORD scattered them abroad over the face of all the earth.

MAIN THOUGHT: So the LORD scattered them abroad from thence upon the face of all the earth: and they left off to build the city. (Genesis 11:8, KJV)

LESSON SETTING
Time: Unknown
Place: Shinar

LESSON OUTLINE
I. The People Build a Tower
(Genesis 11:1-4)
II. God Confuses Their
Language
(Genesis 11:5-9)

UNIFYING PRINCIPLE
Sometimes leaders make plans that will take those they serve in a harmful direction. What can stop this from happening? In Genesis 11, the participants learn that God is aware of misguided plans and will intervene for the greater good of creation.

INTRODUCTION
As we come to this week's text, found in Genesis 11, we might be a bit surprised. Last week's lesson ended on such a hopeful note. Looking at God's renewal of creation in Genesis 9:1-7 and His gift of the covenant sign of the bow in verses 8-17, we might have expected a fresh, new start for humanity, a new era that would leave wickedness of the antediluvian world behind. But that is not, in fact, what happened. On the contrary, the events described in today's text will show that the human capacity for rebellion and wickedness against its Creator is practically limitless.

A few issues must be addressed at the outset. Structurally speaking, it should be pointed out that today's text is embedded in the midst of a series of genealogical tables (see 10:1-32; 11:10-32). Most conservative commentators point out that the events of 11:1-9 precede the events described in the genealogical tables. The fall of the tower and the confusion of the languages, in other words, precipitated the scattering of the nations reflected in the genealogical tables.

A second issue is the origin of the story. Kenneth Mathews points out that "the source of this story has puzzled commentators because it is unique in ancient Near Eastern literature" (Kenneth A. Mathews, *Genesis 1—11:26* [Nashville: Broadman and Holman Publishers, 1996], 469). Writers with prior commitments to source criticism have seen Babylonian or Sumerian traditions in this story. There was, for example, a Sumerian tradition that there was originally one universal language. Others have seen it as a product of Israelite culture, especially considering the strong anti-Babylonian *Tendenz* in the story. Most frequently—and Mathews cites Umberto Cassuto to make this point—commentators "have contended that originally separate motifs (oral) have been joined in this Israelite telling" (ibid.). As we alluded to in previous lessons, it does little good for us to get lost in source-critical questions that do not advance our understanding of the whole passage or our ability to apply it theologically. With Mathews, we affirm that "the exquisite artistry of the pericope … [argues] strongly for an original literary unit" (ibid.).

A third, and final, consideration is the story's historicity. This has been a primary concern for modern commentators, both conservative and liberal, over the past two centuries. In truth, very little can be said about this issue. As Mathews points out, "Although describing a historical event, the account cannot be confidently assigned to a specific historical period" (470). He goes on to say that "those who attempt to specify the historical period point to the collapse of the Third Dynasty of Ur, when Sumerian rule was displaced by Elamites and Amorites of the early second millennium B.C. Sumerian cities boasted of ziggurats, and Ur-Nammu (2062-2046 B.C.), founder of the Third Dynasty, began the construction of Ur's immense ziggurat tower" (ibid.). Whatever we make of this proposal, we do see clear evidence in the story of knowledge on the part of the writer regarding Babylonian and Mesopotamian tradition and religion.

EXPOSITION

I. THE PEOPLE BUILD A TOWER (GENESIS 11:1-4)

After the Flood, the people of the world shared a single language and common speech. But why is it important for us to know this? Brueggemann argues that this text forces us to reflect on the place of language in human life: "Language is decisive for the shape and quality of human community. More than anything else, language determines the way in which human persons care for each other. Language shapes the ways in which human communities conduct their business and arrange power. Language is the way we bestow upon each other the gift of life and death (James 3:10)" (Walter Brueggemann, *Genesis,* Paperback Ed. [Louisville, KY: Westminster John Knox Press, 2010], 102). Language can "coerce, deceive, manipulate, or mystify" (ibid.). It is the power of a common language that allows the people to move this far with their selfish plan.

Man's unity by way of a common tongue is underscored and recognized by God. The phrases "whole world," "one language," and "common speech" reinforce this unity. The phrase "whole world" (v. 2, NIV) translates the Hebrew *kol-ha'arets*. Despite all of this, the tower story more readily brings to mind for us separation from God's providential blessing. Notice the language of verse two: "As men moved eastward, they found a plain in Shinar and settled there" (NIV). This statement may be intended to recall Cain's separation and punishment as he settled for an urban life similar to that of the people of Babel. Mathews points to instances of verbal overlap between the two passages, including Cain's migration toward "Nod, east of Eden" (Gen. 4:16, NIV). Cain came to fear insecurity as a "restless wanderer on the earth" (4:14, NIV). The people of Babel, likewise, feared wandering as a dispersed people (see 11:4). However, both wandering experiences ultimately would lead to God's blessings of "divine protection and propagation of … offspring" (Mathews, 478).

What is meant by "Shinar"? Genesis 10:10, as Mathews notes, records that "the cities located 'in the land of Shinar' are Babylon, Erech, Akkad, and Calneh. Shinar refers to the region 'Babylonia.' It sometimes is translated 'Babylon' or 'Babylonia' in the LXX tradition (cf. Isa 11:11; Zech 5:11). It was the area known in antiquity as the Mesopotamian region 'Sumer and Akkad'" (479). According to Mathews, "The topography of a plain prepares the reader for the erection of the tower that follows … 'settled' is an antonym of the narrative's key idea 'scattered'" (ibid.). The Hebrew word for "settled" (*yasab*) means they had taken permanent residence in the land.

In verses 3-4, human enterprise is at the forefront. The people enjoy a singleness of purpose in these verses. But behind the narrative there is a certain sarcasm. On this point, compare "come, let us make bricks" with "come, let us go down" (vv. 3, 7, NRSV). We also learn something here of the building customs of the people of Babel, which were different from Canaanite customs. Israelite and Canaanite buildings were made of stone commonly found throughout the region. In early Mesopotamia, however, bricks were much more commonly used, especially in monumental structures like the ziggurats.

Verse four indicates that the tower seems to have been the real purpose of the city's construction. The construction of the tower clearly foreshadows Jacob's ladder. If we can view Genesis 11 against the backdrop of Genesis 28:17, we can see that the tower may have been intended as a stairway that provided access to the place of the divine. The people go on to say that they are building the tower "so that [they might] make a name for [themselves]" (v. 4, NIV). They want to secure power and authority via selfish means. They want to be in the place where God resides. In addition to making a name for themselves, they want to prevent themselves from being scattered.

Their words are a mockery of God's promise to Abram that He would make of him a great nation and magnify his name (see Gen. 12). In essence, the people attempted to enact the Abrahamic promise in isolation from God. But they succeeded only in achieving the name of "Babel," or "muddle."

The people's sinful thoughts and actions demonstrate their brokenness. Keil and Delitzsch argue that "the fact that they were afraid of dispersion is a proof that the inward spiritual bond of unity and fellowship, not only 'the oneness of their God and their worship,' but also the unity of brotherly love, was already broken by sin. Consequently the undertaking, dictated by pride, to preserve and consolidate by outward means the unity which was inwardly lost, could not be successful, but could only bring down the judgment of dispersion" (Carl Keil and Franz Delitzsch, *The Pentateuch,* Reprint Ed. [Peabody, MA: Hendrickson Publishers, 1996], 110).

II. GOD CONFUSES THEIR LANGUAGE (GENESIS 11:5-9)

While construction was in progress, the people received a surprise. God came down to see the city and tower that they were building. The frailty of their efforts is highlighted by the text's designation of them as "mortals" (v. 5, NRSV) incapable of attaining to God's level. In fact, God had to come down to their level to see the tower.

God's statement in verse six turns on the people's common language. Mathews notes, "This is the first occurrence of 'people' ('am) in Genesis rather than 'nation' (gôy), which dominates the Table of Nations. 'People' commonly emphasizes kinship ties (e.g., 14:16; 23:7, 11-13), whereas 'nation' tends to indicate geographical and political relations" (483-484). There is a sense of foreboding in the next phrase: "Nothing they plan to do will be impossible for them" (v. 6, NIV). It has been suggested that these words should be read in light of Genesis 3:22. In both instances these words set the stage for what is about to occur. God's action is both preventative and punitive. Even so, as we will see below, it will put the people in a position to be blessed by Him.

Verse seven mocks the builders of the tower. The author skillfully uses inversions of the Hebrew letters in the words *nilbena*—"let us make" (see v. 3)—and *nabela*—"let us confuse" (see v. 7)—to vividly show how God reversed their lot. "Here," writes Mathews, "'confuse' (*bālal*) sets up the following pun concerning the name of the site ('Babel'). Confusion of language results in an absence of 'understanding' that in turn condemns their project" (485). What are we to make of understanding in this text? As Brueggemann notes, "While verse 7 is conventionally translated 'that they may understand,' the word in the text is *shema'*. It permits the rendering, 'that they do not listen to each other'" (103). The first possibility refers to a semantic or a verbal problem. The second possibility is that "the text" is meant to "pose a covenantal, theological issue" (ibid.). Keil and Delitzsch, consistent with their understanding of verse one, argue that when God "resolved to destroy the unity of lips and words by a confusion of the lips … [He] deprived them of the ability to comprehend one another" (110).

Verse eight describes the consequences: "So the LORD scattered them from there over all the earth, and they stopped building the city" (NIV). What they most feared had now occurred. Yet the dispersal disguised the Lord's blessing: they now could achieve the potential He had in mind for them. According to Brueggemann, "The common element of the human proposal (v. 4), of Yahweh's action (v. 8), and the conclusion (v. 9), is the use of the verb 'scatter' (*pus*). Humankind fears scattering and takes action to prevent it. Then, against their will, Yahweh scatters" (98). But again, there is a blessing here. God's scattering helps to enact His creational decree (see 1:28). In the context of judgment, God's Word is to be fulfilled. The good of the scattering surpasses even the negative impact of judgment and punishment. The act itself sets up humanity for the blessing yet to come.

Verse nine brings the tower story full circle. As Kenneth A. Mathews has observed, "This verse brings together the key interpretive elements we have discovered in the account. 'Confused,' 'name,' 'whole world/earth,' 'language,' 'there/from there' and 'scattered' occur again as a crowning crescendo" (485). Nevertheless, the story ends with a scattering that eventually promotes God's blessing. Perhaps Brueggemann is correct when he opines that now "there is a waiting—a waiting for a new word, a new call which will evoke a new community. The whole creation waits to see if Abraham will listen and trust, if Sarah (cf. 11:30) will laugh, if Isaac will be born" (104).

THE LESSON APPLIED

God willed unity for His people. He willed that all people should be in covenant with Him, and Him only. We are called to respond to God and His purposes, depending upon His life-giving power. Today's story represents, in part, a prohibition against all efforts at oneness achieved through human self-sufficiency and autonomy. But it also shows how God works through our rebellion to enact His purposes.

LET'S TALK ABOUT IT

1. What does the Tower of Babel story tell us about the unity of humanity and God's design for us?

In some sense, Genesis 11:1-9 can be read in light of Genesis 2:18-25. As we saw three weeks ago, God said, "'It is not good for the man to be alone. I will make a helper suitable for him'" (Gen. 2:18, NIV). God created woman and, thus, created human community. That community was broken in the garden when the man and the woman sought to be like God by partaking of the fruit. The relationship between man and woman was never again as it had been.

In Genesis 11, we encounter another blow to human community. This time the people are all united in one purpose at the beginning of the story. But that purpose, that unity, is in opposition to God. By the end of the story, they have been scattered and their language has been confused. But even here there are the seeds of redemption and reconciliation. The confusion of their languages anticipates another time much later when there will be a multitude of languages but a singleness of message and purpose. That moment can only come, of course, in the light of Christ's redemptive work on the cross and by the empowerment of the Spirit.

Luke, in the Acts of the Apostles, recounts the birth of the Church on the day of Pentecost, forty days after Jesus' ascension (see Acts 2). After the Holy Spirit descended upon the Apostles, they began to speak. The people who were with them—people from many different places who spoke many different languages—heard the Apostles in their own languages. In this moment, the curse of confusion brought about at Babel was reversed. For us, the day of Pentecost is a harbinger of the day when the fullness of the Kingdom comes and we all join together with one voice to worship God. As Walter Brueggemann notes, "The history of the church [in Acts 2] begins in a new language community where human speech is possible. On the one hand, the new community in Acts 2 regarded its differences of language as no threat or danger, in contrast to the fear of Gen. 11:4. On the other hand, it sought no phony, autonomous unity. It was content with the unity willed by God without overcoming all the marks of scatteredness. And so a new eon begins" (104).

God is concerned for the unity of humanity. It is not His desire that strife and division prevail. We are called to the task of modeling Christ's love in all of our relationships.

HOME DAILY DEVOTIONAL READINGS
SEPTEMBER 30—OCTOBER 6, 2013

MONDAY	TUESDAY	WEDNESDAY	THURSDAY	FRIDAY	SATURDAY	SUNDAY
The Faith of Abraham	The Call of Abram	Settling in the Land	The Land and the Covenant	The Covenant Recounted and Renewed	The Covenant Remembered	The Covenant with Abraham
Hebrews 11:8-16	Genesis 12:1-7	Genesis 13:8-18	Genesis 17:1-8	Joshua 24:1-13	Psalm 105:1-11	Genesis 15:7-21

A PROMISE OF LAND

ADULT TOPIC: A LASTING INHERITANCE	BACKGROUND SCRIPTURES: GENESIS 12:1–7; 13; 15:7–21; 17:8

GENESIS 15:7-21

King James Version

AND he said unto him, I am the LORD that brought thee out of Ur of the Chaldees, to give thee this land to inherit it.

8 And he said, LORD God, whereby shall I know that I shall inherit it?

9 And he said unto him, Take me an heifer of three years old, and a she goat of three years old, and a ram of three years old, and a turtledove, and a young pigeon.

10 And he took unto him all these, and divided them in the midst, and laid each piece one against another: but the birds divided he not.

11 And when the fowls came down upon the carcases, Abram drove them away.

12 And when the sun was going down, a deep sleep fell upon Abram; and, lo, an horror of great darkness fell upon him.

13 And he said unto Abram, Know of a surety that thy seed shall be a stranger in a land that is not theirs, and shall serve them; and they shall afflict them four hundred years;

14 And also that nation, whom they shall serve, will I judge: and afterward shall they come out with great substance.

15 And thou shalt go to thy fathers in peace; thou shalt be buried in a good old age.

16 But in the fourth generation they shall come hither again: for the iniquity of the Amorites is not yet full.

17 And it came to pass, that, when the sun went down, and it was dark, behold a smoking

New Revised Standard Version

THEN he said to him, "I am the LORD who brought you from Ur of the Chaldeans, to give you this land to possess."

8 But he said, "O LORD God, how am I to know that I shall possess it?"

9 He said to him, "Bring me a heifer three years old, a female goat three years old, a ram three years old, a turtledove, and a young pigeon."

10 He brought him all these and cut them in two, laying each half over against the other; but he did not cut the birds in two.

11 And when birds of prey came down on the carcasses, Abram drove them away.

12 As the sun was going down, a deep sleep fell upon Abram, and a deep and terrifying darkness descended upon him.

13 Then the LORD said to Abram, "Know this for certain, that your offspring shall be aliens in a land that is not theirs, and shall be slaves there, and they shall be oppressed for four hundred years;

14 but I will bring judgment on the nation that they serve, and afterward they shall come out with great possessions.

15 As for yourself, you shall go to your ancestors in peace; you shall be buried in a good old age.

16 And they shall come back here in the fourth generation; for the iniquity of the Amorites is not yet complete."

17 When the sun had gone down and it was dark, a smoking fire pot and a flaming torch

MAIN THOUGHT: In the same day the LORD made a covenant with Abram, saying, Unto thy seed have I given this land, from the river of Egypt unto the great river, the river Euphrates. (Genesis 15:18, KJV)

GENESIS 15:7-21

King James Version | *New Revised Standard Version*

King James Version

furnace, and a burning lamp that passed between those pieces.

18 In the same day the LORD made a covenant with Abram, saying, Unto thy seed have I given this land, from the river of Egypt unto the great river, the river Euphrates:

19 The Kenites, and the Kenizzites, and the Kadmonites,

20 And the Hittites, and the Perizzites, and the Rephaims,

21 And the Amorites, and the Canaanites, and the Girgashites, and the Jebusites.

New Revised Standard Version

passed between these pieces.

18 On that day the LORD made a covenant with Abram, saying, "To your descendants I give this land, from the river of Egypt to the great river, the river Euphrates,

19 the land of the Kenites, the Kenizzites, the Kadmonites,

20 the Hittites, the Perizzites, the Rephaim,

21 the Amorites, the Canaanites, the Girgashites, and the Jebusites."

LESSON SETTING
Time: Unknown
Place: Unknown

LESSON OUTLINE
I. **The Cutting of the Covenant (Genesis 15:7-11)**
II. **Abram's Dream (Genesis 15:12-16)**
III. **The Promise of Land (Genesis 15:17-21)**

UNIFYING PRINCIPLE

Many people hope to leave an inheritance for their children. What sort of inheritance has lasting value? God's promise to Abram was the promise of creating a special relationship—a chosen nation—with Abram and Sarai's heirs.

INTRODUCTION

Genesis 15 is perhaps the most critical point in the Abrahamic narrative. Abram and Sarai have been called out of their barrenness through a covenant initiated by God. God's promise stands over against their barrenness. But that promise had not yet been fulfilled. Why should Abram and Sarai continue to believe the promise of God when every circumstance in their lives seemed to contradict that promise?

As Genesis 15 opens, Abram asks God, "'O Lord GOD, what will you give me, for I continue childless, and the heir of my house is Eliezer of Damascus?'" (Gen. 15:2, NRSV). God assures him that the one born in his house, Eliezer, is not his heir; rather the heir will be his own child (see v. 4). The substance of the remainder of Genesis deals with God again showing Abraham that He will keep His promise to Him—He will give Abraham and Sarah a son. (God changes their names in chapter seventeen.)

Most commentaries divide this chapter into two distinct pericopes with verse six as the hinge of the two sections. Brueggemann explains the logic for this division: "In their present form verses 1-6 and 7-21 may be considered as the relation between an *act of commitment* and *dramatic affirmation* of that commitment" (Walter Brueggemann, *Genesis*, Paperback Ed. [Louisville: Westminster John Knox Press, 2010], 148).

In keeping with ancient Near Eastern practice regarding covenants, after calling

Abram out of Ur of the Chaldeans, God made an unconditional covenant with him (sometimes called a royal grant). Abram is to understand that God is the Initiator of the covenant and that he is the beneficiary. That the covenant was unconditional must be firmly understood. This had been so from the outset. God's original command, "'Go from your country'" (Gen. 12:1, NRSV), was thus not a condition, but rather an invitation.

As we will see in today's lesson, the covenant forged between God and Abram featured promise and blessing in several areas. In Genesis 12:1-3, several promises had been made to Abram. Now, all of these promises would be renewed.

EXPOSITION

I. THE CUTTING OF THE COVENANT (GENESIS 15:7-11)

Scholars have pointed out the ways in which today's text foreshadows the making of the covenant at Mount Sinai. We see one of these ways at the very outset of today's text. The opening statement, "'I am the LORD, who brought you out of Ur of the Chaldeans'" (v. 7, NIV), is identical in form to the opening statement of the Sinai covenant, "'I am the LORD your God, who brought you out of Egypt'" (Exod. 20:2, NIV).

God, of course, had a prior relationship with Abram. Today's text builds on the intervening events that had brought them to this particular moment. Abram asks for confirmation of the promise: "'O Lord GOD, how am I to know that I shall possess it?'" (v. 8, NRSV). Consistent with who He is, God responds with a demonstration. Verses 9-11 present the reader with the

details of the demonstration. These are strange rituals, the details of which may well be confusing to the modern reader. In this section, we will discuss the details.

What is most important in these verses is the binding of two parties in an agreement. As in Jeremiah, it may be that the ritual is a sort of blood oath to reinforce the promise visibly (see Jer. 34). In verse nine, God requests five animals for the sacrificial slaughter: a heifer, goat, and ram—each three years old—as well as a dove and a young pigeon. Three of the required animals were used in Israel's sacrificial rituals. Yet, these animals were to be three years old in contrast to Israel's customary practice of sacrificing one-year-olds without defect (e.g., Exod. 29:38; Lev. 1:3; 9:3). One other difference, as noted by Mathews, is that "the term here for 'young pigeon' (gôzāl) is not the customary word describing the bird in Israel's ritual (ben/běnē yônâ, e.g., Lev 1:14; 12:6)" (Kenneth A. Mathews, *Genesis 11:27—50:26* [Nashville: Broadman and Holman Publishers, 2005], 170).

What of these particular animals? Why did God ask for them? Mathews is especially helpful here: "The 'heifer' ('eglâ) was used only on special occasions: the appointment of David (1 Sam 16:2) and a purification rite pertaining to murder (Deut 21:1-9).... The animal was young but old enough to be producing milk" (170-171). The goat (Heb. ēz) was permitted for use in the ritual for Passover and the Day of Atonement (see Gen. 27:9, 16; 30:35; Exod. 12:5; Lev. 16:5). The ram (Heb. 'ayil) "was an important cultic animal (22:13), used in the ordination of the priests (Exod 29:1; Lev 8:18;

9:2) and other sacrifices including guilt offerings (Lev 5:15-18, 25) and the Day of Atonement (Lev 16:3, 5)" (171). The turtledove (Heb. *tōr*) was used in Israel's purification rites.

Abram obeyed God: "He brought [God] all these and cut them in two, laying each half over against the other" (v. 10, NRSV). Due to their small size, the birds were left intact. The animals were then arranged in a manner that would allow the Lord to pass between them.

To understand what is occurring here, it might be helpful to consider a similar account found in Jeremiah 34:18-19. In that passage, according to Mathews, "two wordplays describe the practice.... A calf was 'cut' (*kārat*, v. 18) into pieces, formalizing a covenant that was 'cut' ('made,' NIV, i.e., 'to cut a covenant,' *kārat bĕrît*) between God and the leadership of Judah regarding the freeing of Hebrew slaves" (171). The second wordplay also appears in verse eighteen: "Because they acted treacherously, the people are deemed 'transgressors' (*hā'ōbĕrîm*, NIV 'the men who have violated,' v. 18) who had 'walked between'(*hā'ōbĕrîm*, v. 18) the parts signifying acceptance of the sanctions of transgressing the covenant" (ibid.). Because they had violated the agreement, the threat of death awaited them. In another similarity with Genesis 15, the Lord threatens them that "'the birds of the air and the beasts of the earth'" (Jer. 34:20, NIV) will eat their dead flesh. Having noted all of these similarities, it must be said that there were important differences as well. Most importantly, this is an act that focuses on God's pledge to Abram. Abram himself does not walk through the pieces. The promises made to him are sealed when God Himself passes through the pieces.

II. ABRAM'S DREAM (GENESIS 15:12-16)

The next portion of today's text describes a second night vision: "As the sun was going down, a deep sleep fell upon Abram, and a deep and terrifying darkness descended upon him" (v. 12, NRSV). Notice that the "darkness" is said to be "terrifying" (Heb. *êmâ*). According to Mathews, this provides "the appropriate atmosphere for the gloomy forecast of enslavement for [Abram's] descendants (v. 14)" (173). Abram's deep sleep almost certainly recalls the deep sleep that God brought upon Adam (see Gen. 2:21). As Mathews observes, this sleep is often "associated with divine revelations in dreams and visions (Job 4:13; 33:15; Isa 29:10); here this visionary 'deep sleep' is imposed by the Lord (cf. 2:21; 1 Sam 26:12)" (173).

Abram's concerns, which had been expressed in verse eight, are still present though. God reassures him of His promise: "Then the LORD said to him, 'Know for certain that your descendants will be strangers in a country not their own, and they will be enslaved and mistreated four hundred years'" (Gen. 15:13, NIV). This verse foretells the plight of Abram's descendants. They will settle in Egypt during the time of Joseph. Their servitude there will span four centuries and they will suffer intensely.

But their suffering will not last. God promises to judge and punish the nations that enslaved them. Israel will be victorious over those who oppressed them. Abram is to know that he and his descendants belong to God; He cares for them. There is hope, even in the midst of slavery. Eventually, God's people will be freed with enormous possessions from their captors. God will provide for Abram and his people.

Verse fifteen turns to Abram himself. God promises that Abram will reach old age and will die in peace, probably in Canaan (see Gen. 25:8-9). This is a sign of God's favor upon him.

In verse sixteen, God returns to the people. He tells Abram that they will return to the land in the fourth generation. As Mathews notes, "Hebrew *dôr* ('generation') denotes a span of time, but not necessarily the same fixed number of years.... The reference to 'four hundred years' (v. 13) suggests that 'generation' should also equate to a hundred years. This is supported by Abram's first generation (Isaac) who was born after a hundred years (21:5)" (174-175).

Verse sixteen also speaks of the "sin of the Amorites" (NIV). This has been interpreted in a number of different ways. The term *Amorites* can refer to the entire Canaanite population or to only one of Canaan's peoples. The text tells us that God will punish the Amorites through the Hebrew people. God will exact retribution against their sin when it has "reached its full measure" (ibid.). That God waits so long is a reminder of His forbearance. Moreover, this text reminds us of His concern for all peoples, not just the Israelites.

III. THE PROMISE OF LAND (GENESIS 15:17-21)

God's presence with Abram is symbolized by "a smoking fire pot and a blazing torch" (v. 17, NRSV). God appears in this form, in other words. The act of dividing the animals and walking through them,

as discussed earlier, was a key aspect of ancient contractual agreements. Since God is the One walking between the animals, He is solely responsible for its fulfillment and He obligates Himself as such. The emphasis here is on the unconditional nature of the covenant.

The fire pot, a kind of oven or furnace, "was used for baking bread (Lev 26:26) and roasting grain for sacrifice (Lev 2:14; 7:9). A metaphorical use of 'furnace' (*tannûr*) depicts divine judgment against Israel's enemies" (Mathews, 175). That the fire pot was "smoking" is also significant. Smoke often accompanies the divine presence, functioning as a covering, and can also signify God's wrath (ibid.). The "torch" can also be symbolic of God's presence (see Ezek. 1:13; Dan. 10:6) as well as a picture of destruction (see Judg. 15:5; Zech. 12:6).

Just how the final portion of today's text relates to what has come before is unclear. Does Abram see the events of verse seventeen in the same vision that is recounted in verses 12-16? Perhaps not. It seems more likely that the action of verse seventeen picks up where verse eleven left off. Either way, we are clearly in a different scene in the action of this narrative.

God's words to Abram promise him descendants and land explicitly for the first time in the Abrahamic narrative. The text sets up God's words with this phrase: "On that day the LORD made a covenant with Abram" (v. 18, NIV). Mathews argues that this phrasing "heightens the solemnity of the covenant occasion" (176). He goes on to say that the phrase "'I give this land' reiterates the divine oath promised at Abram's traversing the land (12:7; 24:7)" (ibid.). After God promises to grant the land to Abram and his descendants, He then elaborates in detail on the boundaries of this "reward" (Gen. 15:1, NRSV). These boundaries parallel those of the Garden of Eden. We must keep in mind that verses 18-21 present an idealized picture of Israel's boundaries. Only during the reigns of David and Solomon did the territory of Israel even approach these boundaries. The fact that ten nations are listed may suggest the completeness of Israel's occupancy of the land.

The author's intent seems to be to draw the reader to Mount Sinai. What occurred there was the end point of a plan that was set in motion in the rituals of today's text in Genesis 15. The Abrahamic and the Mosaic covenants both remind us of God's sovereignty, grace, and faithfulness in bringing them to pass.

THE LESSON APPLIED

The promises of God will never fail. God can be trusted to deliver regardless of one's life circumstances. Our faith and trust are on display when we act as if God's promises are true even when situations appear to contradict that belief. The Church does well, for example, to believe and trust God in the midst of great political and economic challenges and uncertainties. He continues to care and moves history toward its fulfillment. When God initiates blessings and promises, He declares that He alone is responsible for bringing them to fruition.

LET'S TALK ABOUT IT

1. **How should we react in the face of seemingly long delays in God's promises?**

Abram had waited for the fulfillment of God's promise for a very long time between the initial promise (see Gen. 12) and the renewal of the promise (see Gen. 15). It was undoubtedly easy for him to believe that the promise would never be fulfilled. Indeed, Abram never saw the total fulfillment of the promise; he only saw its beginnings (as we will see over the next couple of weeks) in the birth of his son Isaac. Much of the narrative that is recounted in these chapters has to do with the nature of trust. Even when it takes a long time, can God still be trusted? Sometimes Abram's trust fails, as when he and Sarai agree that he should have a son by her servant Hagar. They do this, it seems, in order to move God's plan along. Can we blame them, though? How often are we tempted to do the same thing? To take matters into our own hands? We can trust God's promises. Moreover, we can act according to His Word knowing that He will keep all of His promises.

HOME DAILY DEVOTIONAL READINGS
OCTOBER 7–13, 2013

MONDAY	TUESDAY	WEDNESDAY	THURSDAY	FRIDAY	SATURDAY	SUNDAY
A Childless Wife	A Beautiful Wife	A Threatened Wife	The Promise of a Covenant	Dispelling the Competition	Mourning a Beloved Wife	Bearing a Child of Promise
Genesis 11:27-32	Genesis 12:10-20	Genesis 16:1-6	Genesis 17:18-22	Genesis 21:8-14	Genesis 23:1-6	Genesis 17:15-17; 18:9-15; 21:1-7

A PROMISE TO SARAH

ADULT TOPIC:	BACKGROUND SCRIPTURES:
A PROMISE KEPT	GENESIS 17:15–17; 18:9–15; 21:1–7

GENESIS 17:15-17; 18:9-15; 21:1-7

King James Version

AND God said unto Abraham, As for Sarai thy wife, thou shalt not call her name Sarai, but Sarah shall her name be.

16 And I will bless her, and give thee a son also of her: yea, I will bless her, and she shall be a mother of nations; kings of people shall be of her.

17 Then Abraham fell upon his face, and laughed, and said in his heart, Shall a child be born unto him that is an hundred years old? and shall Sarah, that is ninety years old, bear?

• • • 18:9-15 • • •

AND they said unto him, Where is Sarah thy wife? And he said, Behold, in the tent.

10 And he said, I will certainly return unto thee according to the time of life; and, lo, Sarah thy wife shall have a son. And Sarah heard it in the tent door, which was behind him.

11 Now Abraham and Sarah were old and well stricken in age; and it ceased to be with Sarah after the manner of women.

12 Therefore Sarah laughed within herself, saying, After I am waxed old shall I have pleasure, my lord being old also?

13 And the LORD said unto Abraham, Wherefore did Sarah laugh, saying, Shall I of a surety bear a child, which am old?

14 Is any thing too hard for the LORD? At the time appointed I will return unto thee, according to the time of life, and Sarah shall have a son.

New Revised Standard Version

GOD said to Abraham, "As for Sarai your wife, you shall not call her Sarai, but Sarah shall be her name.

16 I will bless her, and moreover I will give you a son by her. I will bless her, and she shall give rise to nations; kings of peoples shall come from her."

17 Then Abraham fell on his face and laughed, and said to himself, "Can a child be born to a man who is a hundred years old? Can Sarah, who is ninety years old, bear a child?"

• • • 18:9-15 • • •

THEY said to him, "Where is your wife Sarah?" And he said, "There, in the tent."

10 Then one said, "I will surely return to you in due season, and your wife Sarah shall have a son." And Sarah was listening at the tent entrance behind him.

11 Now Abraham and Sarah were old, advanced in age; it had ceased to be with Sarah after the manner of women.

12 So Sarah laughed to herself, saying, "After I have grown old, and my husband is old, shall I have pleasure?"

13 The LORD said to Abraham, "Why did Sarah laugh, and say, 'Shall I indeed bear a child, now that I am old?'

14 Is anything too wonderful for the LORD? At the set time I will return to you, in due season, and Sarah shall have a son."

MAIN THOUGHT: For Sarah conceived, and bare Abraham a son in his old age, at the set time of which God had spoken to him. (Genesis 21:2, KJV)

GENESIS 17:15–17; 18:9–15; 21:1–7

King James Version	*New Revised Standard Version*
15 Then Sarah denied, saying, I laughed not; for she was afraid. And he said, Nay; but thou didst laugh.	15 But Sarah denied, saying, "I did not laugh"; for she was afraid. He said, "Oh yes, you did laugh."
• • • 21:1-7 • • •	• • • 21:1-7 • • •
AND the LORD visited Sarah as he had said, and the LORD did unto Sarah as he had spoken.	THE LORD dealt with Sarah as he had said, and the LORD did for Sarah as he had promised.
2 For Sarah conceived, and bare Abraham a son in his old age, at the set time of which God had spoken to him.	2 Sarah conceived and bore Abraham a son in his old age, at the time of which God had spoken to him.
3 And Abraham called the name of his son that was born unto him, whom Sarah bare to him, Isaac.	3 Abraham gave the name Isaac to his son whom Sarah bore him.
4 And Abraham circumcised his son Isaac being eight days old, as God had commanded him.	4 And Abraham circumcised his son Isaac when he was eight days old, as God had commanded him.
5 And Abraham was an hundred years old, when his son Isaac was born unto him.	5 Abraham was a hundred years old when his son Isaac was born to him.
6 And Sarah said, God hath made me to laugh, so that all that hear will laugh with me.	6 Now Sarah said, "God has brought laughter for me; everyone who hears will laugh with me."
7 And she said, Who would have said unto Abraham, that Sarah should have given children suck? for I have born him a son in his old age.	7 And she said, "Who would ever have said to Abraham that Sarah would nurse children? Yet I have borne him a son in his old age."

LESSON SETTING
   Time: Unknown
   Place: Unknown

LESSON OUTLINE
   I. Abraham Laughs
      (Genesis 17:15-17)
   II. Sarah Laughs
      (Genesis 18:9-15)
   III. The Last Laugh
      (Genesis 21:1-7)

UNIFYING PRINCIPLE

We often rejoice at the birth of a new member in the family or community. What does a birth mean to a family or community? Abraham and Sarah saw their child as evidence of God's faithfulness in keeping the promise to create a nation.

INTRODUCTION

Even after the covenant ceremony recounted in Genesis 15, Abram still had difficulty trusting in the promise of God that he and his wife would have a son. God's timing, of course, is not the same as our own. Perhaps, it was the case that Abram and Sarai grew tired of waiting and decided to take matters into their own hands. We see the evidence of this in Genesis 16: "Now Sarai, Abram's wife, bore him no children. She had an Egyptian slave-girl whose name was Hagar, and Sarai said to Abram, 'You see that the LORD has prevented me from bearing children; go in to my slave-girl; it may be that I shall obtain children by her.' And Abram listened to the voice of Sarai" (vv. 1-2, NRSV). Sarai's claim "that the LORD has prevented [her] from bearing children" is dubious, of course. But Abram does not contradict it.

Hagar soon conceives and begins to scorn Sarai. This infuriates Sarai, who does not seem to have considered that Hagar's ability to conceive would arouse jealousy in her own heart. In the argument with Abram that follows, Sarai complains that Hagar now "[looks] on [her] with contempt" (v. 5, NRSV). She deals with this by treating Hagar harshly, thereby causing Hagar to flee into the wilderness. While in the wilderness, an angel appears to her. The angel tells her to name her son Ishmael and tells her something of the life that he will lead. The chapter closes by succinctly noting that "Abram was eighty-six years old when Hagar bore him Ishmael" (v. 16, NRSV).

Despite all this, it would be another thirteen years before God acted to give Abram a son by Sarai (see 16:16—17:1). Before He did this, though, He gave Abram two signs of the covenant that He had made with him. The first of these signs came in the form of a name change for Abram and Sarai. God told Abram: "'You shall be the ancestor of a multitude of nations. No longer shall your name be Abram, but your name shall be Abraham, for I have made you the ancestor of a multitude of nations'" (17:4-5, NRSV). This new name reflects Abraham's covenant relationship with God and signifies his new identity based on God's promise (see Rom. 4:17). The second of the signs was the practice of circumcision. Every male mem-ber of Abraham's house, "'including the slave born in your house and the one bought with your money from any foreigner who is not of your offspring,'" must be circumcised (Gen. 17:12, NRSV). Adherence to God's commands prevents the person from being cut off from His people. Speaking of circumcision, God says, "'My covenant in your flesh is to be an everlasting covenant'" (v. 13, NIV).

EXPOSITION

I. ABRAHAM LAUGHS (GENESIS 17:15-17)

Today's text, which follows the command to circumcise, reveals that Abraham would receive a son through his wife, Sarai. Our text opens as God changes her name: "God also said to Abraham, 'As for Sarai your wife, you are no longer to call her Sarai; her name will be Sarah. I will bless her and will surely give you a son by her. I will bless her so that she will be the mother of nations; kings of peoples will come from her'" (Gen. 17:15-16, NIV). Kenneth A. Mathews points out that, in this story, God "announces blessing directly upon the woman, usually reserved in Genesis for the male progenitors (including Ishmael, v. 20; 12:2; 22:17; 26:24; cp. Luke 1:42)" (*Genesis 11:27—50:26* [Nashville: Broadman and Holman Publishers, 2005], 205). The new name Sarah is simply an alternate form of the earlier Sarai. Both names can be translated "princess." The language here—"'She will be the mother of nations; kings of peoples will come from her'" (v. 16, NIV)—is somewhat reminiscent of what is said about Eve (see Gen. 3:20).

We see in Abraham a range of emotions upon hearing this news: He "fell on his face and laughed, and said to himself, 'Can a child be born to a man who is a hundred years old? Can Sarah, who is ninety years old, bear a child?'" (17:17, NRSV). Delitzsch observes that, for Abraham, "the promise was so immensely great, that he sank in adoration to the ground, and so immensely paradoxical, that he could not help laughing" (Carl Keil and Franz Delitzsch, *The Pentateuch*, Reprint Ed. [Peabody, MA: Hendrickson Publishers, 1996], 144). According to Calvin, it is "'not that he either ridiculed the promise of God, or treated it as a fable, or rejected it altogether'" (ibid.). Torn between joy and wonder, Abraham "'burst out into laughter'" (ibid.). Why would Abraham react this way? Twenty-five years earlier the announcement of a son seemed impossible. It had been thirteen years since Abraham had heard anything from God. This raises the possibility that Abraham's laughter did not arise out of disbelief, but rather from joy. Abraham's laughter, thus, is the laughter of faith.

II. Sarah Laughs (Genesis 18:9-15)

The next portion of today's Scripture opens with God appearing before Abraham by the trees of Mamre as he was sitting in the door of his tent in the heat of the day (see Gen. 18:1). Abraham "looked up and saw three men standing nearby" (v. 2, NIV). But how much of what he saw did Abraham understand? Did he realize that he was in the presence of God? We cannot say. In verse three, Abraham recognizes them with the phrase "my lord" (NIV). Many commentators argue that what Abraham witnessed here was a pre-incarnate manifestation of Christ. As the narrative moves forward, Abraham prepares a special meal for the three and sets it before them under the tree where they eat. The men ask him, "Where is your wife Sarah?" (v. 9, NIV). Some commentators have suggested that during this time women would not have sat at meals with men—least of all strangers. They would have confined themselves to their own quarters. This means that Sarah would have been out of sight, but not out of hearing. The angels' question, "Where is your wife?" indicates that these strangers were no ordinary guests. They clearly knew Abraham well and perceived his situation.

Mathews' comments are helpful here: "Collectively, the trio ('they,' pl.) asked Abraham of Sarah's whereabouts (v. 9); a theophanic messenger also queried Hagar about her travels (16:8; cf. 3:9; 4:9). [Abraham's] response is terse in the Hebrew, *hinnê bā'ōhel*, 'behold, in the tent,' including perhaps a gesture toward it. The spokesman is the Lord, if v. 13 is our guide, who dialogues with Abraham and Sarah in vv. 10-15. 'I will surely return' translates the emphatic Hebrew construction (*šôb 'āsûb*); the certainty of the promise is further enhanced by a specific timetable, 'this time next year' (*kā'ēt hayyâ*, 'at the time of reviving' = spring; cp. 2 Kgs 4:16-17) and by the particle *hinnê*, 'and behold [a son]' (v. 10a)" (217-218).

Although Sarah is not visible, she is listening in the tent. Her facial expression is not described, neither does she speak a word of any sort. The narrator, though, gives us insight into Sarah's heart, thoughts, and actions. Her location is worth noting. She "was listening at the entrance to the tent, which was behind him" (v. 10, NIV). Hearing the promise made by the angel, and knowing the reality of her own situation, she "laughed to herself" (v. 12, NIV). Sarah's laughter is in contrast to Abraham's laughter. Abraham's laughter was a manifestation of joy in faith; Sarah's was a manifestation of doubt and uncertainty.

What she seems to have forgotten is that her pregnancy had nothing to do with her age or fertility. It had everything to do with the power of God. The text emphasizes this in several ways. God alone will be responsible for bringing the promise of a son to pass. The couple is "old and well advanced in years" (v. 11, NIV). Moreover, Sarah was "past the age of childbearing" (ibid.). The message is clear: only God could perform this miracle.

"Pleasure" (v. 12, NIV) often refers to sexual delight or enjoyment. In other contexts, it refers to luxuries or delicacies (see 2 Sam. 1:24; Ps. 36:9; Jer. 51:34). It is possible that she is referring to sexual pleasure here. Just as likely, though, is the possibility that she is referring to the delight and happiness of a newborn child. Sarah laughs at the thought of this. The question she asks in verses 13 is rhetorical in nature. God already knows the answer. The question, however, provides insight into the wisdom of God. He asks in response, "'Is anything too hard for the LORD?'" (v. 14, NIV). Mathews notes that "the Hebrew for 'hard' or 'difficult' (*pala*, v. 14) means 'wonderful' (NAB) in the sense of extraordinary (e.g., Jer 32:17, 27)" (218-219).

III. THE LAST LAUGH (GENESIS 21:1-7)

The scene of our final text is Abraham's dwelling place. As we look at this text, we should recall God's initial promise and the signs of that promise that He gave. The fulfillment of God's Word is indeed awesome. The time has now arrived when God delivers on His Word. The writer begins with a few crucial words: "Now the LORD was gracious to Sarah as he had said, and the LORD did for Sarah what he had promised" (v. 1, NIV). Verses 1-2 transparently show the veracity of God's Word. Notice especially the phrases: "as he had said" (v. 1, NIV); "what he had promised" (ibid.); "at the very time God had promised him" (v. 2, NIV); "as God commanded" (v. 4, NIV).

Verses 3-4 emphasize Abraham's obedience to God's commandments. He names his son Isaac and then circumcises him on the eighth day. Circumcision, as we saw earlier, was the sign of the covenant people: whoever remained uncircumcised could not partake of the hope of the nations, nor could he participate in the worship of Yahweh. Every male who came under Abraham's rule had to be circumcised.

The phrase "the son Sarah bore him" (v. 3, NIV) is used to distinguish Isaac from Ishmael, Hagar's son. The name of Isaac recalls the reaction of Abraham and Sarah at the announcement of the child's coming (see Gen. 17:15-17). The name, according to Mathews, also has reference to the mistreatment and mocking exhibited by Ishmael. He writes that "the Hebrew construction of v. 3 intensifies the identity of the birth mother.... 'Abraham called the name of his son *the one born to him whom Sarah bore to him* Isaac'.... The redundancy 'bore to him' reinforces the significance of the birth mother" (267).

Verse five emphasizes the gap between Abraham's age and that of Isaac. In verse six, the writer inserts "laughter" for Isaac's name and attributes his birth to God who possesses the power and authority to fulfill His promise of a son. The point is that God has provided Sarah with a legitimate heir. Sarah's joy and laughter pervade these verses as she acknowledges that she and Abraham brought forth a child "in [their] old age" (v. 7, NIV). God brought Sarah laughter, and everyone who hears of the birth will laugh with her. Sarah, who once laughed sarcastically, now laughs with joy. Now she knows for sure that the three travelers whom Abraham entertained so many years earlier were divine beings.

THE LESSON APPLIED

God's Word can be trusted completely. Circumstance can neither determine nor deter what God has said. Because of His fulfillment of the promise of a son, Isaac, all other aspects of the covenant will be certain. Often, to be sure, we will experience times of great uncertainty, times when there seems to be no way forward and out of the darkness. Let us hold fast to the promises of God every day.

LET'S TALK ABOUT IT

1. **What can Abraham and Sarah's laughter teach us?**

We do not often think of laughter in theological terms. This tendency, though, is very much to our detriment as pastors and teachers. God laughs in Scripture more often than we might think. Often it is derisive laughter, as when He laughs at human rulers (see Ps. 2) or at the godless and wicked (see Ps. 37:13; 59:8). Human laughter, on the other hand, while sometimes dismissed as "mad" (Eccl. 2:2, NRSV), is also seen as something to be desired (see Job 5:22; 8:21). In the New Testament, the powerful and worldly can laugh (see Luke 6:25), but often that laughter is upended (see Luke 6:21; James 4:9). With Abram and Sarai and Isaac, we get a more complex picture. There is a difference between Abram's laughter and Sarai's laughter—one is the laughter of faith, the other of (perhaps understandable) skepticism. What is really interesting, though, is that the fulfillment of the promise comes in the form of a son named "Laughter" (Heb. *Isaac*), or, translated more colloquially, "Giggles." What does this tell us about the nature of the promise? What might it say about God? What might it say about how we ought to view the future?

HOME DAILY DEVOTIONAL READINGS
OCTOBER 14-20, 2013

MONDAY	TUESDAY	WEDNESDAY	THURSDAY	FRIDAY	SATURDAY	SUNDAY
The Promise of Many Descendants	A Child Born in Affliction	The Symbol of the Covenant	Abraham's Test of Faith	Abraham's Obedience Blessed	The Blessed of the Lord	Blessing Two Family Branches
Genesis 15:1-6	Genesis 16:7-16	Genesis 17:9-14	Genesis 22:1-8	Genesis 22:9-18	Genesis 26:26-31	Genesis 21:13-21; 26:2-5, 12-13

A Blessing for Ishmael and Isaac

ADULT TOPIC:	BACKGROUND SCRIPTURES:
SIBLING RIVALRY	GENESIS 15:1-6; 16; 17:1-14, 18, 20-27; 21:9-21; 26:1-25

Genesis 21:13–14, 17–21; 26:2–5, 12–13

King James Version

AND also of the son of the bondwoman will I make a nation, because he is thy seed.

14 And Abraham rose up early in the morning, and took bread, and a bottle of water, and gave it unto Hagar, putting it on her shoulder, and the child, and sent her away: and she departed, and wandered in the wilderness of Beersheba.

• • • • • •

17 And God heard the voice of the lad; and the angel of God called to Hagar out of heaven, and said unto her, What aileth thee, Hagar? fear not; for God hath heard the voice of the lad where he is.

18 Arise, lift up the lad, and hold him in thine hand; for I will make him a great nation.

19 And God opened her eyes, and she saw a well of water; and she went, and filled the bottle with water, and gave the lad drink.

20 And God was with the lad; and he grew, and dwelt in the wilderness, and became an archer.

21 And he dwelt in the wilderness of Paran: and his mother took him a wife out of the land of Egypt.

• • • 26:2-5, 12-13 • • •

AND the LORD appeared unto him, and said, Go not down into Egypt; dwell in the land which I shall tell thee of:

3 Sojourn in this land, and I will be with thee, and will bless thee; for unto thee, and unto thy seed, I will give all these countries, and I will

New Revised Standard Version

"AS for the son of the slave woman, I will make a nation of him also, because he is your offspring."

14 So Abraham rose early in the morning, and took bread and a skin of water, and gave it to Hagar, putting it on her shoulder, along with the child, and sent her away. And she departed, and wandered about in the wilderness of Beer-sheba.

• • • • • •

17 And God heard the voice of the boy; and the angel of God called to Hagar from heaven, and said to her, "What troubles you, Hagar? Do not be afraid; for God has heard the voice of the boy where he is.

18 Come, lift up the boy and hold him fast with your hand, for I will make a great nation of him."

19 Then God opened her eyes and she saw a well of water. She went, and filled the skin with water, and gave the boy a drink.

20 God was with the boy, and he grew up; he lived in the wilderness, and became an expert with the bow.

21 He lived in the wilderness of Paran; and his mother got a wife for him from the land of Egypt.

• • • 26:2-5, 12-13 • • •

THE LORD appeared to Isaac and said, "Do not go down to Egypt; settle in the land that I shall show you.

3 Reside in this land as an alien, and I will be with you, and will bless you; for to you and to your descendants I will give all these lands, and

MAIN THOUGHT: Then Isaac sowed in that land, and received in the same year an hundredfold: and the LORD blessed him. And the man waxed great, and went forward, and grew until he became very great. (Genesis 26:12-13, KJV)

GENESIS 21:13-14, 17-21; 26:2-5, 12-13

King James Version   *New Revised Standard Version*

perform the oath which I sware unto Abraham thy father;

4 And I will make thy seed to multiply as the stars of heaven, and will give unto thy seed all these countries; and in thy seed shall all the nations of the earth be blessed;

5 Because that Abraham obeyed my voice, and kept my charge, my commandments, my statutes, and my laws.

• • • • • •

12 Then Isaac sowed in that land, and received in the same year an hundredfold: and the LORD blessed him.

13 And the man waxed great, and went forward, and grew until he became very great.

I will fulfill the oath that I swore to your father Abraham.

4 I will make your offspring as numerous as the stars of heaven, and will give to your offspring all these lands; and all the nations of the earth shall gain blessing for themselves through your offspring,

5 because Abraham obeyed my voice and kept my charge, my commandments, my statutes, and my laws."

• • • • • •

12 Isaac sowed seed in that land, and in the same year reaped a hundredfold. The LORD blessed him,

13 and the man became rich; he prospered more and more until he became very wealthy.

LESSON SETTING
Time: Unknown
Place: Canaan

LESSON OUTLINE
I. God Blesses Ishmael
(Genesis 21:13-14, 17-21)
II. God Blesses Isaac
(Genesis 26:2-5, 12-13)

UNIFYING PRINCIPLE

The circumstances surrounding one's birth can affect a child's identity and self-worth. Where does a child find his or her identity and self-worth? Despite the circumstances surrounding Isaac and Ishmael's births, God promised to create great nations through both of them.

INTRODUCTION

Abraham's joy at witnessing the fulfillment of God's covenant promises in the birth of Isaac was tempered by the knowledge that he was responsible for the sons of two mothers who could not live together in peace in the same household.

What would be the end of this conflict? Today's texts give us something of an answer to this question. They demonstrate that God had plans for both of Abraham's sons. He would bless both of them in accordance with the covenant He had made with Abraham. Those blessings would be different, to be sure. Isaac was the chosen one, the son of promise. Ishmael was not. Nevertheless, blessings would come to both of them, because God truly cared for both of them.

But there is more. We should also call attention to what today's texts say about Abraham. They show us, first and foremost, that, just as God cared for both boys, so too did Abraham. Ishmael was the son of a slave, but Abraham loved him. He did not denigrate or abuse him. Moreover, he was "distressed … greatly" (Gen. 21:11, NIV) at Sarah's harsh treatment of Ishmael and his mother. None of this was changed by the fact that Isaac was the chosen son.

EXPOSITION

I. GOD BLESSES ISHMAEL (GENESIS 21:13-14, 17-21)

In Genesis 21, Sarah's laughter (see last week's lesson) is quickly replaced by jealousy. The narrator recounts how Abraham organized a great feast to celebrate the day when Isaac was weaned. On that joyous occasion, "Sarah saw that the son whom Hagar the Egyptian had borne to Abraham was mocking" (v. 9, NIV). Joy gave way to anger. Now Ishmael has become a problem in Abraham's household. There is some controversy about how we should understand this verse. Was Ishmael really "mocking" (NIV; Heb. *mestacheq*) Isaac or was he merely "playing with" him (NRSV)? The former option is to be preferred for two reasons. First, it is difficult to account for Sarah's angry reaction if Ishmael had merely been "playing with" her son. Second, when the Apostle Paul alludes to this story in his letter to the Galatians, he writes that Ishmael "persecuted" (4:29, NRSV; Grk. *ediōken*) Isaac. As Mathews observes, "Exactly what Sarah witnessed is unstated. That Ishmael publicly ridiculed the name of the toddler or the celebratory events surrounding his birth fits well the negative nuance of the term and the obvious wordplay on the name 'Isaac'" (Kenneth A. Mathews, *Genesis 11:27—50:26* [Nashville: Broadman and Holman Publishers, 2005], 268-269). These verses demonstrate how God's providence overruled a family fight to give rise to two great nations.

Sarah's reaction was immediate and very harsh: "She said to Abraham, 'Get rid of that slave woman and her son, for that slave woman's son will never share in the inheritance with my son Isaac'" (v. 10, NIV). Notice Sarah's language: Hagar, who had been her maidservant—and had presumably served her loyally—was now "that slave woman" (ibid.). Even though she had witnessed the fulfillment of God's promise, her insecurity is still palpable in these words. Abraham's own thoughts were different. The narrator tells us that "the matter distressed Abraham greatly because it concerned his son" (v. 11, NIV). His feelings for Ishmael were those of a father for his son. He was grieved by Sarah's request to "get rid" of Hagar and Ishmael. Ishmael was no less dear to Abraham because he had been born to Hagar and not to Sarah.

In light of this, God's instructions to Abraham may surprise us: "But God said to him, 'Do not be so distressed about the boy and your maidservant. Listen to whatever Sarah tells you, because it is through Isaac that your offspring will be reckoned'" (v. 12, NIV). God emphasizes Isaac's place in His scheme of redemption here. But He is not neglecting Abraham's concern for Ishmael. As we come to today's text, which begins in verse thirteen, God tells Abraham that He has something in store for Ishmael.

God tells Abraham, "'I will make the son of the maidservant into a nation also, because he is your offspring'" (v. 13, NIV). As Mathews points out, the word *also* in this verse comes at the head of the sentence in the Hebrew text, connecting the promise made about Isaac with the one made about Ishmael (270).

God would make great nations of both of them and their descendants. In verse thirteen, God explains to Abraham why He will act on behalf of Ishmael even though Ishmael is not the son of the covenant: "'I will make the son of the maidservant into a nation also, because he is your offspring'" (Gen. 21:13, NIV). The promise is extended to Ishmael simply because he is Abraham's son. But Isaac alone is the son of the covenant. This portion of today's text deals with two events: first, the expulsion and salvation of Hagar and her son (vv. 14-19); second, God's plans for Ishmael as he grew to manhood (vv. 20-21).

Abraham arose early the next morning to see Hagar and her son off. Possibly, he wanted to avoid another confrontation with Sarah. Possibly he thought that, by leaving early, they could find asylum before the heat of the day set in. He "took bread and a skin of water, and gave it to Hagar, putting it on her shoulder, along with the child, and sent her away" (v. 14, NRSV). What should we make of these actions? Some have suggested that they resemble the practices of notable Arab chieftains who sent their sons out with limited provisions, often just enough for a few days. According to Keil and Delitzsch, Ishmael would not have been placed on Hagar's shoulder, since he was about the age of 15 or 16 (Carl Keil and Franz Delitzsch, *The Pentateuch,* Reprint Ed. [Peabody, MA: Hendrickson Publishers, 1996], 156). Rather, he was sent off beside his mother. Both were to face the same fate. It might have been best, as some have noted, to send Hagar and Ishmael out with limited provisions so as not to attract brigands who would exploit their weak condition. "Water" (v. 15, NIV) here could be seen as a metaphor for the sustaining provision of God. In the larger narrative, when the water that Abraham gave to Hagar and her son was depleted, God provided sustaining water from a well for Hagar (see v. 19). There she could refill the skins also. For now, though, Hagar "wandered in the desert of Beersheba" (v. 14, NIV), a region on the southern border of Palestine. In this wild expansive desert, they lost their direction.

Verses 15-16 link portions of today's text. These verses describe what occurred when the water Abraham provided for Hagar was depleted. Hagar, we are told, leaves her son under the shade of some bushes, and then removes herself, "about a bowshot away" (v. 16, NIV), to avoid witnessing his death. There she cries. But "God heard the boy crying, and the angel of God called to Hagar from heaven and said to her, 'What is the matter, Hagar? Do not be afraid; God has heard the boy crying as he lies there. Lift the boy up and take him by the hand, for I will make him into a great nation'" (vv. 17-18, NIV). This brings to mind the messenger who had comforted Hagar earlier (see Gen. 16:7-16). Hagar did not know what to do, but God did. We see here how God's grace extended to those outside the covenant. With God there is no impenetrable wilderness where His grace cannot reach. His grace finds Hagar and her son in the wilderness.

Consider the promise made by God in verse eighteen. According to Mathews, the language used by God is "quite similar to the divine promise made to Jacob when entering Egypt (45:3). It nevertheless falls short of the grander promises made to Abraham and his chosen line, who will enjoy an eternal relationship with God, inherit the land, and be a blessing for all peoples (12:2-3; 17:7-8; 18:18; 22:16-18)" (274). But consistent with His grace, God does not forget Hagar and her son.

Verses 20-21 place the responsibility for Ishmael's growth and development squarely upon God. He will be with Ishmael and be responsible for his success. Ishmael, we learn, became an archer in order to survive in the desert. His skills would help him gather food. While residing in the desert of Paran, Hagar secured an Egyptian wife for Ishmael. Some commentators have understood Egypt here as a metaphor for the world and its structures, indicating that Ishmael chose the way of the world over that of God. In this view, marrying the Egyptian was the final step that cut him off from all spiritual potential and made the world his home. Going forward, there would be only hostility and hatred between Isaac and Ishmael.

Other explanations are, perhaps, more likely. Since Paran was located south of Canaan, its proximity to Egypt made it easy for Hagar to secure a wife for her son. It is possible she found his wife among traveling slave merchants. The lesson is clear. Ishmael was a beneficiary of God's grace, but he was not the son of the covenant. He was the son of a slave woman, married to a slave wife, and living in the wilderness apart from civilized life.

II. God Blesses Isaac (Genesis 26:2-5, 12-13)

We now turn to Isaac. The events of Genesis 26 point to several similarities between Isaac's life and Abraham's life. The writer seems to use these similarities to advance the story of how God was faithful to His promise. Scholars have observed, though, that the story of Isaac as recounted here is no accidental duplication of Abraham's story. Rather, the repetition of motifs here is deliberate. The chapter, when seen from the viewpoint of Abraham's life, shows unity of structure and purpose. What happened in Isaac's life rehearses and extends what happened to Abraham. God's faithfulness is front and center here. God, who was faithful in the past, remains faithful now and will continue to be so in the future. What God has done for the father, He will likewise do for the son. But despite these similarities, famine described in Genesis 26 is a new one, not the same one that had forced Abraham into Egypt (see Gen. 12:10). Yet, the manner in which God dealt with Abraham is a good picture of how God will deal with Isaac.

Isaac went to Abimelech, the king of the Philistines, in Gerar, presumably looking for food. He seems to have been on his way to Egypt. (Recall, of course, Abraham's encounter with Abimelech). God tells Isaac explicitly not to go to Egypt but to dwell in the land that He will show him. In spite of the famine, God declares He will be with Isaac to bless him and to fulfill all the promises He had made to Abraham.

God then gives Isaac three exhortations he must obey. First, "'Do not go down to Egypt'" (v. 2, NIV). This brings to mind the fact that Abraham went down to Egypt (see Gen. 12:10). Second, "'live in the land where I tell you'" (v. 2, NIV). The lesson to be gained is that Isaac must wait on the Lord who will provide. Third, Isaac is told to "'stay in this land'" (v. 3, NIV). The KJV's "sojourn" (Heb. *gur*) appears frequently in Genesis and significantly emphasizes the fact that the patriarchs were strangers and foreigners in the lands where they lived (see Gen. 35:27; 37:1; Exod. 6:4).

The Lord was gracious to Abraham because of his obedience and commitment. Abraham was said by God to have "kept [His] requirements, [His] commands, [His] decrees and [His] laws" (v. 5, NIV). The language is very similar to the way obedience to the Sinai covenant is enjoined: "Love the LORD your God and keep his requirements, his decrees, his laws and his commands always" (Deut. 11:1, NIV). Abraham is the ultimate example of obedience to the Law: "'Abraham obeyed [God]'" (Gen. 26:5, NIV). Verses 12-13 drive home the fact that God had blessed Isaac tremendously. He was wealthy and everything he did prospered. The text says: "Isaac sowed seed in that land, and in the same year reaped a hundredfold" (v. 12, NRSV). What is most amazing about this harvest is that it yielded this volume during the first year—immediately. Speaking of the abundance of Israel's crops, Mathews notes that "this feature of Isaac's wealth is in keeping with the chapter's emphasis on the land promise.… The bounty proved that the Lord had 'blessed' Isaac (v. 12; cf. 24:1, 35; 25:11; 39:5)" (408-409). Not only did God bless him with land, the land was a blessing to him. Isaac experienced the blessing in this fashion because of the promise made to Abraham.

THE LESSON APPLIED

The story of Isaac and Ishmael lets us know that God is the God of inclusion. He desires for all to be saved from the penalty of sin. Salvation is offered through His Son, Jesus Christ. He is the ultimate Seed who makes it possible for all families of the earth to be blessed.

LET'S TALK ABOUT IT

1. What would it mean for us to see ourselves as sojourners?

One of the most significant words in today's text occurs in Genesis 26:3, where God tells Isaac to "'stay in this land'" (NIV). As noted in the lesson, the KJV's more evocative "sojourn" is to be preferred to "stay." Sojourning—living in a land as a stranger and a foreigner—was Isaac's call. More importantly, it was the call that God gave to Israel and it is the call He places today upon the Church. We are to be a people whose citizenship and whose fundamental allegiance lies with the Kingdom of God, not with any human society or government. We are to be a people who "have … no continuing city" on this earth, but who "seek one to come" (Heb. 13:14, KJV). How difficult is it for you to think of yourself or your church in this fashion?

HOME DAILY DEVOTIONAL READINGS
OCTOBER 21–27, 2013

MONDAY	TUESDAY	WEDNESDAY	THURSDAY	FRIDAY	SATURDAY	SUNDAY
One Greater than Jacob	The Plot to Gain a Blessing	Planning the Deception	A Blessing Gained Through Deceit	Jacob Received God's Blessing	Jacob's Name Changed to Israel	God's Assurance for Jacob
John 4:1-15	Genesis 27:1-10	Genesis 27:11-17	Genesis 27:18-29	Genesis 32:22-30	Genesis 35:9-15	Genesis 28:1, 10-22

THE BLESSING PASSES TO JACOB

ADULT TOPIC:	BACKGROUND SCRIPTURES:
VISION DREAMS	GENESIS 27:19–29; 28:1–4, 10–22; 32:22–30; 35:9–15

GENESIS 28:1, 10–22

King James Version

AND Isaac called Jacob, and blessed him, and charged him, and said unto him, Thou shalt not take a wife of the daughters of Canaan.

• • • • • •

10 And Jacob went out from Beersheba, and went toward Haran.

11 And he lighted upon a certain place, and tarried there all night, because the sun was set; and he took of the stones of that place, and put them for his pillows, and lay down in that place to sleep.

12 And he dreamed, and behold a ladder set up on the earth, and the top of it reached to heaven: and behold the angels of God ascending and descending on it.

13 And, behold, the LORD stood above it, and said, I am the LORD God of Abraham thy father, and the God of Isaac: the land whereon thou liest, to thee will I give it, and to thy seed;

14 And thy seed shall be as the dust of the earth, and thou shalt spread abroad to the west, and to the east, and to the north, and to the south: and in thee and in thy seed shall all the families of the earth be blessed.

15 And, behold, I am with thee, and will keep thee in all places whither thou goest, and will bring thee again into this land; for I will not leave thee, until I have done that which I have spoken to thee of.

New Revised Standard Version

THEN Isaac called Jacob and blessed him, and charged him, "You shall not marry one of the Canaanite women."

• • • • • •

10 Jacob left Beer-sheba and went toward Haran.

11 He came to a certain place and stayed there for the night, because the sun had set. Taking one of the stones of the place, he put it under his head and lay down in that place.

12 And he dreamed that there was a ladder-set up on the earth, the top of it reaching to heaven; and the angels of God were ascending and descending on it.

13 And the LORD stood beside him and said, "I am the LORD, the God of Abraham your father and the God of Isaac; the land on which you lie I will give to you and to your offspring; 14 and your offspring shall be like the dust of the earth, and you shall spread abroad to the west and to the east and to the north and to the south; and all the families of the earth shall be blessed in you and in your offspring.

15 Know that I am with you and will keep you wherever you go, and will bring you back to this land; for I will not leave you until I have done what I have promised you."

MAIN THOUGHT: And, behold, I am with thee, and will keep thee in all places whither thou goest, and will bring thee again into this land; for I will not leave thee, until I have done that which I have spoken to thee of. (Genesis 28:15, KJV)

GENESIS 28:1, 10–22

King James Version	New Revised Standard Version
16 And Jacob awaked out of his sleep, and he said, Surely the LORD is in this place; and I knew it not.	16 Then Jacob woke from his sleep and said, "Surely the LORD is in this place—and I did not know it!"
17 And he was afraid, and said, How dreadful is this place! this is none other but the house of God, and this is the gate of heaven.	17 And he was afraid, and said, "How awesome is this place! This is none other than the house of God, and this is the gate of heaven."
18 And Jacob rose up early in the morning, and took the stone that he had put for his pillows, and set it up for a pillar, and poured oil upon the top of it.	18 So Jacob rose early in the morning, and he took the stone that he had put under his head and set it up for a pillar and poured oil on the top of it.
19 And he called the name of that place Bethel: but the name of that city was called Luz at the first.	19 He called that place Bethel; but the name of the city was Luz at the first.
20 And Jacob vowed a vow, saying, If God will be with me, and will keep me in this way that I go, and will give me bread to eat, and raiment to put on,	20 Then Jacob made a vow, saying, "If God will be with me, and will keep me in this way that I go, and will give me bread to eat and clothing to wear,
21 So that I come again to my father's house in peace; then shall the LORD be my God:	21 so that I come again to my father's house in peace, then the LORD shall be my God,
22 And this stone, which I have set for a pillar, shall be God's house: and of all that thou shalt give me I will surely give the tenth unto thee.	22 and this stone, which I have set up for a pillar, shall be God's house; and of all that you give me I will surely give one-tenth to you."

LESSON SETTING
Time: Unknown
Place: Bethel

LESSON OUTLINE
I. Jacob's Blessing
   (Genesis 28:1)
II. Jacob's Dream
   (Genesis 28:10-15)
III. Jacob's Response to the Dream
   (Genesis 28:16-22)

UNIFYING PRINCIPLE
When people feel insecure, they look for a place of security and the assurance of not being alone. Where and with whom can they find sanctuary? God assures Jacob of His presence and promises that through Jacob and his offspring, all the families of the earth will be blessed.

INTRODUCTION
Genesis 28 continues the story of Isaac and his family. In last week's lesson, we saw Isaac first as a very young child (see Gen. 21) and later as a prosperous landowner (see Gen. 26). The intervening portion of the narrative introduces us to the irrepressible conflict between Isaac's sons, Jacob and Esau. The narrative recounts how Jacob used trickery (at his mother's urging) to win Isaac's blessing, a blessing that was intended for Esau (see Gen. 27). The consequence that accompanies Jacob's decision is predictable. Considering himself betrayed, Esau pledges to kill Jacob. Jacob then seeks to escape Esau's wrath. So Rebekah directs him to her brother Laban's house in order to get away from Esau and to secure a wife.

While traveling toward Haran, Laban's home, Jacob decides to settle down for the night in a certain place. Here Jacob will directly encounter the God whom he has only heard of heretofore. The dream he has on this night is the crucible of Jacob's transformation. He discovers that Yahweh is a covenant-keeping God, who now reaffirms His promise to Abraham to him personally.

EXPOSITION

I. JACOB'S BLESSING (GENESIS 28:1)

There is a great deal of concern for marriage in verse one. As already mentioned, Jacob's deceit in obtaining a blessing from his father had destroyed his relationship with his brother, Esau. This necessitated that Jacob leave his home in order to escape his brother's wrath. On the advice of his mother, Jacob went to the home of her brother Laban in Haran. The account of that decision closes with a curious statement that Rebekah makes to Isaac: "'I am weary of my life because of the Hittite women. If Jacob marries one of the Hittite women such as these, one of the women of the land, what good will my life be to me?'" (27:46, NRSV).

What are we to make of this statement, which seemingly comes out of nowhere? First and foremost, we must understand it in light of its context. Recall that Jacob received Isaac's blessing by way of trickery: he dressed in skins and went before his father to receive the blessing, his father who was blind and could not tell the difference in that moment between his two sons. In order to escape the consequences of that trickery, Jacob has to flee. Rebekah's words in verse forty-six

provide a plausible motive for Jacob's departure by complaining to Isaac about Esau having married a foreign wife—even though she never mentions Esau by name (see Gen. 26:34-35). As Mathews notes, this is not meant to say "that Rebekah was altogether insincere, since her expectations were most likely to obtain wives for her sons from her native home where she herself volunteered to marry Isaac (24:58)" (Kenneth A. Mathews, *Genesis 11:27—50:26* [Nashville: Broadman and Holman Publishers, 2005], 438). It does, however, highlight an important difference in the two situations. In Isaac's case, Abraham sent a servant to select a wife for him; in Jacob's case, he goes to Paddan Aram and must choose a wife alone.

As Genesis 28 opens, Isaac summons Jacob in order to bless him. As Mathews observes, "the language 'called for Jacob' (v. 1) parallels the introduction in 27:1 when he solicited Esau for the blessing" (439). We should note that this blessing is not meant to duplicate or conflict with Isaac's first blessing of Jacob (see Gen. 27:27-29). Jacob's blessings are based upon what God told Abraham. In truth, nothing new is promised. God has not changed His promise.

II. JACOB'S DREAM (GENESIS 28:10-15)

The text informs us that Jacob went out from Beersheba toward Haran, probably along the route traveled by Abraham's servant who went to find a wife for Isaac. The narrative then notes that "when he reached a certain place, he stopped for the night because the sun had set. Taking one of the stones there, he put it under his head and lay down to sleep" (v. 11, NIV).

There Jacob dreamed of a ladder set up on earth, but the top reached the heavens. Jacob noticed angels ascending and descending on the ladder. They represent the presence of God. As God reaffirms the covenant, it is clear that He will be present with Jacob wherever he goes. Even so, as Walter Brueggemann argues, the "narrative raises difficult questions about the nature of an encounter with God" (Walter Brueggemann, *Genesis*, Paperback Ed. [Louisville: Westminster John Knox Press, 2010], 242). He goes on to say that "the startling element in the narrative is not the *appearance* of God, for religious phenomena are still with us in all sorts of ways. But here, the amazement is not in the appearance. Rather, it is *God*!" (ibid.). The surprise to Jacob is that God is present and available to him in such a way. The wonder is the manner in which God, the sovereign One, attaches to this treacherous fugitive.

According to Brueggemann, verse twelve highlights three visual phenomena in Jacob's dream. First, it is noteworthy that the encounter occurred in a dream. As Brueggemann points out, "The wakeful world of Jacob was a world of fear, terror, loneliness (and, we may imagine, unresolved guilt). Those were parameters of his existence. The dream permits the entry of an alternative into his life" (243). This is a situation, in other words, where Jacob is not in control. In the dream, he is open to different understanding. In the dream, in other words, there is an avenue for the Gospel to penetrate Jacob's life.

The second of the visual aspects of this dream is the ramp, or ladder, between heaven and earth. Brueggemann notes that this ramp was "something like the Mesopotamian ziggurat, a land mass formed as a temple through which earth touches heaven. Such a ramp as a religious figure reflects the imperial religion of the culture. But now it has become a visual vehicle for a gospel assertion" (243). In other words, the good news has come to Jacob; heaven and earth are forever connected. Again Brueggemann says, "Earth is not left to its own resources and heaven is not a remote self-contained realm for the gods. Heaven has to do with earth" (ibid.). Heaven is real; it is accessible. The ramp "symbolically intimat[es] the fact of a real, uninterrupted, and close communication between heaven and earth, and in particular between God in his glory and man in his solitude and sin" (Thomas Whitelaw, *Genesis*, The Pulpit Commentary, Vol. 1, Fifth Ed. [London: C. Kegan Paul & Co., 1881], 349-350). That communication, of course, comes in the person of Jesus Christ. In this text, as commentators have pointed out, there are two possibilities. First, the ramp may be an emblem of Jesus Himself. Second, Jacob may be a type of Christ "in whom the living intercourse between earth and heaven depicted in the vision of the angel-trodden staircase was completely fulfilled" (ibid.).

The third visual aspect of this dream is the presence of angels. They are, as Brueggemann notes, "royal messengers of God who act to do his bidding. As indicated in the promise (vv. 13-15), the message they bear is that the promissory Kingdom of God is now at work. The old kingdom of fear and terror is being overcome" (243-244). They teach us that God can come in such a way as to alter human reality and to give us a new vision of what is possible. Having said that, Brueggemann asserts that the visual elements of this scene are preparatory to the words of the promise recounted in the next verses.

In verses 13-15, the Lord speaks the promise. Jacob has come to this moment while running for his life. At this point in his life, he remains a trickster, searching for an authentic sense of identity. He has not yet emerged into the person God has in store for him. It is in the dream that Jacob is given the grace to change. The promise confirmed to Jacob is the same that was given to Abraham and Isaac. God's words highlight the universality of the covenant promise. There is no room for misunderstanding as to what the promise involves: land for the people of Israel, and well-being for others because of Israel.

Brueggemann observes that there are three main parts to God's promise. First, the Lord says, "I am with you." The fugitive will not be abandoned. The ladder makes the statement that, because of the covenant, God will not abandon Jacob or any others who come under the shadow of the covenant (see Jer. 1:19). Jacob discovered that the God of Abraham and of Isaac was his God too. Note also that "I am with you" is the name given to Jesus of Nazareth. The second part of God's promise is about action: "I will keep you." The allusion is to shepherding or protecting the sheep. God says He will protect the heir of the promise. Not only will Jacob be protected; all of Israel will be under God's divine protection (see Num. 6:24-26; Pss. 91:11-15; 121). The third and final aspect of the blessing is extremely specific, addressed to Jacob alone because of his predicament. It is the promise of homecoming: "I will bring you back to this land." These words show that Jacob's journey into Paddan Aram was not without the Lord's sanction. The lesson is that for those who are abandoned, in exile, and on the run, because of the promise, homecoming can become a reality. God is determined to bring His promise to fruition. He will not abandon Jacob until the promise is completed, "'until I have done what I have promised you'" (v. 15, NIV).

III. JACOB'S RESPONSE TO THE DREAM (GENESIS 28:16-22)

The next several verses deal with Jacob's response to the dream, a response that speaks to the veracity of his experience. Now awakened, Jacob embraces a new reality and a new way of life. Verse seventeen says that Jacob "was afraid" (NRSV), so were Moses (see Exod. 20:18-19), Job (Job 42:5-6), Isaiah (see Isa. 6:5), Peter (see Luke 5:8), and John (see Rev. 1:17, 18)—each at the hearing of God's voice. Jacob describes the place where he had the dream as "awesome" (v. 17, NIV). He realized that wherever this "place" was it was the house of God and the gate of heaven.

In the next verse, Jacob acts purposefully: he "rose early in the morning" (NRSV). He then took the stone he had used for a pillow and set it up as a pillar—not as an object of worship, but as a memorial of the dream experience. Next, he poured oil upon the pillar as an act of sanctification. Jacob called the name of the place *Bethel* (from two Hebrew words meaning "house of God") (see 35:1-5). After Jerusalem, Bethel was perhaps the most important city in the Israelite tradition (cf. 2 Kings 23:15-20; Amos 7:10-17). Luz, from a

Hebrew word meaning "separation," was the earlier name for Bethel. Jacob, who has been separated and estranged from the true God, now finds himself being brought to the house of God in a dream.

In addition to its focus on the "place," the narrative pays attention to the "promise" in a fashion that corresponds to God's statement in verse fifteen. Brueggemann sees a connection between the promises of these verses and the promises of Psalm 23. The phrase "he is with me" echoes verse four of the Psalm 23; "he will keep me" echoes verses 2-3 of Psalm 23; "he will give me bread to eat" echoes verse five of Psalm 23; and the phrase "I come again to my father's house" echoes verse six of Psalm 23 (247-248). These parallels highlight God's action as Provider, Guide, and Protector of Jacob and the nation. Consequently, Jacob makes a vow according to the sovereign God's capacity to deliver. In verse twenty-one, Jacob's desire is to come to his father's house in peace.

Verse twenty-two reads, "'And this stone that I have set up as a pillar will be God's house, and of all that you give me I will give you a tenth'" (NIV). This is the first time a vow is mentioned in the Bible. Then comes the statement that the place where the pillar was erected will become God's house (see 35:1, 15). The vow of the tithe is offered as acknowledgement that the land belongs to its real owner. Jacob is now bound to God, who will continue to be in charge over each detail to come in his life and that of the nation; even Jacob's approaching trickery. God had always been tied to Jacob; now Jacob is tied to God. Jacob will never forget God's place or God's portion.

THE LESSON APPLIED

In our various circumstances, it is good for us to be renewed by the presence of God. When you feel the stress and pressure of life, abandonment, loneliness, and the like, do not forget that you have a friend and brother in Christ Jesus. At the moment of uncertainty and doubt, look to Jesus, "the house of God" and "the gate of heaven" (Gen. 28:17, NIV).

LET'S TALK ABOUT IT

1. **What might we learn from today's story about our own relationship with God?**

God can work through a trickster and deceiver like Jacob, just as well as He can through anyone else. Not everyone is a deceiver, of course. But we are all sinners. Sometimes sinners are pastors and teachers; sometimes they are lay persons. God works through whomever He will, regardless of the distinctions we make in this world.

HOME DAILY DEVOTIONAL READINGS
OCTOBER 28—NOVEMBER 3, 2013

MONDAY	TUESDAY	WEDNESDAY	THURSDAY	FRIDAY	SATURDAY	SUNDAY
Oppression Under a New King	The King's Evil Plan	The Sparing of the Infant Moses	Moses Flees from Pharaoh	The People Worship God	Moses' Encounter with God	Moses' Commission from God
Exodus 1:7-14	Exodus 1:15-22	Exodus 2:1-10	Exodus 2:15-25	Exodus 4:27-31	Exodus 3:1-6	Exodus 3:7-17

PREPARATION FOR DELIVERANCE

| ADULT TOPIC:
GET READY! | BACKGROUND SCRIPTURES:
EXODUS 1—4 |

EXODUS 3:7-17

King James Version

AND the LORD said, I have surely seen the affliction of my people which are in Egypt, and have heard their cry by reason of their taskmasters; for I know their sorrows;

8 And I am come down to deliver them out of the hand of the Egyptians, and to bring them up out of that land unto a good land and a large, unto a land flowing with milk and honey; unto the place of the Canaanites, and the Hittites, and the Amorites, and the Perizzites, and the Hivites, and the Jebusites.

9 Now therefore, behold, the cry of the children of Israel is come unto me: and I have also seen the oppression wherewith the Egyptians oppress them.

10 Come now therefore, and I will send thee unto Pharaoh, that thou mayest bring forth my people the children of Israel out of Egypt.

11 And Moses said unto God, Who am I, that I should go unto Pharaoh, and that I should bring forth the children of Israel out of Egypt?

12 And he said, Certainly I will be with thee; and this shall be a token unto thee, that I have sent thee: When thou hast brought forth the people out of Egypt, ye shall serve God upon this mountain.

13 And Moses said unto God, Behold, when I come unto the children of Israel, and shall say

New Revised Standard Version

THEN the LORD said, "I have observed the misery of my people who are in Egypt; I have heard their cry on account of their taskmasters. Indeed, I know their sufferings,

8 and I have come down to deliver them from the Egyptians, and to bring them up out of that land to a good and broad land, a land flowing with milk and honey, to the country of the Canaanites, the Hittites, the Amorites, the Perizzites, the Hivites, and the Jebusites.

9 The cry of the Israelites has now come to me; I have also seen how the Egyptians oppress them.

10 So come, I will send you to Pharaoh to bring my people, the Israelites, out of Egypt."

11 But Moses said to God, "Who am I that I should go to Pharaoh, and bring the Israelites out of Egypt?"

12 He said, "I will be with you; and this shall be the sign for you that it is I who sent you: when you have brought the people out of Egypt, you shall worship God on this mountain."

13 But Moses said to God, "If I come to the Israelites and say to them, 'The God of your

MAIN THOUGHT: Go, and gather the elders of Israel together, and say unto them, The LORD God of your fathers, the God of Abraham, of Isaac, and of Jacob, appeared unto me, saying, I have surely visited you, and seen that which is done to you in Egypt: And I have said, I will bring you up out of the affliction of Egypt unto the land of the Canaanites, and the Hittites, and the Amorites, and the Perizzites, and the Hivites, and the Jebusites, unto a land flowing with milk and honey. (Exodus 3:16-17, KJV)

Exodus 3:7-17

King James Version	New Revised Standard Version
unto them, The God of your fathers hath sent me unto you; and they shall say to me, What is his name? what shall I say unto them?	ancestors has sent me to you,' and they ask me, 'What is his name?' what shall I say to them?"
14 And God said unto Moses, I AM THAT I AM: and he said, Thus shalt thou say unto the children of Israel, I AM hath sent me unto you.	14 God said to Moses, "I AM WHO I AM." He said further, "Thus you shall say to the Israelites, 'I AM has sent me to you.'"
15 And God said moreover unto Moses, Thus shalt thou say unto the children of Israel, the LORD God of your fathers, the God of Abraham, the God of Isaac, and the God of Jacob, hath sent me unto you: this is my name for ever, and this is my memorial unto all generations.	15 God also said to Moses, "Thus you shall say to the Israelites, 'The LORD, the God of your ancestors, the God of Abraham, the God of Isaac, and the God of Jacob, has sent me to you': This is my name forever, and this my title for all generations.
16 Go, and gather the elders of Israel together, and say unto them, The LORD God of your fathers, the God of Abraham, of Isaac, and of Jacob, appeared unto me, saying, I have surely visited you, and seen that which is done to you in Egypt:	16 Go and assemble the elders of Israel, and say to them, 'The LORD, the God of your ancestors, the God of Abraham, of Isaac, and of Jacob, has appeared to me, saying: I have given heed to you and to what has been done to you in Egypt.
17 And I have said, I will bring you up out of the affliction of Egypt unto the land of the Canaanites, and the Hittites, and the Amorites, and the Perizzites, and the Hivites, and the Jebusites, unto a land flowing with milk and honey.	17 I declare that I will bring you up out of the misery of Egypt, to the land of the Canaanites, the Hittites, the Amorites, the Perizzites, the Hivites, and the Jebusites, a land flowing with milk and honey.'"

LESSON SETTING
   Time: Unknown
   Place: Near Mount Sinai

LESSON OUTLINE
   I. **God Hears the Cry of His People**
      (Exodus 3:7-10)
   II. **Moses' Uncertainty**
      (Exodus 3:11-12)
   III. **God's Name**
      (Exodus 3:13-17)

UNIFYING PRINCIPLE
   When people are called to a new challenge, they must overcome their fears. How can the participants overcome their fears? Before Moses could lead the people to freedom, God repeatedly assured Moses of His persistent help in all the trials to come.

INTRODUCTION
   Our lessons for the month of November will be drawn from the book of Exodus. By way of introduction, we should point out that many years have passed since the days of Jacob and his sons. They settled in Egypt, you will recall, and many generations passed. During this time, the descendants of Jacob grew to be a large number. In time, a pharaoh came to the throne who was not sympathetic to their presence in

Egypt. In fact, he saw them as a threat and he sought to neutralize the threat by enslaving the people of Israel. Today's text opens as God has heard the anguished cries of His people for deliverance from slavery. In today's lesson, we will discuss the call and commission of Moses, the man through whom God would work in order to bring about the deliverance of His people. In a brief ten verses, we will encounter God's strong sense of justice, Moses' recognition of his own inadequacy, and the first hints of God's work to create a covenant people who would glorify His name throughout the world.

The generally agreed-upon location for the events in today's lesson is near Mount Sinai. Moses' attention is drawn to a bright, flaming bush that is burning yet not being consumed. God, of course, could have used any means available to Him in order to gain Moses' attention. Yet He used a burning, flaming bush. Out of this extraordinary sight, God spoke to Moses from the fire. Fire, as we have seen, is frequently a symbol of the presence of the Lord.

God makes a clear statement that the deliverance of His people will be executed by divine power and not by any human instrumentality. God calls Moses' name twice from the bush, demonstrating that His call is intentional and specific (see v. 4). Moses responds, "'Here I am'" (v. 4, NIV). His response is an indication of his openness to hear and to obey God. These same words are spoken in other places in Scripture by Abraham (see Gen. 22:11), Jacob (see Gen. 46:2), and Samuel (see 1 Sam. 3:4).

As the narrative progresses, God asks Moses to come closer and to take off his shoes because he is standing on holy ground. God's presence made the ground holy. That Moses must remove his shoes emphasizes God's transcendence and otherness. God introduces Himself as the God of Abraham, Isaac, and Jacob. We might be inclined to think this unnecessary.

God's holiness and His identity are important because Moses was being sent to a country that worshiped a plethora of gods. Now he is speaking to the one and only God of the universe. In spite of how bad Israel's condition seemed, the unconditional promise God had made to the patriarch would come to pass. Israel's captivity would come to an end as He had promised. First, though, God had to summon a deliverer.

EXPOSITION

I. GOD HEARS THE CRY OF HIS PEOPLE (EXODUS 3:7-10)

As we turn to today's text, we come to the very first time that God speaks in the book of Exodus. As Fretheim has observed about Exodus 3, "This, the first word of God in Exodus, is *programmatic*; it both sets all that follows into motion and reveals the kind of God it is who acts in the narrative to follow" (Terence E. Fretheim, *Exodus* [Louisville: John Knox Press, 1991], 59). God says, "'I have indeed seen the misery of my people in Egypt. I have heard them crying out because of their slave drivers, and I am concerned about their suffering'" (Exod. 3:7, NIV). The language reminds us that God cares about the life and concerns of His people. He understands human sorrow.

God now moves to act on behalf of His people: "'So I have come down to rescue them from the hand of the Egyptians'" (v. 8, NIV). God intervenes in human affairs. He comes down with a purpose—to lead His people to a better land, "'a good and spacious land, a land flowing with milk and honey'" (ibid.). That the land is good means that it is prosperous (see Lev. 20:24; Num. 13:27; Deut. 6:3; 27:3; Josh. 5:6). Moreover, the land would be spacious. This is indicated by the six or, in parallel lists, ten nations who were living there. Israel will possess all the land by God's act and will enjoy the land's abundance.

In verses 9-10, God's call to Moses leads to a double conclusion with the phrases "and now" and "so now" (NIV). This can be compared with 2 Samuel 7:28-29 (NRSV), where the first "now" restates the previous grounds while the second "now" draws a conclusion that calls for a response. In Exodus 3, verse nine repeats verse seven by summarizing the speech and recollecting the circumstances for the divine call, Israel's present need, and God's solution. Verse ten describes the formal commissioning of Moses as God's ambassador to lead His people to a better land.

II. MOSES' UNCERTAINTY (EXODUS 3:11-12)

Moses then questions God: "'Who am I that I should go to Pharaoh, and bring the Israelites out of Egypt?'" (v. 11, NRSV). Moses' first protest against accepting the commission looks back to the time he had spent in the desert. He is certainly not eager to fulfill the role of deliverer. He is keenly aware of his limited capabilities, his inadequacies, and his defects. He has been shepherding flocks, a fugitive on the run, wanted by the Egyptians, and hated

by the Hebrews. But Moses has to understand that God will be the force behind the people's deliverance.

God had time and again promised to be with Abraham, Isaac, and Jacob. Now He promises to do the same for Moses. In verse twelve, God responds to Moses with a reassuring word: "'I will be with you'" (NRSV). God is greater than the pharaoh of Egypt. The tangible sign given to Moses assures him that God will succeed in enacting His promises. He is told that once he has brought the people out of Egypt, he will come again to this same place to worship. The phrase "worship God" (NIV, NRSV) points to becoming "a slave of God" or to "serving God like a slave." The nation is to become slaves for God, rather than slaves for Egypt.

The sign that God gives is confirmatory and appeals to faith rather than to immediate evidence or to the presence of the miraculous. God, at times, gave signs to the people (see Exod. 4:1-9). But in this instance, no such immediate sign is given to Moses. God asks for trust and belief in His promise that He will be present and fulfill His promises. "This sign, which was to be a pledge to Moses of the success of his mission, was one indeed that required faith itself; but, at the same time, it was a sign adapted to inspire both courage and confidence" (Carl Keil and Franz Delitzsch, *The Pentateuch*, Reprint Ed. [Peabody, MA: Hendrickson Publishers, 1996], 286).

III. GOD'S NAME (EXODUS 3:13-17)

In verse thirteen, Moses asks God an important question: "'If I come to the Israelites and say to them, "The God of your ancestors has sent me to you," and they ask me, "What is his name?" what shall I say to them?"'" (NRSV). Verse fourteen records God's response: "God said to Moses, 'I AM WHO I AM' ... 'Thus you shall say to the Israelites, 'I AM has sent me to you'" (NRSV).

There is no shortage of commentary on the meaning of these verses. There was power in knowing a person's name, and this would give one power over another. Moses was searching for something that would assure him of God's presence in the struggle to come. God's name could do that. One must remember that the Hebrew people were living in a polytheistic society, surrounded by the worship of multiple gods. Names were believed not only to identify those to whom they were attached, but also to give clues to their character (see 1 Sam. 25:25).

God responds with a name for Himself that is extremely rich in meaning. It links His name with the verb "to be" (Heb. *hayah*). This name is generally translated, "I AM WHO I AM" (NIV, NRSV). In the English Bible, it is most often rendered "LORD." This practice grows out of the longstanding taboo in Judaism against uttering aloud the name of God. In Hebrew texts, the word *Adonai* is usually substituted.

The traditional understanding of the meaning of the name has recently been challenged. Many leading commentators argue that *ehyeh* is better translated as "I shall be" and so the name should be rendered, "I will be that I will be." No translation, of course, can capture the full range of possible meanings. Also, the name can be understood to mean that

He is self-revealing, self-sustaining, and self-sufficient. The divine name sums up the character of God. The fullness of its meaning could not be comprehended completely by Moses, of course. In essence, what God's name teaches is that He will be present in whatever endeavor we find ourselves. As Israel's circumstances changed, the immutable God remained faithful to His Word. This is what Moses was to convey to the Hebrew people.

More specifically, God's response assures Moses that he is not going to be alone. The gathering of the elders is proof that God intended for Moses to be successful. The promise that the elders will accompany Moses is a sign that he will be able to convince them of his mission and of the authenticity of the revelation he has received.

The elders mentioned are the heads of the various families or tribes (see Exod. 6:14-15, 25; 12:21; Num. 2). Each elder had a tribe to rule. Moses was to transfer God's message to the elders, and they were to accompany Moses before the pharaoh. It would be God who made certain Moses' message was received and accepted by the elders. Note that the message begins with a repetition of the words used by Joseph on his deathbed (see Gen. 50:24): "'I have surely visited you'" (Exod. 3:16, KJV), "'I have watched over you'" (NIV), and "'I have promised to bring you up out of your misery in Egypt'" (v. 17, NIV). God is saying that He would continue to fulfill what He had promised to Joseph. "Misery" used in the text (v. 17, NIV) is a form of the same word used by Abram in Genesis 15:13, where God told him that His people would be "mistreated" (NIV) in Egypt for four hundred years. The same God who told Abram what was to come also told Joseph that He would bring His people out of Egypt. This same God now acted through Moses to do just that.

THE LESSON APPLIED

God continues to call each of us to salvation through Jesus Christ. The Church ought to realize the privilege of being able to worship Him because of who He is. We may not completely comprehend what God is doing, but we can trust Him to be faithful. When adversity arises, we should take courage knowing that ultimately He has the capacity to deliver and save.

LET'S TALK ABOUT IT

1. Where do we see Christ in today's lesson text?

In earlier lessons, we have addressed the problem of how best to read the Old Testament through a Christological lens. The Fathers of the Church wrote extensively about Exodus 3, as did the later Reformers. They observed that "the whole Christological problem emerged in the revelation at the bush. Who was this 'angel' who appeared in the fire in the lowly bush, who spoke for God in executing the redemption from Egypt?" (Brevard Childs, *The Book of Exodus* [Philadelphia: Westminster Press, 1974], 84). Strangely, most modern writers have avoided this question. But in the early centuries of the Church, writers as diverse as Justin, Irenaeus, Eusebius, and Ambrose agreed that the identification of the angel as the Son was "completely obvious" (ibid.).

Whatever we make of this sentiment —however obvious we might find it— it does raise the question of how we read the Old Testament. Is it a dead letter for us? Have we neglected it in our preaching and teaching? Assuming (rightly) that Christ came to fulfill the Law and not to abolish it, how do we read the Old Testament as Christians? Where do we see Christ in it? The early Church's impulse to see Christ in the stories, laws, proverbs, and psalms should caution us against too much trust in historical-critical reconstructions of "what actually happened." The Bible, the Fathers argued, was the Church's book. It speaks of Christ in its entirety.

With that in mind, let us not shy away from the Old Testament in our preaching and teaching. Let us help our congregants to see God at work in these stories for our redemption. In so doing, let us take a part in strengthening them for the trials and challenges they face every day in their desire to live the Christian life.

HOME DAILY DEVOTIONAL READINGS
NOVEMBER 4–10, 2013

MONDAY	TUESDAY	WEDNESDAY	THURSDAY	FRIDAY	SATURDAY	SUNDAY
The Lamb of God	The Troubles Multiply	Broken Spirits and Closed Ears	The Final Plague	The First Passover	The Lord Delivered Israel	The Promise to Pass Over
John 1:29-37	Exodus 5:19-23	Exodus 6:2-9	Exodus 11	Exodus 12:21-28	Exodus 12:43-51	Exodus 12:1-14

BEGINNING OF PASSOVER

ADULT TOPIC: REMEMBER AND CELEBRATE	BACKGROUND SCRIPTURES: EXODUS 6:2–30; 12

EXODUS 12:1-14

King James Version

AND the LORD spake unto Moses and Aaron in the land of Egypt saying,

2 This month shall be unto you the beginning of months: it shall be the first month of the year to you.

3 Speak ye unto all the congregation of Israel, saying, In the tenth day of this month they shall take to them every man a lamb, according to the house of their fathers, a lamb for an house:

4 And if the household be too little for the lamb, let him and his neighbour next unto his house take it according to the number of the souls; every man according to his eating shall make your count for the lamb.

5 Your lamb shall be without blemish, a male of the first year: ye shall take it out from the sheep, or from the goats:

6 And ye shall keep it up until the fourteenth day of the same month: and the whole assembly of the congregation of Israel shall kill it in the evening.

7 And they shall take of the blood, and strike it on the two side posts and on the upper door post of the houses, wherein they shall eat it.

8 And they shall eat the flesh in that night, roast with fire, and unleavened bread; and with bitter herbs they shall eat it.

9 Eat not of it raw, nor sodden at all with water, but roast with fire; his head with his legs, and with the purtenance thereof.

New Revised Standard Version

THE LORD said to Moses and Aaron in the land of Egypt:

2 This month shall mark for you the beginning of months; it shall be the first month of the year for you.

3 Tell the whole congregation of Israel that on the tenth of this month they are to take a lamb for each family, a lamb for each household.

4 If a household is too small for a whole lamb, it shall join its closest neighbor in obtaining one; the lamb shall be divided in proportion to the number of people who eat of it.

5 Your lamb shall be without blemish, a year-old male; you may take it from the sheep or from the goats.

6 You shall keep it until the fourteenth day of this month; then the whole assembled congregation of Israel shall slaughter it at twilight.

7 They shall take some of the blood and put it on the two doorposts and the lintel of the houses in which they eat it.

8 They shall eat the lamb that same night; they shall eat it roasted over the fire with unleavened bread and bitter herbs.

9 Do not eat any of it raw or boiled in water, but roasted over the fire, with its head, legs, and inner organs.

MAIN THOUGHT: And this day shall be unto you for a memorial; and ye shall keep it a feast to the LORD throughout your generations; ye shall keep it a feast by an ordinance for ever. (Exodus 12:14, KJV)

Exodus 12:1-14

<table>
<tr><td>

King James Version

</td><td>

New Revised Standard Version

</td></tr>
</table>

King James Version	*New Revised Standard Version*
10 And ye shall let nothing of it remain until the morning; and that which remaineth of it until the morning ye shall burn with fire.	10 You shall let none of it remain until the morning; anything that remains until the morning you shall burn.
11 And thus shall ye eat it; with your loins girded, your shoes on your feet, and your staff in your hand; and ye shall eat it in haste: it is the LORD's passover.	11 This is how you shall eat it: your loins girded, your sandals on your feet, and your staff in your hand; and you shall eat it hurriedly. It is the passover of the LORD.
12 For I will pass through the land of Egypt this night, and will smite all the firstborn in the land of Egypt, both man and beast; and against all the gods of Egypt I will execute judgment: I am the LORD.	12 For I will pass through the land of Egypt that night, and I will strike down every firstborn in the land of Egypt, both human beings and animals; on all the gods of Egypt I will execute judgments: I am the LORD.
13 And the blood shall be to you for a token upon the houses where ye are: and when I see the blood, I will pass over you, and the plague shall not be upon you to destroy you, when I smite the land of Egypt.	13 The blood shall be a sign for you on the houses where you live: when I see the blood, I will pass over you, and no plague shall destroy you when I strike the land of Egypt.
14 And this day shall be unto you for a memorial; and ye shall keep it a feast to the LORD throughout your generations; ye shall keep it a feast by an ordinance for ever.	14 This day shall be a day of remembrance for you. You shall celebrate it as a festival to the LORD; throughout your generations you shall observe it as a perpetual ordinance.

LESSON SETTING

 Time: ca. 1450 B.C.
 Place: Egypt

LESSON OUTLINE

 I. **The Lord's Calendar**
  (Exodus 12:1-2)
 II. **The Lord's Passover**
  (Exodus 12:3-13)
 III. **The Feast of Unleavened**
  Bread
  (Exodus 12:14)

UNIFYING PRINCIPLE

People who are living under oppression hunger for freedom. What is the meaning of freedom? The freedom God promises to the Hebrew people will create a new beginning in their relationship with God —a beginning they will commemorate for generations to come.

INTRODUCTION

At the conclusion of last week's lesson, Moses had been commissioned to leave the wilderness and return to Egypt. Once there he was to go to his people, the Hebrews, with the message that God had heard their cries and was now moving to deliver them from slavery and mistreatment at the hands of the pharaoh. The narrative of the book of Exodus, of course, covers a considerable amount of ground between that text and today's text. By way of introduction, it will be helpful to summarize the sequence of events that brings us to the institution of the Passover in today's lesson.

Even after he had been given the divine name, Moses' still had fear and uncertainty. He was concerned that the people of Israel would not listen to him (see Exod. 4:1).

In response, God gave him two signs—the staff that turns into the serpent and the leprous hand—that he could use to confirm that his message was from Him. Moses then replied that he was not eloquent enough for the task (see 4:10). In response, God appointed Moses' brother, Aaron, to be his spokesman.

With that, Moses returned to Egypt to appear before the pharaoh (see Exod. 5). The demand he made of the pharaoh was simple: "'Thus says the LORD, the God of Israel, "Let my people go, so that they may celebrate a festival to me in the wilderness"'" (5:1, NRSV). Pharaoh's response was not favorable: "'Who is the LORD, that I should heed him and let Israel go? I do not know the LORD, and I will not let Israel go'" (v. 2, NRSV). After his meeting with Moses and Aaron, the pharaoh actually increased the workload of the Israelites, leading to resentment on the Israelites' part against Moses and Aaron.

In Exodus 7, Moses and Aaron again approached the pharaoh and repeated their original demand to release the people into the wilderness to worship God. This time they accompanied their demand with a sign—the staff that turned into a serpent. As it happened, the pharaoh's court magicians were able to perform the same sign (although Aaron's staff-serpent swallowed up all of the other serpents). The result of this was inconclusive: "Still Pharaoh's heart was hardened, and he would not listen to them, as the LORD had said" (Exod. 7:13, NRSV). This resulted, as is well known, in a series of increasingly severe plagues brought by God against the pharaoh and the people of Egypt: the water turned into blood (see Exod. 7:14-25), the frogs (see 8:1-15), the gnats (see 8:16-19), the flies (see 8:20-32), the plague on the livestock (see 9:1-7), the boils (see 9:8-12), the hail (see 9:13-35), the locusts (see 10:1-20), and the darkness (see 10:21-29).

After the ninth plague—darkness—there is an intermission of sorts in the narrative. God announces to Moses His intentions for what is to come: "'I will bring one more plague upon Pharaoh and upon Egypt; afterwards he will let you go from here; indeed, when he lets you go, he will drive you away'" (Exod. 11:1, NRSV). When Moses announces the nature of this plague—the death of every firstborn child and animal in Egypt—to Pharaoh, his words are very explicit and are spoken "in hot anger" (v. 8, NRSV). They leave no room for confusion. Pharaoh, of course, does not listen, thus setting the scene for today's lesson and the events that follow it.

EXPOSITION

I. THE LORD'S CALENDAR (EXODUS 12:1-2)

The first thing we notice about today's text is that it interrupts the flow of the narrative. It is an "intrusion in to the narrative of [God's] tenth mighty act" (John I. Durham, *Exodus* [Waco, TX: Word Books, 1987], 152). For much of the last two centuries, this seeming interruption has been explained in source-critical terms: most commentators assign Exodus 12:1-20 to the so-called Priestly source (P). This may or may not be true, of course, and its value for our understanding of the passage as a whole is limited. It does, however, forcefully highlight how sudden the transition between chapters eleven and twelve is. But, as Durham argues, "What strikes us as disunified, a patchwork, must be seen in terms of the purpose suggested in the compilation before us, rather than in terms of our own expectation of a logical and coherent sequence" (153). He concludes that there is indeed a purpose to the arrangement of the narrative: "Read in its context, this chapter both interrupts (vv 1-28) and continues (vv 29-42) the narrative without which the requirement of Yahweh's Passover and the feast of the unleavened bread would be arbitrary and puzzling" (ibid.).

But there is another, deeper kind of interruption at work in this text. Whatever can be said about the calendar that the Israelites adhered to prior to this time (in truth, there is no way of knowing, despite the speculation to be found in some commentaries), the institution of the Passover represents a reset of that way of ordering time. God says, "'This month shall mark for you the beginning of months; it shall be the first month of the year for you'" (v. 2, NRSV). But aside from mundane calendrical considerations, this decree by God affirms "the theological importance of Yahweh's Passover" in its "commemoration of Israel's beginning as a people freed by Yahweh" (Durham, 153). Durham goes on to argue that "the Passover month is the 'head' of the months not primarily as the first month of the year in a calendar, either a 'civil' calendar or a 'religious' calendar, but because it is the month during which the Israelites remembered and so actualized their redemption" (ibid.).

II. THE LORD'S PASSOVER (EXODUS 12:3-13)

Instructions for the observance of Passover were given to Israel by the elders of the tribes (see Exod. 12:21). But the ultimate source of these instructions was God. As we move forward with today's text, we come to a large section that deals with the specifics of the observance (see vv. 3-11) and a shorter section that reflects on its meaning (see vv. 12-13). A lamb was to be selected for sacrifice on the tenth day of the month and given care until the fourteenth day of the month. Each man was to select "'a lamb for his family, one for each household'" (v. 3, NIV). The delay likely allowed for the people to thoroughly inspect the animal to be certain it was without blemish.

The animal was to be a year old, male, and, as noted above, without blemish (see v. 5; cf. Lev. 22:20-25; Mal. 1:8, 14). It was to be killed at twilight on the fourteenth day. The blood from the animal was then to be smeared on the doorposts of the home. On that same night, each family was to eat the lamb, roasted with bitter herbs, and unleavened bread. The meat was to be eaten roasted and whole (with the inner parts washed and left inside). It was not to be eaten raw or boiled in water, and all leftovers were to be burned. The meal was to be eaten in haste. Each family member was to have his robe tucked in his belt (i.e., in travelling mode), shoes on, and staff in hand ready to move.

Notice that in this account of the first Passover there is no priest, altar, or tabernacle. Families ate the Passover together—communities in God's presence—around the sacrificial lamb. Some have suggested that the lamb's age, one year old, was correlated to the firstborn who was to die. The bitter herbs also served as a reminder of the harshness of Egyptian bondage and slavery (see Exod. 1:14). The fact that the bread was unleavened was a sign of the haste with which the Israelites were to celebrate. Yeast takes time to ferment, and time was of the essence on this occasion. Moreover, leavened bread was made from a "starter" loaf of dough that was used to leaven the present-day's dough. This was forbidden in Hebrew custom. This was the Lord's Passover, and this was how Israel was to eat it.

We might also observe here that the description given of the Passover meal in Exodus resembles the ritual whereby Aaron and his sons were consecrated as priests (see Exod. 20). That event included the killing of a ram, the sprinkling of its blood, and the consuming of meat with unleavened bread. The significance of these similarities is that Passover functions not only as a means of redemption from Egypt, but as a sign of consecration to God.

With verse twelve, we move from description of the Passover ritual to some reflection on the significance of the event: "'On that same night I will pass through Egypt and strike down every firstborn— both men and animals—and I will bring judgment on all the gods of Egypt. I am the LORD. The blood will be a sign for you on the houses where you are; and when I see the blood, I will pass over you. No destructive plague will touch you when I strike Egypt'" (Exod. 12:12-13, NIV). The blood can be seen as a sign similar to the other signs the people had experienced, namely the nine plagues they had already witnessed against the Egyptians.

Whatever would happen as a result of the Passover, these homes would not be affected by the tenth and final plague. Only the homes of the Egyptians would be affected. Even the Egyptian gods would be judged by the Passover experience. They would be helpless against the God of Abraham, Isaac, and Jacob. These gods, who were often depicted in the form of the animals of the fields, would experience an excruciating blow, all their firstborn would be killed as well.

III. THE FEAST OF UNLEAVENED BREAD (EXODUS 12:14)

The final portion of today's text is brief, but necessarily so. With verse fourteen, we move to an entirely new topic of discussion— the institution of the Feast of Unleavened Bread. The two feasts discussed in this chapter—Passover and Unleavened Bread—are closely connected, but ultimately distinct. At any rate, verses 14-20 are part of a larger unit that discusses how the Feast of Unleavened Bread is to be observed.

The feast was intended to commemorate the same thing that the Passover celebration commemorated: the fact that God spared Israel's firstborn when He moved to kill the firstborn of Egypt. The procedures are given beginning in verse fifteen: "'Seven days you shall eat unleavened bread; on the first day you shall remove leaven from your houses, for whoever eats leavened bread from the first day until the seventh day shall be cut off from Israel'" (NRSV). The seven-day-long festival was bounded on either side—on the first day and the seventh day—with "a solemn assembly" (v. 16, NRSV). The festival was to be observed on specific days: it was to last "from the evening of the fourteenth day [of the month Abib] until the evening of the twenty-first day" (v. 18, NRSV). As to the lasting significance of the festival, Keil and Delitzsch are helpful on this point: "The significance of this feast was in the eating of the *mazzoth*, i.e., of pure unleavened bread. As bread, which is the principal means of preserving life, might easily be regarded as the symbol of life itself…so the *mazzoth*, or unleavened loaves, were symbolical of the new life, as cleansed from the leaven of a sinful nature. But if the eating of mazzoth was to shadow forth the new life into which Israel was transferred, any one who ate leavened bread at the feast would renounce this new life, and was therefore to be cut off from Israel, i.e., 'from the congregation of Israel' (v. 19)" (*The Pentateuch*, Reprint Ed. [Peabody, MA: Hendrickson Publishers, 1996], 333).

THE LESSON APPLIED

The Feasts of Passover and Unleavened Bread discussed in today's lesson remind us that God delivers His people from oppression. In the text, the deliverance was deliverance from bondage in Egypt. In the New Testament, such deliverance is most often spoken of as deliverance from the bondage of sin. This can (and should) be taken to speak of deliverance from both individual and collective sins, sins against personal holiness as well as the sins that infect institutions.

LET'S TALK ABOUT IT

1. **What is the continuing value of Passover for the Church?**

As suggested above, there are continuing lessons in the Passover narrative for the Church. Through the waters of baptism, God has brought us out of the Egypt of sin (see 1 Cor. 10). Christ is also said by Paul to be our Passover Lamb. "Clean out the old yeast so that you may be a new batch, as you really are unleavened. For our paschal lamb, Christ, has been sacrificed" (1 Cor. 5:7). In light of this text, the connections between Passover and the Lord's Supper should be obvious. In our day, some churches hold Passover seders, especially around Easter. These events can certainly be helpful for informational purposes, for helping to get a sense of what this occasion is all about for the Jews. Such seders, though, ought never to take the place of the Lord's Supper, the Eucharist, where we gather around the Lord's table together to share in the commemoration of His death, burial, and resurrection. The new covenant community, the Church, has been given this meal, a meal that looks forward to the great marriage supper of the Lamb (see Rev. 19) where the table will be spread for all who enter into God's kingdom.

HOME DAILY DEVOTIONAL READINGS
NOVEMBER 11–17, 2013

MONDAY	TUESDAY	WEDNESDAY	THURSDAY	FRIDAY	SATURDAY	SUNDAY
Called to Live in Freedom	Setting Apart the Firstborn	Guided by Pillars of Cloud and Fire	Pharaoh's Change of Heart	The Lord Will Fight for You	Guarded from the Approaching Enemy	The Lord Saved Israel that Day
Galatians 5:13-21	Exodus 13:11-16	Exodus 13:17-22	Exodus 14:5-9	Exodus 14:10-14	Exodus 14:15-20	Exodus 14:21-30

BEGINNING OF FREEDOM

ADULT TOPIC:	BACKGROUND SCRIPTURES:
FROM DESPAIR TO DELIVERANCE	EXODUS 13:17–22; 14

EXODUS 14:21-30

King James Version

AND Moses stretched out his hand over the sea; and the LORD caused the sea to go back by a strong east wind all that night, and made the sea dry land, and the waters were divided.

22 And the children of Israel went into the midst of the sea upon the dry ground: and the waters were a wall unto them on their right hand, and on their left.

23 And the Egyptians pursued, and went in after them to the midst of the sea, even all Pharaoh's horses, his chariots, and his horsemen.

24 And it came to pass, that in the morning watch the LORD looked unto the host of the Egyptians through the pillar of fire and of the cloud, and troubled the host of the Egyptians,

25 And took off their chariot wheels, that they drave them heavily: so that the Egyptians said, Let us flee from the face of Israel; for the LORD fighteth for them against the Egyptians.

26 And the LORD said unto Moses, Stretch out thine hand over the sea, that the waters may come again upon the Egyptians, upon their chariots, and upon their horsemen.

27 And Moses stretched forth his hand over the sea, and the sea returned to his strength when the morning appeared; and the Egyptians fled against it; and the Lord overthrew the Egyptians in the midst of the sea.

28 And the waters returned, and covered the chariots, and the horsemen, and all the host

New Revised Standard Version

THEN Moses stretched out his hand over the sea. The LORD drove the sea back by a strong east wind all night, and turned the sea into dry land; and the waters were divided.

22 The Israelites went into the sea on dry ground, the waters forming a wall for them on their right and on their left.

23 The Egyptians pursued, and went into the sea after them, all of Pharaoh's horses, chariots, and chariot drivers.

24 At the morning watch the LORD in the pillar of fire and cloud looked down upon the Egyptian army, and threw the Egyptian army into panic.

25 He clogged their chariot wheels so that they turned with difficulty. The Egyptians said, "Let us flee from the Israelites, for the LORD is fighting for them against Egypt."

26 Then the LORD said to Moses, "Stretch out your hand over the sea, so that the water may come back upon the Egyptians, upon their chariots and chariot drivers."

27 So Moses stretched out his hand over the sea, and at dawn the sea returned to its normal depth. As the Egyptians fled before it, the LORD tossed the Egyptians into the sea.

28 The waters returned and covered the chariots and the chariot drivers, the entire army of

MAIN THOUGHT: Thus the LORD saved Israel that day out of the hand of the Egyptians; and Israel saw the Egyptians dead upon the sea shore. (Exodus 14:30, KJV)

Exodus 14:21–30

King James Version	New Revised Standard Version
of Pharaoh that came into the sea after them; there remained not so much as one of them.	Pharaoh that had followed them into the sea; not one of them remained.
29 But the children of Israel walked upon dry land in the midst of the sea; and the waters were a wall unto them on their right hand, and on their left.	29 But the Israelites walked on dry ground through the sea, the waters forming a wall for them on their right and on their left.
30 Thus the LORD saved Israel that day out of the hand of the Egyptians; and Israel saw the Egyptians dead upon the sea shore.	30 Thus the LORD saved Israel that day from the Egyptians; and Israel saw the Egyptians dead on the seashore.

LESSON SETTING
Time: ca. 1450 B.C.
Place: Pi-hahiroth

LESSON OUTLINE
I. The Lord Divides the Sea (Exodus 14:21-22)
II. The Lord Fights for Israel (Exodus 14:23-25)
III. The Lord Saves Israel (Exodus 14:26-30)

UNIFYING PRINCIPLE

The Israelites may feel themselves in seemingly impossible circumstances while seeking freedom. How can they safely reach freedom? God created a way out when there was no way.

INTRODUCTION

God's promise to deliver His people from Egyptian bondage became a reality. We see that clearly in today's lesson. But we will also see that their deliverance was not the end of the story. There were still obstacles and uncertainties to be faced even after the pharaoh released Moses and the people of Israel to leave. Today's text focuses on the crossing of the Red Sea. As with last week's lesson, there is a significant gap between the Passover

text that we talked about last week and today's text. Therefore, it will behoove us to summarize what occurs in chapters 12-14 as a lead-in to today's lesson. After the description of the rituals for the Passover celebration and the Feast of Unleavened Bread, Moses calls the elders of Israel and instructs them to perform the appropriate rituals: "The Israelites went and did just as the LORD had commanded Moses and Aaron" (Exod. 12:28, NRSV). The narrative then goes on to recount the slaughter of the firstborn (see vv. 29-32). Following that, the narrative moves forward in stages with the Israelites as they journey from Rameses, the place in Egypt where the Israelites seem to have settled, to Succoth to Etham "on the edge of the wilderness" (Exod. 13:20, NRSV) to Pi-hahiroth (see Exod. 14:2). Interspersed with this narrative are further instructions regarding Passover (see 12:43-50), the Feast of Unleavened Bread (see 13:3-10), and the consecration of Israel's firstborn (see 13:11-16).

As the Israelites approached the Red Sea, Pharaoh had a change of heart: "When the king of Egypt was told that the people [of Israel] had fled, the minds of Pharaoh and his officials were changed toward the people, and they said, 'What have we done, letting Israel leave our service?'" (Exod. 14:5, NRSV). As before, the Lord "hardened the heart of Pharaoh" and he sent his chariots to pursue them (v. 8, NRSV). Pharaoh's forces overtook the people of Israel as they "camped by the sea, by Pi-hahiroth, in front of Baal-zephon" (v. 9, NRSV). The people were frightened. As they saw it, they were trapped between the sea and the approaching Egyptian army. In that moment, fear and lack of trust overtook them and they lashed out at Moses: "'Was it because there were no graves in Egypt that you have taken us away to die in the wilderness? What have you done to us, bringing us out of Egypt? Is this not the very thing we told you in Egypt, "Let us alone and let us serve the Egyptians"? For it would have been better for us to serve the Egyptians than to die in the wilderness?'" (vv. 11-12, NRSV).

Moses is unfazed, however. He calls on the people to put aside their fear and to trust in the Lord for deliverance. This makes a great deal of sense to us, of course. We can easily recall that hardly two chapters earlier God through Moses had brought them out of Egypt with a mighty hand. So why, we might ask, could they not remember that? In truth, of course, we do the same thing. Our memories are short; we are frequently tempted to despair at even the slightest setbacks or dangers in our lives. Often, to be honest, this comes from a lack of faith in God's promises. Today's text shows how God acted at a moment when the faith of His people was at a low ebb. It also invites us to renew our faith in His activity in our

lives and in our churches. It also calls us to examine the deeper meaning of God's act of liberation.

One of the more prominent temptations faced by commentators on passages such as this one is the temptation to try to explain the miracle by way of material forces or weather patterns or some other such thing. This is easy to do: for much of the twentieth century, it has been thought by many that the Christian faith would be more readily accepted by non-believers if we simply edited out miracles such as the one described in Exodus 14. That is not, of course, the approach that we will be taking here. But having avoided one ditch, we must not then fall into the other one. If we devote all of our attention to defending the historical veracity (or at least plausibility) of this event, we may well be distracted from seeing the overarching theological message of the story. With that in mind, we will proceed.

EXPOSITION

I. THE LORD DIVIDES THE SEA (EXODUS 14:21-22)

Verse twenty-one speaks of Moses' action: "Then Moses stretched out his hand over the sea" (NIV). This action provided visible evidence to the people that God was with them still. The stretching out of Moses' hand on faith caused an east wind to blow in order for Israel to pass through the sea on dry land. This was the same east wind that brought the locusts to Egypt (see Exod. 10:13). The locusts were driven completely into the Red Sea—not a locust was preserved. The same fate was appointed to the Egyptians. As we will see below, not an Egyptian would survive (see

14:28). God brought the people of Israel to this point and He would deliver them.

The water divided and the people of Israel "went through the sea on dry ground" (v. 29, NIV). The divided waters formed a wall on either side, piled up like a heap. The term *wall* in the text (Heb. *khomah*) connotes a very large wall, such as a city wall, towering well above the Hebrews who marched between the walls of water on dry land. Because of the large walls of water, Pharaoh's forces could attack only from the rear, not from the side. The term *sea* (Heb. *yam*) connotes a body of water of significant depth. The fact that the sea was turned into a valley because of its depth added to the difficulty of the Egyptian assault. It seems that we are meant here to recall an act of creation. As Fretheim points out, "Dry land appears in the midst of chaos, just as in Gen. 1:9-10 (cf. 8:13) at the separation of waters. The divine creative act in the sphere of nature serves as the vehicle for the creation of a liberated people (note also the birthing language—path through water). Creative activity in nature enables creative activity in history. What happens in nature creates new possibilities *for God* within the historical sphere. The work of God as *creator* effects the redemption of a people" (Terence E. Fretheim, *Exodus* [Louisville: John Knox Press, 1991], 159).

In sum, God is at work in nature, in His own creation, to bring about His purposes. As with the plagues, God works through what we see around us.

II. THE LORD FIGHTS FOR ISRAEL (EXODUS 14:23-25)

Israel went through the Red Sea on dry land, and the Egyptians followed them into the midst of the sea. Pharaoh had sent his armies in hopes of bringing back his chief labor source to Egypt. Perhaps he was embarrassed at succumbing to Moses and his God. At any rate, God threw them into confusion. The text tells us that "at the morning watch the LORD in the pillar of fire and cloud looked down upon the Egyptian army" (v. 24, NRSV). God's look is usually one of mercy or, as in this case, of wrath. His look "threw the Egyptian army into panic" (ibid.). This panic, or "confusion" (NIV), is the panic and disarray of an army before a superior challenger, especially when God enters the battle (see Exod. 23:27; Josh. 10:10; Judg. 4:15; 1 Sam. 7:10; Ps. 18:14).

Having followed Israel into the Red Sea, the Egyptians' chariot wheels clogged in mud, making them difficult to drive. With this, they could neither flee nor fight. What is going on here? Some commentators, on the basis of Psalm 78:18-19, argue that a strong storm arose. Others do not follow this line of thought. Keil and Delitzsch suggest that the "look of Jehovah is to be regarded as the appearance of fire suddenly bursting forth from the pillar of cloud that was turned towards the Egyptians" (Carl Keil and Franz Delitzsch, *The Pentateuch*, Reprint Ed. [Peabody, MA: Hendrickson Publishers, 1996], 351). Whatever we conclude about this incident, the Egyptians knew it was not the Israelites whom they were fighting but the Israelites' God. How interesting that Pharaoh had claimed not to know the Lord (see Exod. 5:2), but in the moment of panic at the Red Sea, Pharaoh's soldiers proclaimed Him, using the name of God. Even so, this acknowledgement came too late for the salvation of the Egyptians. The only thing the Hebrew people had to do in this moment was "keep still" (Exod. 14:14, NRSV).

Regardless of what Pharaoh had ordered, what God desired came to fruition. The Egyptians were made to know who God is. Whereas the Egyptians had pursued them on Pharaoh's orders, Israel entered the Red Sea on faith. Just as God had required their faith to place the blood of an unblemished lamb on their doorposts, He now called for Israel's obedience to enter the Red Sea and to fully trust His promise of salvation. He called upon them, moreover, to trust that He would fight for them. The irony here is clear. As Durham notes, "The route so fatal to the Egyptians was a route of deliverance for Israel. They walked as on dry ground, with the waters standing aside for them, a wall to their right and a wall to their left. This language is not conducive to the attempts at naturalistic accounting often pressed upon these verses.... It is the language, rather, of confession. This victory, like the victories in Egypt, is declared to be Yahweh's victory, Yahweh's alone. What we may make of that is our problem. The compositor who set these lines together was speaking from faith and attempting both to address faith and to stimulate faith" (John I. Durham, *Exodus* [Waco, TX: Word Books, 1987], 196-197).

III. The Lord Saves Israel (Exodus 14:26-30)

Again God spoke to Moses, "'Stretch out your hand over the sea, so that the water may come back upon the Egyptians, upon their chariots and chariot drivers'" (v. 26, NRSV). Again, it was Moses who stretched out his hand, but it was God who was acting through him. This was no mere natural phenomenon, as some have tried to argue.

Moses is obedient to God's command and stretches out his hand over the sea. The sea returned to its "normal depth" (v. 27, NRSV) even as the Egyptians were fleeing: "As the Egyptians fled before it, the LORD tossed the Egyptians into the sea. The waters returned and covered the chariots and the chariot drivers, the entire army of Pharaoh that had followed them into the sea; not one of them remained" (Exod. 14:27-28, NRSV). Israel, across the sea and safe from Pharaoh's reach, had only to watch God's judgment and salvation. The water returned, covered the chariots, horsemen, everyone "that had followed them into the sea" (v. 28, NRSV). They all drowned in the Red Sea that day.

The final two verses summarize the miracle of deliverance and bring it to a close. Verse twenty-nine repeats verse twenty-two, emphasizing that the people of Israel walked on dry land in the midst of the Red Sea with protective walls of water on their right and left sides. The Lord "saved" (v. 30, NIV) Israel that day. That day, Israel again saw tangible evidence of God's judgment against the Egyptians. The entire nation of Israel saw the dead bodies of the Egyptians upon the seashore. God destroyed all those who pursued Israel into the sea. Pharaoh and his army saw the great work of God and believed the Lord and His servant Moses.

The Lesson Applied

In situations where there seems to be no escape, we must be willing to "keep still" and wait on God. God wants the world to know and to honor Him for who He is. In worship, we come to know God for who

He is and what He has done for us. Not only did God save and liberate Israel, He did the same for us, the Church.

LET'S TALK ABOUT IT

1. How did the early Church appropriate the story of God's deliverance at the Red Sea?

Early Christian writers frequently made reference to the Exodus. Indeed, it can be argued that the Exodus is a paradigmatic narrative for the New Testament conception of the Christian life. But this is true only because the New Testament writers reshaped the meaning and function of the Exodus for their new context. Perhaps the place where this is seen most clearly is in 1 Corinthians 10, which, according to Childs, "is the most extended reference to the Old Testament tradition" (Brevard Childs, *The Book of Exodus* [Philadelphia: Westminster Press, 1974], 233). As Childs explains there is both a positive and a negative interpretation placed upon the Exodus event in this passage: "Paul employs an allegorical method akin to Philo in speaking of the Old Testament's 'means of grace'. 'Our fathers were all under the cloud, and all passed through the sea, and all were baptized into Moses in the cloud and in the sea ...' The reference to the supernatural Rock which followed

them reflects quite clearly a midrashic tradition.... Yet the major point in Paul's argument was the failure of all of Israel to partake in the divine acts of mercy.... [This] was given as a warning to Christians to take heed lest they also perish" (233-234).

Paul's direct connection between the Red Sea crossing and baptism led to some thought-provoking developments later on. Looking at patristic interpretation of this passage, Daniélou finds a "unanimous tradition which sees here a type of Baptism" (Jean Daniélou, *From Shadows to Reality*, English trans. [London: Burns & Oates, 1960], 171). For early writers like Origen, Tertullian, and Ambrose, "water became a type of judgment from which baptism provided an escape" (Childs, 234). Moreover, the defeat of the Egyptian army at the seashore was "a picture of the need to drown in the waters of baptism all of the sins of greed, pride, and anger which besiege the soul of the Christian" (ibid.). The freedom from Egypt, as we saw in our lesson today, comes to be equated with the freedom from sin. Baptist theology, of course, has traditionally shied away from the full extent of these claims vis-a-vis baptism. Even so, they can help deepen our thinking about both the Exodus and baptism.

HOME DAILY DEVOTIONAL READINGS
NOVEMBER 18–24, 2013

MONDAY	TUESDAY	WEDNESDAY	THURSDAY	FRIDAY	SATURDAY	SUNDAY
Offering Our Possessions	Offering Our Skills	Stirred Hearts and Willing Spirits	Skills for Every Kind of Work	An Overabundance of Offerings	Blessing the Faithful Workers	God Affirms the Completed Work
Exodus 35:4-9	Exodus 35:10-19	Exodus 35:20-29	Exodus 35:30-35	Exodus 36:2-7	Exodus 39:32-43	Exodus 40:16-30, 34, 38

BEGINNING OF THE TABERNACLE

ADULT TOPIC:	BACKGROUND SCRIPTURES:
TRAVELING LIGHT	EXODUS 35—40

EXODUS 40:16–30, 34, 38

King James Version	*New Revised Standard Version*
THUS did Moses: according to all that the LORD commanded him, so did he.	MOSES did everything just as the LORD had commanded him.
17 And it came to pass in the first month in the second year, on the first day of the month, that the tabernacle was reared up.	17 In the first month in the second year, on the first day of the month, the tabernacle was set up.
18 And Moses reared up the tabernacle, and fastened his sockets, and set up the boards thereof, and put in the bars thereof, and reared up his pillars.	18 Moses set up the tabernacle; he laid its bases, and set up its frames, and put in its poles, and raised up its pillars;
19 And he spread abroad the tent over the tabernacle, and put the covering of the tent above upon it; as the LORD commanded Moses.	19 and he spread the tent over the tabernacle, and put the covering of the tent over it; as the LORD had commanded Moses.
20 And he took and put the testimony into the ark, and set the staves on the ark, and put the mercy seat above upon the ark:	20 He took the covenant and put it into the ark, and put the poles on the ark, and set the mercy seat above the ark;
21 And he brought the ark into the tabernacle, and set up the vail of the covering, and covered the ark of the testimony; as the LORD commanded Moses.	21 and he brought the ark into the tabernacle, and set up the curtain for screening, and screened the ark of the covenant; as the LORD had commanded Moses.
22 And he put the table in the tent of the congregation, upon the side of the tabernacle northward, without the vail.	22 He put the table in the tent of meeting, on the north side of the tabernacle, outside the curtain,
23 And he set the bread in order upon it before the LORD; as the LORD had commanded Moses.	23 and set the bread in order on it before the LORD; as the LORD had commanded Moses.
24 And he put the candlestick in the tent of the congregation, over against the table, on the side of the tabernacle southward.	24 He put the lampstand in the tent of meeting, opposite the table on the south side of the tabernacle,
25 And he lighted the lamps before the LORD; as the LORD commanded Moses.	25 and set up the lamps before the LORD; as the LORD had commanded Moses.
26 And he put the golden altar in the tent of the congregation before the vail:	26 He put the golden altar in the tent of meeting before the curtain,
27 And he burnt sweet incense thereon; as the LORD commanded Moses.	27 and offered fragrant incense on it; as the LORD had commanded Moses.

MAIN THOUGHT: For the cloud of the LORD was upon the tabernacle by day, and fire was on it by night, in the sight of all the house of Israel, throughout all their journeys. (Exodus 40:38, KJV)

King James Version	New Revised Standard Version
28 And he set up the hanging at the door of the tabernacle.	28 He also put in place the screen for the entrance of the tabernacle.
29 And he put the altar of burnt offering by the door of the tabernacle of the tent of the congregation, and offered upon it the burnt offering and the meat offering; as the LORD commanded Moses.	29 He set the altar of burnt offering at the entrance of the tabernacle of the tent of meeting, and offered on it the burnt offering and the grain offering as the LORD had commanded Moses.
30 And he set the laver between the tent of the congregation and the altar, and put water there, to wash withal.	30 He set the basin between the tent of meeting and the altar, and put water in it for washing.
• • • • • •	• • • • • •
34 Then a cloud covered the tent of the congregation, and the glory of the LORD filled the tabernacle.	34 Then the cloud covered the tent of meeting, and the glory of the LORD filled the tabernacle.
• • • • • •	• • • • • •
38 For the cloud of the LORD was upon the tabernacle by day, and fire was on it by night, in the sight of all the house of Israel, throughout all their journeys.	38 For the cloud of the LORD was on the tabernacle by day, and fire was in the cloud by night, before the eyes of all the house of Israel at each stage of their journey.

LESSON SETTING
Time: ca. 1450 B.C.
Place: The Wilderness

LESSON OUTLINE
I. **Moses Raises the Tabernacle (Exodus 40:16-30)**
II. **The Cloud and the Glory (Exodus 40:34, 38)**

UNIFYING PRINCIPLE

In the midst of a difficult transition, people look for security and guidance. Where can they find the security and direction they seek? While the Israelites were on their way to the Promised Land, God instructed the people to create the tabernacle—a place where they could always find God's presence and guidance.

INTRODUCTION

Our final lesson for this quarter brings us to the very end of the book of Exodus.

Following God's deliverance of Israel from the hands of the Egyptians at the Red Sea, the narrative follows Israel in the wilderness as she makes her way to Mount Sinai. At Sinai (see Exod. 19:1—24:18), God gives Israel His Law. Also at Sinai, God gives Moses specific instructions for the construction of the Ark of the Covenant and the tabernacle. The final portion of Exodus (see Exod. 25:1—40:38) is concerned with the details of that construction. As Longman and Dillard observe: "Much attention is devoted to the tabernacle in the exodus narrative. Indeed, modern readers often find this section highly repetitious, especially since God's directions to build the tabernacle and the execution of those plans are narrated in detail.... [This section] highlights the importance of the tabernacle to the wilderness generation. These details are lovingly dwelt on because the tabernacle was the primary symbol of God's presence with Israel" (Tremper Longman and Raymond Dillard, *An Introduction to the Old Testament*, Second Ed. [Grand Rapids, MI: Zondervan, 2006], 71). In the midst of these details, it is easy to forget that the concern of the narrative is for the presence of God among His people.

Several different names or designations are given to the tabernacle in the Pentateuch. It is called *hammishkan* (Exod. 25:9) or *mishkan Yahweh* (Lev. 17:4), the dwelling-place or home of the Lord. Elsewhere, it is referred to as *mishkan ha'edut*, the dwelling of the testimony, because it housed the covenant tablets (Exod. 38:21) or *mishkan 'ohel mo'ed*, the tabernacle of tent of meeting, because it served as the appointed meeting place between God and His people (Exod. 39:32). Other names include *miqdash*, sanctuary (Exod. 25:8), and *beth Yahweh*, the house of Yahweh (Exod. 34:26). The sheer range of terminology seen here gives a sense of how the Israelites viewed the tabernacle and the reverence with which they approached it. It will be helpful to recall this as we enter into today's text, a text that on its face value appears to exhibit little in the way of theological interest.

EXPOSITION

I. MOSES RAISES THE TABERNACLE (EXODUS 40:16-30)

Today's text opens with the comment that Moses "did everything just as the LORD had commanded him" (Exod. 40:16, NRSV). This is a key theme of the narrative of the construction of the tabernacle. According to Childs, "The repetition of the phrase 'as Yahweh had commanded Moses,' which

occurs eight times in this section, epitomizes the dominant redactional intention throughout chs. 35—40" (Brevard Childs, *The Book of Exodus* [Philadelphia: Westminster Press, 1974], 637-638). Childs' assertion is backed up by Fretheim, who notes eighteen total occurrences of this language in Exodus 35—40 (Terence Fretheim, *Exodus* [Louisville: John Knox Press, 1991], 313). In other words, throughout the narrative of the construction of the tabernacle, the primary emphasis is on the fact that Moses obeyed God in all things, down to the tiniest and most seemingly insignificant details. Of critical importance in understanding this text is recognizing our own pre-existing biases regarding obedience. In popular theological discourse in America, it is sometimes the case that an insistence on obedience is equated with legalism. Not so in this case. As Fretheim writes: "Given the [Israelites'] apostasy, such obedience is *an external demonstration of loyalty to Yahweh*. Obedience arises out of a heart and spirit properly turned toward God, as the emphasis on that theme makes clear (35:5, 21-22, 29; 36:2). Obedience is thus rooted in faithfulness; the external activity is internally motivated" (314; emphasis in original). That it is external does not make it of lesser value. For the author of the book of Exodus, internal motivation and external action are inextricably linked. With those caveats in place, we move forward with the text at hand.

The tabernacle, we are told, was set up "in the first month in the second year, on the first day of the month" (v. 17, NRSV). This means that the building of the parts took somewhat less than six months. Keil and Delitzsch explain: "On the day mentioned in [Exod. 40:2] the dwelling and court were erected. As not quite nine months had elapsed between the arrival of the Israelites at Sinai, in the third month after the Exodus (ch. 19:1), and the first day of the second year, when the work was finished and handed over to Moses, the building, and all the work connected with it, had not occupied quite half a year" (Carl Keil and Franz Delitzsch, *The Pentateuch*, Reprint Ed. [Peabody, MA: Hendrickson Publishers, 1996], 488). This is interesting purely from an informational standpoint, but it also reminds us just how much time was put into crafting each part of the tabernacle.

As the text moves into a description of the assembly of these pieces, we should remember that the tabernacle was designed to be set up and broken down quickly. After their departure from Egypt, the Israelites were a nomadic people, constantly on the move. This helps us to understand what Moses is doing in this portion of the text: "Moses set up the tabernacle; he laid its bases, and set up its frames, and put in its poles, and raised up its pillars; and he spread the tent over the tabernacle, and put the covering of the tent over it; as the LORD had commanded Moses" (vv. 18-19, NRSV). This process is very much akin to the process of setting up a tent in our own day: there are poles that form the base and poles that support the roof. The "tent" (ibid.) refers to a weatherproof covering, probably made of animal skin, that went over the tabernacle when it was set up.

The text then moves to a discussion of how the furniture of the tabernacle was arranged: "He took the covenant and put it into the ark, and put the poles on the ark,

and set the mercy seat above the ark; and he brought the ark into the tabernacle, and set up the curtain for screening, and screened the ark of the covenant; as the LORD had commanded Moses" (vv. 20-21, NRSV). The "covenant" ("Testimony," NIV) refers to the two tablets of the Decalogue. These were stored inside the Ark. The "mercy seat" refers to the lid of the Ark. The Ark was located in the rear portion of the tabernacle, behind a curtain, concealed from anyone who entered the outer room of the tabernacle (cf. Exod. 25:10-22; 26:31-34). Notice again, as with previous portions of the text, that great emphasis is placed on the fact that Moses did "as the LORD had commanded [him]" (Exod. 40:21, NRSV).

In verses 22-30, we then move to the arrangement of the outer room of the tabernacle. A table was placed in that front room for the bread of the Presence (see Exod. 25:23-30). Again, precision is the order of the day in these instructions. Later portions of the Law give specific instructions about the bread: "You shall take choice flour, and bake twelve loaves of it; two-tenths of an ephah shall be in each loaf. You shall place them in two rows, six in a row, on the table of pure gold. You shall put pure frankincense with each row, to be a token offering for the bread, as an offering by fire to the LORD" (Lev. 24:5-7, NRSV). The level of detail here may seem outlandish to us—instructions about the placement of the bread on the table, for example—but the details remind us of how much care went into the construction of the tabernacle and how much trust Israel placed in the presence of God among them. The details call us to reflection about how we value His presence.

We are then told that Moses placed "the golden altar in the tent of meeting before the curtain, and offered fragrant incense on it; as the LORD had commanded [him]" (Exod. 40:26-27, NRSV). Moses offered burnt offerings and grain offerings on the altar according to God's instruction. Finally, we are told that Moses placed a basin of water for washing in this front room as well. This act, which is where today's text cuts off, was in preparation for what was to come. After the tabernacle had been erected and all of the furniture had been arranged, it was time for priests to be ordained for service in the tabernacle. So Moses, along with Aaron and his sons, "washed their hands and their feet" (v. 31, NRSV). Moreover, "whenever they … approached the altar" (v. 32, NIV), they washed. Durham notes that was "an action in keeping with the requirements given in 30:19-21, and a necessary preparation for any further ministry in the places of Yahweh's Presence" (John I. Durham, *Exodus* [Waco, TX: Word Books, 1987], 500). Thus, this text is something of a prelude to their anointing as priests later on.

II. THE CLOUD AND THE GLORY (EXODUS 40:34, 38)

The climactic moment of the book of Exodus comes in the last four verses of the book. All of the careful description of chapters 25—40 have prepared the way for this moment. The language here, as Durham notes, "is semipoetic … almost hymnic" (500). Structurally, this reference to the descent of the cloud parallels the descent of the cloud at Mount Sinai. Durham says, "The double reference to the cloud covering the Tent of Appointed Meeting and the Glory of Yahweh filling the Tabernacle is

connected with the other cloud and Glory passages in Exodus (cf. 13:21-22; 14:19, 24; 16:10; 24:16-18; 33:9-10, 22; 34:5) and is a particular allusion to the narrative of Yahweh's descent onto Mount Sinai in the sight of Israel in 24:16-18" (ibid.).

Verse thirty-four tells us that God's glory filled the tabernacle. The cloud covering the tabernacle and the glory of God filled the dwelling such that even Moses was unable to enter it. The glory of the Lord is defined as "light and fire, a created splendour, which was the peculiar symbol of God (1 John 1:5)" (Robert Jamieson, A. R. Fausset, and David Brown, *A Commentary, Critical and Explanatory, on the Old and New Testaments,* Vol. 1 [Hartford, CT: S. S. Scranton and Company, 1871], 73). The cloud, God's presence, which had been a guiding, protecting presence of the Lord, now inhabited the tabernacle. The cloud guided the travel itinerary of Israel. As long as the cloud rested on the dwelling, the people could not travel. When the cloud ascended from the tabernacle, they could continue their journey (see Num. 9:15-23).

According to Keil and Delitzsch, "the glory of Jehovah filling the dwelling is clearly distinguished from the cloud coming down upon the tabernacle. It is obvious, however, from Lev. 16:2, and 1 Kings 8:10, 11, that in the dwelling the glory of God was also manifested in a cloud" (490). In the 1 Kings passage just cited, the two concepts—cloud and glory—are used interchangeably. God gave Moses and the people visible evidence of His presence and approval of His dwelling place via the glory and the cloud. The cloud occupied the most holy place above the cherubim atop the Ark of the Covenant. When the cloud departed, Moses and subsequent priests could enter and discharge their duties; the curtains prohibited them from seeing the presence of God in the cloud behind the curtain. The cloud had an external function too: the cloud "was a protection to the sacred edifice from the burning heats of the Arabian climate" (Jamieson, Fausset, and Brown, 73).

Verse thirty-eight informs us that "the cloud of the LORD was on the tabernacle by day, and fire was in the cloud by night, before the eyes of all the house of Israel at each stage of their journey" (NRSV). The cloud at various times and in various places rested exclusively now on the tabernacle. This shows us clearly the special place of the tabernacle. God's presence, guidance, and protection are on stage at each juncture of Israel's travel. God is faithfully providing and fulfilling His promise to His people. He is not functioning under the radar. His desire is for the nation to know of His presence. God is to see them, and they are to see God. Presently, it is primarily in God's holy Word that we discover the true essence and attributes of God.

THE LESSON APPLIED

Exodus 40 is not a readily approachable portion of Scripture for us. It is easy to get lost in the details of the materials and construction of the tabernacle. Today's lesson calls us to focus on what matters most—the presence of God among His people—and to see that the (seemingly insignificant) details of the text point to that reality.

LET'S TALK ABOUT IT

1. **What does today's lesson teach us about the theological importance of place? Does place matter to God? Does it matter to our spiritual lives?**

It is common in Protestant circles to emphasize that the Church is not the building but the people. This is certainly true. The Church is the people of God: it would exist even if there were no physical structures available. Having said that, we also recognize that Christians have been building structures to house their worship assemblies for a very long time. What is the theological significance, if any, of these structures? These structures, to be sure, are not the Church, but they are set apart (sanctified) for the uses of the Church. They themselves are not holy, but what happens in them is holy. Therefore, they carry meaning for us. For that reason, care should be given that these structures contribute to, and not impede, our worship. The same could be said for cultivating an attitude of reverence when we enter these spaces.

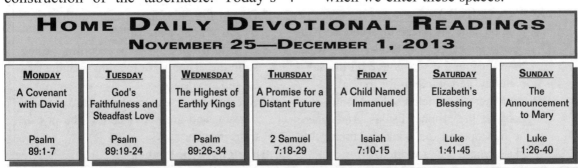

HOME DAILY DEVOTIONAL READINGS
NOVEMBER 25—DECEMBER 1, 2013

MONDAY	TUESDAY	WEDNESDAY	THURSDAY	FRIDAY	SATURDAY	SUNDAY
A Covenant with David	God's Faithfulness and Steadfast Love	The Highest of Earthly Kings	A Promise for a Distant Future	A Child Named Immanuel	Elizabeth's Blessing	The Announcement to Mary
Psalm 89:1-7	Psalm 89:19-24	Psalm 89:26-34	2 Samuel 7:18-29	Isaiah 7:10-15	Luke 1:41-45	Luke 1:26-40

SECOND QUARTER

Lesson material is based on International Sunday School Lessons and International Bible Lessons for Christian Teaching. Copyrighted by the International Council of Religious Education and is used by its permission.

DECEMBER 2013, JANUARY—FEBRUARY 2014

WRITER: REV. DR. PETER DARE

SUGGESTED OPENING EXERCISES

1. **Usual Signal for Beginning**
2. **Prayer (Closing with the Lord's Prayer)**
3. **Singing (Song to Be Selected)**
4. **Scripture Reading:**
   Isaiah 58:6-9 (KJV)

Director: Is not this the fast that I have chosen? to loose the bands of wickedness, to undo the heavy burdens, and to let the oppressed go free, and that ye break every yoke?

School: Is it not to deal thy bread to the hungry, and that thou bring the poor that are cast out to thy house? when thou seest the naked, that thou cover him; and that thou hide not thyself from thine own flesh?

Director: Then shall thy light break forth as the morning, and thine health shall spring forth speedily: and thy righteousness shall go before thee; the glory of the LORD shall be thy reward.

All: Then shalt thou call, and the LORD shall answer; thou shalt cry, and he shall say, Here I am.

Recitation in Concert:
Luke 4:16-21 (KJV)

16 And he came to Nazareth, where he had been brought up: and, as his custom was, he went into the synagogue on the sabbath day, and stood up for to read.

17 And there was delivered unto him the book of the prophet Esaias. And when he had opened the book, he found the place where it was written,

18 The Spirit of the Lord is upon me, because he hath anointed me to preach the gospel to the poor; he hath sent me to heal the brokenhearted, to preach deliverance to the captives, and recovering of sight to the blind, to set at liberty them that are bruised,

19 To preach the acceptable year of the Lord.

20 And he closed the book, and he gave it again to the minister, and sat down. And the eyes of all them that were in the synagogue were fastened on him.

21 And he began to say unto them, This day is this scripture fulfilled in your ears.

CLOSING WORK

1. **Singing**
2. **Sentences:**
   James 2:5-9 (KJV)

   5 Hearken, my beloved brethren, Hath not God chosen the poor of this world rich in faith, and heirs of the kingdom which he hath promised to them that love him?

   6 But ye have despised the poor. Do not rich men oppress you, and draw you before the judgment seats?

   7 Do not they blaspheme that worthy name by the which ye are called?

   8 If ye fulfil the royal law according to the scripture, Thou shalt love thy neighbor as thyself, ye do well:

   9 But if ye have respect to persons, ye commit sin, and are convinced of the law as transgressors.

3. **Dismissal with Prayer**

JESUS' BIRTH FORETOLD

| ADULT TOPIC: SURPRISED AND EXPECTANT | BACKGROUND SCRIPTURE: LUKE 1:26-45 |

LUKE 1:26–40

King James Version

AND in the sixth month the angel Gabriel was sent from God unto a city of Galilee, named Nazareth,

27 To a virgin espoused to a man whose name was Joseph, of the house of David; and the virgin's name was Mary.

28 And the angel came in unto her, and said, Hail, thou that art highly favoured, the Lord is with thee: blessed art thou among women.

29 And when she saw him, she was troubled at his saying, and cast in her mind what manner of salutation this should be.

30 And the angel said unto her, Fear not, Mary: for thou hast found favour with God.

31 And, behold, thou shalt conceive in thy womb, and bring forth a son, and shalt call his name Jesus.

32 He shall be great, and shall be called the Son of the Highest: and the Lord God shall give unto him the throne of his father David:

33 And he shall reign over the house of Jacob for ever; and of his kingdom there shall be no end.

34 Then said Mary unto the angel, How shall this be, seeing I know not a man?

35 And the angel answered and said unto her, The Holy Ghost shall come upon thee, and the power of the Highest shall overshadow thee: therefore also that holy thing which shall be born of thee shall be called the Son of God.

36 And, behold, thy cousin Elisabeth, she hath also conceived a son in her old age: and this

New Revised Standard Version

IN the sixth month the angel Gabriel was sent by God to a town in Galilee called Nazareth,

27 to a virgin engaged to a man whose name was Joseph, of the house of David. The virgin's name was Mary.

28 And he came to her and said, "Greetings, favored one! The Lord is with you."

29 But she was much perplexed by his words and pondered what sort of greeting this might be.

30 The angel said to her, "Do not be afraid, Mary, for you have found favor with God.

31 And now, you will conceive in your womb and bear a son, and you will name him Jesus.

32 He will be great, and will be called the Son of the Most High, and the Lord God will give to him the throne of his ancestor David.

33 He will reign over the house of Jacob forever, and of his kingdom there will be no end."

34 Mary said to the angel, "How can this be, since I am a virgin?"

35 The angel said to her, "The Holy Spirit will come upon you, and the power of the Most High will overshadow you; therefore the child to be born will be holy; he will be called Son of God.

36 And now, your relative Elizabeth in her old age has also conceived a son; and this is the

MAIN THOUGHT: And, behold, thou shalt conceive in thy womb, and bring forth a son, and shalt call his name JESUS. (Luke 1:31, KJV)

LUKE 1:26-40

King James Version	*New Revised Standard Version*
is the sixth month with her, who was called barren.	sixth month for her who was said to be barren.
37 For with God nothing shall be impossible.	37 For nothing will be impossible with God."
38 And Mary said, Behold the handmaid of the Lord; be it unto me according to thy word. And the angel departed from her.	38 Then Mary said, "Here am I, the servant of the Lord; let it be with me according to your word." Then the angel departed from her.
39 And Mary arose in those days, and went into the hill country with haste, into a city of Juda;	39 In those days Mary set out and went with haste to a Judean town in the hill country,
40 And entered into the house of Zacharias, and saluted Elisabeth.	40 where she entered the house of Zechariah and greeted Elizabeth.

LESSON SETTING
Time: 4 B.C.
Place: Nazareth

LESSON OUTLINE
I. **A Grand Announcement (Luke 1:26-28)**
II. **A Grand Announcement Replayed (Luke 1:29-37)**
III. **Mary's Response (Luke 1:38-40)**

UNIFYING PRINCIPLE

People are always amazed and often perplexed when unexpected things happen in their lives. How can Christians handle these unanticipated events that occur? Mary responded at first with surprise and then with dedication to the angel's announcement about the birth of her baby.

INTRODUCTION

If anyone ever thought or believed that this world existed isolated and independent of divine activity, this Gospel account refutes it. Luke places his account within the framework of human history and then reveals from behind the scenes God's interest in human affairs. Suddenly, an angel appears to a young virgin and makes a grand announcement of a divine initiative that points to more than a mere coincidental happening. Careful observation reveals this divine activity is actually the result of God's constant involvement in and evaluation of human affairs since creation. The birth of Jesus Christ is God's answer to the problem of sin and the disenfranchisement of the world.

In this text, a young virgin is targeted by God to become the bearer of God's unique promise of salvation. A member of the angelic host is selected to reveal the Good News to her and, parenthetically, through her to the entire world. She has been chosen by God to be the bearer of salvation. So although the Jewish world is expecting the promised Messiah to come, she never contemplates it would be through her. Startled by the announcement, Mary finally accepts the angelic declaration and subsequently journeys to her older relative's home to verify the announcement that Elizabeth has also received a visit from the divine messenger. The lesson proposes three ideas that demand our attention. First, the text reveals a grand announcement that has universal implications. Second, this grand announcement is repeated and, to some extent, explained to Mary so she will understand the deep significance of the angelic declaration. Finally, the text focuses on Mary's two-part response. These three parts affirm God's keen observation of human affairs and His commitment to direct the course of events according to His purpose.

EXPOSITION

I. A GRAND ANNOUNCEMENT (LUKE 1:26-28)

God sent the angel Gabriel to a pre-determined city at a predetermined time to a pre-selected young woman to fulfill a predetermined purpose. The little known town of Bethlehem was the city, a virgin named Mary was the pre-selected maiden, and the purpose was salvation. Although the text specifically reveals Gabriel as the messenger, in most cases in the biblical record, especially in the Old Testament, angels are unnamed. For example, the angelic being who appeared to announce to Abraham and Sarah the future birth of their son, Isaac, is unnamed. Nor is the angel who appeared to Zorah and Manoah, the parents of Samson, named. Also worthy of note is that this is the first mention of Gabriel in the New Testament.

Gabriel first appears in Daniel 9. Along with Michael, Gabriel seems to be among the highest of the angelic order. Gabriel's presence indicates events of universal importance according to God's purpose. The name Gabriel means "man of God" and relates to the passage as God's "executive assistant" or "spokesperson." Gabriel as the personification of God's presence brings great significance to the occasion and to the message. That is to say, this is no ordinary event for Mary.

In this introductory clause announcing Jesus' pending birth, Luke emphasizes the word *virgin*. The Greek term used for *virgin* in verse twenty-seven is *parthenon*, which in Greek means "chaste and unmarried." This signifies part of the mystery surrounding the virgin Mary's conception. In Jewish culture, if a woman was not a virgin before she was married, then it signified she was not pious, and it would be almost impossible for her to enter into marriage. The miracle of Jesus' birth revolved around the fact that He would be born to a woman who had never been married and had never engaged in any sexual intercourse. A virgin was needed so that Jesus could enter this world sinless, not tarnished with the sin from the lineage of Adam.

Mary's virginity provides God with an opportunity to demonstrate why He alone is God. In Matthew's account of the birth narrative, the problem is not so much Mary's virgin conception as it is Joseph's disbelief that such a conception is even possible (see Matt. 1:18-25). However, God reveals to Joseph that the impossible has indeed happened to him and his proposed bride. It is an indication of the ability of God to work within the course of human affairs to bring about His purpose. Mary and Joseph were given the amazing opportunity of a lifetime, hosting the King of kings. The unbelievable announcement made by Gabriel revolutionized both Mary's purpose and destiny.

II. A GRAND ANNOUNCEMENT REPLAYED (LUKE 1:29-37)

Often when such a grand announcement is made, it is accompanied with disbelief and surprise. A second announcement may be necessary to calm the waters and to reinforce the truth being proclaimed. Such is the case with Mary. Although it is apparent that she favorably entertains the angelic prophecy, Gabriel repeats the announcement to her and provides additional information about her special selection as the subject of divine grace. The angel consoles and reassures her of God's presence and favor.

A theophany or vision could mean destruction was at hand as well as blessings (see 1 Sam. 3:28; Dan. 4:18-33; 5). Gabriel's appearance and announcement to Mary eliminates the former. Mary's theophany focused on a tremendous blessing that alleviated her fears through the understanding that she was not to be afraid. Both angelic beings and Jesus used this comforting formula quite often in Jesus' post resurrection appearances to His Disciples. In Matthew 28:5, the angel at Jesus' gravesite comforts the women who have come to complete the preparation for Jesus' burial. It is followed in Matthew 28:10 by Jesus' own words—a call for them to rejoice and for their fears to be abated. Mark 16:4 has a similar type of meaning, only in this verse Mark uses the word *alarm*, rather than *troubled*, as a way for them to deactivate their fears. The sentence has the effect of saying, "You are in no danger. Do not press the panic button."

The Johannine account, however, takes a different approach to console or to lessen the Disciples' apprehensions. There is no admonition given to the Disciples to not be troubled in the fourth Gospel writer's account of the post resurrection narrative. That admonition had already been given in the pre-crucifixion discourse in John 14–16 with the instruction to the Disciples to guard their hearts against impending trouble that lay on the horizon. But even this periscope, which begins with an admonition against allowing their hearts to be troubled, ends differently than Matthew or Mark.

For John, since Jesus has come to reconcile God and humanity, the stress is on peace. Jesus is God's setting up residence with humanity. He comes to advocate peace between God and His human creatures (see John 1:14; 14:27; 16:33). Repeatedly, John points to Jesus' presence in the world as the establishment of peace between the divine and the human. Therefore, when Jesus appears to the Disciples after His resurrection, it is His presence that overrides any sense of fear. He is the Word of God that dissipates trouble and establishes real peace (see John 20:11-16, 19, 26).

The comfort formula, as noted in the Gospels, is used to focus our attention on a higher level of divine activity taking place in the world. For Mary and the Disciples, it emphasizes the power of God to overcome what was deemed as impossible—the virgin birth and death. Mary has nothing to fear; in fact, she has every reason to rejoice. She has found favor with God. The word *favor* as used here and in Luke 1:28 is the word *charis*. It means

God's unmerited and intentional goodwill of which Mary is the recipient. The common definition of this word is "grace." Mary, relieved from the troubling vision by the comforting words of Gabriel, now engages him in discourse. Her first remark is a question, "How can this happen since I am a virgin?" The contrasting picture here is remarkable. Mary, while engaging in a supernatural conversation, seeks a rational answer to the angel's surprising announcement. Verses 31-37 reveal the unfolding drama as the angel provides the reason for his statement of divine favor.

Mary will be overshadowed by the Holy Spirit and will bear a son, and not just any son, but God's Son. No illusion or reference is made to suggest sexual intercourse. Luke is careful at this point to underscore the conception as the result of the Holy Spirit overshadowing Mary. Jesus' birth is not the result of inappropriate sexual desire as revealed in Genesis 6:1-4 or in Greek mythology. The divine overshadowing carries with it the picture of a cloud filled with rain that gives the water of life to the ground underneath it. In this sense Mary is the channel by which this new life is brought into the world. The picture also carries with it the Old Testament image of God's presence in Exodus. The pillar of cloud (by day) and the pillar of fire (by night) symbolized God's presence during the Exodus and as Moses set up the tabernacle (see Exod. 13:21-22; 40:34-38). The New Testament confirms this divine imagery as indicative of God's presence and approval in the Transfiguration (see Matt. 17:5) Thus, Mary's overshadowing points to God's activity and purpose.

The angel instructs her what to name the child, "His name shall be called Jesus." The name *Jesus* means "God saves." The Hebrew names of Joshua, Isaiah, and Hosea carry a similar meaning. Also, during this time, people were what their names meant. Jesus is the personification of salvation because that is what He came to do. He came to save His people from their sins (see Matt. 1:21). He is what His name proclaims. His shall be the fulfillment of God's promise to continue the kingdom of David.

Scholars agree that both Mary and Joseph were descendants of David. The angel also gives her a bit of information to hold onto that she is able to confirm at a later date. Her aged relative Elizabeth is also pregnant by divine selection. God is working out a pair of miracles simultaneously. It is seldom that miracles take place in isolation, they often occur in multiplicity.

This section of the text closes with a reenactment of the declaration made to the Old Testament couple Sarah and Abraham. It comes in the form of an answer to the rhetorical question presented in Genesis 18:14. The angel notes that nothing would be impossible for God. The angelic message is clear. Virginity, nor barrenness, can interfere with God's power and will to enact salvation.

III. MARY'S RESPONSE (LUKE 1:38-40)

As noted earlier, the imagery used here is an undeniable affront to the doubtful Sarah who laughed when the angel foretold of her impending pregnancy and lays in deep contrast to Mary's response. Sarah laughed at the angelic declaration. Maybe she saw it as a joke or as an injection of divine humor. When confronted by the angel, she denied her laughter. Mary, on the other hand, when faced with a similar impossibility, accepts the angel's words as truth. She accepts by faith what Sarah initially perceived as mere conjecture. At any rate, the text strongly confirms the need for faith in God's ability to do the impossible. It is fair to say that Sarah eventually overcame her lack of faith. But it is also fair to say that her slow progression to faith left her with a serious lapse of faith that would have helped her to develop a more positive relationship with God. God is looking for those who are faithful to accept His grace and power.

THE LESSON APPLIED

This lesson projects three things: First, it reveals that God does not stand idly by while we sin. He has already found a way to redeem us from self-destruction. He comes to us in ways that we do not readily perceive, and He does the impossible. Second, the lesson shows that God takes the time to inform us of what He is doing in our midst, and He announces to us His intentions for our salvation. Third, the text affirms we have a choice in the matter. We can faithfully cooperate with God and receive untold blessings, or we can choose to ignore His interest in our affairs and be left in our sin. Mary chose to accept the angelic blessing and through her faith became a channel for new life for the entire world. She is the perfect example of obedience.

LET'S TALK ABOUT IT

1. Why is barrenness a symbol of secret sin?

The Hebrews developed reasons for everything that happened. For them God was the cause of every good or bad action. Thus, when something good took place in the human life, it was credited with God being pleased with one's lifestyle. On the other hand if something bad happened, then God was punishing the person for his or her sinful activity. Thus, whether good or bad, the action for deciding or judging was based on how well a person was living out the commitment to obey God.

2. Is Mary to be worshiped as the Mother of God?

Mary is the mother of our Lord Jesus. In that respect, she is to be honored and respected. But the Scriptures are clear that Jesus is the pre-existent Word of God who existed before eternity. We read, "And he answered and said unto them, My mother and my brethren are these which hear the word of God, and do it" (Luke 8:21, KJV). Therefore God, who has no beginning or ending, does not have a parental heritage.

HOME DAILY DEVOTIONAL READINGS
DECEMBER 2-8, 2013

MONDAY	TUESDAY	WEDNESDAY	THURSDAY	FRIDAY	SATURDAY	SUNDAY
My Heart Exults in the Lord	O Magnify the Lord with Me	Give Thanks to the Lord	Bless the Compassionate Lord	Praise the Gracious and Merciful Lord	The Lord reigns for All Generations	God Has Done Great Things
1 Samuel 2:1-10	Psalm 34:1-8	Psalm 100	Psalm 103:13-22	Psalm 111	Psalm 146	Luke 1:46-56

MARY'S SONG OF PRAISE

| ADULT TOPIC: | BACKGROUND SCRIPTURE: |
| JUBILANT! | LUKE 1:46-56 |

LUKE 1:46–56

King James Version	*New Revised Standard Version*
AND Mary said, My soul doth magnify the Lord,	AND Mary said, "My soul magnifies the Lord,
47 And my spirit hath rejoiced in God my Saviour.	47 and my spirit rejoices in God my Savior,
48 For he hath regarded the low estate of his handmaiden: for, behold, from henceforth all generations shall call me blessed.	48 for he has looked with favor on the lowliness of his servant. Surely, from now on all generations will call me blessed;
49 For he that is mighty hath done to me great things; and holy is his name.	49 for the Mighty One has done great things for me, and holy is his name.
50 And his mercy is on them that fear him from generation to generation.	50 His mercy is for those who fear him from generation to generation.
51 He hath shewed strength with his arm; he hath scattered the proud in the imagination of their hearts.	51 He has shown strength with his arm; he has scattered the proud in the thoughts of their hearts.
52 He hath put down the mighty from their seats, and exalted them of low degree.	52 He has brought down the powerful from their thrones, and lifted up the lowly;
53 He hath filled the hungry with good things; and the rich he hath sent empty away.	53 he has filled the hungry with good things, and sent the rich away empty.
54 He hath helped his servant Israel, in remembrance of his mercy;	54 He has helped his servant Israel, in remembrance of his mercy,
55 As he spake to our fathers, to Abraham, and to his seed for ever.	55 according to the promise he made to our ancestors, to Abraham and to his descendants forever."
56 And Mary abode with her about three months, and returned to her own house.	56 And Mary remained with her about three months and then returned to her home.

MAIN THOUGHT: And my spirit hath rejoiced in God my Saviour. (Luke 1:47, KJV)

LESSON SETTING
Time: ca. 4 B.C.
Place: Judah

LESSON OUTLINE
I. God Is Savior (Luke 1:46-49)
II. God Blesses Others Through Mary (Luke 1:50-53)

III. God Keeps His Promises (Luke 1:54-56)

UNIFYING PRINCIPLE
People usually respond with great joy when good things happen to them. What is the origin of such joyful responses? Mary responded from the depths of her soul by

praising her God of justice for receiving such a wonderful gift.

INTRODUCTION

How should we react when we are blessed? What is the human response to God's blessings, especially the blessing of salvation? This passage of Scripture is the epitome of what the human reaction should be in light of God's blessings. Mary's expression of praise and thanksgiving to God is what scholars have termed the *Magnificat*. The opening two chapters of Luke's Gospel account, which begin and end with songs of praise, set the tone for this Gospel (see Luke 1:46-55, 68-79; 2:8-14). Mary's song followed by Zechariah's song of praise, which is called by scholars the *Benedictus*, along with Simeon's *Nunc Dimittis*, and the angelic rendition of "Glory to God" surround the events of the announcement and birth of Jesus and place jubilant praise and gratitude as the model response to God's divine initiative. These responses fall in great contrast with the initial human response of disobedience and sin following creation. The first parents disobeyed God and indirectly blamed Him for their sin. Their eldest child Cain became upset with God and refused to accept divine advice on worship and thanksgiving. Humanity attempted to build a tower that extended into the heavens as an enshrinement to itself. Mary's praise, however, is the proper and desired action. As the motif for future Christian behavior, the early Church encased Luke's songs of praise into hymnals to be sung during individual and corporate worship.

Although there is some debate about to whom the song is attributed, Mary or Elizabeth, the testimony of the vast majority of scholars and the early Church denote Mary as the songstress. However, Hannah's song of praise, recorded in 1 Samuel 2:1-10, is the backdrop of Mary's adoration.

Hannah was the barren wife of Elkanah. She desired to have a child and pleaded with God to open her womb. In Hebrew culture, barrenness was a punishment for secret sin. Therefore, Hannah was the subject of public ridicule because her barrenness was evidence of her sin. She also felt shame and guilt as she, to some extent, bought into the theological misinterpretation of that day. Her prayer reveals, however, that she believed God had the power to restore her to a perceived womanly purpose. Absorbed in meditation, Eli thought Hannah was drunk. But she assured him she was immersed deeply in prayer, asking God to relieve her barrenness. Eli extended to her his blessing, and in due time, Hannah conceived and delivered her first child.

Hannah's song is a prayer of thanksgiving and praise to God for overcoming her barrenness and for elevating the status of a woman ridiculed and perceived to be of low estate by others. According to Hannah, only God could deliver her from the sad state of affairs which previously ordered her life. Thus, her song of praise is a reflection of a heart of total praise. She is as absorbed in her praise and thanksgiving to the Lord as she was in her request for Him to fulfill her role as a woman. Evidence of Hannah's continued praise is that she dedicated her child to the service of the Lord for life.

For today's lesson, verses 39-45 serve as a transition to Mary's song. It provides us with Mary's confirmation of the angelic announcement. We cannot say for sure why she made the trip to the Judean hillside, about twenty miles south of Jerusalem. She could have traveled to Elizabeth's home because God was doing great things in the lives of both women and Elizabeth would understand her joy. Also, Mary could have desired to confirm the truthfulness of Gabriel's prophecy. Chances are her journey to see Elizabeth was a combination of the two. It is also significant that upon hearing Mary's voice, Elizabeth's unborn baby leaped for joy in her womb. The unborn John already recognized the holy presence of the Lord within the womb of Mary. Elizabeth repeated the angelic recognition of Mary's special status among women. This transitional passage provides the foundational level for Mary's song of praise. Gabriel's announcement of the birth of her Child coupled with her relative's greeting confirms its veracity and provokes the virgin to praise God.

Mary's song of praise hits on the themes expressed originally by Hannah. First, Mary sees God as her Savior. He delivers her from a state of nothingness to the status of being blessed among women. As the mother of Jesus, she knows she will receive respect from others extending through generations. However, it is careful for us to note that the text reveals no hint of deification for Mary, although she alone holds this honored position. Second, through her blessing she sees God's grace as an extension to others. Mary has come to understand God as a God of reversals. The high and mighty does not compare to Him and their plans are forever thwarted. Third, God keeps His promise to restore Israel. These three truths compose the heart of the *Magnificat* and are solid starting points for us to examine in our quest to model her example.

EXPOSITION

I. GOD IS SAVIOR (LUKE 1:46-49)

The Greek words *sotēr* and *agios* are used to address God by Mary. The former means "to save," the base word for *savior* and the latter means "holy." When addressed to God these words are adjectival nouns that describe two of His attributes. Unlike regular adjectives which merely describe a person, place or thing, this type of adjective reveals the very essence of God's being. Therefore, God is not simply One who is holy or One who has heroic tendencies; rather, He is Holy. He is Savior. He is also both of these at the same time. His being is essentially all that is pure and truthful, and He uses it to accomplish His purpose. "To save" carries with it the idea of Deliverer or Rescuer. Mary's personal testimony of God in this sense is to be applied to Him as the Fulfiller of Israel's destiny. This identification of God as Savior sets the tone of salvation that is a major theme of this Gospel account (see Luke 1:47, 69, 71, 77; 2:11, 30; 3:6; 7:50; 8:48; 17:19; 18:42; 19:9-10; 23:35, 37, 39). Mary's utterance of praise is a direct response to what God has done for her.

Like her Old Testament counterpart Hannah, Mary will no longer be subjected to a humdrum existence because of her selection. She praises God because she will forever be admired and respected as the mother of the world's Savior. She identifies herself as a lowly servant, which is another major theme radiating from Luke. Notice the figures portrayed by Luke in these opening two chapters consist of marginalized people (Elizabeth and Zechariah, Mary and Joseph, the shepherds in the field, Simeon and Anna, etc.). Mary's hymn sounds the alert that this salvation is for all people, including the marginalized. God has remembered her and elevated her status. Therefore, her note of praise has personal overtones for all of those who care to recognize the blessings bestowed upon them by their divine Benefactor. Praise must be rendered to God individually and personally. Also worthy of note is the absence of bragging or self-elevation on the part of Mary. Her soberness lay in deep contrast to any idea of personal accomplishment. Her notoriety was a gift from the Lord which she openly admits in verses 48-49.

II. GOD BLESSES OTHERS
   ## THROUGH MARY
   ## (LUKE 1:50-53)

This passage highlights Mary's praise as an individual and how God's uses her to bless others. Mary acknowledges the blessing given to her by God is not to be hoarded. She is a channel through which God will distribute salvation to others. God's salvation has broader purpose and is inclusive. Mary's acceptance of the angelic announcement is incredible. First of all, she has the faith to receive God's truth as a special anointing that elevates her status among women. Second, she understands to a large degree the impact of her blessing upon the world, especially upon those who stand in awe of God's power and reverence Him. For Mary, God's blessings are continual. Verses 51-55 reveal God

as the divine Initiator of the blessings, bestowing them from one generation to another. In this sense, Mary's statements are reflective as well as futuristic. The song denotes God's past activities wherein He has revealed His abilities to thwart His enemies. But His past deeds remain strong indicators of what He will do. Mary's assessment of God's activities gives credence to the concept of divine strength as perpetual and stable.

Mary's reflection continues. She concludes God is a God who brings about a reversal of fortunes. With His strong arm of power, God has embarrassed the proud and dethroned the high and mighty while simultaneously exalting the lowly. Quite often in Scripture attributes of God are described in anthropomorphic terms, e.g., arm, hand eyes, etc. *Arm*, as used in verse fifty-one, is an allusion to the Old Testament Hebrew word *zeroa,* denoting the divine power and strength of God (see Deut. 4:34; 5:15; Ps. 44; 71:18; 77:15; Isa. 26:11). The picture of strength here is one of a muscular warrior waging war almost single-handedly against a mighty kingdom. Old Testament characters like Gideon, Samson, and David come to mind. Gideon, with only three hundred men, defeated the mighty Midianites (see Judg. 7–8). Also, Samson accomplished a similar feat in destroying the great Philistine army (see Judg. 15:9–16:30). The youthful David, armed with only a pebble and a sling-shot, felled the great military Philistine giant, Goliath, and throughout his life defeated the Philistines and the enemies of Israel repeatedly (see 1 Sam. 17; 2 Sam. 5:17-25; 12:26-31). These men succeeded against huge odds not because of their own power or initiative, but because of the strong arm of the Lord.

Emerging out of this image of strength painted by Mary's praise is that God purposefully uses His strength to bring about a reversal of fortunes for those who trust in Him. The proud are humbled and the humble are exalted. The Apostle Paul, in his correspondence to the Philippian church, argues for the congregation to follow Jesus' model of humility as the way to gain God's approval and subsequent exaltation (see Phil. 2). Matthew and Mark contribute to this concept in their analyses that "the first (the proud) shall be last and the last (the humble) shall be first" (see Matt. 19:30; 20:16; Mark 9:35; 10:31, 42-45). Also, in the parable of the Pharisee and the Publican (tax collector), Luke emphasizes humility (see Luke 18:9-14). Mary identifies herself within this category of persons. Her praise to God for His acceptance of the poor is further echoed in Luke's rendition of Jesus' great sermon (see Luke 6:20-21). Unlike Matthew 5:3-6, Luke's blessing (Greek: *makarios*) is not merely addressed to the poor in spirit, but to the actual poor. The corresponding woes recorded in Luke 6:24-25 also support Mary's reason for rejoicing. Walter Russell Bowie says, "According to Luke, the blessing is upon those who are poor.... For them there shall come a reversal of the human lot. The poor, the hungry, the sad, the oppressed and scorned, whom the world pushes aside with contempt and cruelty, are within the sure compassion of the eternal love. God himself will right their lot" (*The Interpreters Bible*, Vol. VIII [Nashville: Abingdon Press, 1952], 118). Mary rightfully deduces from her blessing that God will bless others through this birth and that those who fear Him will be the beneficiaries of His continued love.

III. GOD KEEPS HIS PROMISES (LUKE 1:54-56)

In conclusion, Mary's hymn of praise points to the theme of God fulfilling His promise. Second Samuel 7:13-16, Isaiah 9:6-7, along with Psalms 2:7 and 89:26-27, point to the establishment of God's deliberate continuation of the Davidic kingdom. Mary confirms this in Luke 1:54. Through Mary, God's promise of the Messiah to deliver Israel has become reality. The keeping of His promise says a lot about God's ability to remember. Unlike the butler who benefitted from Joseph's ability to interpret his dream and forgot to put a good word in for him upon his release, God remembered His promise to Israel (see Gen. 40:12-14, 20-23).

The reference to ancestors and Israel are synonymous and indicates the writer's emphasis on God's favorable remembrance of His people. This promise even goes beyond the promise of continuing the Davidic kingdom because it finds its basis in God's selection of Abraham. Thus, Mary's praise of God has dual bases. First, she praises God for the preservation of the nation of Israel through the Davidic kingdom. Second, she credits God with keeping His promise to Abraham to bless him and his seed forever. God had been consistently faithful to His covenant promises to His people, and Mary offered joyful praise for God's faithfulness to the Israelites.

Mary's song of praise interrupted Luke's narrative of Mary's visit with Elizabeth; therefore, in verse fifty-six, he resumes the story. Mary remained with Elizabeth three more months, which was the duration of Elizabeth's pregnancy. Then she returned home.

THE LESSON APPLIED

Mary's *Magnificat* expresses thanksgiving and jubilance to God for His act of loving-kindness toward her and the people of Israel. Mary recognizes her status among women has been elevated. She also realizes that through her others will also be blessed. Her God is a God of reversals and just as he reversed her situation and others, the implication is He will do so for future generations. Therefore, this hymn of praise becomes a model for the contemporary church to follow. God deserves such praise. He blesses us with one level of grace on top of another (see John 1:16). However, let us be reminded that the greatest blessing we have received is the salvation He offers to us through Jesus Christ.

LET'S TALK ABOUT IT

1. Why does God honor Mary?

Why does God honor any one of us when we are all sinful creatures? We are all special because each person is made in the image of God. Therefore, God cares for all people. However, God's heart is moved when we commit ourselves to living according to His standards. When we honor Him, He honors us. It is fair to say that Mary dedicated herself to holding fast to God's precepts. She honored Him and made herself available to be used by Him. Those who refuse to go along with the crowd and give in to peer pressure will find a special place in God's heart. Mary, as a young girl, found divine favor. Rest assured God is not blind to our activities. When we let God's purposes be born in us, He will honor us with His presence and power.

2. Does Mary indicate she has become deity and, therefore, should be worshiped?

Mary and Elizabeth's statements do not have any hint of Mary's deification. In fact, just the opposite is true. Both exclaim that Mary will be blessed among women. Neither does the angelic announcement recognize any special divine abilities of Mary. Her response to Gabriel was one of humility and a show of deep respect to God. Simply put as the bearer of God's salvation she is to be highly esteemed by her human counterparts, but not worshiped. By faith she becomes an instrument used by God to fulfill His purpose.

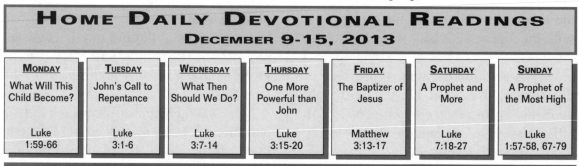

HOME DAILY DEVOTIONAL READINGS
DECEMBER 9-15, 2013

MONDAY	TUESDAY	WEDNESDAY	THURSDAY	FRIDAY	SATURDAY	SUNDAY
What Will This Child Become?	John's Call to Repentance	What Then Should We Do?	One More Powerful than John	The Baptizer of Jesus	A Prophet and More	A Prophet of the Most High
Luke 1:59-66	Luke 3:1-6	Luke 3:7-14	Luke 3:15-20	Matthew 3:13-17	Luke 7:18-27	Luke 1:57-58, 67-79

ZECHARIAH PROPHESIES ABOUT HIS SON JOHN

ADULT TOPIC:	BACKGROUND SCRIPTURE:
OPENING THE WAY	LUKE 1:57-80

LUKE 1:57-58, 67-79

King James Version

NOW Elisabeth's full time came that she should be delivered; and she brought forth a son.

58 And her neighbours and her cousins heard how the Lord had shewed great mercy upon her; and they rejoiced with her.

• • • • • •

67 And his father Zacharias was filled with the Holy Ghost, and prophesied, saying,

68 Blessed be the Lord God of Israel; for he hath visited and redeemed his people,

69 And hath raised up an horn of salvation for us in the house of his servant David;

70 As he spake by the mouth of his holy prophets, which have been since the world began:

71 That we should be saved from our enemies, and from the hand of all that hate us;

72 To perform the mercy promised to our fathers, and to remember his holy covenant;

73 The oath which he sware to our father Abraham,

74 That he would grant unto us, that we being delivered out of the hand of our enemies might serve him without fear,

75 In holiness and righteousness before him, all the days of our life.

76 And thou, child, shalt be called the prophet of the Highest: for thou shalt go before the face of the Lord to prepare his ways;

77 To give knowledge of salvation unto his people by the remission of their sins,

New Revised Standard Version

NOW the time came for Elizabeth to give birth, and she bore a son.

58 Her neighbors and relatives heard that the Lord had shown his great mercy to her, and they rejoiced with her.

• • • • • •

67 Then his father Zechariah was filled with the Holy Spirit and spoke this prophecy:

68 "Blessed be the Lord God of Israel, for he has looked favorably on his people and redeemed them.

69 He has raised up a mighty savior for us in the house of his servant David,

70 as he spoke through the mouth of his holy prophets from of old,

71 that we would be saved from our enemies and from the hand of all who hate us.

72 Thus he has shown the mercy promised to our ancestors, and has remembered his holy covenant,

73 the oath that he swore to our ancestor Abraham, to grant us

74 that we, being rescued from the hands of our enemies, might serve him without fear,

75 in holiness and righteousness before him all our days.

76 And you, child, will be called the prophet of the Most High; for you will go before the Lord to prepare his ways,

77 to give knowledge of salvation to his people by the forgiveness of their sins.

MAIN THOUGHT: And thou, child, shalt be called the prophet of the Highest: for thou shalt go before the face of the Lord to prepare his ways; To give knowledge of salvation unto his people by the remission of their sins. (Luke 1:76-77, KJV)

LUKE 1:57-58, 67-79

King James Version	New Revised Standard Version
78 Through the tender mercy of our God; whereby the dayspring from on high hath visited us,	78 By the tender mercy of our God, the dawn from on high will break upon us,
79 To give light to them that sit in darkness and in the shadow of death, to guide our feet into the way of peace.	79 to give light to those who sit in darkness and in the shadow of death, to guide our feet into the way of peace."

LESSON SETTING
Time: ca. 4 B.C.
Place: Jerusalem

LESSON OUTLINE
I. **John's Birth Fulfills Prophecy (Luke 1:57-58)**
II. **Praise God for Messianic Deliverance (Luke 1:67-75)**
III. **Praise God for John's Calling (Luke 1:76-79)**

UNIFYING PRINCIPLE
When a baby is born, parents usually have high expectations for their new child. What hopes and joys do they usually express? Zechariah prophesied that his son John would prepare the way for the God of justice.

INTRODUCTION
Sunday school students and Bible scholars alike know who John the Baptist was. He is primarily known for preaching repentance in the desert, paving the way for Jesus, and baptizing Him in the Jordan River. However, because of this familiarity, there is real danger in glossing over the full significance of John's work and mission. In today's terms, he was a pacesetter—one who served as a model to be imitated and who set the pace for honoring and committing one's life to Jesus Christ.

John understood his calling. His mission was foretold by Old Testament prophets, as well as by his father Zechariah who, through the power of the Holy Spirit, prophesied from a heart filled with joy. Zechariah praised God because his son had been chosen to fulfill a special and unique purpose. The Messiah would come in his lifetime, and John had been chosen to pave the way for Him.

Luke understands both the birth of John and the birth of Jesus to be the fulfillments of Old Testament prophecies. Centuries before their births, the prophet Isaiah said, "A voice cries out: 'In the wilderness prepare the way of the LORD, make straight in the desert a highway for our God'" (Isa. 40:3, NRSV). Most commentators find in this statement an immediate application to Judah's return from Babylonian captivity. Many, however, also find there a foreshadowing of the work of John the Baptist (see Matt. 3:3; Mark 1:2-3; Luke 3:4-6; John 1:23). As Barry Webb has observed, with the coming of Jesus, these words of Isaiah "sprang to life again with deeper and fuller meaning" (*The Message of Isaiah* [Downers Grove, IL: InterVarsity Press, 1996], 164). Isaiah's prediction reinforces Zechariah's prophecy about his son John the Baptist.

EXPOSITION

I. JOHN'S BIRTH FULFILLS PROPHECY (LUKE 1:57-58)

The account of John's birth is recorded in Luke 1. There it is interwoven with and, to some degree, overshadowed by the events surrounding the birth of Jesus. The angel Gabriel visited Mary announcing her selection as the mother of Christ, but Gabriel first visited Zechariah to announce John's birth.

To understand the significance of God's choice of Zechariah, let us notice a few aspects about him. Zechariah served as a priest in the temple in Jerusalem and "belonged to the priestly order of Abijah" (v. 5, NRSV). It was a once-in-a-lifetime honor for Zechariah, who was chosen by lot to "bring the sacrifice to the altar and clean the ashes off of it" (R. Alan Culpepper, "The Gospel of Luke," in *The New Interpreter's Bible*, Vol. 9 [Nashville: Abingdon Press, 1995], 46).

Gabriel's visit to him took place while he was performing this honor before the Lord at the altar of incense. The angel informs Zechariah that he and his wife Elizabeth would have a son, and he would be named John. Gabriel also says John will "'be great in the sight of the Lord'" (v. 15, NRSV). The angel tells Zechariah more about God's calling on his son John's life: he says John will be Spirit-filled, and that this filling will take place in his mother's womb; he will cause many of his people to turn to God; and in the power of Elijah, he will prepare the people for the coming of Jesus Christ. This proclamation was too much for Zechariah to believe. He questions Gabriel because of the advanced ages of his wife and himself and because Elizabeth is barren. This unbelief results in Zechariah losing his voice. The angel tells him that he will be unable to speak until the child is born.

Today's lesson begins nine months later when John is born in fulfillment of Gabriel's announcement to Zechariah and of Old Testament prophecy. Culpepper writes, "The fulfillment of the announcement of John's birth … serves to heighten the reader's anticipation of the fulfillment of the even greater predictions regarding the birth of Jesus" (58). The ages of Zechariah and Elizabeth, in addition to Elizabeth's barrenness, did not prevent the birth of their son. Rather, it was a wondrous miracle in which they, along with their neighbors and relatives, rejoiced.

II. PRAISE GOD FOR MESSIANIC DELIVERANCE (LUKE 1:67-75)

At the birth of John, Zechariah's mouth is opened, his tongue is loosed, and he begins to praise God in a hymn traditionally called the *Benedictus,* so named because it is the first word in the Latin translation of verse sixty-eight (John MacArthur, *The MacArthur Bible Commentary* [Nashville: Thomas Nelson, 2005], 1275). Zechariah has not been able to speak for nine months, but he opens up his mouth and gives glory to God. MacArthur says, "When Zacharias was struck mute … he was supposed to deliver a benediction. So it is fitting that when his speech was restored, the first words out of his mouth were this inspired benediction" (ibid.). Filled with the Holy Spirit, he prophesies about what the birth of this child John means.

Zechariah begins his song by painting a picture of God's work among the Israelites. He praises God for being personally involved with the Israelites and redeeming them. The Israelites, who are God's covenant people, were promised redemption and deliverance through Abraham (see Gen. 12:1-3; 26:3) and David (see 2 Sam. 7:8-16), both of whom are featured in Zechariah's song.

Zechariah praises God because He "has raised up a horn of salvation for us in the house of his servant David" (v. 69, NIV). A horn was a symbol of strength, and a horn of salvation would be a very powerful instrument that God will use to rescue His people. Zechariah says God has raised up such a horn now "in the house of his servant David" (ibid.). The house of David was the royal line from which Israel's kings came, as prophesied by the prophets of long ago. But the house of David had lain dormant with no Davidic king actively reigning in Israel for hundreds of years. However, the genealogical line was still producing descendants such as Joseph, the earthly father of Jesus. According to John MacArthur, the one of which Zechariah has spoken is not referring to his own son, John, since Zechariah was a priest from the tribe of Levi (1275). The house of David descends from the tribe of Judah; therefore, Zechariah's praise is for the Messiah who will be greater than John. Zechariah knows that Jesus is to be delivered soon because of Mary's visit with Elizabeth. Therefore, he connects the birth of his son to the coming of Jesus Christ.

In verses 72-73, Zechariah continues, "[God] has shown the mercy promised to our ancestors, and has remembered his holy covenant, the oath that he swore to our ancestor Abraham" (NRSV). He moves from the prophecy about the Davidic king to God's promise to Abraham. It is from Abraham that the nation of Israel descends. The Lord God made a covenant with Abraham to bless him and to make of him a great nation (see Gen. 15:5-21). The Lord promised to make Abraham a blessing and said that in him—that is, in his seed, in his offspring—all the nations of the earth would be blessed (see Gen. 22:18), and now that promise is coming to fruition.

Zechariah says, in verses 74-75, that the Israelites will be rescued from their enemies to serve God. Matthew Henry says, "Here seems to be an allusion to the deliverance of Israel out of Egypt" (*Matthew Henry's Commentary on the Whole Bible* [Peabody, MA: Hendrickson Publishers, 1991], 1826). Culpepper notes that the Israelites' deliverance is not merely "from political domination—as important as that is—but the creation of conditions in which God's people can worship and serve God without fear" (59). The Messianic King will deliver people from sin through His perfect sacrifice and will restore them to a right relationship with God.

III. PRAISE GOD FOR JOHN'S CALLING (LUKE 1:76-79)

In the second half of the *Benedictus*, Zechariah turns his attention to his infant son to prophesy about John's God-ordained mission. Only verses 76-77 refer to John the Baptist specifically: "'And you, child, will be called the prophet of the Most High; for you will go before the Lord to prepare his ways, to give knowledge of salvation to his people by the forgiveness of their sins'" (NRSV). Today's parents have hopes and dreams for their children at birth. They want their children to be successful in their chosen profession and so forth. But in John's case, his father had already received a word from the Lord about the specific task his son would perform. He would be a prophet of the Most High, that is a prophet of God with the responsibility of preparing the way for Jesus Christ. He will preach salvation and the forgiveness of sins. John Nolland says, "John granting 'forgiveness of sins,'... is also the central benefit of Jesus' coming.... [For John, it] implies the call to repentance" (*Luke 1–9:20* [Nashville: Thomas Nelson, 2000], 89). John will not be the Messiah, but he will be the forerunner of the Messiah as Malachi promised (see Mal. 3:1). He will prepare people for salvation by preaching repentance. Matthew Henry writes that John will "give people a general idea of the salvation, that they might know, not only what to do, but what to expect" (1827).

Zechariah continues his song of praise, speaking of the "'tender mercy of our God'" (v. 78, NRSV). At this point, Zechariah is not speaking of the greatness of his son any longer but of God's graciousness. Zechariah says the "'dawn,'" who is Jesus, will shine a light on the pathway back to God (ibid.). This alludes to Malachi, who says, "The sun of righteousness will rise, with healing in its wings" (4:2, NRSV). Jesus will shine light on those who live in darkness. What is this darkness? It is the darkness of sin and death, a deadly, willful ignorance of God. The world is filled with sinners who do not know God or do His will because of their fallen state. Trent Butler says, "For too long God's people have lived in the darkness of foreign governments, the darkness of economic oppression, and the darkness of our own sins. We have experienced living death all these years. Now God is changing all that. God will let his sun shine on us. His pathway for us will become clear. No longer will we have to plot war and subversion against the enemy nations. We will know his perfect peace" (*Luke* [Nashville: Broadman and Holman Publishers, 2000], 15).

THE LESSON APPLIED

Today, we know that Zechariah's prophecy was fulfilled in his son John, who prepared the way for Christ. Christ has come with all of the wonderful blessings which were spoken of in the *Benedictus*: redemption, salvation, the forgiveness of sins, the tender mercy of our God, the light that conquers darkness and death, and guidance in the way of peace. He also spoke of the work of Jesus, who has redeemed us with His precious blood and set us free from bondage to sin and death. In Him, we have redemption and the forgiveness of sin. What a marvelous treasure-trove of blessing is found in the *Benedictus*. Through the power of the Holy Spirit, Zechariah foresaw it and sang about it.

Zechariah's song of praise prophesied about his son John. Let us not forget the role of John in preparing for and clarifying Jesus' ministry. When we remember this, we can join Zechariah in singing a song of praise for our salvation. It's not necessary to have a son named John the Baptist to do that. We have only to know the one for whom John prepared the way—Jesus Christ.

LET'S TALK ABOUT IT

1. What does Zechariah's reference to Jesus as the "horn of salvation" (v. 69, NIV) mean for us?

The word *horn* in this passage does not refer to a musical instrument, but is an Old Testament image of strength, power, and victory (see Ps. 92:9-10). This is implied in Micah 4:13 when God says to Jerusalem, "Arise and thresh, O daughter Zion, for I will make your horn iron and your hoofs bronze; you shall beat in pieces many peoples" (NRSV). Micah encouraged the Israelites to trust that God would make His weak people into an army who would rise and thresh God's enemies.

When Zechariah speaks of Jesus as a horn, he means primarily that the Messiah will one day literally destroy his enemies. God's aim in raising a horn of salvation is not merely to liberate an oppressed people, but to also create a holy and righteous people who will trust Him. Therefore, to view Jesus as a horn of salvation is to see Him not only as a national Liberator for the Israelites, but, much more importantly for us now, also as a spiritual Conqueror. If the goal of God's redemption is to be achieved—the gathering of a people who are holy and righteous—then He must and will conquer fear and unrighteousness. The good news of Zechariah's song is that God has raised up a horn of salvation, Jesus Christ, who is the great Horn of salvation for all those who call upon Him as Lord.

2. What can we learn from the life of John the Baptist?

Though not discussed in this lesson, the Scripture goes on to reveal that John fulfilled all that Zechariah prophesied about him. He indeed was the one who prepared the way for the Lord (see Matt. 3:1-3). His life was characterized by complete devotion and utter surrender to Jesus Christ as he prepared the way of the Lord so that others could find Him (see Matt. 3:3). Such devotion and surrender does not come easy for 21st-century Christians, who are distracted by worldly pursuits and everyday busyness. At some point in his life, John knew that the Messiah was coming. He believed this with his whole heart and committed his days to it. By that same token, we, too, know that Jesus is coming again. We should take heed to John the Baptist, who cried out in the wilderness. The day is here when we should devote ourselves to God's calling and Jesus' return.

HOME DAILY DEVOTIONAL READINGS
DECEMBER 16-22, 2013

MONDAY	TUESDAY	WEDNESDAY	THURSDAY	FRIDAY	SATURDAY	SUNDAY
A Child Dedicated to the Lord	Blessing the Children of Israel	Hope for the Coming One	A Ruler from Bethlehem and Judah	God's Blessings on David's Descendants	The Fullness of Time	The Birth of Jesus in Bethlehem
1 Samuel 1:21-28	Numbers 6:22-27	Isaiah 9:1-5	Micah 5:1-5	Psalm 18:46-50	Galatians 4:1-7	Luke 2:1-17

JESUS IS BORN

ADULT TOPIC: A BUNDLE OF JOY	BACKGROUND SCRIPTURE: LUKE 2:1-20

LUKE 2:1-17

King James Version

AND it came to pass in those days, that there went out a decree from Caesar Augustus that all the world should be taxed.

2 (And this taxing was first made when Cyrenius was governor of Syria.)

3 And all went to be taxed, every one into his own city.

4 And Joseph also went up from Galilee, out of the city of Nazareth, into Judaea, unto the city of David, which is called Bethlehem; (because he was of the house and lineage of David:)

5 To be taxed with Mary his espoused wife, being great with child.

6 And so it was, that, while they were there, the days were accomplished that she should be delivered.

7 And she brought forth her firstborn son, and wrapped him in swaddling clothes, and laid him in a manger; because there was no room for them in the inn.

8 And there were in the same country shepherds abiding in the field, keeping watch over their flock by night.

9 And, lo, the angel of the Lord came upon them, and the glory of the Lord shone round about them: and they were sore afraid.

10 And the angel said unto them, Fear not: for, behold, I bring you good tidings of great joy, which shall be to all people.

11 For unto you is born this day in the city of David a Saviour, which is Christ the Lord.

New Revised Standard Version

IN those days a decree went out from Emperor Augustus that all the world should be registered.

2 This was the first registration and was taken while Quirinius was governor of Syria.

3 All went to their own towns to be registered.

4 Joseph also went from the town of Nazareth in Galilee to Judea, to the city of David called Bethlehem, because he was descended from the house and family of David.

5 He went to be registered with Mary, to whom he was engaged and who was expecting a child.

6 While they were there, the time came for her to deliver her child.

7 And she gave birth to her firstborn son and wrapped him in bands of cloth, and laid him in a manger, because there was no place for them in the inn.

8 In that region there were shepherds living in the fields, keeping watch over their flock by night.

9 Then an angel of the Lord stood before them, and the glory of the Lord shone around them, and they were terrified.

10 But the angel said to them, "Do not be afraid; for see—I am bringing you good news of great joy for all the people:

11 to you is born this day in the city of David a Savior, who is the Messiah, the Lord.

MAIN THOUGHT: And she brought forth her firstborn son, and wrapped him in swaddling clothes, and laid him in a manger; because there was no room for them in the inn. (Luke 2:7, KJV)

LUKE 2:1-17

King James Version	New Revised Standard Version
12 And this shall be a sign unto you; Ye shall find the babe wrapped in swaddling clothes, lying in a manger.	12 This will be a sign for you: you will find a child wrapped in bands of cloth and lying in a manger."
13 And suddenly there was with the angel a multitude of the heavenly host praising God, and saying,	13 And suddenly there was with the angel a multitude of the heavenly host, praising God and saying,
14 Glory to God in the highest, and on earth peace, good will toward men.	14 "Glory to God in the highest heaven, and on earth peace among those whom he favors!"
15 And it came to pass, as the angels were gone away from them into heaven, the shepherds said one to another, Let us now go even unto Bethlehem, and see this thing which is come to pass, which the Lord hath made known unto us.	15 When the angels had left them and gone into heaven, the shepherds said to one another, "Let us go now to Bethlehem and see this thing that has taken place, which the Lord has made known to us."
16 And they came with haste, and found Mary, and Joseph, and the babe lying in a manger.	16 So they went with haste and found Mary and Joseph, and the child lying in the manger.
17 And when they had seen it, they made known abroad the saying which was told them concerning this child.	17 When they saw this, they made known what had been told them about this child.

LESSON SETTING
Time: ca. 4 B.C.
Place: Bethlehem

LESSON OUTLINE
I. The Birth of Jesus
(Luke 2:1-7)
II. The Shepherds and the Angels
(Luke 2:8-17)

UNIFYING PRINCIPLE
New parents marvel at the miracle of birth. What makes the birth of a child miraculous? The angels announced to the shepherds the most miraculous birth of all—Jesus, Savior, Messiah, and Lord.

INTRODUCTION
Unlike Matthew, whose birth narrative focuses entirely on Jesus, Luke gives considerable attention to the circumstances surrounding the births of both John and Jesus. He weaves the two stories together tightly, alternating between one and the other in a way that is meant to show how intimately connected the two stories really are. Indeed, it is impossible to fully understand one of these stories apart from the other. Over the past three weeks, we have spent a great deal of time in Luke 1, examining the announcements by Gabriel to Elizabeth and Mary, the song of praise sung by Mary, and the prophetic utterances of Zechariah. In today's lesson, we come to the birth of Jesus. Today's text picks up the narrative of Jesus' birth from where it was "left on hold at [Luke] 1:56" (Joel B. Green, *The Gospel of Luke* [Grand Rapids, MI: Eerdmans, 1997], 124). Luke now resumes the narrative.

Before we turn our attention to the text itself, it will be necessary to deal with a few preliminary matters. First, it is important that we not pass over Luke's ability to craft an effective narrative. From the outset of his Gospel, he has been preparing his readers for the events described in today's text. Green traces movement in the narrative from possibility to probability to event and, finally, to response. He points out that the promise of a son announced by Gabriel to Mary raises a "narrative *possibility* [that] is strengthened by the fulfillment of the sign given Mary—that is, that Elizabeth had conceived in her old age" (120-121). In the songs of Mary and Zechariah—particularly in what they have to say about the son that will be born to her—we move to the "*probability* that the angel's words will come to fruition" (ibid., 121). Today's text brings us to the *event* itself and to the *responses* from the shepherds, angels, and Joseph and Mary, tying together the threads that have come before in a dramatically satisfying way.

Second, we should briefly notice some of the larger interpretive debates that bear upon today's text. Modern scholarship on the Gospel of Luke for much of the nineteenth and twentieth centuries saw Luke as having an essentially benign (if not entirely favorable) view of Roman rule, one that saw Augustus' rule as a positive factor in the spread of the Gospel. Alongside this view came a new appreciation for Luke as an ancient historian. This was a helpful development, to be sure. But it tended to see passages like Luke 2:1-3 as little more than background information or helpful chronology. But these lines of interpretation blinded many scholars and commentators to the overwhelming political (and anti-imperial) overtones of Luke's language. In today's lesson, we will take the time to tease out those implications and the way in which they can improve our understanding of Luke's Gospel. Having addressed those preliminaries, let us now turn our attention to the text.

EXPOSITION

I. THE BIRTH OF JESUS (LUKE 2:1-7)

At the outset, we should note that Luke is an historian. His work displays many of the standard conventions of ancient historiography. His work begins with a preface that is very similar to those found in Polybius, Livy, Diodorus Siculus, and other Hellenistic and Roman historians. He is open about his use of sources (see Luke 1:1-4), and the indirect way in which those sources are "cited" matches the conventions current in his day. Moreover, as we see in today's text, he has a marked interest in chronological detail.

It is worth observing, however, that Luke differs from other ancient historians in some significant ways. The primary difference is that Luke "shows an interest in both history and theology, twin emphases evidenced not only in his attention to the time sequence of events and teachings, but in their topical and theological relationship as well. He writes as a theologian and a pastor, but is directed by the history which preceded him" (Darrell Bock, "Luke, Gospel of," in *Dictionary of Jesus and the Gospels* [Downers Grove, IL: InterVarsity Press, 1992], 498).

In light of all this, it should come as no surprise that Luke opens his narrative of Jesus' birth in this way: "In those days a decree went out from Emperor Augustus that all the world should be registered [Grk. *apographesthai*]. This was the first registration [Grk. *apographē*] and was taken while Quirinius was governor of Syria. All went to their own towns to be registered" (vv. 1-3, NRSV). This is all interesting information. But Luke's references to the registration ("census," NIV) and to Augustus are more than mere background information.

Joel Green, summarizing a major trend in New Testament scholarship over the past two or three decades, argues that these references to Roman rule must be read in light of an overarching anti-imperial thrust found in many, if not all, of the New Testament documents. The name *Augustus*, given to Octavian by the Roman senate in 27 B.C., carried with it distinctly religious overtones. While he demurred when his subjects attempted to venerate him as a god, Augustus was keen to assert the divinity of his adoptive father, Julius Caesar (for epigraphic evidence, see Green, 122 n.6). Consequently, he allowed himself the titles "Son of God" and "Savior," and approved of language that referred to himself as one who had brought peace to "all the world" (ibid.; cf. Luke 2:14).

When the angel of the Lord appeared to the shepherds proclaiming the coming of "good news" (Luke 2:10, NRSV; Grk. *euangelizomai*), Luke and his readers would have thought of another sort of "good news" as well. In the Roman world, "good news" (Grk. *euangelion*) was good news for the imperial court, e.g., the birth of a child to the emperor or a victory in battle for the Roman army. Obviously we should also note that Luke's emphasis on the census—it is mentioned four times in this brief account (vv. 1, 2, 3, 5)—carries ideological weight. The census would have involved two elements: an oath of loyalty to Roman leadership and the payment of a small tribute tax. As Green notes, "Many would have found in the census a disturbing reminder of the alien rule of Rome, and in the ensuing demand of tribute a sign of loyalty to the emperor that compromised fidelity to Yahweh" (123). All of this clearly "sets Jesus in religio-political opposition to the emperor" (ibid.). There is no longer any credible way to claim that Luke supported Roman imperial policy or was attempting to paint a picture of Jesus that would be non-threatening to Roman authorities, as some older commentators asserted.

In contradistinction to Roman imperial claims, Luke presents a family—a husband and his pregnant wife—travelling from a small Galilean village to the man's hometown south of Jerusalem. From the perspective of the Roman authorities, Joseph and Mary were insignificant at best, but that is not how Luke views the situation. He calls attention to Joseph, noting that "he was descended from the house and family of David" (v. 4, NRSV). This points to the royal lineage of both Joseph and the child in Mary's womb. More specifically, it makes a counterclaim to those being made by the Roman authorities on behalf of the emperor. Who is the true "Savior" of the world? Not Augustus. Who brings "good news of great joy" and "peace" (vv. 10, 14, NRSV)? Again, not Augustus. Contrary to every Graeco-Roman claim about the nature of divinity, Jesus was born in circumstances that were anything but divine (at least according to the prevailing pagan notions of divinity in the first century A.D.). Luke's telling of the story bespeaks a very different understanding of what it meant to be divine, to be of royal lineage: while Joseph and Mary were in Bethlehem, "the time came for her to deliver her child. And she gave birth to her firstborn son and wrapped him in bands of cloth, and laid him in a manger, because there was no place for them in the inn" (vv. 6-7, NRSV). Fred Craddock writes that "Luke has kept the story clean of any decoration that would remove it from the lowly, the poor, and the marginal of the earth" (*Luke* [Louisville: John Knox Press, 1990], 35). Luke's concern, as we will see throughout this quarter of study, is precisely for the poor. Here, in very simple terms, he emphasizes the deep connection that the Lord has with the poor and dispossessed at His most vulnerable moment, the moment of His birth.

II. THE SHEPHERDS AND THE ANGELS (LUKE 2:8-17)

From the manger Luke takes us out into the fields in the countryside inhabited by shepherds. Why shepherds, though? Why is it important that shepherds are the first to receive the good news of Jesus' birth? Two things come to mind immediately. First, the shepherds tie Jesus to David, the shepherd-king (see 1 Sam. 16:11-13). Secondly, and perhaps more importantly, we can see here a kind of fulfillment of Isaiah 61:1, which promises that the poor will have the good news preached to them (see Luke 4:16-30). What does this have to do with shepherds? Shepherds, Green observes, "were ... peasants, located toward the bottom of the scale of power

and privilege. That they are here cast in this dress is unmistakable, for the same contrast introduced in Mary's Song—the enthroned versus the lowly (1:52)—is represented here: Augustus the Emperor and Quirinius on one hand (2:1-2), the shepherds on the other" (130-131). That they are thus presented is very significant. In the narrative world of Luke's Gospel, it is shepherds who are honored, not human rulers. Indeed, "[the rulers'] power is relativized and they receive no news of this divine intervention. Good news comes to peasants, not rulers; the lowly are lifted up" (ibid., 131).

What about the angels? As the shepherds were in the fields, "an angel of the Lord stood before them, and the glory of the Lord shone around them, and they were terrified" (Luke 2:9, NRSV). Following the angel's announcement that Jesus had been born, "suddenly there was with the angel a multitude of the heavenly host, praising God and saying, 'Glory to God in the highest heaven, and on earth peace among those whom he favors!'" (vv. 13-14, NRSV). This epiphany has several layers of meaning. First, it undercuts the place of the temple in the religious and cultural life of the temple: "God's glory, normally associated with the temple, is now manifest on a farm!" (Green, 131). The language of the angelic choir's song also points to the universal implications of the advent of Jesus. The "good news" is "for all the people" (v. 10, NRSV)—Jew *and* Gentile; the "peace" God brings in Jesus is peace "on earth" (v. 13, NRSV), not just for Israel. As suggested above, the language of "good news" serves several functions: it draws on Roman imperial propaganda, as well as on the eschatological language of Isaiah 40—66 (e.g., Isa. 40:9). How these two are related for Luke is best put by Green: "Luke, then, has drawn on language embedded in the culture of Roman religion and legitimation of power and in the culture of Jewish trust in divine intervention and rule. He exploits the socio-politico-religious depth of that language in both cultures, *then transforms that language by vesting it in a message about a newborn baby in a manger, spoken to peasant-shepherds"* (134, emphasis added).

The shepherds' response is instructive for us, as is Mary's response. The shepherds, having heard the Good News and having seen Jesus, became some of the earliest evangelists: "When they saw this, they made known what had been told them about this child" (v. 17, NRSV). Mary, on the other hand, "treasured all these words and pondered them in her heart" (v. 19, NRSV). Both responses are good and necessary; neither one should be denigrated or unfavorably compared to the other. Let us attend to both our inner and outer lives, our thoughts and our deeds, so that they might reflect the newness of life in Christ.

THE LESSON APPLIED

We have stressed two things in today's lesson: first, that Luke was an historian and, second, that the Gospel as Luke presents it has strong political overtones. Luke, as strongly as Daniel or any other Old Testament prophet, cautions us against looking to human rulers as savior or deliverer. As Fred Craddock puts it: "Beyond any argument [is] Luke's ... basic conviction that emperors, governments, and laws serve the purpose of God, often without knowing it" (34). Augustus, like Cyrus and Nebuchadnezzar before him, was an instrument of God's will, whether he wanted to be or not. This is God at work in the normal course of human history, entirely without reference to the blasphemous claims of rulers and authorities.

LET'S TALK ABOUT IT
1. **What does today's lesson teach us about Luke's theological concerns?**

For those of us who are pastors and teachers, it is important that we connect today's lesson with what comes before and after, noting how Luke develops certain threads throughout his Gospel. One of these is his concern for the poor and marginalized. Today's lesson demonstrates how God works, not through the powerful, but through the lowly to enact His purposes for the entire world. Today's lesson also emphasizes the fundamentally contradictory claims of God and of Augustus. Both cannot be Lord; both cannot bring good news. Seen from Luke's perspective, our choice is clear.

HOME DAILY DEVOTIONAL READINGS
DECEMBER 23-29, 2013

MONDAY	TUESDAY	WEDNESDAY	THURSDAY	FRIDAY	SATURDAY	SUNDAY
Parents Committed to the Law	Circumcising on the Eighth Day	Offering a Sacrifice to the Lord	Consolation for Israel	The Lord's Comfort and Compassion	A Light to the Nations	Jesus' Presentation in the Temple
Luke 2:21-24	Leviticus 12:1-5	Leviticus 12:6-8	Isaiah 40:1-5	Isaiah 49:8-13	Isaiah 42:1-7	Luke 2:25-38

JESUS IS PRESENTED IN THE TEMPLE

ADULT TOPIC:	BACKGROUND SCRIPTURE:
DREAMS COME TRUE	LUKE 2:21-40

LUKE 2:25–38

King James Version

AND, behold, there was a man in Jerusalem, whose name was Simeon; and the same man was just and devout, waiting for the consolation of Israel: and the Holy Ghost was upon him.

26 And it was revealed unto him by the Holy Ghost, that he should not see death, before he had seen the Lord's Christ.

27 And he came by the Spirit into the temple: and when the parents brought in the child Jesus, to do for him after the custom of the law,

28 Then took he him up in his arms, and blessed God, and said,

29 Lord, now lettest thou thy servant depart in peace, according to thy word:

30 For mine eyes have seen thy salvation,

31 Which thou hast prepared before the face of all people;

32 A light to lighten the Gentiles, and the glory of thy people Israel.

33 And Joseph and his mother marvelled at those things which were spoken of him.

34 And Simeon blessed them, and said unto Mary his mother, Behold, this child is set for the fall and rising again of many in Israel; and for a sign which shall be spoken against;

35 (Yea, a sword shall pierce through thy own soul also,) that the thoughts of many hearts may be revealed.

36 And there was one Anna, a prophetess, the daughter of Phanuel, of the tribe of Aser: she was of a great age, and had lived with an husband seven years from her virginity;

New Revised Standard Version

NOW there was a man in Jerusalem whose name was Simeon; this man was righteous and devout, looking forward to the consolation of Israel, and the Holy Spirit rested on him.

26 It had been revealed to him by the Holy Spirit that he would not see death before he had seen the Lord's Messiah.

27 Guided by the Spirit, Simeon came into the temple; and when the parents brought in the child Jesus, to do for him what was customary under the law,

28 Simeon took him in his arms and praised God, saying,

29 "Master, now you are dismissing your servant in peace, according to your word;

30 for my eyes have seen your salvation,

31 which you have prepared in the presence of all peoples,

32 a light for revelation to the Gentiles and for glory to your people Israel."

33 And the child's father and mother were amazed at what was being said about him.

34 Then Simeon blessed them and said to his mother Mary, "This child is destined for the falling and the rising of many in Israel, and to be a sign that will be opposed

35 so that the inner thoughts of many will be revealed—and a sword will pierce your own soul too."

36 There was also a prophet, Anna the daughter of Phanuel, of the tribe of Asher. She was of a great age, having lived with her husband seven years after her marriage,

MAIN THOUGHT: For mine eyes have seen thy salvation, Which thou hast prepared before the face of all people. (Luke 2:30–31, KJV)

LUKE 2:25-38

King James Version	*New Revised Standard Version*
37 And she was a widow of about fourscore and four years, which departed not from the temple, but served God with fastings and prayers night and day. 38 And she coming in that instant gave thanks likewise unto the Lord, and spake of him to all them that looked for redemption in Jerusalem.	37 then as a widow to the age of eighty-four. She never left the temple but worshiped there with fasting and prayer night and day. 38 At that moment she came, and began to praise God and to speak about the child to all who were looking for the redemption of Jerusalem.

LESSON SETTING
> Time: ca. 4 B.C.
> Place: Jerusalem

LESSON OUTLINE
  I. **Simeon in the Holy Spirit (Luke 2:25-28)**
  II. **Simeon's Words (Luke 2:29-35)**
  III. **The Prophet Anna (Luke 2:36-38)**

UNIFYING PRINCIPLE

All people desire to live in freedom. In what way and through whom is this desire fulfilled? Simeon and Anna anticipated the presentation of the baby Jesus in the temple because they recognized Jesus as the just fulfillment of the prophecy of the coming Messiah.

INTRODUCTION

The Gospel according to Luke is the only one which presents this story of the infant Jesus in the temple in Jerusalem (see 2:21-38). Several key Lukan themes are present in this story, including Jerusalem as the geographical goal and focus, the work of the Holy Spirit, the role of women, the fulfillment of God's promises, and worship. This story about Jesus in Jerusalem as a baby sets the stage for much of what will follow in Luke.

Our verses today fall within a narrative frame, which is intended to show that "Jesus grew up in a family that meticulously observed the law of Moses" (Fred B. Craddock, *Luke* [Louisville: John Knox Press, 1990], 38). Luke 2:21-24 highlights Mary and Joseph's adherence to rituals for circumcising and naming Jesus (one a longstanding sign of the covenant for the Jewish people, the other a special revelation given by an angel which they obeyed), Mary's purification after childbirth through sacrifice, and the importance of the temple in Jerusalem for all these events. Luke 2:39 states that Mary and Joseph completed the steps the Law required of them following the birth of their first child. Verse forty says simply that, like His cousin John (see 1:80), Jesus "grew and became strong, filled with wisdom; and the favor of God was upon him" (Luke 2:40, NRSV). In these ways, Luke shows definitively that Jesus will be raised in a devout Jewish family who obeyed not only God's special commands for them, but also the everyday laws and rituals that were put in place generations ago. Both parents took the task of raising the Messiah very seriously and did so in the best way they knew: by following God's Law.

EXPOSITION

I. SIMEON IN THE HOLY SPIRIT (LUKE 2:25-28)

Verses 25-26 show that Simeon was a man whose words could be trusted. He was a "righteous and devout" man (Luke 2:25, NRSV). *Righteous* implies that Simeon acted correctly toward other people (being merciful, being just, etc.), and *devout* suggests that he acted correctly toward God (keeping the Sabbath, making appropriate sacrifices, keeping feast days, etc.). In addition to these traits, however, was the fact that "the Holy Spirit rested on [Simeon]" (ibid.). In fact, the Holy Spirit was active in Simeon's life, having informed him that "he would not see death before he had seen the Lord's Messiah" (v. 26, NRSV). It was the Holy Spirit in Simeon's life in conjunction with Mary and Joseph's adherence to the Law that led to the fulfillment of these words.

In Luke 2:27, Mary and Joseph are doing nothing unusual; in fact, they are faithfully following through with the necessary rites after Jesus' birth, which had been practiced through generations since the Law was given. What they are doing is decidedly unremarkable. Although he does not make this explicit, it is clear from context that Luke intends for the reader to understand that only through the Holy Spirit's guidance could Simeon possibly understand that the infant before him was the Messiah he had been waiting for. After recognizing Him, Simeon holds the infant Jesus in his arms and begins to praise God. "The scene is a moving one: an old man now ready to die holding a six-week-old baby who is, at long last, 'the consolation of Israel'" (Craddock, 39).

II. SIMEON'S WORDS (LUKE 2:29-35)

Numerous commentators note that the *Nunc dimittis* (Simeon's song of praise, "Now you are dismissing," so called because of the first two words in the Latin translation) closely mirrors language found in Isaiah 40—55. In verse twenty-nine, Simeon begins his song, addressing God as "'Master'" and referring to himself as a "'servant,'" setting the tone for the verses to follow (NRSV).

This is not unusual language to use when speaking of or to God; what is striking is how the Master acts toward the servant. First, He had made a promise to His servant, and second, He has kept that promise and allowed Simeon to see "'[his] salvation,'" referring to Jesus the Messiah (v. 30, NRSV). As the Master, nothing and no one could force God to keep a promise made to Simeon. The promise given was God's good choosing, and His keeping it testifies to God's faithfulness. This is why Simeon sings and declares that he can now die in peace, knowing that God is finally doing what Israel has been expecting.

To this point, the passage (including the framing story) has focused only on Jewish customs and tradition. At this juncture, however, Simeon's song takes on a global concern. This Messiah will be "'a light for revelation to the Gentiles, and for glory to [the] people Israel'" (v. 32, NRSV). While this may seem surprising, the inclusion of all nationalities is not absent from the Old Testament. Simeon's words carry an echo of Zechariah's own: "Many peoples and strong nations shall come to seek the LORD of hosts in Jerusalem, and to entreat the favor of the LORD" (Zech. 8:22, NRSV).

The phrases about "light" and "glory" parallel one another. For the Gentiles, Jesus will finally illuminate the truth that they have been looking for, consciously or not; for Israel, He will be the culmination of her history, the fulfillment of the Law and the Prophets, and will accomplish all that God intended her to be. While the reverse could also be said (Jesus is the best of what any Gentile culture or worship could strive for; He reveals truth about God which was otherwise distant or not explicit in Israel), the primary need of both groups of people differed, and so the parallel includes both people needing light and glory while acknowledging that they both came from different starting points.

Mary and Joseph were "amazed" (v. 33, NRSV) about what Simeon was saying concerning Jesus. Luke does not explain why, although after all that they have already been through, it is perhaps more astounding that they could still be amazed than if they were not. Simeon's words seemed to have "opened up possibilities requiring further development and clarification" for Jesus' parents (Joel B. Green, *The Gospel of Luke* [Grand Rapids: Eerdmans Publishing, 1997], 146). Luke agrees with Simeon's assessment of Jesus' mission as being for Israel and also for the whole world. This truth had not been explicitly stated before and very well could explain Mary and Joseph's reaction. Again, mandate exists throughout the Old Testament for the inclusion of all nations, but, just as today we sometimes read the Old Testament as exclusively concerned with Israel, so too Israel oftentimes read her own stories as though the blessings that came to her were meant for her own benefit only. Maybe for the first time, Mary and Joseph are receiving a fuller picture of Jesus' importance.

After his song, Simeon turns to Jesus' parents and blesses them. Then he speaks specifically, not to Joseph, but to Mary. Green asserts that this speech is "the first explicit manifestation of the reality that God's purpose will not be universally supported, and the first candid portent that the narrative to follow will be a story of conflict" (149). Simeon echoes Isaiah's talk of "God as the stone that causes God's own people to stumble" (ibid.) when he says that Jesus "'is destined for the falling and the rising of many in Israel, and to be a sign that will be opposed so that the inner thoughts of many will be revealed'" (Luke 2:34-35, NRSV). This will be played out time and again in this Gospel, especially in the various accounts of Pharisees in which Jesus brings their inner thoughts to light by examining their actions.

Unfortunately for Mary, this news does not end with Israel in general: "'and a sword will pierce your own soul too'" (v. 35, NRSV). This already foreshadows Jesus' brutal death. Because He is the Light of the world, all people who heard of Him or met Him, Jew and Gentile alike, would be thrown into a "crisis of decision … [of which] rising and falling, life and death, result" (Craddock, 39). Simeon's words inject a dose of reality into what has to this point been predominately hopeful proclamations. He sets the stage for the conflicts to come, especially between Jesus and the powerful religious leaders of the day. Having heard the story so often before, readers might forget that

Mary was not aware from the beginning that Jesus would be killed, nor was it a foregone conclusion that she would be alive to see it happen. Simeon's words surely added to the new mother's anxiety about raising her first child, and the words will return to her when she begins to see their fulfillment.

III. THE PROPHET ANNA
(LUKE 2:36-38)

Luke states matter-of-factly that "there was also a prophet, Anna" (v. 36, NRSV). Female prophets were not unheard of before her, but, certainly, men dominated the profession. Her designation as "the daughter of Phanuel, of the tribe of Asher" (ibid.) serves to show her Jewish heritage. Phanuel could be "a variant of 'Peniel' [meaning] 'face to face … with God'" and serve in a subtle way to further legitimate Anna as one to whom God spoke (David Lyle Jeffrey, *Luke* [Grand Rapids: Brazos Press, 2012], 48). She, alongside Simeon, also belongs to the nation of Israel. Taken together, Simeon and Anna become "male-female counterparts, who represent the best of expectant Israel and testify to the central place Jesus already occupies in God's redemptive plan" (Green, 143).

Besides intimating that Anna is wise, her age and the length of years spent in widowhood recall the Jewish ideal of marrying only one time and devoting one's self to God after the death of a spouse. For more than eighty years, Anna worshiped in the temple "with fasting and prayer night and day" (Luke 2:37, NRSV). The hyperbole shows her utter devotion to God. Green suggests that her fasting "constitutes a form of protest, an assertion that all is not well" (Green, 151). Indeed, there was much to be protested. Like the prophets before her, likely her protests were over the injustice she saw committed against the poor, the nation's failure to care for the orphan, the widow, and the foreigner, perhaps even about the loathsome Roman Empire, which held Israel in its grasp as so many other oppressive empires had done before.

Seeing Jesus, however, she "began to praise God and to speak about the child to all who were looking for the redemption of Jerusalem" (v. 38, NRSV). Like Simeon, she recognized Jesus' importance for Israel when he was presented to her. She, like the true prophets before her, was led by the Spirit. Perhaps after the sight of Him, she knew her years of fasting and prayer had been answered; no longer could she protest God's apparent inaction. A new thing was happening, and His name was Jesus.

Where the end of Simeon's speech focused on those in Israel who would not accept Jesus and the pain it would cause Mary and her Son, Anna's speech centers on those "who [are] looking for the redemption of Jerusalem" (ibid.). This points to the existence of others in Israel who, like Simeon and Anna, would recognize the Lord's Messiah when they met Him. Although Simeon's speech ended on quite a somber note, Anna's speech puts receptive Israel in the spotlight. Not all would reject this one sent by the Lord. Men like Zechariah and Simeon—even shepherds—and women such as Elizabeth and Anna, who had been barren and widowed, respectively, would accept Jesus and praise God for His arrival and call Jesus "Emmanuel" ("God with us").

THE LESSON APPLIED

Until this point in Luke, Jesus' life only led people to praise God and recognize Jesus as the Lord's Messiah. Simeon's speech points to the conflicts to come: not all people would recognize that Jesus was from the Lord. Anna's speech circles back, however, and reassures the reader that it would also not be true that all people would reject Jesus. In the Jerusalem context, both Anna and Simeon kept God's laws and were led by the Spirit, who allowed them to see their long-hoped-for Messiah, even in their advanced years. He fulfilled His promises to them and to Israel, and they reacted appropriately—with praise.

We who live on the other side of this story know where it is going. Jesus would minister to His people, and yet He would also be betrayed, flogged, ridiculed, and finally killed. Imagine how Simeon and Anna might have reacted—this precious Jesus, now grown, their hope for the future, was executed as a common criminal.

What of God's promise then? Mary carries their expectations for the Messiah into the future, suffers as Simeon and Anna would have, and lives to see her Son resurrected. God more than kept His promise, and even today, He can surprise us with the twists and turns He is willing to take in order to bring about His purposes.

LET'S TALK ABOUT IT

1. **Why is it significant that Luke chose to use both a man and a woman to announce Jesus in the temple?**

Throughout his Gospel, Luke presents stories that highlight women in Jesus' life. For example, women are the first ones to find out about Jesus' resurrection (see Luke 24:1-12). In today's lesson, Mary and Elizabeth were noted for their worship to God for the roles they will play in the salvation of Israel. Their male counterparts, Joseph and Zechariah, have also contributed to these themes. Both Simeon and Anna speak in the Spirit prophetically.

This pairing takes the reader all the way back to creation, when "God created humankind in his image, in the image of God he created them; male and female he created them" (Gen. 1:27, NRSV). In order for humankind to be represented, both men and women must be heard; neither gender can stand for the entire population alone. Together, Simeon and Anna, male and female, "are Israel in miniature, and Israel at its best: devout, obedient, constant in prayer, led by the Holy Spirit, at home in the temple, longing and hoping for the fulfillment of God's promises" (Craddock, 40).

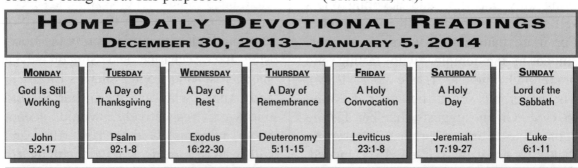

HOME DAILY DEVOTIONAL READINGS						
DECEMBER 30, 2013—JANUARY 5, 2014						
MONDAY	**TUESDAY**	**WEDNESDAY**	**THURSDAY**	**FRIDAY**	**SATURDAY**	**SUNDAY**
God Is Still Working	A Day of Thanksgiving	A Day of Rest	A Day of Remembrance	A Holy Convocation	A Holy Day	Lord of the Sabbath
John 5:2-17	Psalm 92:1-8	Exodus 16:22-30	Deuteronomy 5:11-15	Leviticus 23:1-8	Jeremiah 17:19-27	Luke 6:1-11

HONORING THE SABBATH

ADULT TOPIC:	BACKGROUND SCRIPTURE:
LIVING WITH JUSTICE AND MERCY	LUKE 6:1-47

LUKE 6:1–11

King James Version

AND it came to pass on the second sabbath after the first, that he went through the corn fields; and his disciples plucked the ears of corn, and did eat, rubbing them in their hands.

2 And certain of the Pharisees said unto them, Why do ye that which is not lawful to do on the sabbath days?

3 And Jesus answering them said, Have ye not read so much as this, what David did, when himself was an hungred, and they which were with him;

4 How he went into the house of God, and did take and eat the shewbread, and gave also to them that were with him; which it is not lawful to eat but for the priests alone?

5 And he said unto them, That the Son of man is Lord also of the sabbath.

6 And it came to pass also on another sabbath, that he entered into the synagogue and taught: and there was a man whose right hand was withered.

7 And the scribes and Pharisees watched him, whether he would heal on the sabbath day; that they might find an accusation against him.

8 But he knew their thoughts, and said to the man which had the withered hand, Rise up, and stand forth in the midst. And he arose and stood forth.

9 Then said Jesus unto them, I will ask you one thing; Is it lawful on the sabbath days to do good, or to do evil? to save life, or to destroy it?

New Revised Standard Version

ONE sabbath while Jesus was going through the grainfields, his disciples plucked some heads of grain, rubbed them in their hands, and ate them.

2 But some of the Pharisees said, "Why are you doing what is not lawful on the sabbath?"

3 Jesus answered, "Have you not read what David did when he and his companions were hungry?

4 He entered the house of God and took and ate the bread of the Presence, which it is not lawful for any but the priests to eat, and gave some to his companions?"

5 Then he said to them, "The Son of Man is lord of the sabbath."

6 On another sabbath he entered the synagogue and taught, and there was a man there whose right hand was withered.

7 The scribes and the Pharisees watched him to see whether he would cure on the sabbath, so that they might find an accusation against him.

8 Even though he knew what they were thinking, he said to the man who had the withered hand, "Come and stand here." He got up and stood there.

9 Then Jesus said to them, "I ask you, is it lawful to do good or to do harm on the sabbath, to save life or to destroy it?"

MAIN THOUGHT: Then said Jesus unto them, I will ask you one thing; Is it lawful on the sabbath days to do good, or to do evil? to save life, or to destroy it? (Luke 6:9, KJV)

LUKE 6:1-11

King James Version	*New Revised Standard Version*
10 And looking round about upon them all, he said unto the man, Stretch forth thy hand. And he did so: and his hand was restored whole as the other.	10 After looking around at all of them, he said to him, "Stretch out your hand." He did so, and his hand was restored.
11 And they were filled with madness; and communed one with another what they might do to Jesus.	11 But they were filled with fury and discussed with one another what they might do to Jesus.

LESSON SETTING
Time: A.D. 33
Place: Capernaum

LESSON OUTLINE
I. Jesus Declares His Authority Over the Sabbath (Luke 6:1-5)
II. Jesus Proves His Authority Over the Sabbath (Luke 6:6-11)

UNIFYING PRINCIPLE
Often, rules and limitations set by others make it difficult for us to help one another. What causes us to want to help others? Jesus, who is Lord of the Sabbath, teaches that acts of mercy and justice should be practiced all the time.

INTRODUCTION
Today's lesson begins a new unit that takes a look at Luke's account of Jesus as He initiates His Father's new Kingdom on earth. Today's passage of Scripture fits well into a balanced account of healing stories, discipleship stories, and controversy stories found in Luke 5:1—6:16. For example, the calling of Levi in Luke 5:27-32 and the twelve Disciples in Luke 6:12-16 are balanced, and the stories of Jesus' healing of a leper and a paralytic in Luke 5:12-26 are balanced well by the Sabbath controversy stories (R. Alan Culpepper, "The Gospel of Luke" in *The New Interpreter's Bible*, Vol. 9 [Nashville: Abingdon Press, 1995], 133). In the first Sabbath controversy in Luke's account, Jesus pronounces His authority over the Sabbath. In the second story, Jesus proves His authority over the Sabbath.

Before beginning today's study, a review of the importance of the Sabbath is paramount. Of course, the command to honor the Sabbath originates with the Ten Commandments from Sinai (see Exod. 20:8-11). Over time, differing interpretations regarding how ardently one should honor the Sabbath arose. According to Joel Green, "Although one can locate references to Sabbath observance throughout Israel's history, Sabbath observance increased in its importance during the period of the Second Temple ... along with circumcision and dietary restrictions" (*The Gospel of Luke* [Grand Rapids: Eerdmans, 1997], 252). Green contends that the Jews valued the Sabbath observance so much that they almost elevated it to the same level of importance as circumcision in being an identity marker for God's chosen people. As a result of this almost fanatical devotion to the Sabbath, the Pharisees and scribes prescribed Sabbath rules and regulations based on their interpretations of Exodus 20:8-11 and other Levitical passages related to Sabbath observance.

EXPOSITION

I. JESUS DECLARES HIS AUTHORITY OVER THE SABBATH (LUKE 6:1-5)

Today's passage in Luke finds a parallel account in Mark 2:23-28. Mark mentions that these events take place in Capernaum, whereas Luke implies that Jesus is continuing His Capernaum ministry which began in Luke 4. On a particular Sabbath day, Jesus and His Disciples are traveling through a grain field, when out of hunger, the Disciples begin to pluck the grain, rub the kernels in their fingers, and eat them. The description of the Disciples' rubbing the grain signifies how the grain was separated from the chaff (Culpepper, 133). Some Pharisees see what the Disciples are doing, and they ask, "'Why are you doing what is not lawful on the sabbath?'"(Luke 6:2, NRSV). The Pharisees are not upset about the Disciples' taking the grain from someone's field; rather, they are upset that the Disciples have been perceived as working on the Sabbath day.

Just to clarify, the Disciples are also not stealing grain from someone's field. According to the Law of Moses, "If you go into your neighbor's standing grain, you may pluck the ears with your hand, but you shall not put a sickle to your neighbor's standing grain" (Deut. 23:25, NRSV). And of further note, the Disciples have not technically broken the Fourth Commandment of the Decalogue. According to Exodus 34:21, the Israelites were forbidden from harvesting or plowing on the Sabbath. The Disciples had merely plucked the grain to eat. As stated earlier, the religious leaders of the day had been enforcing their own interpretations of the Decalogue on the people, and they viewed the Disciples' actions of plucking and rubbing as harvesting and reaping (Culpepper, 133).

Jesus responds to the accusations of the Pharisees and scribes by recounting the story of David found in 1 Samuel 21:1-6: "'Have you not read what David did when he and his companions were hungry? He entered the house of God and took and ate the bread of the Presence, which it is not lawful for any but the priests to eat, and gave some to his companions?'"(Luke 6:3-4, NRSV). Centuries prior, while David was on the run from King Saul, he had stopped in Nob and met with the priest Ahimelech. David lied to the priest and told him that Saul had sent him and his men on a secret mission. David requested that the priest give him and his men some bread to eat. Ahimelech said he only had the holy bread that had been set aside for the priests to eat as prescribed in Leviticus 24:5-9. The only way David and his men could eat this bread was if they were sexually pure in accordance with purity holiness laws. David asserted that he and his men had kept themselves pure in recent days as was typical of rules of holy war when men were fighting and kept themselves free of sexual activity. On a side note, Bruce Birch points out the irony of David's insisting he and his men had kept themselves pure and Uriah's refusing to sleep with his wife, Bathsheba during war time in 2 Samuel 11:11-12 ("The First and Second Books of Samuel" in *The*

New Interpreter's Bible, Vol. 2 [Nashville: Abingdon Press, 1998], 1140). Ahimelech acquiesced to David's wishes and gave the men the bread to eat.

Culpepper points out how Luke's inclusion of Jesus' referencing King David further emphasizes the connection between Jesus and David. Luke notes how Jesus is from the "house of David" twice in the nativity story (see Luke 1:27, 32); he recounts how a blind man calls Jesus the "'Son of David'" in Luke 18:38-39; and Luke writes of Jesus' assertion that He is greater than David (see Luke 20:41-44) (Culpepper, 134). According to Culpepper, Jesus' purpose in referencing David in today's passage is to tell the Pharisees and scribes that "hunger—human need—is given priority over ritual observance of what God has decreed as sacred" (133-134). Jesus illustrates that practicality must be used in observance of the Law. One shouldn't allow someone to hunger or thirst just to observe the Sabbath laws in their entirety; God would rather this person be satisfied physically.

Jesus then pronounces His authority over the Sabbath: "'The Son of Man is Lord of the Sabbath'" (Luke 6:5, NIV). With these words, Jesus tells the Pharisees that He is "God's authorized agent to determine what was appropriate on the Sabbath" (Green, 254). If He wants the Disciples to be able to pluck and eat grain on the Sabbath, then He has the authority to allow them to do so because He created the Sabbath. Luke omits Jesus' further words which are found in the parallel account in Mark 2:27: "'The Sabbath was made for man, not man for the Sabbath'" (NIV). Culpepper explains Jesus' words: "The effect of this

saying is to clarify that Sabbath observance was intended as a gift for humanity, not as an onerous duty. The Sabbath could, therefore, be violated by work when that work met a real human need" (134). God intended the Sabbath to be a day of rest that could be enjoyed; He never intended for it to become the Pharisaical behemoth that denied people practical comforts and food in times of need. Luke does not give the Pharisees' reaction to Jesus' words in Luke 6:1-5, but the next Sabbath controversy story strikes an even deeper nerve in the religious leaders.

II. Jesus Proves His Authority Over the Sabbath (Luke 6:6-11)

While Jesus declared His authority over the Sabbath in the first Sabbath controversy account, He now illustrates His authority as the Lord of the Sabbath in Luke 6:6-11. Luke begins with his reoccurring theme of Jesus' teaching in the synagogue that started in Luke 4:25. While teaching in the temple on "another Sabbath" (Luke 6:6, NIV), a man with a withered right hand is present as well as some scribes and Pharisees who see an opportunity to trap Jesus. According to Culpepper, the stage is set for a miracle, and "Jesus seizes a teachable moment and teaches not just with words but by means of a dramatic life situation" (134). Culpepper also explains the significance of Luke's specifying that the man's right hand is withered: "Luke adds that it was the man's right hand, the hand normally used for work, gesturing, and greeting. Since one performed chores of bodily hygiene with one's left hand, that hand was not to be presented in public. The man had lost the use of his good hand, presumably forcing him to use his left hand in public, thereby adding shame to his physical disability" (ibid.). The handicapped man is in need of divine healing, and he has encountered the Messiah; unfortunately, the day happens to be the Sabbath day.

The religious leaders in the temple are likely licking their chops in anticipation of Jesus' next move. Culpepper perceives they have Jesus in what appears to be an obvious dilemma. If Jesus heals the man on the Sabbath, then they can accuse Him of breaking the Sabbath laws. On the other hand, if Jesus refuses to help the man, they can say that Jesus has "complied with their authority and denied his mission to 'release the captives'" (134) as He had publicly stated in the synagogue at Nazareth in Luke 4:18. In Luke 6:8, Luke says Jesus knows exactly what the Pharisees and scribes are thinking, which Green notes as perhaps being a reference to Simeon's prophecy in Luke 2 about "'the inner thoughts of many [being] revealed'" (v. 35, NRSV) (255). In spite of knowing the religious leaders are waiting to trap Him, Jesus commands the man to stand up in the middle of everyone, thus, making a public spectacle of the healing that is to occur.

Jesus then asks a question, "'I ask you, is it lawful to do good or to do harm on the sabbath, to save life or to destroy it?'" (Luke 6:9, NRSV). This question serves to disarm the Pharisees just as Jesus' question did before healing the paralyzed man in Luke 5:22-23 (Culpepper, 135). Culpepper writes that in Jesus' question, "Sabbath observance is defined positively, not in terms of what one will not do, but in terms of what one must do" (ibid.). The Sabbath should not be about forsaking doing good for others if keeping the Law entirely demands so. Green explains further, "Jesus refuses to represent Sabbath observance as a litmus test for faithfulness to God. More fundamental for him is God's design to save—a purpose that is not incompatible with Sabbath observance but, in fact, is embodied in God's purpose for the Sabbath" (256). God's chief aim for humanity is for the betterment of all individuals. He created the Sabbath as a gift for men and women. Why would He be upset if someone didn't heed the Law entirely in order to better others?

The Pharisees and scribes do not respond to Jesus' question as He "[looks] around at all of them" (v. 10, NRSV), waiting for an answer. Then Jesus commands the handicapped man, "'Stretch out your hand'" (ibid.). The man obeys, and his hand is completely "restored" (ibid.). Green notes that the rendering of the verb restore (Grk. *apekatestathē*) in the LXX also carries the connotation "to save" and refers to the restoration of Israel (256). Thus, Green asserts, "In this one scene, with reference to this one man with a crippled hand, we are to see an expression of Jesus' mediation of God's eschatological redemption" (ibid.). God's overall purpose in restoring all of Israel as well as all of humanity back to Himself is an undertone of the healing story. The work of salvation is made possible for all men and women—even on the Sabbath day.

By healing the man's withered hand, Jesus was publicly showing everyone that He has all authority over the Sabbath. Luke records the religious leaders' reaction in verse eleven. The men are "filled with fury and [discuss] with one another what they might do to Jesus"(NRSV). In his parallel account, Mark adds that the Pharisees begin to plot with the Herodians how they might kill Jesus (see Mark 3:6).

THE LESSON APPLIED

Today's lesson speaks about the importance of not placing too much emphasis on duty and values at the expense of helping those who are in need. How often do Christians become so busy with activities at church and at home that they neglect the true purpose of the church in being a light to the community? Christians might preach about helping the less fortunate but never actually put their words into action. This is unacceptable.

Remember James' words that faith without works is dead in James 2:14-26. Culpepper writes in reference to Jesus' question in Luke 6:9, "To refuse to do good, to save life, is tantamount to a decision to do evil, to destroy life. From this perspective, rather than defining piety negatively—by what one does not do or what one opposes—Jesus' challenge calls us to demonstrate our faith by the good and beneficial things we do"(136). The world will see Christians' faith when their faith is in action.

LET'S TALK ABOUT IT

1. Do Jesus' actions in Luke 6:1-11 show that He wants to do away with the Law of Moses?

Jesus' actions do not mean the Law should be abolished. Jesus' famous saying in Matthew 5:17-18, "'Do not think that I have come to abolish the law or the prophets; I have come not to abolish but to fulfill. For truly I tell you, until heaven and earth pass away, not one letter, not one stroke of a letter, will pass from the law until all is accomplished'"(NRSV). The Old Testament Law anticipates the coming of the Messiah all throughout its writings. When Jesus finally comes, He aims to fulfill the Law's prophecies regarding His coming as well as to teach the people to live by the spirit of the Law rather than the letter of the Law. He teaches the revolutionary concept that hatred in one's heart is just as sinful as murder. The same holds true for having lustful thoughts being the equivalent of committing adultery in God's eyes. God cares more about people's hearts and motivations in keeping His commandments rather than dutiful obedience that lacks love and compassion. Jesus intends to show people how to follow the Law the way God intended it to be followed—with a willing heart.

HOME DAILY DEVOTIONAL READINGS
JANUARY 6-12, 2014

MONDAY	TUESDAY	WEDNESDAY	THURSDAY	FRIDAY	SATURDAY	SUNDAY
Judged by the Righteous God	The Righteous and Upright	Enslaved to God	Living As God's Servants	Forgiveness and Mercy	Blessings and Woes	Do Not Judge
Psalm 7:7-17	Proverbs 11:3-11	Romans 6:16-23	1 Peter 2:11-17	Matthew 18:21-35	Luke 6:20-26	Luke 6:27-42

HOW TO LIVE AS GOD'S PEOPLE

ADULT TOPIC:	BACKGROUND SCRIPTURE:
LIVING JUSTLY WITH OTHERS	LUKE 6:17-36

LUKE 6:17-31

King James Version

AND he came down with them, and stood in the plain, and the company of his disciples, and a great multitude of people out of all Judaea and Jerusalem, and from the sea coast of Tyre and Sidon, which came to hear him, and to be healed of their diseases;

18 And they that were vexed with unclean spirits: and they were healed.

19 And the whole multitude sought to touch him: for there went virtue out of him, and healed them all.

20 And he lifted up his eyes on his disciples, and said, Blessed be ye poor: for yours is the kingdom of God.

21 Blessed are ye that hunger now: for ye shall be filled. Blessed are ye that weep now: for ye shall laugh.

22 Blessed are ye, when men shall hate you, and when they shall separate you from their company, and shall reproach you, and cast out your name as evil, for the Son of man's sake.

23 Rejoice ye in that day, and leap for joy: for, behold, your reward is great in heaven: for in the like manner did their fathers unto the prophets.

24 But woe unto you that are rich! for ye have received your consolation.

25 Woe unto you that are full! for ye shall hunger. Woe unto you that laugh now! for ye shall mourn and weep.

26 Woe unto you, when all men shall speak well of you! for so did their fathers to the false prophets.

New Revised Standard Version

HE came down with them and stood on a level place, with a great crowd of his disciples and a great multitude of people from all Judea, Jerusalem, and the coast of Tyre and Sidon.

18 They had come to hear him and to be healed of their diseases; and those who were troubled with unclean spirits were cured.

19 And all in the crowd were trying to touch him, for power came out from him and healed all of them.

20 Then he looked up at his disciples and said: "Blessed are you who are poor, for yours is the kingdom of God.

21 Blessed are you who are hungry now, for you will be filled. Blessed are you who weep now, for you will laugh.

22 Blessed are you when people hate you, and when they exclude you, revile you, and defame you on account of the Son of Man.

23 Rejoice in that day and leap for joy, for surely your reward is great in heaven; for that is what their ancestors did to the prophets.

24 But woe to you who are rich, for you have received your consolation.

25 Woe to you who are full now, for you will be hungry. Woe to you who are laughing now, for you will mourn and weep.

26 Woe to you when all speak well of you, for that is what their ancestors did to the false prophets.

MAIN THOUGHT: But I say unto you which hear, Love your enemies, do good to them which hate you. (Luke 6:27, KJV)

Luke 6:17-31

King James Version	New International Version
27 But I say unto you which hear, Love your enemies, do good to them which hate you,	27 But I say to you that listen, Love your enemies, do good to those who hate you,
28 Bless them that curse you, and pray for them which despitefully use you.	28 bless those who curse you, pray for those who abuse you.
29 And unto him that smiteth thee on the one cheek offer also the other; and him that taketh away thy cloak forbid not to take thy coat also.	29 If anyone strikes you on the cheek, offer the other also; and from anyone who takes away your coat do not withhold even your shirt.
30 Give to every man that asketh of thee; and of him that taketh away thy goods ask them not again.	30 Give to everyone who begs from you; and if anyone takes away your goods, do not ask for them again.
31 And as ye would that men should do to you, do ye also to them likewise.	31 Do to others as you would have them do to you."

LESSON SETTING
Time: A.D. 33
Place: Capernaum

LESSON OUTLINE
I. **God's Blessings on the Poor (Luke 6:17-26)**
II **Love Your Enemies (Luke 6:27-30)**
III. **The Golden Rule (Luke 6:31)**

UNIFYING PRINCIPLE

People experience both love and hate from others around them. How are Christians to respond to those who hate them? Jesus teaches that justice does not always appear in the way people treat one another, but His followers are to love people regardless of what they do or say.

INTRODUCTION

Last week's lesson covered Luke 6:1-11. In these verses, we looked at two Sabbath controversy stories that involved Jesus. In the first one, the Disciples plucked grain from the field and ate on the Sabbath day. The Pharisees accused the men of breaking the Sabbath, but Jesus recalled the story of David's men eating the holy bread while on the run from Saul. Jesus then proclaimed Himself the "'Lord of the Sabbath'" (Luke 6:5, NIV). Next, Jesus was teaching in the synagogue when He healed a man with a withered hand. The Pharisees accused Him of working on the day of rest, and Jesus responded by asking whether it was better to save a life or destroy a life on the Sabbath. His point was that God intended the Sabbath to be a gift for men and women. Also, by healing the man's hand, Jesus proved that He was, indeed, the "'Lord of the Sabbath'" (ibid.).

Today's passage covers Luke 6:17-31, but first we need to recognize the context of Jesus' words. Luke 6:12 informs us that Jesus goes up to the mountain to spend the night in prayer with God. Afterwards, He chooses twelve men to serve as His Apostles. Then, He descends from the mountain (some scholars see a possible reference to Moses' descending from Mount Sinai with the Decalogue) and begins to speak with three groups of people: "a great crowd of his disciples and a great multitude of people from all Judea, Jerusalem, and the coast of Tyre and Sidon. They [have] come to hear him and to be healed of their diseases; and those who [are] troubled with unclean spirits" (vv. 17-18, NRSV).

EXPOSITION

I. GOD'S BLESSINGS ON THE POOR (LUKE 6:17-26)

These people serve as a sharp contrast to Jesus' previous audience in the first part of chapter six: the scribes and Pharisees. Instead of looking to trap Jesus, these people are actively seeking to hear Jesus' teachings and be healed of their infirmities. Verse nineteen then says that Jesus heals all of the people (through the aid of the Holy Spirit) who need His touch. R. Alan Culpepper points out that Luke's mentioning of the healing and unclean spirits introduces a common theme in Luke as well as the next phase of Jesus' Galilean ministry (see Luke 7:21; 8:2, 26-39; 9:37-43) ("The Gospel of Luke" in *The New Interpreter's Bible*, Vol. 9 [Nashville: Abingdon Press, 1995], 142).

After healing the people, Jesus delivers what is now known as the Sermon on the Plain in verses 20-49; this sermon parallels much of Jesus' Sermon on the Mount in Matthew 5—7. Joel Green argues this sermon reinforces the theme of discipleship in Luke (which actually began in verse twelve). He writes, "Jesus gives instructions on the way of discipleship that serve as an invitation and challenge to all.... All are welcome, but to stay, to be able to name Jesus as 'Lord,' Jesus' gracious invitation must be joined by obedience" (*The Gospel of Luke* [Grand Rapids: Eerdmans,

1997], 261). Jesus is going to invite His followers to partake in a radical reworking of the ethics common of His day. Those who claim to follow Jesus will have to act in a way that is contrary to everything they have ever been taught.

Luke also records some of the same Beatitudes that appear in Matthew 5:1-12, but Luke's account differs in that his Beatitudes are given in the second person rather than the third person and that Luke emphasizes true socioeconomic needs rather than spiritual needs (ibid.). After offering blessings to the poor, Jesus then gives what Green calls "'anti-beatitudes'" (265) to the rich. Jesus pronounces woes on those who are enraptured only in their pursuit of material possessions and riches. Their arrogant attitudes are deplorable to God, and Jesus warns, "'Woe to you who are rich, for you have received your consolation. Woe to you who are full now, for you will be hungry. Woe to you who are laughing now, for you will mourn and weep'" (Luke 6:24-25, NRSV). He also warns them about paying too much attention to flattery because that is how their ancestors spoke to the false prophets of old. Culpepper notes that Luke warns of the dangers of great wealth more than any other Gospel writer (144).

II. LOVE YOUR ENEMIES (LUKE 6:27-30)

Whereas the first part of Jesus' sermon detailed God's blessings on the poor, the second section tells Jesus' followers how to treat their enemies. Green explains that this section naturally follows the prior because it "continues to define the new conditions of existence in Jesus' community ... and unveils the general perspectives and practices that will characterize those who participate in this community" (269). Jesus begins this new section by saying, "'But I say to you that listen, Love your enemies, do good to those who hate you, bless those who curse you, pray for those who abuse you'"(vv. 27-28, NRSV). This passage parallels Jesus' words in Matthew 5:44, but slight variations are present. Jesus' words are likely quite shocking to His listeners. Why would anyone go above and beyond to do good to those who cause harm and suffering? What makes one's enemies worthy of blessing and prayer? Culpepper notes that such a command went entirely against the conventional wisdom of Luke's day. For example, the Essenes at Qumran taught their followers to love or hate their enemies based on their adherence to the Council of God or the Vengeance of God. Also, someone's blessing those who cursed him or her was the direct opposite of what the men of Belial practiced (147). And last but not least, the Old Testament itself taught "Anyone who maims another shall suffer the same injury in return: fracture for fracture, eye for eye, tooth for tooth; the injury inflicted is the injury to be suffered" (Lev. 24:19-20, NRSV). Thus, Jesus' words go against everything His listeners have ever known.

Green writes that Jesus' command to love one's enemies "[lacks] any commonly held ethical base and can only be understood as an admonition to conduct inspired by God's own graciousness"(272). Just as God shows grace to His followers when they sin, so should His followers show grace to those who sin against them. Also, Fred Craddock aptly points out that Jesus'

words assume that His "listeners are victims, not victimizers" (*Luke* [Louisville: John Knox Press, 1990], 89). Jesus does not say what to do when His followers have harmed or abused others because "such behavior, it is assumed, is foreign to those who live under the reign of God" (89-90). Those who claim Christ should not be characterized in such a manner.

Jesus then gives four examples of how one should show love to his or her enemies: "'If anyone strikes you on the cheek, offer the other also; and from anyone who takes away your coat do not withhold even your shirt. Give to everyone who begs from you; and if anyone takes away your goods, do not ask for them again'" (Luke 6:29-30, NRSV). In biblical times, to strike someone on the cheek was a serious insult. According to Culpepper, striking someone in such a way was "a physical expression of cursing or reviling" (147). Thus, Jesus teaches that when one allows his or her enemy to do the same to the other cheek, it "is an equally dramatic and physical form of non-retaliation that breaks the cycle of violence and rejects the principle of retaliation" (ibid.). Turning the other cheek promotes humility and peace in the face of conflict.

At first glance, Jesus appears to be talking about allowing someone to steal one's shirt if the coat is taken, but more than likely Jesus is referencing legal action or the payment of a debt. Deuteronomy 24:10-13 gives instructions about not taking advantage of someone who has given a coat as a pledge of payment (Culpepper, 147). Also, when Jesus says to give to those who ask for things or take without asking, He is more than likely not talking about giving to the poor and needy; rather, He is talking about giving in to the requests of superiors, thus promoting even more humility amongst His followers (Culpepper, 146). Thus, love is shown to one's enemies in action more than anything else. Green writes, "Love is expressed in doing good—that is, not by passivity in the face of opposition but in proactivity: doing good, blessing, praying, and offering the second cheek and shirt along with the coat" (272). Jesus teaches that His followers are not to stand idly when facing opposition. They should especially be proactive in showing love and humility even when some might just remain passive.

III. THE GOLDEN RULE (LUKE 6:31)

Jesus then tells His listeners what has become famously known as the Golden Rule: "'Do to others as you would have them do to you'" (v. 31, NRSV). Jesus says that Christians should treat others as they would like to be treated. Craddock notes that variations of the Golden Rule have existed all throughout ancient civilizations prior to Christianity. Variations can be found in Homer, Seneca, Tobit, etc. (90). Craddock also says that "If anyone is disturbed that the saying is not unique to Jesus, remember that the universal embrace of a principle does not make it any less true, any less valid, or any less binding"(ibid.). Augustine wrote in *On Christian Doctrine* that even the beliefs of pagans can have elements of truth in them, thus, the fact that the Golden Rule expands through so many secular philosophies further strengthens the truth of Jesus' teaching.

Although today's selected verses end with verse thirty-one, the full context of the passage continues through verse thirty-six. In these verses, Jesus gives the motivation for why one should love his or her enemies. Jesus begins by saying just loving those who treat people well offers no benefit: "'If you love those who love you, what credit is that to you? For even sinners love those who love them. If you do good to those who do good to you, what credit is that to you? For even sinners do the same. If you lend to those from whom you hope to receive, what credit is that to you? Even sinners lend to sinners, to receive as much again'" (vv. 32-34, NRSV). Green writes that Jesus' use of the word *sinners* refers to those who do good for others only with the expectation of reciprocation: "Pictured are essentially closed groups, whose members are free to give only to one another since integral to their gifts is the obligation of return in kind" (273). Those who follow Christ should expect nothing in return for doing good to others because doing good is the virtue by itself.

Thus, Jesus says, "'But love your enemies, do good, and lend, expecting nothing in return'" (v. 35, NRSV). And for today's passage, this especially applies to how one treats his or her enemies. Jesus then tells the result of what will happen if His followers love their enemies and treat them well: "'Your reward will be great, and you will be children of the Most High; for he is kind to the ungrateful and the wicked'" (Luke 6:35, NRSV). Those who love their enemies will be rewarded by their heavenly Father and known as His children. Green also notes that in Lukan society, patrons often did good for the community and were revered for their monetary contributions and service. People were placed in the debt of patrons for their beneficent deeds. Green argues, though, that "in this new economy, however, the patron gives without strings attached, yet is still repaid, now by a third party, God, the great benefactor, the protector and the benefactor of those in need" (274). Jesus concludes this section by commanding His followers to "'be merciful, just as your Father is merciful'" (Luke 6:36, NRSV). Christians are to show mercy just as they were shown mercy by their heavenly Father. The rest of Jesus' Sermon on the Plain tells His followers not to judge others, the importance of bearing good fruit, and the parable of the Foolish Man who built his house on the sand.

THE LESSON APPLIED

Today's lesson contained some of the toughest commands to follow in the entire Bible. Jesus instructed His followers to treat their enemies the exact opposite way that society taught. The same applies even to today's culture. When someone harms another, the immediate response is to seek revenge or payback, yet Jesus taught that love should be the initial retort. Culpepper gives some practical advice on how to love one's enemies: "The imperative to love one's enemies can have a range of meanings, depending on its context: Win over your opponent by kindness; take the moral high road; shame your enemy by your superior goodness; deflect hostility or prevent further abuse by offering no resistance; rise above pettiness; or demonstrate a Christ-like character as a Christian witness" (147). Knowing the right way to react is easy; putting the right response into action is not so easy.

LET'S TALK ABOUT IT
1. Do Jesus' words teach pacifism?

Some Christians interpret Jesus' words to teach that Christians should never respond in a severe manner whatever the situation may be, but such a response is not entirely pragmatic. In Luke 6:27-36, Jesus is speaking about levels of personal insults and minor conflicts. When it comes to legal issues, justice should always be sought, but vengeance should not. If someone commits murder, the victim's friends and family should seek justice—but through the right legal channels and not in their own hands. Also, if someone is physically attacking an individual, this individual has the right to defend him or herself. The question then becomes how severe a response is acceptable. One cannot forget that God is a God of love, but He is also a God of justice. Justice will always be served whether in this life or the next.

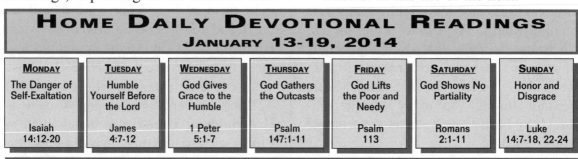

HOME DAILY DEVOTIONAL READINGS
JANUARY 13-19, 2014

MONDAY	TUESDAY	WEDNESDAY	THURSDAY	FRIDAY	SATURDAY	SUNDAY
The Danger of Self-Exaltation	Humble Yourself Before the Lord	God Gives Grace to the Humble	God Gathers the Outcasts	God Lifts the Poor and Needy	God Shows No Partiality	Honor and Disgrace
Isaiah 14:12-20	James 4:7-12	1 Peter 5:1-7	Psalm 147:1-11	Psalm 113	Romans 2:1-11	Luke 14:7-18, 22-24

JESUS TEACHES ABOUT RELATIONSHIPS

ADULT TOPIC:	BACKGROUND SCRIPTURE:
WELCOMING ALL PEOPLE	LUKE 14:7-24

LUKE 14:7-18, 22-24

King James Version	*New Revised Standard Version*
AND he put forth a parable to those which were bidden, when he marked how they chose out the chief rooms; saying unto them.	WHEN he noticed how the guests chose the places of honor, he told them a parable.
8 When thou art bidden of any man to a wedding, sit not down in the highest room; lest a more honourable man than thou be bidden of him;	8 "When you are invited by someone to a wedding banquet, do not sit down at the place of honor, in case someone more distinguished than you has been invited by your host;
9 And he that bade thee and him come and say to thee, Give this man place; and thou begin with shame to take the lowest room.	9 and the host who invited both of you may come and say to you, 'Give this person your place,' and then in disgrace you would start to take the lowest place.
10 But when thou art bidden, go and sit down in the lowest room; that when he that bade thee cometh, he may say unto thee, Friend, go up higher: then shalt thou have worship in the presence of them that sit at meat with thee.	10 But when you are invited, go and sit down at the lowest place, so that when your host comes, he may say to you, 'Friend, move up higher'; then you will be honored in the presence of all who sit at the table with you.
11 For whosoever exalteth himself shall be abased; and he that humbleth himself shall be exalted.	11 For all who exalt themselves will be humbled, and those who humble themselves will be exalted."
12 Then said he also to him that bade him, When thou makest a dinner or a supper, call not thy friends, nor thy brethren, neither thy kinsmen, nor thy rich neighbours; lest they also bid thee again, and a recompence be made thee.	12 He said also to the one who had invited him, "When you give a luncheon or a dinner, do not invite your friends or your brothers or your relatives or rich neighbors, in case they may invite you in return, and you would be repaid.
13 But when thou makest a feast, call the poor, the maimed, the lame, the blind:	13 But when you give a banquet, invite the poor, the crippled, the lame, and the blind.
14 And thou shalt be blessed; for they cannot recompense thee: for thou shalt be recompensed at the resurrection of the just.	14 And you will be blessed, because they cannot repay you, for you will be repaid at the resurrection of the righteous."
15 And when one of them that sat at meat with him heard these things, he said unto him, Blessed is he that shall eat bread in the kingdom of God.	15 One of the dinner guests, on hearing this, said to him, "Blessed is anyone who will eat bread in the kingdom of God!"

MAIN THOUGHT: For whosoever exalteth himself shall be abased; and he that humbleth himself shall be exalted. (Luke 14:11, KJV)

King James Version	*New Revised Standard Version*
16 Then said he unto him, A certain man made a great supper, and bade many:	16 Then Jesus said to him, "Someone gave a great dinner and invited many.
17 And sent his servant at supper time to say to them that were bidden, Come; for all things are now ready.	17 At the time for the dinner he sent his slave to say to those who had been invited, 'Come; for everything is ready now.'
18 And they all with one consent began to make excuse. The first said unto him, I have bought a piece of ground, and I must needs go and see it: I pray thee have me excused.	18 But they all alike began to make excuses. The first said to him, 'I have bought a piece of land, and I must go out and see it; please accept my regrets.'"
• • • • • •	• • • • • •
22 And the servant said, Lord, it is done as thou hast commanded, and yet there is room.	22 "And the slave said, 'Sir, what you ordered has been done, and there is still room.'
23 And the lord said unto the servant, Go out into the highways and hedges, and compel them to come in, that my house may be filled.	23 Then the master said to the slave, 'Go out into the roads and lanes, and compel people to come in, so that my house may be filled.
24 For I say unto you, That none of those men which were bidden shall taste of my supper.	24 For I tell you, none of those who were invited will taste my dinner.'"

LESSON SETTING

Time: ca. A.D. 30

Place: Judea

LESSON OUTLINE

I. **Where to Sit**
   (Luke 14:7-11)

II. **Who Should Be Invited to Dinner**
   (Luke 14:12-14)

III. **Who Will Come to Dinner**
   (Luke 14:15-18, 22-24)

UNIFYING PRINCIPLE

Homogeneity is the standard by which people invite others to social events. What inhibits Christians' ability to invite those who are different from them? Jesus has a message of social justice that reverses the custom and compels people to welcome all people.

INTRODUCTION

Luke 14:1-24 relates the story of a meal at a Pharisee's house which is unique to this Gospel, having no overlap with either Matthew or Mark (David Lyle Jeffrey, *Luke* [Grand Rapids, MI: Brazos, 2012], 185). This meal is part of a pattern in Luke's Gospel, as he frequently highlights them. Meals as teaching opportunities were found in Greco-Roman literature and "called *symposia*, where a figure of wisdom shares his knowledge with others" (Darrell L. Bock, *Luke* [Grand Rapids, MI: Zondervan, 1996], 391). In addition to the text today, Luke specifically discusses Jesus' eating with Levi (see Luke 5:29-32), twice with Pharisees (see 7:36-50, 11:37-52), the Last Supper (see 22:7-38), and two meals after His resurrection (see 24:30-35, 41-43) (ibid.).

The meal in these verses is the final invitation Jesus receives from the Pharisees, although it is surprising that He was invited even a second time, let alone a third, given what has transpired in His previous meals with them (David E. Garland, *Luke,* Vol.

3 [Grand Rapids, MI: Zondervan, 2011], 563). At the first meal, Jesus forgave a sinful woman's sins, which mortified His host, Simon (see Luke 7:47-49). Perhaps Jesus was unclear the first time about His priorities, and so when for a second time He ate with the Pharisees, He made Himself perfectly clear: "'Woe to you Pharisees! For you tithe mint and rue and herbs of all kinds, and neglect justice and the love of God'" (11:42, NRSV). When a lawyer spoke up in protest, Jesus spoke again: "'Woe also to you lawyers! For you load people with burdens hard to bear, and you yourselves do not lift a finger to ease them'" (v. 46, NRSV). Unsurprisingly, after the second meal, "the scribes and the Pharisees began to be very hostile toward him and to cross-examine him about many things, lying in wait for him, to catch him in something he might say" (vv. 53-54, NRSV). Each meal afforded Jesus the opportunity to teach about God's Kingdom, especially concerning who will be counted among His people.

The meal in today's lesson occurs on a Sabbath, and Jesus has already put His Pharisaic hosts on edge by healing a man (see Luke 14:1-6). Certainly, He has established a pattern of such behavior, and this final meal with them will be no different. From the Pharisees' perspective, He is failing to play by the rules—healing on the Sabbath and now lecturing them about humility and invitations for feasts, which they recognize for the thinly veiled criticisms that they are.

In the ancient Near East, honor and shame were of the utmost importance to a person. Honor could be turned to shame in a moment, and with it a person's entire reputation was affected. When Jesus discusses shame in these verses, then, it must be understood as more than mere embarrassment. One's entire life could change based on earning shame or honor. This is not a purely Greco-Roman concept. Jesus' teaching in these verses closely echoes a maxim found in Proverbs 25: "Do not put yourself forward in the king's presence or stand in the place of the great; for it is better to be told, 'Come up here,' than to be put lower in the presence of a noble" (vv. 6-7, NRSV).

EXPOSITION

I. WHERE TO SIT (LUKE 14:7-11)

Jesus does not begin speaking until He has observed the Pharisees' choosing their seats, especially vying for the seats of honor, which would be nearest to the host. What He says directly contradicts their practice: "'Do not sit down at the place of honor, in case someone more distinguished than you has been invited by your host'" (Luke 14:8, NRSV). This, given the honor/shame system, is simply common sense. If the person of highest honor showed up last (as often happened), then Jesus' illustration of being kicked out of the place of honor becomes frighteningly realistic. By the time this other person has shown up, however, the host is unlikely to rearrange seating around the one who was too proud, and so that person ends up, not where he should have been all along, but at the lowest place because that is all that is still available. His self-exaltation results in great disgrace.

What to do instead, however, is not so eminently practical. Jesus does not say,

"Choose the seat which most realistically approximates your position at the dinner." Rather, He tells the Pharisees to "'sit down at the lowest place'" (v. 10, NRSV). This is a counterintuitive move—He is telling them to consider themselves the least important person at the meal. Yet the move is savvy, for "'when your host comes, he may say to you, "Friend, move up higher"'" (ibid.). The guest has either chosen correctly and thus reduced the shame of being in the lowest place by not drawing attention to his position, or he has set himself up to be honored by the host who knows he belongs in a better seat. Thus, "humility is also a form of prudential wisdom; by sitting in the lowest seat the wise person avoids both offense and embarrassment" (Jeffrey, 185).

In verse eleven, it becomes clear that in this scenario, honor and shame are outside of the guest's control. The host will be the one to raise or lower the guest's position. The verbs themselves are passive, showing that the action is performed by the host. For Jesus, the dinner "serves as both a metaphor for relationships in God's reign and a warning of God's judgment" (Garland, 577). In the Kingdom, God decides whom to honor and whom to humble, so the best course of action is to remain humble in hopes of being counted among "'those who humble themselves [who] will be exalted'" (v. 11, NRSV).

II. WHO SHOULD BE INVITED TO DINNER
(LUKE 14:12-14)

Now Jesus changes the scenario and advises the host on whom to invite for his dinners. He begins by excluding everyone who would ordinarily be invited: friends, siblings, other family members, or wealthy neighbors. This should not be understood as a permanent command, such that one could never invite these people to dinner again (Garland, 577). Instead, such as these must not be the only ones who ever merit an invitation because they cannot repay the honor of being invited with the honor of a return invitation and so pad each other's social résumés (ibid.).

Those to be invited, then, offer no social incentives: "'When you give a banquet, invite the poor, the crippled, the lame, and the blind'" (v. 13, NRSV). As Garland explains, "This command echoes the Deuteronomic commands to invite the Levites, the resident aliens, the orphans, and the widows, so that they 'may come and eat and be satisfied, and so that the LORD your God may bless you in all the work of your hands' (Deut. 14:29)" (Garland, 578). Again, whereas humbling and exaltation were received from God as a result of one's actions, inviting these lowly ones to dinner results in blessing "'because they cannot repay you, for you will be repaid at the resurrection of the righteous'" (Luke 14:14, NRSV).

In churches today, "righteousness" is a nebulous word, not given a clear definition and assumed to be unattainable. This was not so in Israel, even in Jesus' day. The righteous person was the one who practiced justice and mercy, including, but not limited to, caring for those who could not care for themselves, whether economically, physically, or in any other way. Righteousness was rooted in right action toward other people. It meant ensuring that the courts were unbiased and that no one living in God's land went hungry, especially when others had plenty. Thus, "'the resurrection of the righteous'" (ibid.) implicitly includes people who take care of the lower echelons of society because right action is the basis of righteousness. God's Kingdom is made up of the righteous and gives special concern to those in society who are neglected by others.

III. WHO WILL COME TO DINNER (LUKE 14:15-18, 22-24)

The guest who speaks to Jesus is apparently looking to smooth over what has become an awkward social situation, saying, "'Blessed is anyone who will eat bread in the kingdom of God!'" (v. 15, NRSV). Bock paraphrases him thus: "'Despite our differences, won't it be nice for all of us to experience the blessing of sitting in fellowship before God when he reasserts his rule fully?'" (394). Jesus reorients the discussion, calling into question who it really is that will "'eat bread in the kingdom of God'" (v. 15, NRSV), and He wastes no time beginning His parable.

The background for the story is a man's throwing a huge dinner with many guests invited. The conflict comes when the slave is sent to announce that the meal is ready and to gather the guests. Suddenly, everyone is making excuses which Jeffrey calls "both disingenuous and lame" (187). In verses 18-20, three guests offer their justifications for the rudeness of turning down the invitation once the food has already been prepared: the first needs to finalize the purchase of some land, the second to finalize the purchase of oxen, and the third is constrained by his recent marriage. Rather than waste the food, the host tells

the slave to ""'Go out at once into the streets and lanes of the town and bring in the poor, the crippled, the blind, and the lame'"" (v. 21, NRSV), which is the exact list Jesus has already said must be invited by the righteous for dinner.

After these guests have arrived, the house is still not full, so the host sends his slave again. This time he goes "'out into the roads and lanes [in order to] compel people to come in'" (v. 23, NRSV). Garland suggests that the people outside of the city would have been of even lower social standing than those found within and would include "ethnic groups, tanners, traders, beggars, [and] prostitutes" (591). These people from outside the city need some special convincing, perhaps because they have never heard of this man and so distrust his motives. "They must be convinced it is a genuine invitation and not a cruel prank or an attempt to subjugate them further" (Garland, 591).

Presumably, these last ones fill the house because the story ends when the man tells them with finality that none of those who made excuses will enjoy his dinner. In the Greek, *you* is plural, suggesting that Jesus is now speaking as Himself, no longer as the narrator. As such, He is making a statement about who will eat with Him in His Kingdom although the Pharisees will not realize this is His intent and will perhaps hear only a social snub—they will not be invited when He throws a party. On the other hand, Jesus is once again displaying a marked disdain for the Pharisees' customs and status. From a faithful post-crucifixion stance especially, the first group can be read as representing Israel, who will forfeit its special invitation, while the second and third round of invitees represents Gentiles who will be called in when the original guests decide they have better things to do.

THE LESSON APPLIED

In God's Kingdom, it matters how "the least of these" are treated. As Jeffrey puts it, "It is not just that the poor matter to God and must be served but also clearly that 'worth' as measured in human eyes does not correspond to the way God sees things'" (185). While it is true that all people have worth in God's eyes and He loves everyone, some experience inordinate amounts of love from their fellow humans as well, whether because they are powerful, beautiful, or talented. Humility opens the door for God's honor, and a large part of the humility defined by Jesus in these verses means giving up one's social right for honor and status and choosing to side with those who not only do not offer such perks but may also lower one's own social standing. These people hold a special place in God's heart. Citizenship in God's Kingdom requires humility which results in righteous living. Micah sums up both points nicely: "'He has told you, O mortal, what is good; and what does the LORD require of you but to do justice, and to love kindness, and to walk humbly with your God?'" (6:8, NRSV).

LET'S TALK ABOUT IT

1. **Who will eat bread in the Kingdom of God?**

The Church for centuries has celebrated the Lord's Supper, eating the bread of which Jesus said, "'This is my body, which is given for you. Do this in remembrance of me'" (Luke 22:19, NRSV). In this communion, the Kingdom of God is acted out as the poor and the rich, the healthy and the ill of all nationalities eat together the bread which is Jesus' body. Paul's condemnation of the Corinthian practice of the meal is that they "show contempt for the church of God and humiliate those who have nothing" (1 Cor. 11:22, NRSV). They obscure the Good News which is inherent in the common bond Christians have through the Holy Spirit by giving priority to the wealthy when celebrating the Lord's Supper.

As the bread points to the past, considering Jesus' life, death, and resurrection, so it also points to the future in which God's Kingdom will come in its fullness and we will understand how it was that the meal instituted at Jesus' last Passover on earth declared God's future reality. It will be a glorious reality where believers will feast with Jesus in heaven for all eternity.

HOME DAILY DEVOTIONAL READINGS
JANUARY 20-26, 2014

MONDAY	TUESDAY	WEDNESDAY	THURSDAY	FRIDAY	SATURDAY	SUNDAY
An Open Hand to the Poor	The Cry of the Poor and Afflicted	False Concern for the Poor	I Will Give to the Poor	Shrewdness and the Future	Master of the Heart	Comfort and Agony
Deuteronomy 15:7-11	Job 34:17-30	John 12:1-8	Luke 19:1-10	Luke 16:1-9	Luke 16:10-18	Luke 16:19-31

JESUS TEACHES COMPASSION FOR THE POOR

ADULT TOPIC: COMPASSION AND GENEROSITY AT THE GATE	BACKGROUND SCRIPTURE: LUKE 16

LUKE 16:19–31

King James Version

THERE was a certain rich man, which was clothed in purple and fine linen, and fared sumptuously every day:

20 And there was a certain beggar named Lazarus, which was laid at his gate, full of sores,

21 And desiring to be fed with the crumbs which fell from the rich man's table: moreover the dogs came and licked his sores.

22 And it came to pass, that the beggar died, and was carried by the angels into Abraham's bosom: the rich man also died, and was buried;

23 And in hell he lift up his eyes, being in torments, and seeth Abraham afar off, and Lazarus in his bosom.

24 And he cried and said, Father Abraham, have mercy on me, and send Lazarus, that he may dip the tip of his finger in water, and cool my tongue; for I am tormented in this flame.

25 But Abraham said, Son, remember that thou in thy lifetime receivedst thy good things, and likewise Lazarus evil things: but now he is comforted, and thou art tormented.

26 And beside all this, between us and you there is a great gulf fixed: so that they which would pass from hence to you cannot; neither can they pass to us, that would come from thence.

27 Then he said, I pray thee therefore, father, that thou wouldest send him to my father's house:

28 For I have five brethren; that he may testify unto them, lest they also come into this place of torment.

New Revised Standard Version

"THERE was a rich man who was dressed in purple and fine linen and who feasted sumptuously every day.

20 And at his gate lay a poor man named Lazarus, covered with sores,

21 who longed to satisfy his hunger with what fell from the rich man's table; even the dogs would come and lick his sores.

22 The poor man died and was carried away by the angels to be with Abraham. The rich man also died and was buried.

23 In Hades, where he was being tormented, he looked up and saw Abraham far away with Lazarus by his side.

24 He called out, 'Father Abraham, have mercy on me, and send Lazarus to dip the tip of his finger in water and cool my tongue; for I am in agony in these flames.'

25 But Abraham said, 'Child, remember that during your lifetime you received your good things, and Lazarus in like manner evil things; but now he is comforted here, and you are in agony.

26 Besides all this, between you and us a great chasm has been fixed, so that those who might want to pass from here to you cannot do so, and no one can cross from there to us.'

27 He said, 'Then, father, I beg you to send him to my father's house—

28 for I have five brothers—that he may warn them, so that they will not also come into this place of torment.'

MAIN THOUGHT: He that is faithful in that which is least is faithful also in much: and he that is unjust in the least is unjust also in much. (Luke 16:10, KJV)

LUKE 16:19-31

King James Version	New Revised Standard Version
29 Abraham saith unto him, They have Moses and the prophets; let them hear them.	29 Abraham replied, 'They have Moses and the prophets; they should listen to them.'
30 And he said, Nay, father Abraham: but if one went unto them from the dead, they will repent.	30 He said, 'No, father Abraham; but if someone goes to them from the dead, they will repent.'
31 And he said unto him, If they hear not Moses and the prophets, neither will they be persuaded, though one rose from the dead.	31 He said to him, 'If they do not listen to Moses and the prophets, neither will they be convinced even if someone rises from the dead.'"

LESSON SETTING
Time: ca. A.D. 30
Place: Judea

LESSON OUTLINE
I. The Beggar Lazarus and the Miserly Rich Man (Luke 16:19-21)
II. A Reversal of Fortune (Luke 16:22-26)
III. A Plea for Brothers (Luke 16:27-31)

UNIFYING PRINCIPLE
Selfishness motivates the attitudes and behaviors of many people. How does selfishness blind Christians to the needs of others? Jesus tells the story of Lazarus and the rich man to teach his followers to put their selfish desires aside so they can help the poor.

INTRODUCTION
The narrative of the rich man and Lazarus is the last in a series of parables that Luke records beginning in chapter fifteen which includes the parables of the lost sheep, the lost coin, and the prodigal son. The more immediate context for the text today is the parable told to the Pharisees of the shrewd manager from which Jesus concludes "'You cannot serve God and wealth'"

(Luke 16:13, NRSV). Immediately following this, "the Pharisees, who were lovers of money, heard all this, and they ridiculed him" (v. 14, NRSV). As in the previous lesson, Jesus does not shy away from correcting the Pharisees' undeniably flawed interpretations of God's Law from the Old Testament which were never about outward appearances, but rather, about Israel's relationship to God and her people's relationships to one another. These covenant relationships (Israel to God, individuals to God, individuals to others) were recorded in the Law and the Prophets. The Pharisees should have known that the love of money was a grievous error.

The Law has numerous injunctions against abusing the poor, including leaving part of the harvest in the field for the poor to glean, not charging interest on loans, and being fair to both rich and poor in the courts (see Lev. 19:10, Deut. 24:12, 14, Exod. 23:6, etc.). However, these regulations would not be the end of poverty. "Since there will never cease to be some in need on the earth, I [Yahweh] therefore command you, 'Open your hand to the poor and needy neighbor in your land'" (Deut. 15:11, NRSV). Amos prophesied to Israel before she went into exile saying,

"Hear this, you that trample on the needy, and bring to ruin the poor of the land, saying, 'When will the new moon be over so that we may sell grain; and the Sabbath, so that we may offer wheat for sale? We will make the ephah small and the shekel great, and practice deceit with false balances, buying the poor for silver, and the needy for a pair of sandals, and selling the sweepings of the wheat'" (8:4-6, NRSV). Israel and Judah had both already been judged for a love of money, and yet the Pharisees did not learn.

To show the error of their thinking, Jesus tells them the story of the rich man and Lazarus. As per usual, Jesus does not tiptoe around issues but addresses them definitively. Every part of the story is a corrective to the Pharisees' thinking, from the importance of ceremonial cleanliness to God's blessing of riches, from whom Abraham blessed to what evidence is needed to know God's will.

Before getting into the story, a note should be made concerning the characters' names. There is power in naming; we need only look to examples wherein people's names are forcibly changed or discarded in order to understand the truth of this. In the same way, failing to give a name at all can indicate any myriad of intentions, most of which are at least unflattering. Thanks to the Latin translations of the New Testament, the rich man in this story has traditionally been given the name Dives. While there is nothing inherently wrong with the tradition, the power of the story is blunted when the rich man is named. As Jesus tells the story, the only character named is Lazarus. In fact, Lazarus is the only man given a name in any of Jesus' parables other than Abraham, who is identified in this parable as the patriarch. This suggests from the beginning that, whereas the rich man had both a name and a reputation in his life, his mistreatment of the man Lazarus (who is humanized through naming) has resulted in his eternal punishment.

EXPOSITION

I. THE BEGGAR LAZARUS AND THE MISERLY RICH MAN (LUKE 16:19-21)

These first verses contain an unusual amount of description for Jesus' parables. The rich man, though unnamed, wore "purple and fine linen" (v. 19, NRSV). His clothing was so nice that it was made of "the most delicate and most expensive fabric known to the ancient world" (David E. Garland, *Luke*, Vol. 3 [Grand Rapids, MI: Zondervan, 2011], 669). In addition, he "feasted sumptuously every day" (v. 19, NRSV), not just on special occasions. This was a man who was not just well off, but rich beyond reckoning.

Contrasted to this opulence is the poor man, Lazarus. The name *Lazarus* is a Greek form of the Hebrew name *Eleazar*, meaning "God helps." For Lazarus, this name was highly ironic. Lazarus was a beggar "'covered with sores ... [which] the dogs would come and lick'" (v. 20-21, NRSV). Dogs in the ancient world were a far cry from man's best friend; Lazarus' proximity to them made him unclean and, thus, contemptible to the Jewish elite. He lay at the rich man's gate, a state which indicates not only Lazarus' utter destitution, but also, the rich man's great wealth as the specific Greek word used here indicates a gate which "advertises his wealth and keeps out undesirable riffraff" (Garland, 670). The Greek terminology may also indicate that Lazarus was put at the gate by others, suggesting that he may have been lame.

Despite his proximity to Lazarus and Lazarus' obvious need, the rich man never satisfied Lazarus' desire to eat "'what fell from the rich man's table'" (v. 21, NRSV). He did not expect to be a guest or have a seat at the table. Rather, Lazarus merely wanted to eat the food on the floor; even this was denied him.

II. A Reversal of Fortune (Luke 16:22-26)

Now that the characters have been introduced, the story moves forward. Both men died and Lazarus "'was carried away by the angels to be with Abraham'" (v. 22, NRSV), perhaps contrasting with his family or friends' carrying him to the gate before. "'The rich man also died and was buried'" (ibid., NRSV). The brevity of the announcement of his death foreshadows what is to come. Whereas he lived lavishly, death for the rich man was an existence stripped of grandeur.

In Matthew 19, Jesus says "'It will be hard for a rich person to enter the kingdom of heaven. Again I tell you, it is easier for a camel to go through the eye of a needle than for someone who is rich to enter the kingdom of God'" (vv. 23-24, NRSV). His Disciples were aghast and wondered who would be in heaven if not the rich. The same reaction should be expected of the Pharisees when Jesus says that Lazarus was by Abraham's side but not the rich man. Despite his heritage as a son of Abraham and his earthly blessings from God (which were thought to indicate his favor in this life and the next), the rich man found himself in hell. From his place in hell, he could see Abraham and Lazarus together in heaven.

When the rich man called Abraham "'father'" (v. 24, NRSV), the patriarch did not refer to him in like manner. Instead, Abraham called him not "'son'" but the generic, neuter word for "'child'" (Luke 16:25, NRSV), which identified him as a person in need of instructions. As if the rich man's place in hell were not enough, Abraham's chilly demeanor confirmed that something about the rich man's actions in life was horribly wrong for him to be suffering torment. Likely, the man assumed that calling Abraham "father" necessarily meant that he would also be called "son." In another conversation with the Pharisees recorded in Matthew 3, John speaks to this entitled notion, saying that "'God is able from these stones to raise up children to Abraham'" (see v. 9, NRSV). The mishap of one's birth does not determine one's standing before God.

The rich man's request to Abraham was for Lazarus to show mercy to him in the afterlife such as had not been shown to the poor man before death. His request was for Lazarus to deliver water to refresh his heat-tortured condition. Garland sees this not as a request but an order, with the rich man thinking that "Abraham [would] send Lazarus to be his lackey" (672).

More distressingly, the rich man here reveals that he had known Lazarus' name all along and still did not help him! No longer could his actions be justified. In life, the rich man was very well aware of Lazarus and knowingly neglected him, feeling no responsibility for the plight of his fellow man. All of these things point to the audacity of the rich man to call himself a son of Abraham and assume he would be comforted, even in hell.

In Luke 16:25, Abraham reminded the rich man of the good things he received in his lifetime and the bad things that Lazarus received, but now the fortunes have been reversed. Nowhere is it suggested that Lazarus was a righteous man and should have been brought to Abraham's side; rather, because of the harsh treatment he suffered in life, he was brought to Abraham's side. Nor was it mentioned that the rich man got his wealth by fraud or deceit. The rich man's lack of concern for even the most basic needs of his fellow man merited the punishment he received, especially given the excess in which he had lived.

Abraham also revealed that there was a chasm or a gaping hole that prevented passage. No one could travel from heaven to hell, and no one could cross from hell to heaven. Who it was that might want to go down to visit the rich man is not specified; Lazarus did not pipe up and say, "Send me!" In another instance of parallelism in this story, the chasm parallels the rich man's gate with a key difference: whereas the gate could be opened and closed to seal off the residence or opened to people coming and going, the chasm was fixed and will not be removed. No one passed through, across, or around it. The rich man's fate was sealed.

III. A PLEA FOR BROTHERS (LUKE 16:27-31)

The rich man hadn't given up yet. Since he could not improve his own situation, he settled for warning his brothers who were still alive. As he continued to call Abraham "father," Abraham dropped even the "child" from his replies. His answers were the final word; once he has said this last part, there would be nothing left to be said.

Once again, the rich man tried to send Lazarus on an errand—this time, to his five brothers to warn them. The message is implied from the circumstances of the story: they needed to be told not to neglect the needs of the poor, especially those literally on their doorstep. This warning may not be motivated by brotherly affection, as might be assumed from the text, but rather, in keeping with his rather self-centered character. The rich man was merely looking out for his family "as an extension of himself" (Garland, 673). To this request, Abraham delivered the key to Jesus' argument against the Pharisees. He told the rich man they have Moses and the Prophets, and they should listen to them. Moses here stands for the Law, such that Abraham was saying that all the Law and all the Prophets were enough to teach each of the rich man's brothers (and each Pharisee) how to live righteously.

The coup de grâce occurred when the rich man persisted, telling Abraham that his brothers would repent if they were confronted by someone who had risen from the dead. At this point, Abraham had enough and ended the conversation by pointing out a truism: they would not listen to neither Moses and the Prophets nor a person from the dead.

The story ends here. Abraham (and by extension Jesus) made his point. Lazarus never said a word in this story; he was vindicated by none other than the father of the faith, Abraham. Even when the rich man wanted Lazarus to speak to the five living brothers, Abraham spoke for Lazarus.

In effect, when Jesus rises from the dead, these Pharisees will also not believe the Good News He has preached to the poor. What Lazarus lacked in life he gained in death: a powerful advocate who will speak on his behalf. For the rich, good news for the poor likely means bad news for their own wealth and standing; their disdain for the Gospel results from the love of money Jesus warns them against.

No reaction from the Pharisees is recorded, but based on previous episodes and the plot to kill Jesus, one can assume they hear loud and clear that Jesus is saying they are not sons of Abraham because they do not care for the poor. Instead of repenting, however, they become vengeful.

THE LESSON APPLIED

The same danger that Israel ran into and which the Pharisees faced is a danger very much alive and well in the United States today. Too often, we celebrate God's blessing of wealth without holding it in an open hand in order to help the poor of our own communities. God has given us plenty, but we act as though we have achieved our wealth without help. While riches can be a sign of God's blessing, the rich man learned that riches are not a blessing to be squandered on one's own interests.

Rather, the blessing is for the sake of the world, as are all of the blessings God gives. We ought to beware of our comfort in this life, lest we count ourselves among Abraham's children and receive only rebuke on the other side of the grave!

LET'S TALK ABOUT IT

1. Since our salvation is based on faith alone, what good are works?

It is true that salvation is based on faith alone, but Jesus also said, "'Not everyone who says to me, "Lord, Lord," will enter the kingdom of heaven, but only the one who does the will of my Father in heaven'" (Matt. 7:21, NRSV). Faith, which is more than intellectual consent, is demonstrated by our actions. Again Jesus said, "'Do not think that I have come to abolish the law or the prophets; I have come not to abolish but to fulfill'" (Matt. 5:17, NRSV).

What God required from His people in the Old Testament regarding the love of God and love of people still holds true; we cannot claim to love God without acting in love towards our fellow humans, and the love required is to take care of one another, especially when God blesses us for the task.

HOME DAILY DEVOTIONAL READINGS
JANUARY 27—FEBRUARY 2, 2014

MONDAY	TUESDAY	WEDNESDAY	THURSDAY	FRIDAY	SATURDAY	SUNDAY
A People Who Will Not Listen	A Lamp to Lighten My Darkness	The Voice of the Living God	Neither Add nor Take Away Anything	Denying God by Actions	Love in Truth and Action	Hearers and Doers of the Word
Jeremiah 7:21-28	2 Samuel 22:26-31	Deuteronomy 5:22-27	Deuteronomy 4:1-10	Titus 1:10-16	1 John 3:14-20	James 1:19-27

HEAR AND DO THE WORD

ADULT TOPIC:	BACKGROUND SCRIPTURE:
COMMITTED TO ACTION	JAMES 1:19-27

JAMES 1:19–27

King James Version	New Revised Standard Version
WHEREFORE, my beloved brethren, let every man be swift to hear, slow to speak, slow to wrath:	YOU must understand this, my beloved: let everyone be quick to listen, slow to speak, slow to anger;
20 For the wrath of man worketh not the righteousness of God.	20 for your anger does not produce God's righteousness.
21 Wherefore lay apart all filthiness and superfluity of naughtiness, and receive with meekness the engrafted word, which is able to save your souls.	21 Therefore rid yourselves of all sordidness and rank growth of wickedness, and welcome with meekness the implanted word that has the power to save your souls.
22 But be ye doers of the word, and not hearers only, deceiving your own selves.	22 But be doers of the word, and not merely hearers who deceive themselves.
23 For if any be a hearer of the word, and not a doer, he is like unto a man beholding his natural face in a glass:	23 For if any are hearers of the word and not doers, they are like those who look at themselves in a mirror;
24 For he beholdeth himself, and goeth his way, and straightway forgetteth what manner of man he was.	24 for they look at themselves and, on going away, immediately forget what they were like.
25 But whoso looketh into the perfect law of liberty, and continueth therein, he being not a forgetful hearer, but a doer of the work, this man shall be blessed in his deed.	25 But those who look into the perfect law, the law of liberty, and persevere, being not hearers who forget but doers who act—they will be blessed in their doing.
26 If any man among you seem to be religious, and bridleth not his tongue, but deceiveth his own heart, this man's religion is vain.	26 If any think they are religious, and do not bridle their tongues but deceive their hearts, their religion is worthless.
27 Pure religion and undefiled before God and the Father is this, To visit the fatherless and widows in their affliction, and to keep himself unspotted from the world.	27 Religion that is pure and undefiled before God, the Father, is this: to care for orphans and widows in their distress, and to keep oneself unstained by the world.

MAIN THOUGHT: But be ye doers of the word, and not hearers only, deceiving your own selves. (James 1:22, KJV)

LESSON SETTING
Time: ca. A.D. 55
Place: Jerusalem

LESSON OUTLINE
I. Quick Listening, Slow Speech
(James 1:19-21)

II. Doers, Not Mere Hearers
(James 1:22-25)

III. Pure Religion
(James 1:26-27)

UNIFYING PRINCIPLE

People often talk about what will help others, but they do not take action. What will help them take action? James says that those who are both hearers and doers of the word practice justice.

INTRODUCTION

This unit will contain four lessons on the letter of James. The recent history of this letter is marked by either neglect or unfair comparison to the letters of Paul. James is a book that was accepted later than other books into the canon due not to questions about content, but due to uncertainty concerning the authorship. The question about authorship concerned not whether James wrote the book, but which James wrote it. This question is not easily answered by looking at the book itself since the James mentioned in the opening address is not specified. The question of which James wrote the book is concerned with the apostolic authorship of the book. One of the criteria of a book's acceptance into the canon of the New Testament was that the author of the book had to be an Apostle or closely connected to an Apostle (e.g., the Gospel of Mark was accepted because of Mark's connection to Peter, and the Gospel of Luke and the book of Acts were accepted because of Luke's connection to Paul). The book gained its acceptance as being written by James, the brother of Jesus, and the leader of the Jerusalem church.

The content of the epistle of James was not questioned by a major Christian thinker until Martin Luther. Luther assigned the epistle a secondary status due to a misunderstanding in which he saw a contrast between the teachings of Paul and James concerning the relationship between grace, faith, and works. Luke Timothy Johnson explains that Martin Luther's view of James is one that stands in opposition to the view of the early church. Further, his view of James also contradicts the view of many of the reformers. "John Calvin, for instance, wrote an appreciative commentary on James. Influential critics of the nineteenth century, however, forcefully adopted Luther's position, interpreting this letter as part of the historical dialectic between Pauline and Judaizing movements in early Christianity.... Although such an interpretation is rarely advanced today, James continues to be studied almost entirely in terms of its relationship to Paul. This is doubly unfortunate. It unfairly makes Paul the sole criterion for canonical acceptance, and it disastrously reduces the significance of James to a few misunderstood verses. Those who have managed to read James on its own terms discover in it a writing of rare vigor and life, which interprets the 'faith of our Lord Jesus Christ of glory' (2:1) in a distinctive and compelling manner" (Johnson, *The Writings of the New Testament* [London: SCM Press, 1999], 507). In order to engage this letter in a way that does not simply contrast it with the writings of Paul, there must be some understanding of the background of the writer of this letter.

James, the leader of the church in Jerusalem and the brother of Jesus, was a Christian who was deeply formed by the Jewish faith. "For our letter the most important element of background is the imagery of James as a conservative Jewish Christian very loyal to observing the Law.

He was not an extreme legalist, for both Acts 15 and Gal 2 agree that he sided with Paul in declaring that the Gentiles did not have to be circumcised when they came to believe in Christ. Yet the speech that appears on his lips in Acts 15:13-21 offers the most traditional reason for that acceptance of Gentiles by applying to them elements of Lev 17—18 applicable to strangers living within Israel" (Raymond E. Brown, *An Introduction to the New Testament* [New York: Doubleday, 1997], 727). It is thus fitting that "the NT letter that bears his name echoes in many ways traditional Jewish belief and piety" (ibid.).

It is also likely that James is writing to Christians who have also been deeply formed by the Jewish faith. If this is the case, it is worthwhile to keep these two ideas in mind as we read this epistle. "We might be well advised, then, to think of the addressees as Christians strongly identified by the Jewish heritage" (ibid., 728). However, despite the assertions of some scholars, the epistle of James is not merely a Jewish epistle reappropriated for the early Christian church. The references to God as Father and "the coupling of 'God' and 'the Lord Jesus Christ' in the first line shows the traditional Christian faith of the writer" (ibid.).

This brings us to the specific section we will engage today. This part of the letter addresses concerns that will be more fully addressed throughout the letter. This serves as a means of outlining the concerns of this epistle but also giving these concerns a sense of coherence. "This section … opens with a survey of five themes in swift succession…. The first is the wisdom teaching that places a restraint on a hasty and impetuous desire to promote God's cause, seen here as 'divine righteousness.' … [The second and third are the] two major interests [that] then motivate James' counsel: the advocacy of practical obedience to God's message, which must be not only received with humility (v. 21) but also acted upon. Fourth, there is concern for the defenseless members of the community, linked with, fifth, a deliberate turning aside from 'the ways of the world' (v. 27)" (Ralph W. Martin, *James* [Nashville: Thomas Nelson, 1988], 47). It is the hope that the following discussion will show how these different themes give a coherent picture of the Christian life.

EXPOSITION

I. QUICK LISTENING, SLOW SPEECH (JAMES 1:19-21)

Today's section begins with an exhortation that is common to wisdom literature in setting up a contrast between being "quick to listen" and "slow to speak" (James 1:19, NRSV). This quickness to listen and slowness to speak is also connected to being "slow to anger" (ibid.). Quickness in listening entails attention to others who are speaking, but there is also a connection to "the implanted word that has the power to save [our] souls" (v. 21, NRSV). This ability to listen would also imply that one possesses the humility that is necessary for accepting this "implanted word." The ability to listen attentively to others and the Word of God is necessary for the Christian life. It allows words to have a transformative effect, forming disciples of Jesus Christ to understand what is desired of them by God and by others in the community of faith. It allows believers to see more clearly how they should act.

"'Hearing and doing' God's will, with the corollary that believers should not be quick to follow their own desires and designs, is a common theme in the Wisdom literature" (Martin, 47). James argues that those who do not listen but speak and become angry quickly are those who are following their misdirected desires. These desires are those that will lead them to destruction. The quickness to speech and anger leads the disciple away from the source of life: God's righteousness. It is not that the righteousness of God is dependent upon the faithfulness of believers—God is always righteous—it is that those who follow their desires are led away from that which produces the righteousness of God within them. In this way, they deprive themselves of the source of all life.

James follows the lead of those who wrote the wisdom literature of the Old Testament in telling his readers to be slow to speak. Hasty speech is the downfall of those who do not take time to listen and learn. The books of Proverbs and Ecclesiastes discuss the foolishness of hasty speech (see Prov. 10:8, 19; 13:3; 15:1; 29:20; Eccl. 7:9; 9:17—10:1; 10:12-14). "These texts…instill a prudential ethic that only a fool will be unguarded in his speech and he will learn to rue the day of intemperate statements. Far better, the wisdom teachers say, to be considerate and to listen first before making rash statements" (Martin, 47). Being quick in listening and slow in speech develops the character that is necessary for the disciple of Christ.

However, it is not simply that the foolish person brings ruin on him or herself through hasty speech, but the hasty speaker may bring about the ruin of the larger faith community through a lack of consideration. "The quiet words of the wise are more to be heeded than the shouting of a ruler among fools. Wisdom is better than weapons of war, but one bungler destroys much good. Dead flies make the perfumer's ointment give off a foul odor; so a little folly outweighs wisdom and honor" (Eccl. 9:17—10:1, NRSV). The hasty speech of one person in the community could undo much of the wise work that has been accomplished to bring the church together. James' concern about speech is then not only about the individual, but also about the effect that an individual's speech has on the entire community. This discussion will be further expanded by James in 3:1-12.

II. DOERS, NOT MERE HEARERS (JAMES 1:22-25)

Grace is God's gift that makes a claim upon His followers. Grace requires something of us, demands a faith that works. "Theoretical correctness counts for little if one's life does not conform to the truth one espouses. The notion that some sort of profession/confession of belief or conviction could be significant if it were not demonstrated by a consistent pattern of behavior is not, in James' world, to be taken seriously" (Luke Timothy Johnson, *The Letter of James* [New York: Doubleday, 1995], 213). Confession without action is mere deception. It is necessary for the faith of the Christian disciple to lead to action that embodies the content of that confession. Confession of a faith that does not require any action would be inconsistent with God the Son who enters the world as a human and gives His life for the life of the world.

James works to further explain the problem of faith without change through the image of a man looking into a mirror. James' image of the one who looks into a mirror and forgets signifies the person who is not transformed by the confession of faith. Those who hear the Word without allowing it to take hold deny the true transformative power of the Word. They hear and they confess that they believe it, but their lives show no indication that this word has had any effect. The transformation wrought by the Word requires endurance. Thus, those who look into the Law not only look, but also persevere. It is thus not mere hearing or mere looking, but the perseverance and endurance in action that also demonstrates faith.

III. Pure Religion (James 1:26-27)

James revisits the importance of the control of speech in the Christian faith as he will again later in the letter. Faithful speech must be accompanied by faithful action or it becomes false speech. Thus, those who claim the Christian religion can do so truthfully only if they live lives that embody that religion. James is concerned with speech because speech must be consonant with the person's true nature. If the disciple of Christ cannot engage in truthful speech, this person will cause many to distrust the speech of the faithful and diminish the witness to Christ. The actions and speech of the believer are the way that those in the world see the God of the believer. Thus, if one acts in ways that run counter to the concerns of God, this person could cause others to doubt that this is a God who is good. This means, then, that the speech and action of the believer needs to be consistent with the concerns of the God in whom he or she has faith. The proclamation of religious faith must be accompanied by religious action. For James, pure religion consists of caring for those who are on the edges of society: the orphans and the widows.

This discussion of care for orphans and widows introduces an important theme that runs throughout the letter of James. James is concerned with the contrasting treatment those of differing economic statuses receive. He will later address the preference that is shown to wealthy over the poor in the assembly. This concern places him firmly within the teachings of the Torah and the concern God has for the marginalized. This concern is clearly demonstrated in the life of Jesus as He shows care for those who are on the margins. He teaches often that those who are typically excluded are the ones who will enter His Kingdom first. This indicates a reversal of the way the world typically works. James locates true religion in the means that religion is lived. "The person who 'thinks/considers' himself religious without the corresponding behavior has a religion that is 'foolish/vain' and perhaps even … idolatrous" (Johnson, Letter, 214). If one who professes the faith fails to live out the faith, that person's religion is false.

The Lesson Applied

As the epistle of James moves forward, each of the themes addressed in this section will be expanded upon. This section thus provides a framework for reading the rest of the epistle. James, here, is concerned with the practical implications of the declaration of faith in Jesus Christ. For James, the only faith that matters is one that is embodied in the life to which Jesus calls His disciples. Thus, James calls his audience to action. He calls them to listen quickly instead of speaking quickly, to not become angry quickly, to do what the Word of God requires of them, to control their tongues, to care for orphans and widows, and to not let the world defile them. All of these practices are not ends in themselves but means that draw believers more fully into God's righteousness. James' explanation of this demonstrates that those who work to faithfully embody this life will not be left alone in these pursuits. God's righteousness and implanted Word will form the character of disciples in ways that help them pursue faithful lives.

It is also important that the communal nature of these practices is recognized. The person in the community does not simply pursue these practices for the sake of oneself, but also for the health of the entire community. Being quick to listen and slow to speak allows the Church to grow in faithfulness. It prevents the unnecessary discord that can result from hasty speech. This, therefore, allows the Word of God to take a firm hold of the life of the community, resulting in works that honor God. This can then be the Church that faithfully embodies the Gospel she proclaims to the world.

LET'S TALK ABOUT IT

1. How should we read James and Paul?

Since the time of Luther, many Christians have interpreted the writings of Paul and James in contrast—even in conflict—with one another. This line of interpretation has set Paul's message of "grace" at odds with James' message of "works," leading to a devaluing of the letter of James. This has diminished our ability to see the moral force and the beauty of the exhortation of James. Rather than reading Paul and James in this way, we need to see how their emphases varied as they responded to differing situations in the Church. While Paul argues strenuously against certain elements (i.e., "works") of Judaism being bound upon Gentile Christians (e.g., circumcision and certain food laws), it is not true to say that he is unconcerned with our works. Likewise, James' emphasis on our deeds is not meant to devalue the centrality of trusting faith. Both Paul and James are concerned with how the gift of God's grace is borne out in the lives of the faithful. Both men are ultimately consistent with one another in their teaching that the grace of God embodied in the life, death, and resurrection of Jesus demands that those who have this faith must live lives that exemplify it.

HOME DAILY DEVOTIONAL READINGS
FEBRUARY 3-9, 2014

MONDAY	TUESDAY	WEDNESDAY	THURSDAY	FRIDAY	SATURDAY	SUNDAY
Judging Rightly and Impartially	Judging on the Lord's Behalf	Giving Justice to the Weak	Showing Partiality Is Not Good	God Shows No Partiality	Put on the Lord Jesus Christ	Faith and Favoritism
Deuteronomy 1:9-18	2 Chronicles 19:1-7	Psalm 82	Proverbs 28:18-22	Acts 10:34-43	Romans 13:8-14	James 2:1-13

TREAT EVERYONE EQUALLY

ADULT TOPIC:	BACKGROUND SCRIPTURE:
PLAYING FAVORITES	JAMES 2:1-13

JAMES 2:1-13

King James Version

MY brethren, have not the faith of our Lord Jesus Christ, the Lord of glory, with respect of persons.

2 For if there come unto your assembly a man with a gold ring, in goodly apparel, and there come in also a poor man in vile raiment;

3 And ye have respect to him that weareth the gay clothing, and say unto him, Sit thou here in a good place; and say to the poor, Stand thou there, or sit here under my footstool:

4 Are ye not then partial in yourselves, and are become judges of evil thoughts?

5 Hearken, my beloved brethren, Hath not God chosen the poor of this world rich in faith, and heirs of the kingdom which he hath promised to them that love him?

6 But ye have despised the poor. Do not rich men oppress you, and draw you before the judgment seats?

7 Do not they blaspheme that worthy name by the which ye are called?

8 If ye fulfil the royal law according to the scripture, Thou shalt love thy neighbour as thyself, ye do well:

9 But if ye have respect to persons, ye commit sin, and are convinced of the law as transgressors.

10 For whosoever shall keep the whole law, and yet offend in one point, he is guilty of all.

11 For he that said, Do not commit adultery, said also, Do not kill. Now if thou commit no adultery, yet if thou kill, thou art become a transgressor of the law.

New Revised Standard Version

MY brothers and sisters, do you with your acts of favoritism really believe in our glorious Lord Jesus Christ?

2 For if a person with gold rings and in fine clothes comes into your assembly, and if a poor person in dirty clothes also comes in,

3 and if you take notice of the one wearing the fine clothes and say, "Have a seat here, please," while to the one who is poor you say, "Stand there," or, "Sit at my feet,"

4 have you not made distinctions among yourselves, and become judges with evil thoughts?

5 Listen, my beloved brothers and sisters. Has not God chosen the poor in the world to be rich in faith and to be heirs of the kingdom that he has promised to those who love him?

6 But you have dishonored the poor. Is it not the rich who oppress you? Is it not they who drag you into court?

7 Is it not they who blaspheme the excellent name that was invoked over you?

8 You do well if you really fulfill the royal law according to the scripture, "You shall love your neighbor as yourself."

9 But if you show partiality, you commit sin and are convicted by the law as transgressors.

10 For whoever keeps the whole law but fails in one point has become accountable for all of it.

11 For the one who said, "You shall not commit adultery," also said, "You shall not murder." Now if you do not commit adultery but if you murder, you have become a transgressor of the law.

MAIN THOUGHT: Hearken, my beloved brethren, Hath not God chosen the poor of this world rich in faith, and heirs of the kingdom which he hath promised to them that love him? (James 2:5, KJV)

JAMES 2:1-13

King James Version

New Revised Standard Version

King James Version | **New Revised Standard Version**

12 So speak ye, and so do, as they that shall be judged by the law of liberty.
13 For he shall have judgment without mercy, that hath shewed no mercy; and mercy rejoiceth against judgment.

12 So speak and so act as those who are to be judged by the law of liberty.
13 For judgment will be without mercy to anyone who has shown no mercy; mercy triumphs over judgment.

LESSON SETTING
Time: ca. A.D. 55
Place: Jerusalem

LESSON OUTLINE
I. **Do Not Show Favoritism**
   (James 2:1-4)
II. **The Gift of the Poor**
   (James 2:5-7)
III. **The Royal Law**
   (James 2:8-13)

UNIFYING PRINCIPLE
People show partiality toward others for a variety of reasons. How can we avoid favoritism? James reminds his followers of the importance of justice practiced through taking care of the poor and loving their neighbors as themselves.

INTRODUCTION
The letter of James has many similarities to the wisdom literature of the Old Testament (including certain psalms, Job, Proverbs, and Ecclesiastes). The primary source that orients both the wisdom literature and the letter of James is the doctrine of creation found in the Pentateuch. There we learn that God's creation is designed to work in a particular way. Drawing on this, the wisdom writings instruct us in how to live in a world that is faithfully ordered toward God's will. However, because of human rebellion, the promised gifts of living according to the life described in the wisdom literature often do not come to fruition. The letter of James shares a kinship with these writings, but James is focused on the question of living faithfully within the Christian community.

Thus, James imparts wisdom that is consonant with the life of Jesus Christ. "Much of the moral exhortation of antiquity dealt with finding and keeping one's place in the world as a means to success and honor. James has none of those concerns, but deals exclusively with moral attitudes and behavior" (Luke Timothy Johnson, "The Letter of James," in *The New Interpreter's Bible,* Vol. 12 [Nashville: Abingdon Press, 1998], 179-180). James is not concerned with the achievement of status. In fact, there is much in James that critiques the desire to achieve an elevated status.

Today's text is one that critiques desire for status. It is closely connected to Leviticus 19:15, 18, as this is interpreted through the life and ministry of Jesus. "[James'] attention is exclusively devoted to an *ekklēsia* gathered by common values and convictions, summarized by faith in Jesus Christ (2:1)" (Johnson, "Letter," 180). Uppermost is his concern for the holiness of the community. Holiness in this context should be understood as something being set apart for the purposes of God. These specific purposes are embodied in the life and ministry of Jesus Christ.

James is thus calling the Church to a way of life that faithfully reflects the life of Jesus Christ.

EXPOSITION

I. DO NOT SHOW FAVORITISM (JAMES 2:1-4)

Today's text opens with a question: "Do you with your acts of favoritism really believe in our glorious Lord Jesus Christ?" (James 2:1, NRSV). This opening question does create some difficulty in translation with the phrase "our glorious Lord Jesus Christ." One possible translation for this phrase is "'our Lord of glory, Jesus Christ'" (Ralph P. Martin, *James* [Nashville: Thomas Nelson, 1988], 60). This translation provides a "parallel, at least in thought but not in precise wording" (Martin, 60) to 1 Cor. 2:8: "None of the rulers of this age understood this; for if they had, they would not have crucified the Lord of glory" (NRSV). It could be inferred from the common usage of the title *Lord of Glory* by James and Paul that this is one way the early Christians are beginning to speak of Jesus.

Another possible translation is "'faith in our glorious Lord Jesus Christ'" (Martin, 60). Martin puts forth a theological interpretation of this translation that shares some kinship with the description of Jesus in Philippians 2. "The point of the ascription 'glorious' will be a paradoxical one: Christian faith centers, for James, in the person of a glorious figure who nonetheless abased himself to identify with the poor and cast in his lot with the despised and oppressed to whom the kingdom is promised" (Martin, 60). If this is the most appropriate translation of this passage,

the contrast would be striking. Jesus, who shares in the glory of God gives up that glory, impoverishing Himself by becoming human. In His ministry, He often goes to the outsider, the marginalized, the oppressed. However, those who are now claiming to be His followers are appealing to the wealthy while despising the poor. Jesus relinquishes the status to come into this world and save people from their poverty (not simply material, but spiritual poverty as well), but His disciples are showing favor to the wealthy while despising the poor. This is in contradiction to the ministry of Jesus Christ.

This text serves to expand upon James 1:9-11: "Let the believer who is lowly boast in being raised up, and the rich in being brought low, because the rich will disappear like a flower in the field. For the sun rises with its scorching heat and withers the field; its flower falls, and its beauty perishes. It is the same way with the rich; in the midst of a busy life, they will wither away" (NRSV). Through exposing their hypocrisy in showing preference to the wealthy to the exception of the poor, James is also demonstrating that this community is choosing something non-eternal.

James is concerned with turning this community back to faithful practices. So he asks a question that connects the nature of their belief with their ethical practices. "James seeks to hold the community to its professed ideals. Do the readers claim as their own the 'faith of Jesus' that announced to the poor an elect place in the kingdom? Then they cannot adopt the standards of the world that scorns the poor and treats them with contempt. Do the readers claim as their own the 'law of love' associated with Jesus' preaching of the kingdom? Then they must live out that love consistently and not practice the sort of discrimination against the poor that the very law quoted by Jesus itself condemns" (Luke Timothy Johnson, *The Letter of James* [New York: Doubleday, 1995], 219).

There is also a question of the setting in which this discrimination is taking place. The setting could be one of a worship assembly or some type of ecclesial legal proceeding. If it is a worship assembly, this behavior denies the equality that all possess before God. The practice of partiality would demonstrate a striking disobedience to the teachings of Jesus especially if it takes place in the gathering that is set aside for the purpose of worshiping Him.

If, however, it is a legal proceeding, the poor in this instance may be seeking justice but are instead placed at a disadvantage and shamed by those attending and overseeing the proceeding. "The usage in Lev 19:15 makes it clear that the original context of the language was that of judging cases in the community: unjust judgment was that based on appearances rather than on the merits of the case" (Johnson, *Letter*, 221). These acts of favoritism counter the claim made upon the community by Leviticus 19: "You shall not render an unjust judgment; you shall not be partial to the poor or defer to the great: with justice you shall judge your neighbor.... You shall not take vengeance or bear a grudge against any of your people, but you shall love your neighbor as yourself: I am the LORD" (vv. 15, 18, NRSV).

With the legal proceeding being the most likely setting James has in mind, James is demonstrating that in the one place where the poor should receive a fair hearing they are being discriminated against before they can even say a word. This is a community that has become enamored with status. In this infatuation, they have denied their calling as disciples of Jesus Christ and become no different from the rest of the world in how it approaches those who have wealth and those who do not. They have become judges who inflict evil when they should be showing mercy.

II. THE GIFT OF THE POOR (JAMES 2:5-7)

James is likely drawing from the same teachings that have been passed on as the Sermon on the Mount (see Matt. 5:3; Luke 6:20). The connection between the poor and their inheritance of the Kingdom of God demonstrates that James was drawing upon a teaching that was significant in the life of the early Church. Indeed, this is a teaching that is essential to understanding the ongoing, faithful life of the Church. James is concerned that those who have material poverty are being discriminated against. However, for James this promise to the poor is not simply because of their poverty. "There is a promise for the poor, but inasmuch as their poverty is accompanied by faith and the love of God, and as they are chosen in order that it should be so" (Sophie Laws, *A Commentary on the Epistle of James* [Peabody, MA: Hendrickson Publishers, 1987], 103).

This neglect of God's chosen ones is even more grievous in that the preference the people are showing is for those who actively persecute them. The wealthy to whom they are showing deference are the ones who are causing strife in the community by dragging the impoverished into the courts. This is where the courtroom setting becomes even more relevant. The poor are dragged into the courts by the rich and the people who are overseeing the courts have also been dragged into the courts by the rich, but they are now showing a preference for the wealthy. They may be doing this to escape further persecution from the wealthy, but in their actions they deny justice to the poor. This further exacerbates a situation that is already marked by much suffering for the impoverished.

This goes even further because it blasphemes the name that identifies them. Blasphemy of Jesus' name is essentially the act of slandering Jesus. In bearing the Name of Christ, James' audience is called to faithfully reflect the image of Christ to the world. However, in their acts of favoritism, they misrepresent Christ through judgment according to the standards of the world. They have essentially denied their belief in Christ while clinging to His name. They have also denied sharing the gift of Christ that has been given to them with others.

III. THE ROYAL LAW
(JAMES 2:8-13)

We now come to the essential thrust of James' argument. James identifies the royal command as the one Jesus identifies as the second command (see Mark 12:28-34). For James as with Jesus, the command to "love your neighbor" is intimately connected to the command to love God. This fits with the theme of James' writing thus far. James is concerned that their professed love for God is not being embodied in their actions, so James shows that there is a clear connection between their active love for others and their confession of Jesus as Lord.

Therefore, James moves to the negative side of this teaching: failure to embody one part of the teaching of the Law means that one is guilty of the entire Law. Thus those who would appeal to their keeping of the other Commandments have no ground on which to stand because they have failed to uphold the teaching that defines the essential nature of the Law. The Law is bound together as one because there is One who gave the entirety of the Law. Thus failing to uphold any aspect of the Law is a failure to honor the One who gave the Law. "[James] is not speaking theoretically but practically. The person who claims to live by the law of love, yet practices the sort of discrimination that the law of love itself forbids has broken the law of love entirely" (Johnson, "Letter," 193).

The members of this community should thus act in ways that embody the teaching of the Royal Law. They are called to love their neighbors in ways that do not show discrimination. They have been given a gift through the grace of Jesus Christ that must be passed on to those they come in contact with. If they fail to uphold this law, they will be judged by it. So they are called to demonstrate mercy instead of partiality. They are to deal justly with those seeking justice. They should not let their assemblies become marked by division and strife. They should not allow their worship to become a practice that is abhorrent to God. They should instead heed the words of the prophet Amos, "Let justice roll down like waters, and righteousness like an ever-flowing stream" (5:24, NRSV). The worship of the Church should be accompanied by lives that embody mercy.

THE LESSON APPLIED

The attitudes of those we have encountered in today's text are attitudes that persist today. In the Church, we too often defer to the wealthy to the exclusion of the poor. The poor are thus denied any place in the Church. "When the poor cannot find a place in a Christian church, that church no longer has any connection to Jesus" (Johnson, "Letter," 195). This denial of a place for the poor is connected with our lust for a place of standing and power for the Church. This can be seen in congregations that make decisions based on who has wealth and power. In an effort to not offend the wealthy and powerful, those in the Church will often speak and make decisions in ways that soothe the egos of the powerful. This hampers the Church's ability to speak clearly and prophetically concerning the nature of wealth (which often comes through the oppression of others). In this, the Church denies her call to embody God's gift of grace and mercy to this world. Indeed, in so doing, the Church becomes a place where God's mercy can no longer be seen.

LET'S TALK ABOUT IT

1. Do the poor inherit the Kingdom of God simply because of their poverty?

This is a difficult question because Scripture often shows a clear preference for the poor. However, it is worth noting the particular text that forms the basis for today's text: "You shall not render an unjust judgment; you shall not be partial to the poor or defer to the great: with justice you shall judge your neighbor" (Lev. 19:15, NRSV). James is calling the people to show no partiality in either direction. However, partiality works in the favor of the wealthy more often than not. And this is the particular situation that James is facing. What, then, does he mean when he says that the poor have been chosen to be heirs of the Kingdom of God? Those who are poor often demonstrate a greater faith in God because they see clearly that they can only depend on God. Thus, through their faith, they demonstrate clearly what it means to be faithful to God. They are thus afforded an important place in the community of faith because they help others draw closer to God. In denying the poor a place in the Church, we deny ourselves an important way to draw closer in communion with God and one another.

HOME DAILY DEVOTIONAL READINGS
FEBRUARY 10-16, 2014

MONDAY	TUESDAY	WEDNESDAY	THURSDAY	FRIDAY	SATURDAY	SUNDAY
The Work of Faith with Power	Faith Distracted by Loving Money	Completing What's Lacking in Faith	An Example of Great Faith	A Faith That Saves	Living Your Life in Christ	Faith Demonstrated Through Works
2 Thessalonians 1:3-12	1 Timothy 6:6-12	1 Thessalonians 3:4-13	Luke 7:1-10	Luke 7:36-50	Colossians 2:1-7	James 2:14-26

SHOW YOUR FAITH BY YOUR WORKS

ADULT TOPIC:	BACKGROUND SCRIPTURE:
LIVE WHAT YOU BELIEVE	JAMES 2:14-26

JAMES 2:14-26

King James Version

WHAT doth it profit, my brethren, though a man say he hath faith, and have not works? can faith save him?

15 If a brother or sister be naked, and destitute of daily food,

16 And one of you say unto them, Depart in peace, be ye warmed and filled; notwithstanding ye give them not those things which are needful to the body; what doth it profit?

17 Even so faith, if it hath not works, is dead, being alone.

18 Yea, a man may say, Thou hast faith, and I have works: shew me thy faith without thy works, and I will shew thee my faith by my works.

19 Thou believest that there is one God; thou doest well: the devils also believe, and tremble.

20 But wilt thou know, O vain man, that faith without works is dead?

21 Was not Abraham our father justified by works, when he had offered Isaac his son upon the altar?

22 Seest thou how faith wrought with his works, and by works was faith made perfect?

23 And the scripture was fulfilled which saith, Abraham believed God, and it was imputed unto him for righteousness: and he was called the Friend of God.

24 Ye see then how that by works a man is justified, and not by faith only.

25 Likewise also was not Rahab the harlot justified by works, when she had received the

New Revised Standard Version

WHAT good is it, my brothers and sisters, if you say you have faith but do not have works? Can faith save you?

15 If a brother or sister is naked and lacks daily food,

16 and one of you says to them, "Go in peace; keep warm and eat your fill," and yet you do not supply their bodily needs, what is the good of that?

17 So faith by itself, if it has no works, is dead.

18 But someone will say, "You have faith and I have works." Show me your faith apart from your works, and I by my works will show you my faith.

19 You believe that God is one; you do well. Even the demons believe—and shudder.

20 Do you want to be shown, you senseless person, that faith apart from works is barren?

21 Was not our ancestor Abraham justified by works when he offered his son Isaac on the altar?

22 You see that faith was active along with his works, and faith was brought to completion by the works.

23 Thus the scripture was fulfilled that says, "Abraham believed God, and it was reckoned to him as righteousness," and he was called the friend of God.

24 You see that a person is justified by works and not by faith alone.

25 Likewise, was not Rahab the prostitute also justified by works when she welcomed

MAIN THOUGHT: For as the body without the spirit is dead, so faith without works is dead also. (James 2:26, KJV)

JAMES 2:14-26

King James Version	New Revised Standard Version
messengers, and had sent them out another way?	the messengers and sent them out by another road?
26 For as the body without the spirit is dead, so faith without works is dead also.	26 For just as the body without the spirit is dead, so faith without works is also dead.

LESSON SETTING
    Time: ca. A.D. 55
    Place: Jerusalem

LESSON OUTLINE
  I. **Faith and Works Must Be Congruent**
    (James 2:14-19)
  II. **Two Examples of Faith in Action**
    (James 2:20-26)

UNIFYING PRINCIPLE

People often make great declarations of faith but show no evidence of them in their actions. What gives evidence of faith? James states that faith, which by itself is dead, becomes active when carried out through works of justice.

INTRODUCTION

Today's lesson is a natural progression from last week's exhortation from James about fulfilling the Royal Law. James commanded his readers in James 2:1-13 to avoid partiality and to show equal love to everyone, thus fulfilling the second greatest commandment quoted by Jesus: "Thou shalt love thy neighbour as thyself" (Matt. 22:39, KJV). In showing love to others, followers of Jesus will show that they are truly His followers: "'By this everyone will know that you are my disciples, if you have love for one another'" (John 13:35, NRSV). In like manner, in James 2:14-26, the author argues that faith must be supported by works. Acts of love and hospitality for the less fortunate exhibit

the love of Christ. If one does not show any love to others, then what good is this person's faith? Luke Timothy Johnson argues that James 2:14-26 is essentially the Apostle's building upon his earlier assertion that Christians cannot only be "hearers" of the Word; rather, they must be "doers of the word" (James 1:22, NRSV) and, in doing so, prove their faith in action ("The Letter of James" in *The New Interpreter's Bible*, Vol. 12 [Nashville: Abingdon Press, 1998], 196).

While James 2:14-26 may not seem too complicated to most contemporary Christians, such has not always been the case in Church history. This passage in James was a catalyst of great debate, especially among contemporaries of Martin Luther and John Calvin. Paul's writing is often compared to the book of James because similar vocabulary as well as the use of Abraham as an example is found in Galatians 5 and Romans 4. Because of his earlier Catholic background, Luther vehemently detested the book of James and claimed that James "drives us back to the law" (qtd. in Johnson, 197), believing that James 2 emphasized works instead of faith for obtaining salvation. Conversely, Calvin "read James and Paul as applying the same convictions to different circumstances" (ibid., 197).

As a result of the great controversy surrounding James' epistle, the book became greatly marginalized and often viewed as lesser in the biblical canon. Much of James was virtually ignored—even the areas where Paul and James plainly agree. Today, though, most contemporary Christians are able to recognize that James is not contradicting Paul at all. Johnson explains, "Paul and James use the figure of Abraham to make their respective arguments concerning the good news to the Gentiles and the necessity of acting out faith, with language that converges enticingly at the semantic level yet diverges just as decisively at the conceptual level" (ibid.). Today's lesson will hopefully illustrate this truth.

EXPOSITION

I. FAITH AND WORKS MUST BE CONGRUENT (JAMES 2:14-19)

James begins this section with a series of questions: "What good is it, my brothers and sisters, if you say you have faith but do not have works? Can faith save you?" (James 2:14, NRSV). He continues in verse fifteen by giving the example of someone who claims to be a Christian yet fails to offer food and nourishment to a brother or sister in need and only offers the unfortunate soul best wishes in the process. What kind of faith is this? James declares that such "faith by itself, if it has no works, is dead" (v. 17, NRSV). It has no purpose or vitality.

Luther read this passage in James and only saw the argument that works were required for salvation. This is not what James is saying, though. He is rather saying that one's faith is supported by acts of love and hospitality. Johnson explains, "James' topic is not really soteriology;

he has already declared that it is the 'implanted word' from God that 'is able to save your souls' (1:21). The issue is, rather, how to be a 'doer' of the word" (197). James is not concerned about Christians' being able to fulfill the Law through works to gain righteousness; instead, he is concerned about Christians' faith being evident through their righteous works. When a Christian sees a brother or sister in need, the natural reaction should be to feed or clothe such an individual. Such an act of love fulfills the royal law mentioned earlier.

Recall also the similar language of Jesus in John 15: "'I am the vine, you are the branches. Those who abide in me and I in them bear much fruit, because apart from me you can do nothing. Whoever does not abide in me is thrown away like a branch and withers; such branches are gathered, thrown into the fire, and burned'" (John 15:5-6, NRSV). Jesus plainly states that those who profess to be followers of Him yet bear no fruit are useless to Him. They are like branches cast to the side and forgotten.

Johnson asserts that Christian thinkers such as Origen and Calvin correctly understood James' argument for the congruency of faith and works as expressed in Paul's writings in Galatians 5:6: "For in Christ Jesus neither circumcision nor uncircumcision counts for anything; the only thing that counts is faith working through love" (NRSV). In his letter to the Galatians, Paul is writing specifically to repudiate the teachings of the Judaizers who were teaching that Gentile converts to Christianity must adhere to all the teachings of the Law—including circumcision—to fully obtain salvation. Paul denounces this erroneous understanding by arguing that circumcision in and of itself accomplishes nothing. Righteousness is not gained by adhering to the works of the Law. The righteousness of Christ is imputed to believers through faith, and their faith is then exhibited through works of love shown to others.

Furthermore, a Christian who lacks such love for others is a prime example of one who practices the type of religion that James despises. In James 1:26, the Apostle asserts that those who cannot control their tongues possess a "worthless" religion (NRSV). Instead, those who possess "pure and undefiled" religion are the ones who seek "to care for orphans and widows in their distress, and to keep [themselves] unstained by the world" (v. 27, NRSV). The Christian who cannot take the time to help others in need simply has a dead faith that lacks any worth or vitality.

James then uses a rhetorical device to emphasize his point in 2:18. He imagines someone opposing his argument that faith and works are necessarily compatible by saying, "'You have faith and I have works'" (NRSV). The Apostle then immediately retorts to this foolish proposition, "Show me your faith apart from your works, and I by my works will show you my faith. You believe that God is one; you do well. Even the demons believe—and shudder" (vv. 18-19, NRSV). According to Johnson, for James, faith without any works to offer support is just "intellectual assent" (198). Believing in God is not equivalent to living a life for God. James' tone turns sarcastic as he asserts, "You believe in God? Good for you! So do

the demons. What's your point?" Such an inadequate amount of faith becomes reproachable, especially when one realizes that the opposing forces of God's Kingdom have the same kind of "faith." Johnson summarizes this pitiful level of faith quite well: "This is a parody of faith rather than the response of those who love God" (198). Such use of a rhetorical device by James helps to drive his point home even harder.

II. TWO EXAMPLES OF FAITH IN ACTION (JAMES 2:20-26)

James continues to address this imaginary antagonist. He proclaims: "Do you want to be shown, you senseless person, that faith apart from works is barren?" (v. 20, NRSV). James doesn't hold back in declaring someone who holds to this view as being devoid of sense and wisdom. He also uses this device to set up two exemplars of individuals from the Old Testament who demonstrated genuine faith through their actions. Furthermore, these two individuals were heavily celebrated in Jewish tradition for their hospitality, a point that James surely had in the back of his mind after his discussion of Christians' needing to show loving hospitality to those in need (Johnson, 198).

James begins by asking, "Was not our ancestor Abraham justified by works when he offered his son Isaac on the altar?" (v. 21, NRSV). This story is a perfect example for James to use because Abraham's obedience to God in this instance was predicated by faith. In Genesis 22, the story is recorded of God's testing of Abraham to offer his only son as a sacrifice. Without a word of dissent, Abraham obeyed while knowing the heartwrenching task that awaited him appeared to be the undoing of God's covenant made to him in Genesis 15. If Isaac died, then whence would the great nation promised to Abraham spring? Yet Abraham trusted God and believed that God would still remain faithful to His promise. Abraham demonstrated his great faith by acting in accordance with what God commanded him to do.

James then explains how Abraham's work (his obedience in being willing to sacrifice his son) and faith were congruent: "You see that faith was active along with his works, and faith was brought to completion by the works" (v. 22, NRSV). Abraham's faith was perfected in his obedience. Johnson explains, "In other words, faith is the subject from beginning to end. Deeds do not replace faith; they complete it" (198). As a result of Abraham's faith being made complete, James says, "Thus the scripture was fulfilled that says, 'Abraham believed God, and, it was reckoned to him as righteousness,' and he was called the friend of God. You see that a person is justified by works and not by faith alone" (vv. 23-24, NRSV).

James, like Paul in Galatians 3:6, has quoted from Genesis 15:6 to explain how Abraham's faith justified him before God. Yet James' emphasis is slightly different than Paul's. Whereas Paul emphasized that Abraham's faith in God in general was what justified him, James emphasizes that this giant act of obedience demonstrated Abraham's righteous faith fully. Regarding the book of James, Johnson writes, "Thus the translation of 2:21 might better be that Abraham was 'shown to be righteous'" (198). While believing in

God is what attained righteousness for Abraham, his act of obedience proclaimed this faith publically.

Furthermore, along with being declared righteous before God, Abraham was deemed as being a "friend of God" (v. 23, NRSV). The phrase "friend of God" is not found in Genesis. Instead, the phrase appears to be a combination of 2 Chronicles 20:7, where Jehoshaphat asks, "'Did you not, O our God, drive out the inhabitants of this land before your people Israel, and give it forever to the descendants of your friend Abraham?'" (NRSV), and Isaiah 41:8 where God assures Israel of forthcoming aid: "But you, Israel, my servant, Jacob, whom I have chosen, the offspring of Abraham, my friend" (NRSV; Johnson, 198). The Greeks' understanding of friendship involved a "close sharing of all material and spiritual things" (ibid.), signifying to James' readers the close relationship that existed between Abraham and God.

Also, James' invoking of friendship with God in this passage will serve as a nice juxtaposition to one who considers himself a friend of the world in James 4:4 (ibid.). Johnson writes, "Abraham's willingness to give back to God what God had gifted him with demonstrates and perfects his faith and shows what 'friendship with God' means" (199). Such an intimate closeness with God makes being entangled in the pursuits of the world impossible for a believer.

James concludes this section by harkening to another Old Testament hero of great faith: Rahab. As stated earlier, both Rahab and Abraham were honored in Jewish tradition for their great hospitality.

Rahab's showing hospitality to the two spies who were sent to scope out Jericho in Joshua 2:2-21 was a great demonstration of faith for James: "Likewise, was not Rahab the prostitute also justified by works when she welcomed the messengers and sent them out by another road?" (v. 25, NRSV). Rahab risked her life in protecting the spies from the pursuers who approached her door and did so because she had recognized that the Jews' God was the one true God. Because of her great faith, Rahab and her family were spared when the Jews defeated Jericho.

Johnson writes that James' using both Rahab and Abraham as examples parallels those who would serve the brother and sister in need in James 2:14-15. Unlike the wicked judges who speak in James 2:2-4, the uncaring believer who offers useless words in James 2:16, and the foolish words of the man in James 2:18, Rahab and Abraham are silent, and their actions speak much louder than any words could (199).

James then concludes this section with an aphorism that echoes verse seventeen: "For just as the body without the spirit is dead, so faith without works is also dead" (v. 26, NRSV). Just as a man without the breath of life is dead, so is a Christian who claims to have faith but no works to exhibit his or her faith.

THE LESSON APPLIED

Today's lesson is a stark reminder that Christians are not to sit idly by in their walk with God. They must be active participants. Their lives should constantly be producing fruit. People should notice a difference in the lives of Christians. Remember that good works do not merit salvation, but works do show others that salvation has truly transformed someone's life into a new creation. Are people able to see the results of such a transformation in your life? How can you produce better fruit in your life?

LET'S TALK ABOUT IT

1. Why do works not merit salvation?

A common misconception among many unbelievers is that being a good person makes someone worthy enough to go to heaven. The Bible is very clear, though, that salvation only comes through faith in Christ and not of works (see Eph. 2:8-9). Nothing men and women can do is good enough to cancel the debt of sin. God is holy and cannot tolerate sin of any kind in His presence. The only proper atonement that can be attained is through the shed blood of Christ. Asking for forgiveness of sins and placing one's trust in Christ is the only way to restore one's broken relationship with God.

HOME DAILY DEVOTIONAL READINGS
FEBRUARY 17-23, 2014

MONDAY	TUESDAY	WEDNESDAY	THURSDAY	FRIDAY	SATURDAY	SUNDAY
Lying and Flattering Lips	Words That Intimidate	Words That Lead to Repentance	Words That Lead to Mourning	Words That Lead to Worship	Words Guided by Wisdom	Taming the Tongue
Psalm 12	1 Samuel 17:1-11	2 Chronicles 15:1-12	Nehemiah 1	Genesis 24:42-52	Proverbs 18:2-13	James 3:1-12

CONTROL YOUR SPEECH

ADULT TOPIC: UNFORK YOUR TONGUE	BACKGROUND SCRIPTURE: JAMES 3:1-12

JAMES 3:1-12

King James Version

MY brethren, be not many masters, knowing that we shall receive the greater condemnation.

2 For in many things we offend all. If any man offend not in word, the same is a perfect man, and able also to bridle the whole body.

3 Behold, we put bits in the horses' mouths, that they may obey us; and we turn about their whole body.

4 Behold also the ships, which though they be so great, and are driven of fierce winds, yet are they turned about with a very small helm, whithersoever the governor listeth.

5 Even so the tongue is a little member, and boasteth great things. Behold, how great a matter a little fire kindleth!

6 And the tongue is a fire, a world of iniquity: so is the tongue among our members, that it defileth the whole body, and setteth on fire the course of nature; and it is set on fire of hell.

7 For every kind of beasts, and of birds, and of serpents, and of things in the sea, is tamed, and hath been tamed of mankind:

8 But the tongue can no man tame; it is an unruly evil, full of deadly poison.

9 Therewith bless we God, even the Father; and therewith curse we men, which are made after the similitude of God.

10 Out of the same mouth proceedeth blessing and cursing. My brethren, these things ought not so to be.

11 Doth a fountain send forth at the same place sweet water and bitter?

New Revised Standard Version

NOT many of you should become teachers, my brothers and sisters, for you know that we who teach will be judged with greater strictness.

2 For all of us make many mistakes. Anyone who makes no mistakes in speaking is perfect, able to keep the whole body in check with a bridle.

3 If we put bits into the mouths of horses to make them obey us, we guide their whole bodies.

4 Or look at ships: though they are so large that it takes strong winds to drive them, yet they are guided by a very small rudder wherever the will of the pilot directs.

5 So also the tongue is a small member, yet it boasts of great exploits. How great a forest is set ablaze by a small fire!

6 And the tongue is a fire. The tongue is placed among our members as a world of iniquity; it stains the whole body, sets on fire the cycle of nature, and is itself set on fire by hell.

7 For every species of beast and bird, of reptile and sea creature, can be tamed and has been tamed by the human species,

8 but no one can tame the tongue—a restless evil, full of deadly poison.

9 With it we bless the Lord and Father, and with it we curse those who are made in the likeness of God.

10 From the same mouth come blessing and cursing. My brothers and sisters, this ought not to be so.

11 Does a spring pour forth from the same opening both fresh and brackish water?

MAIN THOUGHT: Out of the same mouth proceedeth blessing and cursing. My brethren, these things ought not so to be. (James 3:10, KJV)

JAMES 3:1-12

King James Version

12 Can the fig tree, my brethren, bear olive berries? either a vine, figs? so can no fountain both yield salt water and fresh.

New Revised Standard Version

12 Can a fig tree, my brothers and sisters, yield olives, or a grapevine figs? No more can salt water yield fresh.

LESSON SETTING
　　Time: ca. A.D. 55
　　Place: Jerusalem

LESSON OUTLINE
　I. **Speech and Action**
　　(James 3:1-5)
　II. **A Divided Tongue**
　　(James 3:6-12)

UNIFYING PRINCIPLE

Often people speak without thinking about the impact their words will have on others. How can Christians be sure that their words will benefit those who hear them? James speaks of justice within the context of controlling a person's tongue because both blessings and curses can come from the same mouth.

INTRODUCTION

In James, the convergence of speech and action is important. Speech and action are to be oriented toward the same end. Speech can shape action. Thus, divided speech brings an end to faithful action even before one can begin. This is the problem James is countering throughout his letter. He is concerned, first, that the profession of faith (speech) is not leading to faithful action. However, he is also concerned that even the speech of his audience is incoherent. They speak contradictory words with the same tongue. Thus, a tongue that is created to bless is set on fire by hell and curses those created in God's image.

This should lead us to some questions about the nature of speech. What does the nature of our speech reveal about us? Is speech merely an arbitrary practice that reveals nothing about the inner nature of the person? Speech and language are intimately linked with identity. Speech contains within it layers of meaning that have developed over the course of a history of a people. Thus, speech can both reveal and reshape attitudes without a people consciously reflecting on the effect speech has.

In today's text, we will see how James describes the effect of the tongue on our actions. James uses the tongue as a metaphor in a way that is similar to how other biblical writers use the heart as a metaphor. For these writers, the heart is the seat of intention. The biblical writers use the imagery of the heart as a metaphor for what defines our true, inner nature. In the same way, the tongue for James is more than just a member of the body. The tongue is equated with speech, but it also extends beyond this understanding. The tongue is intimately connected to the heart as the tongue reveals the nature of the heart. Thus, the tongue connects intention, speech, and action.

It is worth noting that James does not give a firm answer to how to control the tongue in this section. He will address this question at the end of the letter. "In

5:12-20, James will develop the proper modes of speech within the community of faith" (Luke Timothy Johnson, *The Letter of James* [New York: Doubleday, 1995], 255). The discussion of speech that is truthful and undivided is important for James as he seeks to define what this community is called to be.

EXPOSITION

I. SPEECH AND ACTION (JAMES 3:1-5)

James opens his extended discussion of speech with a warning to those who want to become teachers. While an initial reading may not see a connection between this verse and the following discussion, "the first verse should not ... be treated as a separate saying, but seen as introducing the general topic by reference to a particular instance. Teachers being men of words *par excellence* are particularly exposed to the danger of sins of speech" (Sophie Laws, *A Commentary on the Epistle of James* [Peabody: Hendrickson Publishers, 1980], 140). Part of the problem that James may be addressing here is that many in the community desire to become teachers because of the status it will give them in the church (Laws, 141). James, however, responds to this desire for status by showing that teachers will be held to a higher standard. It may be that some were rising to the position of a teacher and being careless with the words they were using. Thus, they did harm to the community through careless teaching simply because they desired a place of standing in the community.

In James 2, James already discussed the problem of discrimination based on wealth and social standing. The warning against teaching seems to continue to address the desire for standing while moving into the discussion of speech. False and flattering speech reveals that this is a community that does not faithfully control its actions. Thus, James 3 is a pivotal point in the letter as James explicitly connects speech to control of the body, i.e., the ability to control the tongue means that one can control the entire body. James describes this as working from multiple aspects.

First, if the teacher can control his or her tongue in teaching, he or she can impart teaching that conveys the truth of the Christian faith. "The teacher would ... be responsible for passing on the various traditions accurately and thoroughly, for their legitimate re-interpretation and application, and hence to a large degree for the guidance of the community in many aspects of its life (intellectual, spiritual and liturgical as well as moral). It is important that aspirants to that position should be fit for it, though James supplies no criteria for assessing this" (Laws, 143-144). Teaching, though, is not limited simply to speech. Teaching also comes about through the actions of the teacher. Thus truthful teaching does not simply mean that the teacher says the correct words to explain the Christian faith. Truthful teaching also comes through the words spoken by the teacher being consonant with the teacher's life. The teacher must both speak and act in ways that are faithful to the teachings that have been passed on to him or her.

"Error in speech may be particularly crucial for the teacher, but it is not a problem for him alone. In view of the destructive power James attributes to the tongue it is surprising that he should use here only the verb *ptaiō,* to trip or make a mistake. If the choice is deliberate, it may be in order to associate with the danger apparently trivial failures as well as blatant offences" (Laws, 144). For James, character is formed in the insignificant, mundane activities. This is characteristic of the larger wisdom tradition as well. Thus, seemingly small mistakes in speech can lead to greater sin down the road. This is particularly important for the teacher who is charged with passing on the teachings that have been passed on to him or her. The teacher who fails to faithfully pass on the teachings that have been given to him or her will speak in ways that are harmful to the church. Habits of speech are, therefore, particularly important as the teacher gives faithful direction to the community.

James 3:2 indicates that one who can control the tongue will be able to control all other aspects of life. This is made explicit by comparing the ability to control speech to a bridle being placed in a horse's mouth. The driver can control the direction of the horse through the placement and movement of the bridle. This image is built upon by demonstrating that a small part of a large ship, the rudder, gives the ship direction. Both of these comparisons lead James to a discussion of the power of a small member of the body, the tongue, in directing the body. The ability to master the tongue is indeed mastery over the entire body because the tongue is exceptionally difficult to control.

James 3:1 and 3:5 seem to bracket this section well. James instructs his readers that not many should become teachers because of the easy possibility of making mistakes in speech. He closes by noting that although the tongue is small, "it boasts of great exploits" (James 3:5, NRSV). Although there is a positive assessment of the tongue's ability to direct the rest of the body, it is clear from the beginning of this argument that the tongue is not a member that is easily controlled.

This brings us to the second aspect of speaking truthfully. The inability to control the tongue is connected to its tendency to boast "of great exploits" (ibid.). Though the tongue is a small member of the body, the tongue is the part of the body that can speak to what the body can do. The tongue, however, often overestimates its own abilities and the abilities of the body. This could come through the tongue's claiming things that it believes the body should be able to do without understanding the limitations of a particular body. However, the tongue likely speaks in a way that comes from the pride and arrogance of the speaker. The tongue claims things the speaker knows not to be true in order to make the speaker look good in the sight of others. The tongue is thus giving a false representation of the speaker. Speaking truthfully demands that the tongue give a true representation of the speaker. This is accomplished through the confession of our faith in Christ and of our failings in representing Christ faithfully to the world.

II. A DIVIDED TONGUE (JAMES 3:6-12)

Although the ability to control the tongue indicates an ability to control the body, James does not paint a hopeful picture of the ability to control the tongue. "How great a forest is set ablaze by a small fire! And the tongue is a fire. The tongue is placed among our members as a world of iniquity; it stains the whole body, sets on fire the cycle of nature, and is itself set on fire by hell…. No one can tame the tongue—a restless evil, full of deadly poison" (James 3:5-6, 8, NRSV). James' description of the tongue in this section may lead the reader to believe that control of the tongue is hopeless. The even greater concern is that it seems James gives no means of counteracting this uncontrollable member. This brings us to another aspect of truthful speech.

This aspect is embodied in the ability to speak blessings without also speaking curses. James is concerned throughout his letter with the divided minds of his audience. This divided mind most clearly reveals itself in divided speech. And this divided speech comes about through the tongue's speaking blessing in the worship of God and then cursing those made in the image of God. The words spoken about those made in God's image may reveal something about the true nature of the speaker's attitude toward God. It may be that this divided speech reshapes and reveals the attitude of the speaker. As the speaker continues to speak curses of those made in God's image, the speaker not only begins to see other people as worthless, he or she may also begin to see God as worthless as well.

There is something of a liturgical point to this passage as well. If the mouth is blessing God in worship, then the mouth that has been defiled by cursing those made in God's image needs some manner of purification. This mouth should refrain from cursing those made in God's image because, in so doing, the mouth is cursing God. Thus, cursing those made in God's image leads down a deadly path. This should recall some of the deficient practices of worship of the Israelites that were announced by the prophets. "These people draw near with their mouths and honor me with their lips, while their hearts are far from me" (Isa. 29:13, NRSV).

As we have seen, James' readers have practices that run counter to what they confess in their speech. "The proper and improper uses of speech are of central concern to James. Before this essay, we have seen as negative modes of speech the self-justifying claim that one is tempted by God (1:13), the flattering speech that reveals partiality toward the rich and shames the poor (2:3-6), the careless speech of those who wish well toward the poor but do not help them (2:16), the superficial speech of the one claiming to have faith even without deeds (2:18). After this essay, we shall see these other examples of improper speech: judging and slandering a brother (4:11), boasting of one's future plans without regard for God's will (4:13), grumbling against a brother (5:9)" (Johnson, 254-255). The attitudes and actions of the people in the community have led the people to a type of worship that does not truly honor the God they confess as Lord.

THE LESSON APPLIED

For James, speech is an important aspect of the life of the Church. The ability to speak truthfully allows the Church to faithfully reflect the God it worships. However, it is too often the case that the Church does not speak carefully and truthfully about the nature of the God we serve and the nature of the community that serves God. This inability to speak truthfully leads the Church to ways that are unfaithful to the Church's calling. "The accommodated character of the church is at least partly due to the failure of the clergy to help those they serve know how to speak Christian. To learn to be a Christian, to learn the discipline of the faith, is not just similar to learning another language. It *is* learning another language" (Stanley Hauerwas, *Working with Words* [Eugene: Cascade Books, 2011], 87). This inability to faithfully pass on the language of the faith comes about because the Church has let other forces outside it determine the language it speaks. We have failed to faithfully consider the teachings that have been passed down to us and have, thus, lost the ability to discern what is truly faithful to the nature of the Christian faith. Faithful habits of speech must be learned so that we can faithfully speak God's Word to the world.

LET'S TALK ABOUT IT

1. How do we develop faithful habits of speech?

One of the primary ways we can develop faithful habits of speech is through prayer. Prayer, however, is not something we innately know how to do. It is something that must be learned. "We learn to speak to God because God has spoken and speaks to us. In the language of the Father in heaven God's children learn to speak with God. Repeating God's own words, we begin to pray to God. We ought to speak to God, and God wishes to hear us, not in the false and confused language of our heart but in the clear and pure language that God has spoken to us in Jesus Christ" (Dietrich Bonhoeffer, *Prayerbook of the Bible*, James H. Burtness, trans. [Minneapolis: Fortress Press, 2005], 156). The language that we have received to speak to God is taught to us in the life of Jesus Christ. In Luke 11, one of Jesus' Disciples asks Him to teach them to pray. Jesus does this by teaching them the prayer referred to as the Lord's Prayer. Jesus does not give the Disciples a description of prayer; He gives the Disciples the words for prayer. Jesus is the definitive teacher of the truthful speech of God because He is the Word of God incarnate. We can take the words Jesus prays, in the Lord's Prayer and the Psalms, as instruction in how we should pray to and speak about God. We can only learn to speak truthfully by speaking the words God has given to us.

HOME DAILY DEVOTIONAL READINGS
FEBRUARY 24—MARCH 2, 2014

MONDAY	TUESDAY	WEDNESDAY	THURSDAY	FRIDAY	SATURDAY	SUNDAY
The Lord Is King	You Are My Son	An Eternal Throne	God's Heritage	God's Steadfast Love and Faithfulness	The Messiah Will Reign Forever	A Throne Established Forever
Psalm 93	Psalm 2	Psalm 45:1-9	Psalm 94:8-15	Psalm 98	Revelation 11:15-19	2 Samuel 7:4-16

THIRD QUARTER

Lesson material is based on International Sunday School Lessons and International Bible Lessons for Christian Teaching. Copyrighted by the International Council of Religious Education, and is used by its permission.

MARCH, APRIL, MAY 2014

WRITER: DR. ROBERT J. HOLMES

SUGGESTED OPENING EXERCISES

1. **Usual Signal for Beginning**
2. **Prayer (Closing with the Lord's Prayer)**
3. **Singing (Song to Be Selected)**
4. **Scripture Reading:**
   Psalm 110 (KJV)

Director: The LORD said to my Lord, Sit thou at my right hand, until I make thine enemies thy footstool. The LORD shall send the rod of thy strength out of Zion: rule thou in the midst of thine enemies.

School: Thy people shall be willing in the day of thy power, in the beauties of holiness from the womb of the morning: thou hast the dew of thy youth.

Director: The LORD hath sworn, and will not repent, Thou art a priest for ever after the order of Melchizedek.

School: The Lord at thy right hand shall strike through kings in the day of his wrath.

Director: He shall judge among the heathen, he shall fill the places with the dead bodies; he shall wound the heads over many countries.

All: He shall drink of the brook in the way: therefore shall he lift up the head.

Recitation in Concert:
Isaiah 9:2-7 (KJV)

2 The people that walked in darkness have seen a great light: they that dwell in the land of the shadow of death, upon them hath the light shined.

3 Thou hast multiplied the nation, and not increased the joy: they joy before thee according to the joy in harvest, and as men rejoice when they divide the spoil.

4 For thou hast broken the yoke of his burden, and the staff of his shoulder, the rod of his oppressor, as in the day of Midian.

5 For every battle of the warrior is with confused noise, and garments rolled in blood; but this shall be with burning and fuel of fire.

6 For unto us a child is born, unto us a son is given: and the government shall be upon his shoulder: and his name shall be called Wonderful, Counsellor, The mighty God, The everlasting Father, The Prince of Peace.

7 Of the increase of his government and peace there shall be no end, upon the throne of David, and upon his kingdom, to order it, and to establish it with judgment and with justice from henceforth even for ever. The zeal of the LORD of hosts will perform this.

CLOSING WORK

1. **Singing**
2. **Sentences: Leviticus 19:18 (KJV)**
   18 Thou shalt not avenge, nor bear any grudge against the children of thy people, but thou shalt love thy neighbor as thyself: I am the LORD.
3. **Dismissal with Prayer**

AN ETERNAL KINGDOM

ADULT TOPIC: A CHANGE OF PLANS	BACKGROUND SCRIPTURE: 2 SAMUEL 7:1-17

2 SAMUEL 7:4-16

King James Version

AND it came to pass that night, that the word of the LORD came unto Nathan, saying,

5 Go and tell my servant David, Thus saith the LORD, Shalt thou build me an house for me to dwell in?

6 Whereas I have not dwelt in any house since the time that I brought up the children of Israel out of Egypt, even to this day, but have walked in a tent and in a tabernacle.

7 In all the places wherein I have walked with all the children of Israel spake I a word with any of the tribes of Israel, whom I commanded to feed my people Israel, saying, Why build ye not me an house of cedar?

8 Now therefore so shalt thou say unto my servant David, Thus saith the LORD of hosts, I took thee from the sheepcote, from following the sheep, to be ruler over my people, over Israel:

9 And I was with thee whithersoever thou wentest, and have cut off all thine enemies out of thy sight, and have made thee a great name, like unto the name of the great men that are in the earth.

10 Moreover I will appoint a place for my people Israel, and will plant them, that they may dwell in a place of their own, and move no more; neither shall the children of wickedness afflict them any more, as beforetime,

11 And as since the time that I commanded judges to be over my people Israel, and have caused thee to rest from all thine enemies. Also the LORD telleth thee that he will make thee an house.

New Revised Standard Version

BUT that same night the word of the LORD came to Nathan:

5 Go and tell my servant David: Thus says the LORD: Are you the one to build me a house to live in?

6 I have not lived in a house since the day I brought up the people of Israel from Egypt to this day, but I have been moving about in a tent and a tabernacle.

7 Wherever I have moved about among all the people of Israel, did I ever speak a word with any of the tribal leaders of Israel, whom I commanded to shepherd my people Israel, saying, "Why have you not built me a house of cedar?"

8 Now therefore thus you shall say to my servant David: Thus says the LORD of hosts: I took you from the pasture, from following the sheep to be prince over my people Israel;

9 and I have been with you wherever you went, and have cut off all your enemies from before you; and I will make for you a great name, like the name of the great ones of the earth.

10 And I will appoint a place for my people Israel and will plant them, so that they may live in their own place, and be disturbed no more; and evildoers shall afflict them no more, as formerly,

11 from the time that I appointed judges over my people Israel; and I will give you rest from all your enemies. Moreover the LORD declares to you that the LORD will make you a house.

MAIN THOUGHT: And thine house and thy kingdom shall be established for ever before thee: thy throne shall be established for ever. (2 Samuel 7:16, KJV)

2 Samuel 7:4-16

King James Version	New Revised Standard Version
12 And when thy days be fulfilled, and thou shalt sleep with thy fathers, I will set up thy seed after thee, which shall proceed out of thy bowels, and I will establish his kingdom.	12 When your days are fulfilled and you lie down with your ancestors, I will raise up your offspring after you, who shall come forth from your body, and I will establish his kingdom.
13 He shall build an house for my name, and I will stablish the throne of his kingdom for ever.	13 He shall build a house for my name, and I will establish the throne of his kingdom forever.
14 I will be his father, and he shall be my son. If he commit iniquity, I will chasten him with the rod of men, and with the stripes of the children of men:	14 I will be a father to him, and he shall be a son to me. When he commits iniquity, I will punish him with a rod such as mortals use, with blows inflicted by human beings.
15 But my mercy shall not depart away from him, as I took it from Saul, whom I put away before thee.	15 But I will not take my steadfast love from him, as I took it from Saul, whom I put away from before you.
16 And thine house and thy kingdom shall be established for ever before thee: thy throne shall be established for ever.	16 Your house and your kingdom shall be made sure forever before me; your throne shall be established forever.

LESSON SETTING

Time: circa 1000 B.C.
Place: Jerusalem

LESSON OUTLINE

I. **The Freedom of Yahweh**
   (2 Samuel 7:4-7)
II. **Yahweh Is King, David Is Prince**
   (2 Samuel 7:8-11)
III. **Yahweh Will Establish David's House**
   (2 Samuel 7:12-16)

UNIFYING PRINCIPLE

Many people value permanence and seek to build things that will outlast themselves, but how do people seek to build a legacy? When David wanted to build a house for God, God promised to build a house for David—a dynasty, a tradition of royalty.

INTRODUCTION

The books of 1 and 2 Samuel were originally one book. When the Hebrew text was translated into Greek, it was divided into two books "to accommodate the work to the length of scrolls typically used in classical antiquity. The books of Samuel are concerned primarily with the establishment of the monarchy in Israel under Saul, followed by the rise and reign of David." (Brian E. Kelly, "Samuel, Books of," in *Dictionary for Theological Interpretation of the Bible* [Grand Rapids, MI: Baker Academic, 2005], 717). The books display an ambivalent attitude toward the monarchy. Although God allows the Israelites to have a king, this request for "a king to govern [the Israelites], like other nations" (1 Sam. 8:5, NRSV) is understood to be a rejection of the Lord (see 1 Sam. 8:4-9). "The book is…skeptical (at least) about human kingship, which is not fundamental to Yahweh's rule or Israel's identity, and is sometimes inimical to these, especially when the prophetic word is spurned" (Kelly, 720).

While the books are generally skeptical about human kingship, they are more specifically critical of a kingship that presumes upon Yahweh's intentions. The king is to be subject to Yahweh and rule in the way Yahweh desires. Saul is rejected as king because he does not conform to obedience of Yahweh. David is accepted because he is concerned, at least initially, with being obedient to Yahweh and readily repents when he is confronted with his sins and presumptions. David's later reign, however, is plagued with problems brought about by his own failures. "David in his later years fails to realize the blessings promised to his own kingship. His rule is beneficial only insofar as he submits himself to Yahweh and his commands. The various intrigues involving a wayward David and his equally wayward sons indicate that politics (both sexual and power) posited on a calculating worldly wisdom leads only to disaster" (Kelly, 719).

The questions of Yahweh's sovereignty and human kingship are at the heart of today's passage. Yahweh has provided for David, taking him "from the pasture, from following the sheep to be prince over [Yahweh's] people Israel" (2 Sam. 7:8, NRSV). Yahweh, in His freedom, has chosen David to be prince over His people. David, being given rest from His enemies by Yahweh and established in his palace in Jerusalem, now assumes that he needs to build a temple for Yahweh. He speaks to his advisor, the prophet Nathan, concerning this proposal, and Nathan approves without bringing this before Yahweh in prayer. Yahweh's prophets and princes should take nothing for granted when they claim to be acting on behalf of His Name.

EXPOSITION

I. THE FREEDOM OF YAHWEH (2 SAMUEL 7:4-7)

After Nathan approves David's plans without consulting Yahweh, Yahweh addresses Nathan with correction that very evening. Yahweh tells Nathan to speak to his servant. Yahweh's addressing David as His servant illuminates two ideas that are important for interpreting this passage. First, in correcting David, Yahweh is not rejecting David as the leader of His people because He still sees David as His servant. Second, though David is leader of Israel, he is still subject to Yahweh and must follow Yahweh's intentions for the nation of Israel. This is a reminder to both David and Nathan that they do not have the final say in Israel. Both David and Nathan must submit faithfully to the rule of Yahweh in order to faithfully lead and serve Yahweh's people, Israel.

A brief word should be said here about the prophet Nathan, this is his first appearance in Samuel. "Although his origin is unknown, the present passage indicates that he and David knew each other, and that David sought his counsel in religious matters" (John T. Willis, *First and Second Samuel* [Austin, TX: Sweet Publishing Company, 1982], 329). As is seen later in Samuel, Nathan is not a false (court) prophet who speaks words that simply approve the king's acts (see 2 Sam. 11:1—12:15). However, in this instance, Nathan speaks without consulting Yahweh. "Even though Nathan was a true prophet, it was not his prerogative to speak for God when God had not spoken" (Willis, 329). Although Nathan often speaks truthfully concerning the nature of Yahweh's will, he is only able to do this when he has faithfully consulted Yahweh concerning His will. Yahweh demands the same obedience from both His prophets and His kings.

Yahweh's questioning of David's desire to build a house (temple) relies on a play between *house* and *tent and tabernacle*. The Hebrew word *bayith* (house) plays a critical role throughout 2 Samuel 7. "It is readily apparent that this chapter relies on a word play, involving the variant meanings of a single word, to convey its central theme. The common Hebrew noun [*bayith*] can, depending on context, mean 'house,' 'dwelling,' 'palace,' 'temple,' or 'dynasty.' All of these meanings may play a role in 2 Sam 7:1-17, but the crucial theological focus is on the relationship between temple and dynasty" (Bruce C. Birch, "The First and Second Books of Samuel," in *The New Interpreter's Bible*, Vol. 2 [Nashville: Abingdon, 1998], 1254). *House* symbolizes locating Yahweh to a fixed place, while *tent and tabernacle* are consonant with Yahweh's freedom. While David's intentions may be good, David's locating Yahweh to a fixed place may be an attempt to control Yahweh and ensure that Yahweh remains on the side of the Israelites. Yahweh's specific references to *house* and *tent and tabernacle* indicate that at least part of Yahweh's concern is that the newly placed king is now attempting to manipulate Him.

Yahweh's rebuke to David and Nathan concerns their presumption. They attempt to build Yahweh a temple because they assume He desires one from their hands. They are attempting to rely on their own initiative in a way that undercuts Yahweh's freedom in leading Israel. Yahweh has asked no leaders before David to build Him a temple, and David's assumption that he should build a temple may indicate a desire to point to his own glory. Yahweh's freedom, however, will not be inhibited by a king's desire for glory. Yahweh will accomplish things in His time.

II. Yahweh Is King, David Is Prince (2 Samuel 7:8-11)

It is Yahweh's initiative that has placed David as a leader over Israel. Yahweh has taken David "from the pasture, from following the sheep to be prince over [Yahweh's] people Israel" (2 Sam. 7:8, NRSV). It is important that Yahweh does not refer to David here as king (*melek*) over Israel. The word *nagid* used to describe David's place in Israel means "chief, leader, sovereign ... prince" (William Holladay, *"nagid"* in *A Concise Hebrew and Aramaic Lexicon of the Old Testament* [Grand Rapids, MI: Eerdmans, 1988], 226). This is not a term that describes a king who holds absolute sovereignty, but a ruler who leads by the appointment of someone more powerful. David, therefore, is not a king like those of other nations, but is a prince who is to carry out faithfully the commands of Yahweh. David only leads at the appointment of Yahweh, and his power is thus limited.

Instead of allowing David to build the temple for Him, Yahweh describes everything He has done and will continue to do on behalf of David. David is thus moved from being the active one, drawing attention to himself, to the passive recipient of Yahweh's grace. This serves to remind

David that there is no inherent worthiness on his part for the blessings he has received. David has only arrived at this place because of Yahweh's gracious provision. So Yahweh recounts the gracious acts he has done on David's behalf: "I took you from the pasture, from following the sheep to be prince over my people Israel; and I have been with you wherever you went, and have cut off all your enemies from before you" (2 Sam. 7:8-9, NSRV). In the Hebrew text, the agency of Yahweh is emphasized through the use of the first person singular pronoun in conjunction with the first person singular verb. This serves to make it clear that it is *Yahweh* who has acted and will continue to act graciously on behalf of David and the Israelites.

Yahweh's promise to make David's name great recalls the promise made to Abram in Genesis 12:1-3. This new promise Yahweh makes to David in conjunction with the promise to establish the people of Israel in a place should serve to remind David and the reader of Deuteronomy 7:7-8: "It was not because you were more numerous than any other people that the Lord set his heart on you and chose you— for you were the fewest of all peoples. It was because the Lord loved you and kept the oath that he swore to your ancestors, that the Lord has brought you out with a mighty hand, and redeemed you from the house of slavery, from the hand of Pharaoh king of Egypt" (NRSV). Like Israel, David was not chosen because of his outstanding qualities. He is the youngest son of Jesse, and Jesse does not consider David at first when Samuel comes to anoint one of Jesse's sons as king. David, like Israel,

is an afterthought (see 1 Sam. 16:1-13). Yahweh chooses David and Israel in His freedom, and they are not chosen based on their merits. Yahweh blesses them so that they may bring honor to His Name before the nations. David's actions will only be blessed when they are submitted to Yahweh's will. Thus David will always be prince to the King, Yahweh.

III. Yahweh Will Establish David's House (2 Samuel 7:12-16)

Yahweh now reveals His intentions for David. Instead of David building a house (temple) for Yahweh, Yahweh will establish a house (dynasty) for David. Once again, Yahweh is demonstrating that He will act in divine freedom to graciously bless David. This gracious blessing does not come about because of anything David has done. Yahweh has thus far been the primary actor in placing David on the throne. And Yahweh will continue to be the primary actor ensuring the continuation of the royal line of David. David's royal line will be continued in Solomon. Solomon will be the one who builds the temple for Yahweh (see 1 Kings 5:3-5). In this passage, Solomon also notes that another reason David could not build the temple was because of the constant warfare in which David was engaged (cf. 2 Chron. 22:2-19; 28:3; note that David says the reason he could not build was because of the blood he had shed). David does not get to determine the timeline for the building of the temple, the temple will be built at Yahweh's discretion. There will be no limit on Yahweh's freedom.

Yahweh will ensure the Davidic line, and the sons of David will be as sons to

Yahweh. They will be subject to Yahweh and will suffer punishment if they turn from Yahweh's intentions for Israel. The establishment of the throne of David forever sets up a messianic expectation for the people of Israel. Israel begins to expect, particularly in the exile, the emergence of a king like David who will restore Israel. The basis for this expectation lies in the promise made by Yahweh to David in this passage. The story playing out through the books of Samuel and Kings demonstrates that the rebellious line of kings that descended from David will end in exile. However, there is still hope for a Davidic king who will restore the fortunes of Israel.

THE LESSON APPLIED

Christians understand that this expectation for the coming King is fulfilled in the person of Jesus Christ. Jesus, however, does not fulfill expectations in the way the Israelites anticipated. This is a theme that remains consistent throughout Scripture: God confounds human expectations. In Jesus Christ, the Israelites did not receive a King who overthrew the Roman Empire. Instead, Jesus Christ is the King who fully submits Himself to the will of His Father, going to the cross and exposing that the powers of this world do not have the final say. The vindication of the Kingship of Jesus Christ lies in His resurrection that defeats the grave, death and ushers in a new age.

LET'S TALK ABOUT IT

1. How should Christians understand their relationship to human governments?

The story of the kingship in Israel provides an interesting entry into the discussion of the relationship between God's people and human governments. In 1 Samuel 8:4-9, Yahweh explains that Israel's desire for a king like the nations is a rejection of Him. Yahweh, however, later chooses a king for himself, choosing David. The picture that comes through most forcefully in Samuel is that kings and governments only do well when they submit themselves fully to Yahweh.

This, however, does not necessarily justify the desire to get those who follow God in power because the parallel lesson throughout the books of Samuel and Kings are that political power often corrupts. There are few kings who faithfully embody what Yahweh expects of the kings of Israel, and even those few tend to stray from Yahweh's commands. Political power often works from a place of presumption, a place that often excludes the voice of God.

HOME DAILY DEVOTIONAL READINGS
MARCH 3-9, 2014

MONDAY	TUESDAY	WEDNESDAY	THURSDAY	FRIDAY	SATURDAY	SUNDAY
A Son Named Emmanuel	The King of the Jews	Is This the Son of David?	Hosanna to the Son of David	Whose Son Is the Messiah?	Following the Son of David	The Son of David
Matthew 1:22-25	Matthew 2:1-6	Matthew 12:15-23	Matthew 21:12-17	Matthew 22:41-45	Mark 10:46-52	Psalm 89:35-37; Isaiah 9:6-7; Matthew 1:18-21

SON OF DAVID

ADULT TOPIC: FAMILY CONNECTIONS	BACKGROUND SCRIPTURES: PSALM 89:3-14, 30-37; ISAIAH 9:1-7; MATTHEW 1:18—2:6; MARK 12:35-37; LUKE 1:26-33

PSALM 89:35-37; ISAIAH 9:6-7; MATTHEW 1:18-21

King James Version

ONCE have I sworn by my holiness that I will not lie unto David.

36 His seed shall endure for ever, and his throne as the sun before me.

37 It shall be established for ever as the moon, and as a faithful witness in heaven. Selah.

• • • Isaiah 9:6-7 • • •

FOR unto us a child is born, unto us a son is given: and the government shall be upon his shoulder: and his name shall be called Wonderful, Counsellor, The mighty God, The everlasting Father, The Prince of Peace.

7 Of the increase of his government and peace there shall be no end, upon the throne of David, and upon his kingdom, to order it, and to establish it with judgment and with justice from henceforth even for ever. The zeal of the LORD of hosts will perform this.

• • • Matthew 1:18-21 • • •

NOW the birth of Jesus Christ was on this wise: When as his mother Mary was espoused to Joseph, before they came together, she was found with child of the Holy Ghost.

19 Then Joseph her husband, being a just man, and not willing to make her a public example, was minded to put her away privily.

New Revised Standard Version

ONCE and for all I have sworn by my holiness; I will not lie to David.

36 His line shall continue forever, and his throne endure before me like the sun.

37 It shall be established forever like the moon, an enduring witness in the skies." Selah

• • • Isaiah 9:6-7 • • •

FOR a child has been born for us, a son given to us; authority rests upon his shoulders; and he is named Wonderful Counselor, Mighty God, Everlasting Father, Prince of Peace.

7 His authority shall grow continually, and there shall be endless peace for the throne of David and his kingdom. He will establish and uphold it with justice and with righteousness from this time onward and forevermore. The zeal of the LORD of hosts will do this.

• • • Matthew 1:18-21 • • •

NOW the birth of Jesus the Messiah took place in this way. When his mother Mary had been engaged to Joseph, but before they lived together, she was found to be with child from the Holy Spirit.

19 Her husband Joseph, being a righteous man and unwilling to expose her to public disgrace, planned to dismiss her quietly.

MAIN THOUGHT: And she shall bring forth a son, and thou shalt call his name JESUS: for he shall save his people from their sins. Now all this was done, that it might be fulfilled which was spoken of the Lord by the prophet. (Matthew 1:21-22, KJV)

PSALM 89:35-37; ISAIAH 9:6-7; MATTHEW 1:18-21

King James Version	*New Revised Standard Version*
20 But while he thought on these things, behold, the angel of the LORD appeared unto him in a dream, saying, Joseph, thou son of David, fear not to take unto thee Mary thy wife: for that which is conceived in her is of the Holy Ghost. 21 And she shall bring forth a son, and thou shalt call his name JESUS: for he shall save his people from their sins.	20 But just when he had resolved to do this, an angel of the Lord appeared to him in a dream and said, "Joseph, son of David, do not be afraid to take Mary as your wife, for the child conceived in her is from the Holy Spirit. 21 She will bear a son, and you are to name him Jesus, for he will save his people from their sins."

LESSON SETTING

Time: Unknown;
circa 725 B.C.; 4 B.C.

Place: Judea

LESSON OUTLINE

I. The Firstborn Son
(Psalm 89:35-37)
II. Characteristics of the Son and His Reign
(Isaiah 9:6-7)
III. Joseph Names His Son
(Matthew 1:18-21)

UNIFYING PRINCIPLE

People have expectations and hopes regarding their descendants. What assurance do people have that their line of descendants will continue? As God promised David and as Isaiah prophesied, Matthew reports that the birth of Jesus fulfills the traditional expectation that a descendant of David would be coming as the Savior.

INTRODUCTION

Psalm 89 is a royal psalm consisting of a hymn about God's kingship, an oracle about His covenant with David, and a lament concerning a military defeat (Craig C. Broyles, *Psalms* in *New International*

Biblical Commentary [Peabody, MA: Hendrickson, 1999], 355). Based on various factors pertaining to the lament section and his assertions that the psalm has not been edited, Ward dates this psalm broadly to pre-exilic days after Solomon's reign and during the divided kingdom, likely between Rehoboam and Zedekiah (James M. Ward, "The Literary Form and Liturgical Background of Psalm 89" in *Vetus Testamentum* 11.3 [July 1, 1961], 339). Mullen claims that "while contacts between 2 Sam. 7:14-16 and Ps. 89:20-38 appear indisputable, it is impossible to demonstrate the direction of any possible literary dependency" (E. Theodore Mullen, Jr., "The Divine Witness and the Davidic Royal Grant: 0. 89:37-38" in *Journal of Biblical Literature* 102.2 [June 1, 1983], 209). Part of the difficulty is the Deuteronomistic influence found in 2 Samuel 7 which is absent from Psalm 89 (ibid., 208). Psalms were used in liturgy, such that this particular psalm would have been used at least in part to remember God's faithfulness to covenant.

Isaiah dates further into Israel's monarchical history, covering the years circa B.C. 745 to 701. During this time, the

Northern Kingdom falls to Assyria and Judah approaches the same fate (Walter Brueggemann, *Isaiah 1-39* in *Westminster Bible Companion* [Louisville, KY: Westminster John Knox, 1998], 1). Several themes run throughout the text of Isaiah, among them God's covenant loyalty which will be finally expressed in the person of a "significant agent of God who is at times described by terms appropriate for deity" (Terry Briley, *Isaiah Vol. 1* in *The College Press NIV Commentary* [Joplin, MO: College Press, 2000], 22-23). This theme is particularly evident in Isaiah 9.

Matthew draws on the expectations of texts like these in his birth narrative to confirm that Jesus is the fulfillment of prophecy. Scholars generally accept that Matthew was written between A.D. 80-100. The documentary theory plays a role in this date, positing that Matthew uses Mark's gospel and the hypothetical document Q as sources and thus must have been written after them, but before the Didache or Ignatius' writings circa A.D. 110 (M. Eugene Boring, "Gospel of Matthew" in the *New Interpreter's Bible* [Nashville, TN: Abingdon Press, 1995], 105-106).

EXPOSITION

I. THE FIRSTBORN SON (PSALM 89:35-37)

Verses 35-37 are found in the oracle section concerning the line of the Davidic kingship. Broyles notes an intensification from the promises as stated in 2 Samuel 7 to those found in the preceding verses. From being a son to being the firstborn son, from a great king to the most exalted king with an empire and a dynasty, this Davidic king is the most glorious fulfillment possible for God's promises (see 19ff). Verses 35-37 especially stress the eternal nature of God's covenantal promise to David and its fulfillment (ibid., 357).

Keep in mind the relationship between parties which is assumed when speaking of covenant. This is not an agreement made between equals; rather, the party with power condescends to the other, vowing to take care of him (or them, in the case of Israel) in return for fidelity to the terms of the covenant. God has always been the Sovereign who blesses His people in exchange for fidelity to Him as is demonstrated throughout Israel's history (see Exod. 19:3-6, Josh. 8:30-35, etc.).

God swears by His holiness in Psalm 89:35 to fulfill the covenant He made with David and "does not merely say it (as in v. 19), or merely promise it (as in v. 3)" (John Goldingay, *Psalms Vol. 2: Psalms 42-89* in *Baker Commentary on the Old Testament: Wisdom and Psalms* [Grand Rapids, MI: 2008], 682). Goldingay argues that this is an escalation from the previous ways of speaking about God's covenant with David; He puts His "own personal being" on the line to demonstrate His seriousness to His promises (ibid.). In poetic parallel to this, God "will not lie to David" (v. 35, NRSV).

Mullen considers the mention of the sun and the moon a naming of God's witnesses (210). In Micah, God calls on the mountains to be witnesses in his trial against Samaria and Judah concerning who is guilty of disloyalty to covenant—Himself or the nation (see Mic. 6:1-5). These appeals are not made to nature but to the way the universe as created by

God functions. In Israelite cosmology, the mountains held up the dome of the sky and so were integral to the integrity of the earth. Thus, the witness of the sun and the moon in the heavens suggests the witness of the entire universe and the very systems of existence which Israel daily depended upon. Their very stability speaks to God's faithfulness and will bear witness to the truth of His promise to David.

II. CHARACTERISTICS OF THE SON AND HIS REIGN (ISAIAH 9:6-7)

Isaiah likely understands his prophecies as looking beyond exile for their fulfillment. The use of prophetic past (speaking of a future occurrence in the past tense, as though it had already happened) bolsters this analysis (J. Alec Motyer, *The Prophecy of Isaiah: An Introduction & Commentary* [Downers Grove, IL: IVP Academic, 1993], 98). The chapter offers hope to a people facing significant political turmoil from within and without.

In their original historical context, these verses may refer to the birth of Hezekiah, especially as a foil to his evil father Ahaz (see Isa. 9:6). His was a much more faithful reign than his father's (Brueggemann 82). Assuming that Hezekiah was the original king Isaiah had in mind, Brueggemann argues that "the well-known series of royal names for 'the new king' is likely ritualized hyperbole," meaning these were not believed to be literally true but rather indicative of the ideal type of a king, perhaps originating in Egyptian liturgy (83-84). (Keep in mind that the capitalization in English translations of Hebrew was not present in the original texts.) In order to make this position tenable, Brueggemann interprets the titles "wonderful counselor," "mighty god," "everlasting father," and "prince of peace" as ideals of a real king—he is wise, father of a great dynasty, and able to restrain political chaos (83).

Two crippling problems arise, however. First and most obviously is this reference to the king as "mighty god." Brueggemann tries to find a way around this by claiming that the king would have great power, especially militarily (ibid.). The fact remains that Isaiah the prophet wrote these words, and no true prophet of God would ever claim that any man was also a god. This is further complicated by the second issue—borrowing liturgy from Egypt. This is not in itself a totally unrealistic possibility for the population at large, which was given to syncretism throughout its existence. However, one cannot assume that Isaiah also engaged in syncretism, or especially that he would adopt a formula from Egypt without even amending the reference to a god besides Yahweh.

A more acceptable position argues that these verses were from the first Messianic, since no person could fully embody these traits, nor would Isaiah have expected it given the language he used (Briley, 140). *Pele'*, translated *wonder*, "frequently refers to the impact created by a supernatural act of God" (ibid.). *Mighty God* itself is used of Yahweh in Isaiah 10:21. God declares Himself David's Father in His promise of a lasting kingdom (ibid., 140-141). Brueggemann acknowledges that if these verses were first applied to Hezekiah, they did not find their final fulfillment until Christ's coming (82).

"His authority shall grow continually, and there shall be endless peace for the throne of David and his kingdom" (v. 7, NRSV). The NIV translates verse seven "Of the increase of his government and peace there will be no end" (qtd. in Briley, 137). What the NIV draws out is a paradox—who has ever heard of a government's influence growing outside of its national borders without violence? Yet, looking forward again to Jesus and his claim on Christian lives, one sees that His Kingdom does not advance through violence or coercion but rather through the faithful, loving witness of His followers. He reigns "with justice and with righteousness from this time onward and forevermore" (v. 7, NRSV; see Rev. 5). All of this is accomplished in "the zeal of the Lord of hosts" (v. 7, NRSV), not through human ability or even desire.

III. JOSEPH NAMES HIS SON (MATTHEW 1:18-21)

Matthew works diligently to show that Jesus is the fulfillment of prophecy (R. T. France, "The Gospel of Matthew" in *The New International Commentary on the New Testament* [Grand Rapids, MI: Eerdmans, 2007], 40). He opens with Joseph's genealogy, which in itself presents an issue which Matthew intends to clarify—namely, if Jesus is born of Mary and is not biologically Joseph's son, how can He then be considered part of David's lineage?

As is often noted, the engagement period for Jews in the first-century was vastly different from today's dominant Western notion. It was a legally binding relationship which was not yet the consummated marriage. Thus, if Mary was guilty of sleeping with another man (since Joseph knew she hadn't slept with him, this seemed the only other option),

she was guilty of adultery under Jewish law. However, Matthew informs us in the same breath as the announcement of her pregnancy that the child is "from the Holy Spirit," leaving no time for suspicion on the reader's part (Matt. 1:18, NRSV).

Joseph wasn't yet privy to the origin of the pregnancy and was "a righteous man and unwilling to expose her to public disgrace" (v. 19, NRSV). Typically in Jewish thinking, a righteous man was one who adhered to the law, but in this case Joseph was commended for erring on the side of mercy by desiring a quiet divorce and minimizing Mary's public shame (Craig S. Keener, *A Commentary on the Gospel of Matthew* [Grand Rapids, MI: Eerdmans, 1999], 92-93). Like engagement, shame was a different concept in Israel and the wider Roman world at this time than in the West today. Whole lives were lived in pursuit of honor and could be destroyed in moments through one shameful deed. Mary's pregnancy would have been the end of her good reputation.

Before he could follow through, however, "an angel of the Lord appeared to him in a dream" (v. 19, NRSV). France notes that "specific emphasis is placed both in the angel's message and in the subsequent narrative on Joseph's role in naming Jesus" (48; see Matt. 2:13, 19). In verses 20-21, the angel reiterates what Matthew has already told his reader, and then adds the key to the question of lineage: "you are to name him Jesus, for he will save his people from their sins" (Matt. 1:21, NRSV). Both the name and the naming are significant here. "Jesus" is a Hellenization of the Hebrew "Joshua" which Matthew takes to mean "Yahweh saves" (Boring,

135). The name recalls Moses' successor Joshua and the post-exile high priest as well, both of whom led the people during important transition times (see Deut. 31:1-8, Josh. 3, Zech. 6:9-15, Hag. 1:12-14, 2:1-9). Furthermore, by giving Joseph the specific task of naming, the angel in essence tells Joseph to adopt the child. Joseph became Jesus' legal father and "ensured the official status of the son and heir" (France 48). In this way, Matthew concludes his apologetic for identifying Jesus as the coming King who had been promised from long ago.

THE LESSON APPLIED

The psalmist and Isaiah lived in times when it would have been easy to forget God's promises or assume that He had finished with His chosen people. They had worshipped other gods, appointed their own kings, depended on their own military might and political allegiances, and forgotten to care for the widow, the orphan, and the alien. These breeches of covenant carried curses for the unfaithful. Indeed, exile was coming, but this was not a mere punitive punishment; rather, judgment was meant to recall the people to their covenant with God, to remind them of His blessings so that they could be restored to those blessings. His faithfulness in sending Jesus justifies the hope that both the psalmist and Isaiah saw from a distance and which Matthew declared had finally arrived for Israel and ultimately the entire world. He kept His covenant with Israel and continues to keep covenant today with His Church.

LET'S TALK ABOUT IT

1. How can we trust that God will remain faithful?

God has made promises to the Church which have not yet been fulfilled, especially concerning the coming fullness of His Kingdom on earth. Violence wrecks havoc in old traditional ways and in new, creative ways every day. One environmental crisis after another threatens the vitality of all life the world over. The Church so often seems fragmented, led by earthly leaders in search of power rather than servitude and participating in communal patterns based on socioeconomics rather than God's love for the other. In such times, it is easy to lose hope in the good future God has promised. Yet, in similar situations, Israel waited more than seven-hundred years from when Psalm 89 was written to when Jesus walked the earth. We on the other side of the cross have seen the climax of history and live in the now and not-yet of God's future. We the Church are the sign that God is faithful to His promises as we grow into His intended future for the sake of the world.

HOME DAILY DEVOTIONAL READINGS						
MARCH 10-16, 2014						
MONDAY	**TUESDAY**	**WEDNESDAY**	**THURSDAY**	**FRIDAY**	**SATURDAY**	**SUNDAY**
Protect Me, O God	Show Me the Path of Life	Freed from the Fear of Death	The Power of the Resurrection	The Heavenly Call of God	Made Both Lord and Messiah	Placed on David's Throne
Psalm 16:1-6	Psalm 16:7-11	Hebrews 2:14-18	Philippians 3:7-11	Philippians 3:12-16	Acts 2:33-36	Psalm 110:1-4; Acts 2:22-24, 29-32

PETER'S REPORT

ADULT TOPIC:	BACKGROUND SCRIPTURES:
LOOKING FORWARD AND LOOKING BACK	PSALM 110; ACTS 2:22-36

PSALM 110:1-4; ACTS 2:22-24, 29-32

King James Version

THE LORD said unto my Lord, Sit thou at my right hand, until I make thine enemies thy footstool.

2 The LORD shall send the rod of thy strength out of Zion: rule thou in the midst of thine enemies.

3 Thy people shall be willing in the day of thy power, in the beauties of holiness from the womb of the morning: thou hast the dew of thy youth.

4 The LORD hath sworn, and will not repent, Thou art a priest for ever after the order of Melchizedek.

• • • Acts 2:22-24 • • •

YE men of Israel, hear these words; Jesus of Nazareth, a man approved of God among you by miracles and wonders and signs, which God did by him in the midst of you, as ye yourselves also know:

23 Him, being delivered by the determinate counsel and foreknowledge of God, ye have taken, and by wicked hands have crucified and slain:

24 Whom God hath raised up, having loosed the pains of death: because it was not possible that he should be holden of it.

• • • • • •

29 Men and brethren, let me freely speak unto you of the patriarch David, that he is both dead and buried, and his sepulchre is with us unto this day.

New Revised Standard Version

THE LORD says to my lord, "Sit at my right hand until I make your enemies your footstool."

2 The LORD sends out from Zion your mighty scepter. Rule in the midst of your foes.

3 Your people will offer themselves willingly on the day you lead your forces on the holy mountains. From the womb of the morning, like dew, your youth will come to you.

4 The LORD has sworn and will not change his mind, "You are a priest forever according to the order of Melchizedek."

• • • Acts 2:22-24 • • •

"YOU that are Israelites, listen to what I have to say: Jesus of Nazareth, a man attested to you by God with deeds of power, wonders, and signs that God did through him among you, as you yourselves know—

23 this man, handed over to you according to the definite plan and foreknowledge of God, you crucified and killed by the hands of those outside the law.

24 But God raised him up, having freed him from death, because it was impossible for him to be held in its power."

• • • • • •

29 "Fellow Israelites, I may say to you confidently of our ancestor David that he both died and was buried, and his tomb is with us to this day.

MAIN THOUGHT: He seeing this before spake of the resurrection of Christ, that his soul was not left in hell, neither his flesh did see corruption. (Acts 2:31, KJV)

Psalm 110:1-4; Acts 2:22-24, 29-32

King James Version

30 Therefore being a prophet, and knowing that God had sworn with an oath to him, that of the fruit of his loins, according to the flesh, he would raise up Christ to sit on his throne;

31 He seeing this before spake of the resurrection of Christ, that his soul was not left in hell, neither his flesh did see corruption.

32 This Jesus hath God raised up, whereof we all are witnesses.

New Revised Standard Version

30 Since he was a prophet, he knew that God had sworn with an oath to him that he would put one of his descendants on his throne.

31 Foreseeing this, David spoke of the resurrection of the Messiah, saying, 'He was not abandoned to Hades, nor did his flesh experience corruption.'

32 This Jesus God raised up, and of that all of us are witnesses."

LESSON SETTING

Time: Unknown; circa A.D. 29

Place: Jerusalem

LESSON OUTLINE

I. **The Right Hand of Yahweh (Psalm 110:1-4)**

II. **The Father Vindicates the Crucified Son (Acts 2:22-24)**

III. **Witnesses of the Resurrection (Acts 2:29-32)**

UNIFYING PRINCIPLE

People need to understand what they have received as a legacy for them to perceive any value in it. How can people correlate tradition and legacy? Peter interpreted the coming of Jesus, which the followers witnessed, as Jesus' fulfillment of the prophecy for a savior descending from the line of David.

INTRODUCTION

Today we are studying Psalm 110 and its connection to Peter's sermon on the Day of Pentecost. Psalm 110 is one of the more frequently used psalms in the New Testament. This psalm is particularly important because of Jesus' use of this psalm in the Gospels to describe His

relationship to David (see Matt. 22:41-46; Mark 12:35-37; Luke 20:41-44). Jesus places the psalm in the voice of David. This causes some difficulty for modern interpreters because it does not conform to their expectations concerning acceptable forms of interpretation. However, this should not cause us to discount the methods that Jesus and the New Testament writers use to interpret the Old Testament. Jesus' use of this psalm to describe Himself is a typological use of the psalm. In identifying Himself as the King and Priest of the psalm, Jesus demonstrates that He fulfills the psalm more fully than David or any other king. In Jesus' application of the psalm to Himself, He brings meaning to the psalm that was not previously seen. Jesus fulfills the type of King-Priest described in the psalm. In drawing on the messianic expectations that had developed concerning this psalm, Jesus identifies Himself as Messiah. Jesus thus identifies Himself as Lord of David.

Our second text for today is Acts 2:22-24, 29-32. This is a section of Peter's sermon on the day of Pentecost when the apostles were filled with the Holy Spirit. Peter draws on the Old Testament throughout his sermon. Here is an instance where we see the apostles beginning to reinterpret the Old Testament in light of the life of Jesus Christ. Consequently, this is also a place where the witnesses to Jesus' life, death, and resurrection, explore the connection of Psalm 110 and the life of Jesus more extensively.

EXPOSITION

I. THE RIGHT HAND OF YAHWEH (PSALM 110:1-4)

Our task in explicating this psalm lies first in explaining the psalm as it stands before us. Then we may be able to have a greater understanding of Jesus' use of this particular psalm. Jesus' use of this psalm as self-description should certainly change our approach to the psalm. But it is necessary to first take the psalm on its own terms, and then move to the connection of Jesus Christ.

The psalm begins with a formula that is typically associated with the prophets. There is, therefore, a prophetic nature already present in the psalm. The speaker in the psalm is somewhat difficult to discern. "'My lord' is a standard term of respect, the way anyone would speak of any superior; it is what follows that suggests it designates the king. It is again a term that would come more easily to the lips of a minister at the royal sanctuary than to the kind of prophet who needed to keep a measure of independence over against the administration" (John Goldingay, *Psalms*, Vol. 3 [Grand Rapids, MI: Baker Academic, 2008], 293). This is likely a psalm composed in the royal court, thus explaining the identification of the psalm with David.

A difficulty is created by placing the lord of Psalm 110:1 (NRSV) at the right hand Yahweh. This creates a difficulty because in this instance Yahweh is described as having a body (in this case a right hand). However, it more appropriate to understand Yahweh as having no body. This is the reason that there can be no images made of Yahweh. Thus the description of the lord sitting at the right hand of Yahweh must take on some other meaning. This is where it is helpful to draw on the nature of metaphor in the bodily descriptions of Yahweh. "To sit at someone's right hand is to sit in a position of prestige and authority. One would expect someone sitting there to be one with the support of the earthly king, or in this case the heavenly King, as his servant" (Goldingay, 293-294). The metaphor of the right hand of Yahweh being a place of prestige allows us to understand the place of this lord. The one described as sitting at the right hand of Yahweh is the one who has the support of Yahweh's power.

The image of Zion in this psalm further reinforces the idea that the lord in this psalm has the support of Yahweh. "Zion is the place where Yahweh lives with his faithful people in the absence of sin and danger" (Paul House, "Obadiah, Book of," in *Dictionary for Theological Interpretation of the Bible* [Grand Rapids, MI: Baker Academic, 2005], 543). Zion is, therefore, a place of refuge for those who are faithful to Yahweh. The picture of the lord in this psalm is one of a faithful servant of Yahweh who can reside and rule from His holy city. Zion is the city of the future hope of the Israelites where Yahweh dwells with His people.

The mention of Zion is hopeful as is the mention of *dew*. "The figurative comparison with the dew of the dawn implies the life-giving hope (in a land noted for summer's dryness) at the king's coronation" (Craig C. Broyles, *Psalms* [Peabody, MA: Hendrickson, 1999], 414-415). If this is a psalm that accompanies the coronation of a king, the psalm expresses hopefulness for the king's reign. The hope is that the king will faithfully embody what Yahweh desires of the king.

However, the hopefulness seen here extends beyond the king faithfully embodying his reign. This lord, or king, is called to the priesthood. In the Old Testament, the image of the priest-king is most fully embodied in Melchizedek, the mysterious king of Salem who provides aid to Abram in Genesis 14:18. Just as he is identified in this psalm as a king who has an everlasting priesthood, Melchizedek is later discussed in Hebrews 5—7 as the prototype for the priesthood of Jesus. The writer of Hebrews uses Psalm 110:4 and Genesis 14:18 to build a typological parallel between Melchizedek and Jesus. "First, Melchizedek blessed Abraham. Since a superior always blesses an inferior, Melchizedek must be the prototype of the only real High Priest, Jesus Christ, who can claim superiority even to Abraham. Second, Melchizedek can be such a type for Jesus Christ because he is 'without father or mother or genealogy, and has neither beginning of days nor end of life (Heb. 7:3)'" (Walter Brueggemann, *Genesis* [Louisville, KY: John Knox, 1982], 139). Jesus' use of Psalm 110:4 indicates that this lord is truly the Lord of all, Jesus Christ.

In this context, the right hand of God takes on fuller significance, as well. Jesus not only sits at the right hand of God as King but also as Priest. "To sit at God's 'right hand' involves both royal and priestly power. The 'right hand' of God is the just and merciful 'ruling and judging' of the God who is love. In this sense, as Aquinas says (quoting Augustine), God is nothing but 'right hand.'" (Matthew Levering, *Jesus and the Demise of Death* [Waco, TX: Baylor University Press, 2012], 50-51). Therefore, Jesus can truly be identified as the right hand of God—the power of God.

II. THE FATHER VINDICATES THE CRUCIFIED SON (ACTS 2:22-24)

As we move into the second passage for today, we come to the Day of Pentecost where Peter is delivering a sermon in Jerusalem. In Acts 1, the apostles witness the ascension of Jesus, and they are promised by Jesus that the Holy Spirit will come upon them. Acts 2 opens with the arrival of the Holy Spirit and the apostles speaking in other languages. Peter, therefore, delivers this sermon through the power of the Holy Spirit, and as a response to the people gathered in Jerusalem.

Peter's desire is to make the case that Jesus is the One to whom the teachings of the Law and the Prophets point. So Peter's case lies in vindicating Jesus through connecting Him to God the Father. Peter affirms that God validates Jesus' ministry through Jesus' works of power. God reveals the true nature of Jesus "with deeds of power, wonders, and signs" (Acts 2:22, NRSV). Because of his belief that God has vindicated Jesus through these actions, Peter does not hesitate in pointing out that Jesus is from Nazareth. "There is no attempt to hide that Jesus is from Nazareth, undoubtedly a controversial point that would have ruled out his being Messiah in some minds. Yet human opinion is not really important because Jesus was accredited by God in several ways" (Ben Witherington III, *The Acts of the Apostles: A Socio-Rhetorical Commentary* [Grand Rapids, MI: Eerdmans, 1998], 144). Peter clearly understands that God works through those we least expect.

Peter then identifies the plan to kill Jesus as something that was not outside the scope of God's foreknowledge. In this instance, Peter is saying that it is no accident that Jesus was handed to those who killed Him. "In v. 23 we see the juxtaposition, common in various parts of the NT, of God's divine plan with human actions for which humans are held responsible. One and the same event, Jesus' being handed over to be killed, can be said to be 'according to God's definite plan and foreknowledge' and at the same time is seen as a blameworthy sin on the part of some of Jesus' fellow Jews" (Witherington, 144-145). The people are not innocent in the killing of Jesus, but God—Father, Son, and Holy Spirit—intended the death of the Son from the beginning. This does not mean that the Son on earth does not have the desire to avoid this particular event. He can only embrace His humanity fully by experiencing the doubt and uncertainty that humans experience. Jesus willingly gives Himself over to be beaten and crucified because He knows that this is the only way to free mankind from the power of death brought about by sin. His victory was ultimately in the hands of the God that He had made known.

The death of Jesus, however, was not the last word in His life and ministry. "The point is that God was not going to allow Jesus' ministry and work to end in this fashion. Indeed, v. 24b suggests that Jesus was such a righteous and powerful person that death had no permanent power over him and his body" (Witherington, 145). Death will not be victorious because Jesus Christ is God made human. In taking on the life of a human, Jesus Christ is able to defeat death's grip through His resurrection. This resurrection comes about through the very life the Son shares with the Father. This is the ultimate vindication of the ministry and life of Jesus Christ.

III. WITNESSES OF THE RESURRECTION (ACTS 2:29-32)

Peter moves on to demonstrate the superiority of Jesus over David through his witnessing the resurrection of Jesus. The grave of David would have been a place that would have been easily visible or accessible to those in the audience. So the apostles could attest to Jesus being no longer in the grave, while the people could clearly see that David was still in the grave.

In proclaiming himself as witness to the resurrection, Peter serves doubly as a witness. "Peter does not merely proclaim the resurrection, he claims with the Eleven to have been a witness of the resurrection appearances. Thus Peter himself is in a double sense a witness—one who has seen and one who reports or bears witness" (Witherington, 147).

Although the next passage is not included in today's lesson proper, it is necessary to go a little further to fully explain the content of Peter's sermon. This is the section where Peter draws explicitly upon Psalm 110 to further explain the nature of Christ. Peter notes that not even the resurrection of Jesus fully explains the Person of Jesus Christ. Peter draws on Psalm 110 to explain that Jesus was not only raised from the dead, but He also ascended into heaven to the right hand of the Father. This ascension of Jesus to the right hand of the Father gives a clear indication of the nature of Jesus Christ. Jesus is not merely a good man who embodied the teachings of God fully. Jesus, in fact, participates in the divine life. As discussed above, God is all right hand—God is all powerful. Jesus' ascension to the right of God demonstrates that Jesus shares in the power of God because He is God.

THE LESSON APPLIED

In proclaiming the resurrection of Jesus Christ, Peter and the other apostles are witnesses to the resurrection in a double sense. They are the ones who have seen and been with the risen Christ, and they are now proclaiming this experience to any who will hear. These apostles will also become witnesses, martyrs, and living spectacles through how they live and die. They will become witnesses through their lives because they will live lives that are shaped by their encounter with the risen Lord. They will witness in their deaths because they will go to those deaths proclaiming that death does not have the last word. The apostles find an assurance of life in the resurrection of Jesus. This hope for life gives them the ability to endure any persecution that may come their way.

LET'S TALK ABOUT IT

1. How should the resurrection reshape our understanding of life?

The resurrection of Jesus Christ serves as the vindication of Jesus' ministry on earth and His continuing ministry through His Church. The resurrection also serves to indicate that death will ultimately be defeated. This should reshape the vision of life for the disciple of Jesus Christ. In knowing that death has ultimately been defeated through Jesus' resurrection, the Christian should find ways of living in the world that are not death-dealing but life-giving. This is the witness of the continuing ministry of the body of Christ on earth. The resurrection of Jesus Christ is the ultimate expression of the holiness of God. Death is defeated, and we no longer live by its ways. This is the holiness that Jesus' disciples seek to embody in living in the light of the resurrection.

HOME DAILY DEVOTIONAL READINGS
MARCH 17-23, 2014

MONDAY	TUESDAY	WEDNESDAY	THURSDAY	FRIDAY	SATURDAY	SUNDAY
Sheep Without a Shepherd	The One at God's Right Hand	The Lord Cares for the Flock	The Wrath of the Lamb	Salvation Belongs to Our God	The Lamb Will Be Their Shepherd	Worthy Is the Lamb
Matthew 9:35—10:1	Psalm 80:8-19	Zechariah 10:1-5	Revelation 6:12-17	Revelation 7:9-12	Revelation 7:13-17	Revelation 5:5-13

WORTHY IS THE LAMB

REVELATION 5:6-13

King James Version

AND I beheld, and, lo, in the midst of the throne and of the four beasts, and in the midst of the elders, stood a Lamb as it had been slain, having seven horns and seven eyes, which are the seven Spirits of God sent forth into all the earth.

7 And he came and took the book out of the right hand of him that sat upon the throne.

8 And when he had taken the book, the four beasts and four and twenty elders fell down before the Lamb, having every one of them harps, and golden vials full of odours, which are the prayers of saints.

9 And they sung a new song, saying, Thou art worthy to take the book, and to open the seals thereof: for thou wast slain, and hast redeemed us to God by thy blood out of every kindred, and tongue, and people, and nation;

10 And hast made us unto our God kings and priests: and we shall reign on the earth.

11 And I beheld, and I heard the voice of many angels round about the throne and the beasts and the elders: and the number of them was ten thousand times ten thousand, and thousands of thousands;

12 Saying with a loud voice, Worthy is the Lamb that was slain to receive power, and riches, and wisdom, and strength, and honour, and glory, and blessing.

13 And every creature which is in heaven, and on the earth, and under the earth, and such as are in the sea, and all that are in them, heard

New Revised Standard Version

THEN I saw between the throne and the four living creatures and among the elders a Lamb standing as if it had been slaughtered, having seven horns and seven eyes, which are the seven spirits of God sent out into all the earth.

7 He went and took the scroll from the right hand of the one who was seated on the throne.

8 When he had taken the scroll, the four living creatures and the twenty-four elders fell before the Lamb, each holding a harp and golden bowls full of incense, which are the prayers of the saints.

9 They sing a new song: "You are worthy to take the scroll and to open its seals, for you were slaughtered and by your blood you ransomed for God saints from every tribe and language and people and nation;

10 you have made them to be a kingdom and priests serving our God, and they will reign on earth."

11 Then I looked, and I heard the voice of many angels surrounding the throne and the living creatures and the elders; they numbered myriads of myriads and thousands of thousands,

12 singing with full voice, "Worthy is the Lamb that was slaughtered to receive power and wealth and wisdom and might and honor and glory and blessing!"

13 Then I heard every creature in heaven and on earth and under the earth and in the sea, and all that is in them, singing, "To the one

MAIN THOUGHT: Saying with a loud voice, Worthy is the Lamb that was slain to receive power, and riches, and wisdom, and strength, and honour, and glory, and blessing. (Revelation 5:12, KJV)

REVELATION 5:6–13

King James Version   *New Revised Standard Version*

I saying, Blessing, and honour, and glory, and power, be unto him that sitteth upon the throne, and unto the Lamb for ever and ever.

seated on the throne and to the Lamb be blessing and honor and glory and might forever and ever!"

LESSON SETTING
    Time: A.D. 95
    Place: Patmos

LESSON OUTLINE
  I. Setting the Scene
    (Revelation 5:6)
 II. The Lamb Is Worthy
    (Revelation 5:7-10)
III. Heaven and Earth Joined in
    Worship
    (Revelation 5:11-13)

UNIFYING PRINCIPLE

When long-hoped-for dreams come about, people express their joy in celebration. In what ways do people celebrate? The result of the fulfillment of the salvific tradition is the extravagant praise and worship of God by the multitude of the redeemed.

INTRODUCTION

The book of Revelation is a book that often either suffers abuse at the hands of certain interpreters or neglect because of the strange imagery. It is a book that can be disorienting due to visions that are difficult to understand. "The very fluidity of John's images strongly suggests that he was aware of the inadequacy of all forms of religious language to express the ineffable being of God" (G. B. Caird, *The Revelation of St. John the Divine*, 2nd ed. [London: A & C Black (Publishers) Limited, 1987], 61). The strange imagery of the book then serves to convey the mystery of God, while also revealing something about the divine life in the heavenly courts. The book of Revelation is often misinterpreted due to a lack of attention to the orienting picture of worship that opens the apocalypse proper. "Structurally the first three chapters are a covering letter to accompany and introduce the account of John's apocalyptic visions.... But John intended his readers to come to the visions with their minds prepared by what they had read in the letters" (ibid., 60). The book, therefore, is structured in such a way that the first three chapters introduce the book and John's reasons for writing the book. The primary orienting vision of the book is the vision of worship in Revelation 4—5.

The context of worship is important to the interpretation of the book of Revelation. "Revelation was probably composed for oral reading at a Christian service of worship. Each of the three scrolls in Revelation mentions the true worship of God. The 'last battle' is not between good and evil as abstractly conceived but between worshippers of the beast and worshippers of God" (Francesca Aran Murphy, "Revelation, Book of," in *Dictionary for Theological Interpretation of the Bible* [Grand Rapids, MI: Baker Academic, 2005], 687). The theme of worship, therefore, should shape any interpretation of the book. In fact, it may helpful to see the visions of Revelation playing out again and again in the presence and context of the worship of the heavenly court in Revelation 4—5.

Worship as an orienting vision in the book of Revelation also gives context to the "call for the endurance of the saints" (Rev. 14:12; see also 13:10). "Patient endurance" is an important theme in the first chapters of the book (see 1:9; 2:2; 2:19; 3:10). The book of Revelation is intended to help the Church endure either the hardship of persecution (particularly Smyrna and Philadelphia) or a lazy discipleship due to a privileged status (particularly Sardis and Laodicea). The constant message is that those who align themselves with the slain Lamb will endure. This alignment with the Lamb comes about through the grace God bestows in the worship of the Lamb. We will now turn to the scene of the worship of the Lamb.

EXPOSITION

I. SETTING THE SCENE (REVELATION 5:6)

In Revelation 4—5, John describes a scene of worship in the heavenly court. He has entered the heavenly court and seen several images that express the centrality of worship in the heavenly life. "The heaven which is the scene of John's visions … is part of the created universe, but a part which is entered by the opening of the spiritual eye rather than by any more literal form of transit" (Caird, 62). As the scene opens in chapter four, John sees a door to heaven and is invited to come and see what will take place. So John enters in the Spirit, sees the throne, and sees the One seated on the throne. The figure sitting on the throne is only given a vague description (see Rev. 4:2-3). This vague description of the One on the throne reinforces a sense of mystery. The throne serves as a point of orientation in this scene of worship. The One who sits on the throne is worthy of worship, and the creatures and the elders direct their worship toward Him. "The first thing that John sees in heaven is a throne. From first to last John's vision is dominated by this symbol of divine sovereignty. The final reality which will still be standing when heaven and earth have disappeared is the great white throne [Rev. 20:11]" (Caird, 62). Around this throne are twenty-four other thrones where the twenty-four elders are seated. They "are either angels representing all saints or the heads of the twelve tribes together with the twelve apostles, representing thus all the people of God" (G. K. Beale, *The Book of Revelation* [Grand Rapids, MI: Eerdmans, 1999], 322). There are four living creatures that surround the throne, and they sing without ceasing, "'Holy, holy, holy, the Lord God the Almighty, who was and is and is to come'" (Rev. 4:8, NRSV). When the creatures sing this, the twenty-four elders fall before the throne, worship, and cast their crowns before the One seated on the throne, singing, "'You are worthy, our Lord and God, to receive glory and honor and power, for you created all things, and by your will they existed and were created'" (Rev. 4:11, NRSV). The four living creatures serve as precentors. A *precentor* is one who directs worship, particularly through singing concurrently with the congregation or singing a line and having the congregation sing in response. The twenty-four elders then serve as the responding congregation in this instance. The language of the refrains and the depiction of the scene make it clear that God is the One who is on the throne. God is the Creator of all things and the One who lives forever. This scene of worship of God gives context for the scene that will follow.

In the following scene, there is a dilemma. There is a scroll with seven seals, "and no one in heaven or on earth or under the earth was able to open the scroll or look into it" (Rev. 5:3, NRSV). In the desperate search for the One who is able to open the seals of the scroll, one of the elders consoles John by saying, "'Do not weep. See, the Lion of the tribe of Judah, the Root of David, has conquered, so that he can open the scroll and its seven seals'" (Rev. 5:5, NRSV). The striking contrast comes about in the elder's description and John's vision. The elder has said that the *Lion* of Judah has conquered and now John sees a *Lamb* that has been slaughtered. The image of the slaughtered Lamb is connected to the lambs sacrificed for the Passover and the image in Isaiah 53:7, "like a lamb that is led to the slaughter" (NRSV; Beale, 351). It also builds further on the imagery of the Gospel of John where Jesus' crucifixion occurs at the same time the lambs are slaughtered for the Passover feast (see John 19:16-37). Of course, the Lamb standing in the midst of the heavenly court is Jesus Christ. The scandalous claim that is made about the nature of Jesus Christ in this scene is that He has conquered through death. The paradoxes, therefore, continue, thus revealing that the world as it appears is not the true nature of the world. The Lamb conquering

through being slaughtered reveals the ultimate powerlessness of those who believe they have control over life and death.

The Lamb is also described as "having seven horns and seven eyes, which are the seven spirits of God sent out into all the earth" (Rev. 5:6, NRSV). The horn is a symbol of strength, with seven indicating perfection in strength. The eye is a symbol of knowledge, with seven eyes indicating the omniscience of the Lamb. The seven eyes of the Lamb are also the seven spirits of God. "The seven spirits of God... have formerly been confined to the heavenly throne room... implying that they are agents only of God operating throughout the earth.... But, as a result of the death and resurrection, these spirits also become Christ's agents throughout the earth, who figuratively represent the Holy Spirit himself. The Spirit carries out the sovereign plan of the Lord" (Beale, 355). The Holy Spirit along with the One on the throne (the Father) and the slaughtered Lamb (the Son) is one of the fuller expressions of Trinitarian theology in the Bible. In this passage, we get a glimpse (though still shrouded in mystery) of the interaction of the Three Persons of the Trinity. Worship, again, plays a role in helping to identify these *Three as One*.

II. THE LAMB IS WORTHY (REVELATION 5:7-10)

Now that the Lamb enters the scene, the Lamb takes "the scroll from the right hand of the one who was seated on the throne" (Rev. 5:7, NRSV). As discussed in the previous lesson, the right hand of God should be understood as the power of God. The scroll is connected to the power of God. The Lamb's ability to take the scroll from the right hand of the One on the throne further reinforces the divine nature of the Lamb and the intimate connection between the Lamb and the One on the throne.

Now that the Lamb takes the scroll from the right hand of the One on the throne, the elders fall down in worship to the Lamb. This is a new occurrence in the book of Revelation. No one other than the One on the throne is worshiped throughout the book. John is in fact commanded twice not to worship the angel showing him the visions (see 19:10; 22:8-9). John also falls at the feet of the "one like the Son of Man" (1:13, NRSV) in Revelation 1:17, but this is likely not a scene of worship. It seems more likely that John falls "as though dead" out of fear (1:17, NRSV). This is made clear by the "one like the Son of Man" telling him, "'Do not be afraid'" (Rev. 1:17, NRSV). All of this demonstrates the special place of the Lamb as One who is worthy of being worshiped.

The elders fall before the Lamb with "each holding a harp and golden bowls full of incense, which are the prayers of the saints" (Rev. 5:8, NRSV). The harps clearly indicate the elders' worship of the Lamb. The golden bowls of incense are identified with the prayers of the saints. In identifying the bowls of incense with the prayers of the saints, John is drawing from the imagery of Psalm 141:2, "Let my prayer be counted as incense before you" (NRSV). There is a further connection between the prayers of the saints and the prayer of Psalm 141. The psalmist is crying for vindication from the Lord in the presence of His enemies. "The saints' prayers are to be identified with those of 6:9-11 and 8:4ff., which call for divine vindication of martyred believers and which are both directly linked to judgment of the ungodly. Therefore, the prayers mentioned here are not just praises but especially requests that God defend the honor of his reputation for justice by judging the persecutors of his people" (Beale, 357).

In response to the Lamb taking the scroll, the elders sing a "new song" (Rev. 6:9, NRSV). "In the OT a 'new song' is always an expression of praise for God's victory over the enemy, sometimes including thanksgiving for God's work of creation. In this case, the 'new song' celebrates the defeat of the powers of evil and sin" (Beale, 358). In this scene, the *new song* celebrates the victory of the Lamb in ushering in a new age through His death and resurrection. In this new age, the Lamb also creates a new people who are marked by the identity of being "a kingdom and priests" (Rev. 6:10, NRSV).

III. HEAVEN AND EARTH JOINED IN WORSHIP (REVELATION 5:11-13)

The worship escalates so that many angels join their voices to the creatures and the elders. They sing the same song about the Lamb that they sing about the One sitting on the throne. Every creature in heaven, on earth, and under the earth joins in the chorus. The song now connects the One seated on the throne to the Lamb. "The hymns in vv 9-12 emphasize Jesus' deity more than most other passages in the NT, addressing the Lamb in the same way as God is addressed in 4:11 and 5:13, especially in the clause 'worthy are you'" (ibid., 358). The Lamb is worthy because He has conquered death through His resurrection. "The Lamb's overcoming through death is a presupposition for his worthiness to receive sovereign authority" (Beale, 358-359). This is a further affirmation of the Lamb's deity in that the Lamb is declared worthy because the Lamb alone is able to open the seals.

In this image of all creation in heaven and earth and under the earth joining in the worship of the Lamb and the One on the throne, the reader should experience a sense of being overwhelmed. This is a point where worship is experienced in its full beauty and majesty. The entirety of creation joins in the worship. The picture is so powerful that all should be brought to their knees in worship of God—Father, Son, and Holy Spirit.

THE LESSON APPLIED

The worship that occurs in this scene is indicative of the ongoing victory of Jesus Christ, the slaughtered Lamb, over the powers of this world. In worship, the Church is to continue to proclaim and reenact this victory. Worship then moves the body of Christ through the entire drama of the history of the world. In worship, we proclaim the creation of the world through God's speech. We confess the sinfulness of rebellious humanity. We proclaim the ongoing decisive acts of the victory of God through the exodus, the crucifixion, and the resurrection. We cry out in prayer for the vindication of God's faithful. We praise God in song. We anticipate God's final victory in the experience of the Lord's Table. "If we are to know God at all, we must know him as the unfathomable mystery, a mystery to be explored only by the humility of worship" (Caird, 63).

LET'S TALK ABOUT IT

1. How should we approach reading the book of Revelation?

As pastors and teachers, we confront a difficult situation when it comes to encouraging our students and congregants to read the book of Revelation. Due to the difficult imagery of the book, we may even shy away from teaching from Revelation. As discussed above, the book of Revelation likely held a place of being read aloud in the context of worship. It may be helpful when approaching the teaching and reading of this book to read the entirety of it aloud in one sitting. This means also that the book needs to be read aloud and heard. It would be best then to have a group of people come together to experience the reading of the book aloud. There is a reality that only can be appreciated when the Word is spoken out loud.

HOME DAILY DEVOTIONAL READINGS
MARCH 24-30, 2014

MONDAY	TUESDAY	WEDNESDAY	THURSDAY	FRIDAY	SATURDAY	SUNDAY
The Lord Enthroned As King	The Lord Protects	The Lord Gives Victory	Loud Songs of Joy	Your Salvation Comes	Coming in the Lord's Name	The Triumphal Entry
Psalm 29	Zechariah 9:10-15	Psalm 20	Psalm 47	Isaiah 62:8-12	Psalm 118:21-29	Zechariah 9:9; Matthew 21:1-11

TRIUMPHANT AND VICTORIOUS

ADULT TOPIC:	BACKGROUND SCRIPTURES:
JOY AND CELEBRATION	ZECHARIAH 9:9-10; MATTHEW 21:1-11

ZECHARIAH 9:9; MATTHEW 21:1-11

King James Version

REJOICE greatly, O daughter of Zion; shout, O daughter of Jerusalem: behold, thy King cometh unto thee: he is just, and having salvation; lowly, and riding upon an ass, and upon a colt the foal of an ass.

• • • Matthew 21:1-11 • • •

AND when they drew nigh unto Jerusalem, and were come to Bethphage, unto the mount of Olives, then sent Jesus two disciples,

2 Saying unto them, Go into the village over against you, and straightway ye shall find an ass tied, and a colt with her: loose them, and bring them unto me.

3 And if any man say ought unto you, ye shall say, The Lord hath need of them; and straightway he will send them.

4 All this was done, that it might be fulfilled which was spoken by the prophet, saying,

5 Tell ye the daughter of Sion, Behold, thy King cometh unto thee, meek, and sitting upon an ass, and a colt the foal of an ass.

6 And the disciples went, and did as Jesus commanded them,

7 And brought the ass, and the colt, and put on them their clothes, and they set him thereon.

8 And a very great multitude spread their garments in the way; others cut down branches from the trees, and strawed them in the way.

9 And the multitudes that went before, and that followed, cried, saying, Hosanna to the son of David: Blessed is he that cometh in the name of the Lord; Hosanna in the highest.

New Revised Standard Version

REJOICE greatly, O daughter Zion! Shout aloud, O daughter Jerusalem! Lo, your king comes to you; triumphant and victorious is he, humble and riding on a donkey, on a colt, the foal of a donkey.

• • • Matthew 21:1-11 • • •

WHEN they had come near Jerusalem and had reached Bethphage, at the Mount of Olives, Jesus sent two disciples,

2 saying to them, "Go into the village ahead of you, and immediately you will find a donkey tied, and a colt with her; untie them and bring them to me.

3 If anyone says anything to you, just say this, 'The Lord needs them.' And he will send them immediately."

4 This took place to fulfill what had been spoken through the prophet, saying,

5 "Tell the daughter of Zion, Look, your king is coming to you, humble, and mounted on a donkey, and on a colt, the foal of a donkey."

6 The disciples went and did as Jesus had directed them;

7 they brought the donkey and the colt, and put their cloaks on them, and he sat on them.

8 A very large crowd spread their cloaks on the road, and others cut branches from the trees and spread them on the road.

9 The crowds that went ahead of him and that followed were shouting, "Hosanna to the Son of David! Blessed is the one who comes in the name of the Lord! Hosanna in the highest heaven!"

MAIN THOUGHT: And the multitudes that went before, and that followed, cried, saying, Hosanna to the son of David: Blessed is he that cometh in the name of the Lord; Hosanna in the highest. (Matthew 21:9, KJV)

ZECHARIAH 9:9; MATTHEW 21:1-11

King James Version

10 And when he was come into Jerusalem, all the city was moved, saying, Who is this?
11 And the multitude said, This is Jesus the prophet of Nazareth of Galilee.

New Revised Standard Version

10 When he entered Jerusalem, the whole city was in turmoil, asking, "Who is this?"
11 The crowds were saying, "This is the prophet Jesus from Nazareth in Galilee."

LESSON SETTING
Time: ca. A.D. 32
Place: Jerusalem

LESSON OUTLINE
I. The King Is Coming
   (Zechariah 9:9)
II. The King Prepares His Entrance
   (Matthew 21:1-6)
III. The King Has Come
   (Matthew 21:7-11)

UNIFYING PRINCIPLE

People of every generation and from every country have traditional rituals for welcoming dignitaries or heads of state. What is the most fitting way to celebrate the arrival of an honored person? The crowds who welcomed Jesus into Jerusalem spread out their cloaks on the road as a special gesture to recognize him as Messiah.

INTRODUCTION

This week's lesson concludes the study of the Davidic covenant with the familiar narrative about Jesus' Triumphal Entry into Jerusalem. Although no explicit reference is made to David in Zechariah 9:9, the return of the King to Zion/Jerusalem should recall to the minds of the readers the messianic hope of a Davidic king in 2 Samuel 7. This connection is made more explicit in Jesus' Triumphal Entry into Jerusalem as the crowd connects this entry

to Jesus being the Son of David. Jesus exemplifies His messianic Kingship by His entrance into the city.

That the Triumphal Entry narrative has been captured by all of the Gospels speaks to its importance (see Mark 11:1-10; Luke 19:29-44; John 12:12-19). Matthew's Gospel broadly chronicles the life of Jesus from His miraculous birth to His sacrificial death, resurrection, and ascension. The Triumphal Entry falls toward the end of Matthew's account and takes place early in the week prior to Jesus' crucifixion as He and His Disciples make their way to Jerusalem.

Matthew identifies Jesus as the Son of David throughout his Gospel. He identifies Jesus in this way to open the genealogy (see Matt. 1:1); the angel of the Lord calls Joseph son of David (see Matt. 1:20); Jesus is called out to in this way five times in connection with healing (two blind men twice, first in Matt. 9:27, then in 20:30-31; the crowds wonder if He is the Son of David after the healing of the demoniac who was blind and mute in 12:22-23; the Canaanite woman calling for mercy for her daughter who was being tormented by a demon in 15:22; healing in the temple after the Triumphal Entry and cleansing of the temple in 21:15); and finally the Pharisees respond to Jesus' question about the Messiah by identifying the Messiah as the Son of David (see Matt. 22:41-46). The Triumphal Entry thus serves as a turning point in Jesus' explicit self-identification as the Son of David. He thus entered Jerusalem in this way, knowing it would lead to His death. We know of this foreknowledge of Jesus through His predicting His death three times in Matthew (16:21; 17:22-23; 20:17-19). The Triumphal Entry attests that Jesus is also the Messiah—the anointed One—who would be Ruler over all. Thus the crowd in Jerusalem celebrates His entry into the city with palms.

EXPOSITION

I. THE KING IS COMING (ZECHARIAH 9:9)

The Triumphal Entry is celebrated by many churches on Palm Sunday one week before Easter. Palm Sunday is the first day of Holy Week, which reenacts Jesus' entry into Jerusalem, the last supper and the foot washing, the crucifixion, the burial, and the resurrection. This is a deeply formative, orienting period in the Church's year as we experience the culmination of the Law and the Prophets in the Person of Jesus. The Triumphal Entry of Jesus was prophesied by Zechariah, who was both a prophet and a priest. The ministry of Zechariah overlapped the ministry of Haggai as both prophets preached to the Israelites in Jerusalem after spending approximately seventy years in captivity in Babylon.

The reader of the book of Zechariah may note its complex and seemingly disjointed structure as Zechariah wrote using a mixture of genres, including sermons, poetry, oracles of judgment, and apocalyptic literature (George L. Klein, *Zechariah*,

[Nashville: Broadman & Holman, 2008], 27). Based on its messages, the book can be divided into two sections with chapters 1—8 containing dated visions and sermons, and chapters 9—14 containing poetic oracles and descriptions of judgment and blessings (ibid.). Although some scholars identify Zechariah as being written by two different writers because of the differing styles of the first and second sections, the reader does not have to assume that this is the case. "The differences between the two portions of Zechariah should not be underestimated. Nevertheless, one may challenge whether these differences represent adequate grounds for postulating divergent authorship as well. The book of Jeremiah, whose authorship has remained relatively unchallenged, illustrates that a single biblical author may fully employ significantly diverse genres" (ibid.).

The first half of Zechariah 9 (vv. 1-8) is the pronouncement of judgment on Israel's enemies while Israel enjoys deliverance. Verses 9-17 describe the advent of Israel's King and the blessings that are in store for God's people. The writer draws on other Old Testament texts to not only help the Israelites envision the future, but also to "portray the future as a recapitulation and thus as a restoration" of the hopes of Israel's past (Ben C. Ollenburger, "The Book of Zechariah" in *The New Interpreter's Bible*, Vol. 7 [Nashville, TN: Abingdon Press, 1996], 740).

After suffering through defeat and a long captivity at the hands of their enemies, the news of a coming King as described by Zechariah in verse nine had to be a welcome message of hope. Zechariah paints a vivid picture of the entrance of the King and begins by instructing the Israelites to celebrate. Ollenburger says shouting and rejoicing for joy were connected with the celebration of God as King (see Psalms 47; 96; 98). However, "Zechariah … instructs Zion/Jerusalem to rejoice and shout at the entrance of a human King, not of Yahweh as king" (Ollenburger, 807). Though Zechariah does not provide a name for the future King, the language of verse nine makes it clear that He will be from the house of David.

Next Zechariah provides a description of the character of the coming King. He says the King will be "righteous" (NIV). Other translations use the word "just" (KJV) and "triumphant" (NRSV); however, Ollenburger says "legitimate" may be a better translation (807). The Hebrew term used here is *tsadiq*, which "is used in Jer. 23:5 to describe the 'Branch,' specifically to say that he will be a legitimate heir of David" (ibid.). This legitimacy needs to be understood in terms of righteousness. Righteousness is defined by having a faithful relationship with God. Therefore, the legitimate heir of David, in whom Israel and the world has their hopes, would be the King who relates faithfully to God the Father.

Finally, verse nine says the coming King will be "riding on a donkey," specifically, "on a colt, the foal of a donkey" (NIV). Of note here, the King will make His entrance on a young animal, and not the adult mule. In the Old Testament, the mule was the choice mount of nobility (see 1 Kings 1:33, 38, 44). However, the starker contrast would be between how the kings of the nations enter a city they have conquered and how this King would enter Jerusalem. The kings of the nations would enter the city riding on a war-horse, a symbol of their power. This King, however, is humble and rides into the city on the foal of a donkey.

II. THE KING PREPARES HIS ENTRANCE (MATTHEW 21:1-6)

In the Gospel of Matthew, Jesus is with His Disciples near Bethphage and is making arrangements for His entry into Jerusalem. Though the Triumphal Entry narrative is recorded in all four Gospels, Matthew relies on the Markan account as the source for much of his content (M. Eugene Boring, "The Gospel of Matthew" in *The New Interpreter's Bible*, Vol. 8 [Nashville, TN: Abingdon Press, 1996], 403). In most places, Matthew follows the Markan text closely but deviates on some points. For example, Matthew identifies that the entrance into Jerusalem occurred on Monday, while Mark identifies the day as Sunday. Boring writes, "In both Mark and Matthew, the first identifiable day of the week is Wednesday, 'the two days before the Passover' of Mark 14:1 = Matt. 26:1" (400). With the Passover beginning on Thursday evening and "by counting backward from Wednesday … we arrive at Monday for the Triumphal Entry in Matthew, which was a Sunday in Mark." Boring contends that when Matthew rewrote the narrative, he reduced two Markan days to one, but this does not change the meaning as both writers were demonstrating the connection to the Passover (400).

In verses 1-2, Jesus and His Disciples are journeying to Jerusalem. They traveled seventeen miles from Jericho (see Matt. 20:29) and arrived at Bethany. They pause just before they reach Bethphage, which is near the Mount of Olives. Matthew is intentional about including the Mount of Olives in his narrative because of Zechariah's mention of an eschatological event there (Boring, 403; see also Zech. 14:4). Jesus gives instructions to two of His disciples: "'Go to the village ahead of you, and at once you will find a donkey tied there, with her colt by her. Untie them and bring them to me'" (v. 2, NIV).

Matthew makes explicit reference to the prophecy of Zechariah in verses 4-5. However, he "omits Zechariah's characterization of the king as 'righteous and saving' ... in order to place all the emphasis on Jesus as the 'humble' and 'gentle' ... king who redefines the nature of kingship" (Boring, 403). Matthew mentions a donkey and a colt while the other Gospel writers mention only the colt. Some commentary writers believe the reason for this difference is that Matthew misunderstood the parallelism in Zechariah 9:9; however, Matthew is likely relying on rabbinic methods to show that Jesus fulfilled the prophecy down to the smallest detail (Boring, 403).

III. THE KING HAS COME (MATTHEW 21:7-11)

The Disciples follow Jesus' instructions and bring "the donkey and the colt" to Him (v. 7, NIV). They place their cloaks on the animals for Jesus to sit on. The crowds gather for Jesus' entry to Jerusalem. "These crowds pave Jesus' way into the city with shouts of acclamation and with their own cloaks and branches.... In their acclamation of Jesus, the crowds use words from Ps. 118:25-26, the last of the Hallel psalms sung at Passover. 'Hosanna'...was originally a prayer, 'Save I/we beseech you,' but by the first century had become a contentless, festive shout, something like a religious 'hurrah,' with no more literal meaning than 'Good-bye' (also originally a prayer, 'God be with you')" (Boring, 403). The crowd calls Jesus "Son of David." This is the fifth time that Matthew has shown Jesus being proclaimed the Son of David by regular people.

While the crowds use the proper language to address Jesus as He enters Jerusalem, they still misunderstand the claim Jesus' ministry is making upon them. They offer their praise to Jesus, but they also attempt to drive away the blind men who proclaim Jesus as the Son of David and ask for healing (see Matt. 20:29-34). These are the same the crowds who will later cry out for the crucifixion of Jesus. While Jesus embodies the righteous King entering the city of Jerusalem from Zechariah 9:9, the crowds misunderstand the nature of this King. Their eyes will need to be opened to this reality (relying here on Boring, 403-404).

THE LESSON APPLIED

Throughout his Gospel, Matthew records the works of Jesus, who preached and taught about the Kingdom of heaven with unmatched wisdom and authority. Jesus taught about the nature of life in the Kingdom (see Matt. 5). He also gave lessons on how to pray and fast (6:5-18). Beyond that Jesus performed many miracles of healing people of devastating diseases such as leprosy (8:2-3) and paralysis (9:2-7) to feeding five thousand people with "five loaves and two fish" (14:15-21, NIV). Because of all that He did, Jesus deserved accolades, but He did not exalt Himself (see Phil. 2:6-11). He avoided public recognition until the time was right.

As presented in our lesson, that time came when Jesus mounted a colt and rode into Jerusalem, making His Triumphal Entry. The statement He made to the crowd that day is one He continues to make—I am the Messiah, the King of kings, and the Lord of lords. In recognition of His messiahship, the people laid palm branches and their clothing upon Jesus' path, giving Him the highest praise. In the end, this same crowd of people rejected Jesus, denying His rule over them. These were empty words of praise. Often, today's Christians treat the words of worship in the same manner. We hold onto sin and have not sacrificially committed it all to Him. Yet at the same time, we shout and sing praises to Him. It's time to lay everything at the feet of Jesus.

LET'S TALK ABOUT IT

1. What difference does it make that Jesus presented Himself as a humble King rather than a demanding Ruler?

The opposite of humility is pride, which is often taught in today's culture as a virtue. However, the Old Testament reveals God hates "a proud look" (Prov. 6:16-17, KJV) and promises to "destroy the house of the proud" (Prov. 15:25, KJV). In the New Testament, James builds on this wisdom tradition, writing, "'God opposes the proud, but gives grace to the humble'" (4:6, NRSV). Throughout biblical history, people have fallen because of pride. Consider King Uzziah. The writer of Chronicles writes, "When he had become strong he grew proud, to his destruction" (2 Chron. 26:16, NRSV). Although, Uzziah did not turn away from God to worship other gods, he became prideful in his manner of serving God so he was struck with leprosy for the rest of his life (see 2 Chron. 26:1-23).

Prideful people value themselves more than others, are more concerned about their own comfort, and can make sharp, hurtful statements. In contrast, a humble person has an attitude of being gentle, kind, gracious, and putting others before self. Jesus humbly embodies these characteristics through sharing in the divine life. If Jesus had denied Himself (which is impossible), and presented Himself as an arrogant, demanding King, we would still be lost and without hope. The Lamb that was slain for our sins had to be without blemish (see 1 Pet. 1:18-19). If He did not live the perfect life, His death, burial, and resurrection would not have had their desired effect.

HOME DAILY DEVOTIONAL READINGS
MARCH 31—APRIL 6, 2014

MONDAY	TUESDAY	WEDNESDAY	THURSDAY	FRIDAY	SATURDAY	SUNDAY
The Holy Temple	The House of the Lord	I Cried for Help	My Prayer Came to You	Something Greater Than the Temple	A Holy Temple in the Lord	A House of Prayer
Habakkuk 2:18-20	Psalm 27:1-5	Psalm 18:1-6	Jonah 2:1-9	Matthew 12:1-8	Ephesians 2:11-22	Isaiah 56:6-7; Jeremiah 7:9-11; Mark 11:15-19

JESUS CLEANSES THE TEMPLE

ADULT TOPIC:	BACKGROUND SCRIPTURES:
PRESERVING PLACES OF HERITAGE	ISAIAH 56:6-8; JEREMIAH 7:8-15; MARK 11:15-19

ISAIAH 56:6-7; JEREMIAH 7:9-11; MARK 11:15-19

King James Version

ALSO the sons of the stranger, that join themselves to the LORD, to serve him, and to love the name of the LORD, to be his servants, every one that keepeth the sabbath from polluting it, and taketh hold of my covenant.

7 Even them will I bring to my holy mountain, and make them joyful in my house of prayer: their burnt offerings and their sacrifices shall be accepted upon mine altar; for mine house shall be called an house of prayer for all people.

••• Jeremiah 7:9-11 •••

WILL ye steal, murder, and commit adultery, and swear falsely, and burn incense unto Baal, and walk after other gods whom ye know not;

10 And come and stand before me in this house, which is called by my name, and say, We are delivered to do all these abominations?

11 Is this house, which is called by my name, become a den of robbers in your eyes? Behold, even I have seen it, saith the LORD.

••• Mark 11:15-19 •••

AND they come to Jerusalem: and Jesus went into the temple, and began to cast out them that sold and bought in the temple, and overthrew the tables of the moneychangers, and the seats of them that sold doves.

16 And would not suffer that any man should carry any vessel through the temple.

17 And he taught, saying unto them, Is it not written, My house shall be called of all nations

New Revised Standard Version

AND the foreigners who join themselves to the LORD, to minister to him, to love the name of the LORD, and to be his servants, all who keep the sabbath, and do not profane it, and hold fast my covenant—

7 these I will bring to my holy mountain, and make them joyful in my house of prayer; their burnt offerings and their sacrifices will be accepted on my altar; for my house shall be called a house of prayer for all peoples.

••• Jeremiah 7:9-11 •••

WILL you steal, murder, commit adultery, swear falsely, make offerings to Baal, and go after other gods that you have not known,

10 and then come and stand before me in this house, which is called by my name, and say, "We are safe!"—only to go on doing all these abominations?

11 Has this house, which is called by my name, become a den of robbers in your sight? You know, I too am watching, says the LORD.

••• Mark 11:15-19 •••

THEN they came to Jerusalem. And he entered the temple and began to drive out those who were selling and those who were buying in the temple, and he overturned the tables of the money changers and the seats of those who sold doves;

16 and he would not allow anyone to carry anything through the temple.

17 He was teaching and saying, "Is it not written, 'My house shall be called a house of prayer

MAIN THOUGHT: Is this house, which is called by my name, become a den of robbers in your eyes? Behold, even I have seen it, saith the LORD. (Jeremiah 7:11, KJV)

Isaiah 56:6-7; Jeremiah 7:9-11; Mark 11:15-19

King James Version

the house of prayer? but ye have made it a den of thieves.

18 And the scribes and chief priests heard it, and sought how they might destroy him: for they feared him, because all the people was astonished at his doctrine.

19 And when even was come, he went out of the city.

New Revised Standard Version

for all the nations'? But you have made it a den of robbers."

18 And when the chief priests and the scribes heard it, they kept looking for a way to kill him; for they were afraid of him, because the whole crowd was spellbound by his teaching.

19 And when evening came, Jesus and his disciples went out of the city.

LESSON SETTING

>   Time: ca A.D. 32
>   Place: Jerusalem

LESSON OUTLINE

I. **Welcome to the House of Prayer**
    (Isaiah 56:6-7)

II. **Corruption in the House of Prayer**
    (Jeremiah 7:9-11)

III. **Cleansing the House of Prayer**
    (Mark 11:15-19)

UNIFYING PRINCIPLE

When an activity becomes rote, the original helpful intents and purposes may be lost and replaced by new, harmful ones. How can a good activity be prevented from evolving into an unintended harmful result? Jesus' angry action in the temple called attention to the ways in which the priests and worshipers had lost sight of the tradition of God's dwelling place as a house of prayer for all peoples.

INTRODUCTION

This second unit of lessons is the study of biblical prophecies foretold and fulfilled, specifically concerning the life of Jesus. This first lesson focuses on Jesus' cleansing of the temple.

The nature of prophecy in the Old Testament as it relates to how the life of Jesus is narrated in the New Testament is a complicated matter. Prophecies often do not work in a straightforward prediction-fulfillment manner, and this is true of today's texts. The prophecies of Isaiah and Jeremiah were addressed to specific circumstances in their time. We can see this most easily in the text from Jeremiah, in which Jeremiah compares the use of the temple by people in his day to robbers going to a hideout after committing their theft. As we engage the prophets and Jesus' interpretations of their writings in His life, we will see that Jesus often draws out fuller meaning from the prophetic writings than the original writers may have anticipated. This should not serve as a means of discounting the foresight of the prophets, but should serve to remind us that Jesus, God Incarnate, works in ways that confound the understanding of those in His time on earth and those of our time as well.

In the context of this lesson, Jesus refers to the temple as the "house of prayer" (Mark 11:17). This name has historical significance. The temple in Jerusalem was destroyed and rebuilt several times.

Solomon began building the temple in 966 B.C. and completed it seven years later. This first temple was destroyed by the Babylonian army in 586 B.C. (Geoffrey Wigoder, et al., eds., *Illustrated Dictionary & Concordance of the Bible* [Jerusalem: G.G. The Jerusalem Publishing House Ltd., 1986], 975-6). However, the temple was rebuilt after the Israelites returned from Babylonian exile. "The rebuilt (Second) Temple, which was more modest than the first, was defiled and rededicated during the Hasmonean period and was eventually demolished and totally rebuilt as a magnificent new structure by King Herod. Herod's Temple was destroyed by Roman legions in A.D. 70" (ibid., 976). The temple in Mark 11 is Herod's temple.

When Solomon dedicated the temple, he devoted a large portion of his dedication to prayer, asking God to hear the prayers of those who pray in or toward the temple (see 1 Kings 8:22-53). God responded, "'I have consecrated this temple, which you have built, by putting my Name there forever. My eyes and my heart will always be there'" (1 Kings 9:3, NIV). It was a sacred place that had been dedicated to God and God promised to remain there. Prayer was important in the temple, as it was intended to orient the prayer on the Lord's desires.

EXPOSITION

I. WELCOME TO THE HOUSE OF PRAYER
(ISAIAH 56:6-7)

The temple was first referred to as the "house of prayer" in the Old Testament. One particular occasion was in Isaiah 56:6-7. In this passage, God expands the vision of the temple to include Israelites and those who were previously excluded (foreigners and eunuchs) in the service of the Lord. It is a clear demonstration of the nature of God's grace. In restoring the Israelites to their calling of being God's representatives in the world, God also shows grace to the outsiders to whom the Israelites are called to demonstrate God's glory. God communicates this message through the prophet Isaiah.

Isaiah received his call during the latter reign of King Uzziah (see Isa. 6). Isaiah prophesies judgment on Israel for their wicked deeds, but also hope for a restored future in which God makes all things right. It is difficult to determine sharp breaks in the text that clearly define the different time periods of Isaiah's ministry. It is beyond the scope of this commentary to engage the larger discussion of how to divide the time periods of the book. However, we will work with a basic outline of Isaiah 1—39 (pre-exilic), 40—55 (exilic), and 56—66 (post-exilic). During the pre-exilic period Isaiah received a vision concerning the Israelites' activities (see Isa. 1:2-31). He saw Israel's guilt of turning away from God, and as a result, they were broken and desolate (vv. 2-9).

During the exile, Isaiah spoke words of comfort to the displaced Israelites as they wondered if God had forsaken them. Isaiah comforts them by speaking of God's promise that their suffering is coming to an end and they will be restored. This is possible because the Lord's power exceeds all others and will not be limited by the nations or other gods (see Isa. 40:1-31).

Although today's passage could be roughly identified with the post-exilic period of Isaiah's ministry, it is important to note that the themes of judgment and restoration run throughout the book. The particular focus of this text is that of the Lord welcoming non-Israelites and other outsiders into His house of prayer. This is the original intention of the Lord's calling the Israelites to be His people. This is the command implicit in God's original call and blessing of Abram (see Gen. 12:1-3). This is why the failure to uphold the Lord's commands caused the Israelites to go into exile. The Israelites had been freed from physical captivity in Babylon but were still separated from God because of sin. Thus God sets the conditions of their return. "'Maintain justice and do what is right, for my salvation is close at hand and my righteousness will soon be revealed. Blessed is the man who does this, the man who holds it fast, who keeps the Sabbath without desecrating it, and keeps his hand from doing any evil'" (NIV).

This passage also serves as a message of hope for eunuchs and foreigners. To the eunuchs who obey, God promises to give "an everlasting name that will not be cut off" (v. 5, NIV). Similarly, God will bless foreigners. They are required to love the name of God, become God's servant, and keep the Sabbath (v. 6, NIV). "Both 56:1-8 and 65—6 . . . not only give foreigners access to the temple (56:7; 66:21 by implication), but also permit them into the priesthood. With respect to the latter point, Isaiah 56:6 indicates the priestly duty of the foreigner with the expression [*sharat Yahweh*], this verb with human as subject and God as direct object is always otherwise being used of priests. Likewise, Isaiah 66:21 promises access to the priesthood for foreigners participating in the

return ('I will also take some of them to be Levitical Priests')" (Jacob Stromberg, *Isaiah After Exile* [New York: Oxford University Press, 2011], 14).

Finally, in verse seven, God promises to bring those who heed Isaiah's message to "my holy mountain" (v. 7, NIV). This verse not only gives foreigners access to the temple, but also permits them into the priesthood because they will be accepted at God's altar. "The Lord . . . chose Jerusalem as the sacred place and its center, Mt. Zion, as the place where the Lord would encounter the people in the Temple" (Gene M. Tucker, "The Book of Isaiah 1—39" in *The New Interpreter's Bible*, Vol. 6 [Nashville: Abingdon Press, 2001], 38). The temple or the house of prayer for all nations is where all will be accepted and given joy, including foreign worshipers, who have fully joined themselves to Israel's Lord.

II. CORRUPTION IN THE HOUSE OF PRAYER (JEREMIAH 7:9-11)

A key theme in today's text is the nature of true worship in the temple. As discussed earlier, the temple plays a prominent role in the history of Israel. Its destruction often accompanies Judah's falls. The temple is thought to be a safeguard against all enemies, but the destruction of the temple indicates that the temple provided no means of safety if the people had rebelled against God. Jeremiah is prophesying the coming destruction of the temple because God's people have used their worship as an attempt to manipulate the Lord.

The prophet has received a word from God, who instructed Jeremiah to preach His message from the temple gate, speaking to the people of Judah as they entered the temple. Jeremiah addressed the people twice from this location—first in this passage, and again in Jeremiah 26. However, on the second occasion the prophet is nearly killed by the hearers because of his message.

In Jeremiah 7, Jeremiah is standing at the gates of the temple, proclaiming a message from the Lord concerning the nature of worship in the temple. This message, or sermon, "addresses two perennial and interrelated issues in the Judean community: (1) the incongruity between the worship of the people and their way of life and (2) the inviolability of the Temple. The underlying question was whether the continued existence of the Temple as God's dwelling place ... constituted a security blanket over the land, especially Jerusalem, ensuring God's protection from harm for Zion, no matter what the people did or how they behaved" (Patrick D. Miller, "The Book of Jeremiah," in *The New Interpreter's Bible*, Vol. 6 [Nashville: Abingdon Press, 2001], 635). However, Jeremiah preached this was not true and gave "a clear and emphatic no to the widespread assumption that Zion was secure, and that God would never let anything happen to the Temple" (ibid.).

Jeremiah's presence in the temple, preaching God's message of judgment upon the people essentially transforms the scene into a courtroom. Jeremiah is announcing the various sins—theft, murder, adultery, false witness, and idolatry—of which the people are guilty. In the guilt incurred by these sins, the people are also guilty of breaking covenant with the Lord. Their continued worship in the temple only serves to intensify the problem, as it demonstrates a lack of concern for their actions. "What is astonishing in the Lord's eyes is that the people can violate the most fundamental of the covenantal stipulations and yet go into worship in the Temple ... and go right back out to commit the same crimes and sins" (Miller, 637).

Jeremiah makes an inevitable determination: the temple is no longer a place of worship. It has now become a "den of robbers," a place to hide out after doing their misdeeds. Because of the abuse of this temple, it will be subject to destruction. Those who have abused the temple will no longer have sanctuary in the place they have defiled. Their sins have driven God's special presence from the temple.

III. CLEANSING THE HOUSE OF PRAYER (MARK 11:15-19)

In the Gospel of Mark, Jesus first enters the temple after the triumphal entry simply to observe what is happening. He returns the next day and denounces the money changers and dove sellers by overturning their tables and benches. "This episode is commonly referred to as the 'Cleansing of the Temple,' even though it does not involve ritual purification of a sanctuary that has been defiled" (Pheme Perkins, "The Gospel of Mark," in *The New Interpreter's Bible*, Vol. 8 [Nashville: Abingdon Press, 1995] 661). Instead, *cleansing* refers to Jesus driving out those who defiled the temple.

This cleansing occurs the week before Passover. Therefore, travelers are buying sacrificial animals for offerings in the temple. However, Jesus took issue because business was being conducted in the outer

Court of the Gentiles. Donald English writes, "The bone of contention is that the place intended for Gentiles ('*all nations*') to pray, was being misused by the Jews for trade (and profit)" (*The Message of Mark* [Downers Grove, IL: InterVarsity Press, 1992], 190). Jesus' prophetic action would not allow anyone to pass through.

After throwing out the money changers, Jesus explains His actions to His Disciples by quoting from Isaiah 56:7 and Jeremiah 7:11. "Those in charge of the Temple, the chief priests and scribes, perceive this teaching as an attack on them" (Perkins, 663). Therefore, they began to look for ways to kill Him. According to English (190), this may prove to be a difficult task "because the whole crowd was amazed at his teaching" (Mark 11:18, NIV). The cleansing of the temple was a messianic act that established Jesus' authority and ownership of the temple. He is not just Lord of the Sabbath (Mark 2:28), but also Lord of the temple.

THE LESSON APPLIED

The concern in today's texts is the relationship between worship and ethics. Isaiah paints the picture of the temple where those who were previously excluded can come to the temple to worship the Lord. Isaiah also affirms that those who come to worship must bind themselves to the Lord's commands. Jeremiah's concern is that those who are worshiping in the temple are doing so in a way that disgraces the Name of the Lord. Jesus has both of these pictures in mind as He drives out the buyers and sellers from the temple. In identifying the temple as "a den of robbers," Jesus echoes the prophecy of Jeremiah, which signaled the end of the first temple. The temple that Jesus enters will also be destroyed because it has not fulfilled the call to be "a house of prayer for all nations." This is a call that now lives on in the Church as we are called to be people who faithfully embody God's desires for His people. ///

LET'S TALK ABOUT IT

1. Why was Jesus' anger not counted as sin?

The anger of Jesus Christ in the temple is consistent with the anger of the Lord in the Old Testament when the Israelites rebelled against His purposes. The anger of the Lord in the Old Testament and the anger of Jesus in the temple are both concerned with the restoration of a people in rebellion. Thus it is not that Jesus is angry simply for the sake of being angry. Rather, His anger is derived from a desire to restore a faithful practice of worship in the temple. Therefore, this should be construed as holy anger.

HOME DAILY DEVOTIONAL READINGS
APRIL 7-13, 2014

MONDAY	TUESDAY	WEDNESDAY	THURSDAY	FRIDAY	SATURDAY	SUNDAY
An Established Throne Forever	Light Has Dawned	Seated on the Throne of Glory	The Kingdom of God's Beloved Son	A Better Hope	King of Kings, Lord of Lords	Here Is the Man
1 Chronicles 17:7-14	Matthew 4:12-17	Matthew 19:23-30	Colossians 1:9-14	Hebrews 7:11-19	Revelation 19:11-16	Jeremiah 23:5-6; Zechariah 6:9-14; John 19:1-5

A MESSIANIC PRIEST-KING

ADULT TOPIC:
A PERCEIVED THREAT

BACKGROUND SCRIPTURES:
JEREMIAH 23:5–6; ZECHARIAH 6:9–15;
JOHN 19:1–5; HEBREWS 7:13

JEREMIAH 23:5–6; ZECHARIAH 6:9–15; JOHN 19:1–5

King James Version

BEHOLD, the days come, saith the LORD, that I will raise unto David a righteous Branch, and a King shall reign and prosper, and shall execute judgment and justice in the earth.

6 In his days Judah shall be saved, and Israel shall dwell safely: and this is his name whereby he shall be called, THE LORD OUR RIGHTEOUSNESS.

• • • Zechariah 6:9-15 • • •

AND the word of the LORD came unto me, saying,

10 Take of them of the captivity, even of Heldai, of Tobijah, and of Jedaiah, which are come from Babylon, and come thou the same day, and go into the house of Josiah the son of Zephaniah;

11 Then take silver and gold, and make crowns, and set them upon the head of Joshua the son of Josedech, the high priest;

12 And speak unto him, saying, Thus speaketh the LORD of hosts, saying, Behold the man whose name is The BRANCH; and he shall grow up out of his place, and he shall build the temple of the LORD:

13 Even he shall build the temple of the LORD; and he shall bear the glory, and shall sit and rule upon his throne; and he shall be a priest upon his throne: and the counsel of peace shall be between them both.

New Revised Standard Version

THE days are surely coming, says the LORD, when I will raise up for David a righteous Branch, and he shall reign as king and deal wisely, and shall execute justice and righteousness in the land.

6 In his days Judah will be saved and Israel will live in safety. And this is the name by which he will be called: "The LORD is our righteousness."

• • • Zechariah 6:9-15 • • •

THE word of the LORD came to me:

10 Collect silver and gold from the exiles—from Heldai, Tobijah, and Jedaiah—who have arrived from Babylon; and go the same day to the house of Josiah son of Zephaniah.

11 Take the silver and gold and make a crown, and set it on the head of the high priest Joshua son of Jehozadak;

12 say to him: Thus says the LORD of hosts: Here is a man whose name is Branch: for he shall branch out in his place, and he shall build the temple of the LORD.

13 It is he that shall build the temple of the LORD; he shall bear royal honor, and shall sit upon his throne and rule. There shall be a priest by his throne, with peaceful understanding between the two of them.

MAIN THOUGHT: And said, Hail, King of the Jews! and they smote him with their hands. (John 19:3, KJV)

King James Version	*New Revised Standard Version*
14 And the crowns shall be to Helem, and to Tobijah, and to Jedaiah, and to Hen the son of Zephaniah, for a memorial in the temple of the LORD.	14 And the crown shall be in the care of Heldai, Tobijah, Jedaiah, and Josiah son of Zephaniah, as a memorial in the temple of the LORD.
15 And they that are far off shall come and build in the temple of the LORD, and ye shall know that the LORD of hosts hath sent me unto you. And this shall come to pass, if ye will diligently obey the voice of the LORD your God.	15 Those who are far off shall come and help to build the temple of the LORD; and you shall know that the LORD of hosts has sent me to you. This will happen if you diligently obey the voice of the LORD your God.

• • • John 19:1-5 • • •

THEN Pilate therefore took Jesus, and scourged him.	THEN Pilate took Jesus and had him flogged.
2 And the soldiers platted a crown of thorns, and put it on his head, and they put on him a purple robe,	2 And the soldiers wove a crown of thorns and put it on his head, and they dressed him in a purple robe.
3 And said, Hail, King of the Jews! and they smote him with their hands.	3 They kept coming up to him, saying, "Hail, King of the Jews!" and striking him on the face.
4 Pilate therefore went forth again, and saith unto them, Behold, I bring him forth to you, that ye may know that I find no fault in him.	4 Pilate went out again and said to them, "Look, I am bringing him out to you to let you know that I find no case against him."
5 Then came Jesus forth, wearing the crown of thorns, and the purple robe. And Pilate saith unto them, Behold the man!	5 So Jesus came out, wearing the crown of thorns and the purple robe. Pilate said to them, "Here is the man!"

LESSON SETTING

Time: 605 B.C. (JEREMIAH); 520 B.C. (ZECHARIAH); A.D. 30 (JOHN)

Place: Jerusalem

LESSON OUTLINE

I. **A Righteous King** (Jeremiah 23:5-6)

II. **A Crown for the King** (Zechariah 6:9-15)

III. **King of the Jews** (John 19:1-5)

UNIFYING PRINCIPLE

People tend to lash out at perceived threats to their established power. How do people form a perception of threat? The perception of Jesus as a king who would exercise political rule and power made him seem to be a threat to the existing Roman and Jewish powers.

INTRODUCTION

These three books are separated in time by approximately seven hundred years. The book of Jeremiah follows the prophet's ministry, which began between 627 and 622 B.C. during Josiah's reign and continued through the subsequent kings, the sacking of Jerusalem with its attendant deportations, and Jeremiah's exile in Egypt (Patrick D. Miller, "The Book of Jeremiah" in *The New Interpreter's Bible,*

Vol. 6 [Nashville: Abingdon Press, 2001], 555, 561). On the other hand, dating John is difficult, such that any time from just before A.D. 70 to the beginning of the second century has scholarly backing (Leon Morris, *The Gospel According to John,* Revised Ed. [Grand Rapids: Eerdmans, 1995], 25-30). Zechariah falls between the other two books, beginning with his ministry in post-exile Judah ca. 520 B.C. ("Zechariah" in Pamela J. Scalise, *Minor Prophets II* [Grand Rapids: Baker Books, 2009], 180).

It is too easy to forget that the claims of Jesus' kingship were political in nature, threatening both the Jewish elite and the Roman Empire. The Old Testament writers were understandably looking for an earthly fulfillment of God's political promises of a Davidic king while John believed Jesus to be the fulfillment of these and other prophecies and so reigns in a very real, albeit unexpected, way. All three texts accept that God's coming king will be a political power to whom all of the world will one day bow.

EXPOSITION

I. A RIGHTEOUS KING (JEREMIAH 23:5-6)

Recall God's promise to David: "Your house and your kingdom shall be made sure forever before me; your throne shall be established forever" (2 Sam. 7:16, NRSV). Jeremiah reminds the people of this promise in verses 5-6, which comprise the second in a series of three prose sermons found at the beginning of Jeremiah 23 (Miller, 744). Together, the sermons reflect primarily on the judgment of the kings of Judah and offer hope for the future of the monarchy (ibid.).

According to Leslie Allen, "The poem promises a future Davidic monarchy, but it is not 'eschatological' in the sense that it contains anything that deviates from the course of ongoing human history under Yahweh's providential control" (*Jeremiah* [Louisville: Westminster John Knox Press, 2008], 259).

The verses begin by talking respectively about "'the days'" and "'his days'" (vv. 5-6, NRSV), recalling other prophetic language about the day of the Lord which would be a day of rejoicing for those who kept covenant and a day of terror for those who did not (see Amos 5:18; Ezek. 30:3; Zeph. 1:14.). These two verses also play on the Hebrew root *tsdq*, which frequently translates as "righteousness" (Allen, 258). The same root appears in the name of Judah's last king, Zedekiah (Heb. *Tsideqiyyahu*, "the Lord is my righteousness"). This root is not used explicitly in either verse but may be meant as a foil to the new King's name, *Yahweh tsidqenu*, "'the LORD is our righteousness'" (Heb. *Yahweh tisdqenu*) (ibid., 259). The repetition and wordplay create cohesion in the verses. Jeremiah's audience knows Zedekiah well, as he was placed on the throne by Babylon. Jehoiachin, his nephew, had been king until his exile in Babylon; many expected him to return and take the throne. Zedekiah was a weak ruler who neither opposed Jeremiah nor offered support. After being forced into a rebellion by the powerful Judean upper class, Zedekiah saw his children executed and then had his eyes put out—a heinous punishment (Miller, 559-560).

The king to come will not be like Zedekiah. Instead, this king He "shall reign as king and deal wisely, and execute justice and righteousness in the land" (Jer. 23:5, NRSV). It is unlikely that a king like this will be bribed into obstructing justice. Further, "in his days Judah will be saved and Israel will live in safety" (v. 6, NRSV). It is doubtful that this new king will be bullied into insurrection, especially against God. The "Branch" (v. 5, NRSV) language found here is echoed in Zechariah's prophecies, and will be examined in the next section.

II. A CROWN FOR THE KING (ZECHARIAH 6:9-15)

Zechariah carefully reminds his audience that the words he speaks are from God, not from himself. "The word of the LORD came to me" introduces the oracle of these verses (Zech 6:9, NRSV). At the close of the oracle, Zechariah does this again by saying, "You shall know that the LORD of hosts has sent me to you. This will happen if you diligently obey the voice of the LORD your God" (v. 15, NRSV).

"This" (ibid.) refers to the body of the oracle. Zechariah is told by God to "collect silver and gold ... and make a crown" (vv. 10-11, NRSV). The Hebrew actually has *crowns* (plural), which O'Brien explains as indicating that one was meant for a priest and another for the Davidic king (Julia M. O'Brien, *Nahum, Habakkuk, Zephaniah, Haggai, Zechariah, Malachi* [Nashville: Abingdon Press, 2004], 205). Against this, Homer Hailey interprets the use of the plural as indicating that the single crown was made of two metals and symbolized the unity of the priestly and kingly roles of the coming king (*A Commentary on the Minor Prophets* [Grand Rapids: Baker Book House, 1972], 351-352). The gold

and silver for the crown come from three men (Heldai, Tobijah, and Jedaiah) who had been born in exile and brought with them from Babylon riches which were given to them. These men, along with Josiah the son of Zephaniah, will witness the crowning. In verse fourteen, they will be given the crown to keep "as a memorial in the temple of the LORD" (NRSV).

The crown is integral to the "sign-act" to come—namely, crowning "a proxy rather than the new king himself" (Scalise, 241). The high priest Joshua stands in as the king at what must have been a private event, as a public one would risk misunderstanding and trouble from Babylon on account of apparent rebellion (ibid., 242). Since "Jesus" is a Hellenized version of the Hebrew name "Joshua," it is particularly fitting that a man of this name was representing the man to come. One key element which is missing at this ceremony is the anointing. In the past, a prophet from God would anoint the man He had chosen, and that one would be king. Priests were also anointed, so it is likely that Joshua had been anointed at one time, since he was a priest, but the lack of anointing here indicates to the audience that this is a mere symbol of what was to come.

In other royal inaugurations when God spoke, He spoke directly to His Messiah, indicated by the use of second person pronouns. In this text, however, the king is spoken of in the third person, as though he is not present, which is exactly what was intended. God says, "Here is a man whose name is Branch" (v. 12, NRSV) even though the crowned Joshua is only the sign of the one to come. The man is not present, and will not be until Jesus walks the earth. Centuries later, all of this will come to fruition at Jesus' baptism, when He is anointed with the Holy Spirit and God speaks to him: "'You are my Son, the Beloved; with you I am well pleased'" (Mark 1:11, NRSV).

In a play on words which is retained in English translations, the man is called "Branch: for he shall branch out in his place, and he shall build the temple of the Lord" (Zech. 6:12, NRSV). Zerubbabel's absence here is conspicuous, as he was the one who was rebuilding the temple (see Zech. 4:9). A common explanation among some scholars is that the text has been emended to strike Zerubbabel's name from the passage. This may indicate that, for whatever reason, Zerubbabel had fallen out of power (William P. Brown, *Obadiah Through Malachi* [Louisville: Westminster John Knox Press, 1996], 157). The Branch's role in building the temple is stressed into verse thirteen and comes back in verse fifteen when "those who are far off shall come and help to build the temple of the Lord" (NRSV). In context, this likely indicates exiles who will return (Brown, 158). Understanding that Jesus is the Priest, however, gives the verse fuller meaning and hints at the inclusion of all nations, not just ethnic Jews.

Our understanding of Jesus as fulfilling this prophecy as both King and Priest is not found explicitly in the text. Rather, the king "shall [have] a priest by his throne, with peaceful understanding between the two of them" (Zech. 6:13, NRSV). The two men will be "working in mutual cooperation in a bicameral form of government" (Brown, 158). From our point of view, however, we see that Jesus fills both

roles and does so better than any two men could have ever done.

III. King of the Jews (John 19:1-5)

Now, we transition to the Gospel of John to see the crowning of the Messiah. After Pilate's examination of Jesus, he finds no reason to punish Him and yet he has "him flogged" (John 19:1, NRSV), likely with a leather whip studded with bone or metal (Morris, 699). Morris postulates that by having Jesus flogged, Pilate was hoping to avoid executing Him. On the one hand, he may have been motivated to ridicule Jesus and was thus trying to show how pitiful Jesus seemed after the Romans had finished with him and how absurd the charges against Him really were. On the other hand, he could have been trying to cause the Jewish leaders to take pity on Jesus and rescind their accusations (ibid., 698). Whatever the motivation, even the brutality of the beating would not sway the Jewish crowd.

Next the soldiers make a crown of thorns and put it on Jesus' head and clothe him in a purple robe. After the flogging, this gesture was intended to add insult to injury. Both the crown and the purple robe suggest royalty, which of course neither the soldiers nor Pilate actually believed Jesus was. How else could they proclaim "'Hail, King of the Jews!'" and then slap that king in the face (v. 3, NRSV)?

After all of this, Pilate goes to the Jews and maintains his belief in Jesus' innocence: "'I find no case against him'" (v. 4, NRSV). However, the innocence of a Jewish man makes little different to Pilate. Ancient sources attest to his tenuous relationship with the people he governed in Jerusalem and how he often struggled for control in that backwoods province. More than likely, these things were on his mind, along with a bias towards the Jews as a people, or else he would not have ordered Jesus to be flogged, nor would he allow the Christ to be crucified without basis. Certainly if Jesus, like Paul, had been a Roman citizen, these crimes could not have been committed by the Roman governor.

Pilate maintains Jesus' innocence and presents Him to the crowd, saying, "'Here is the man!'" (v. 5, NRSV). Calling Jesus "'the man'" (ibid.) is as close to Jesus' self-designation "'Son of Man'" (Luke 5:24, NRSV) as Pilate could come (J. Ramsey Michaels, *John* [Peabody, MA: Hendrickson, 1989], 317-318). "Like the high priest Caiaphas (11:51-52), Pilate is understood here as speaking more wisely than he knows" (ibid.). He never found Jesus guilty, but neither did he come to any real understanding of who He was treating as a mere criminal. Pilate tries to avoid crucifying Jesus for a time, but the pressure from the Jewish leaders and the crowd proves to be too much. He must keep the peace, so Jesus must die.

THE LESSON APPLIED

These prophecies from Jeremiah and Zechariah, along with many others, understandably led the Jews to an understanding of the Messiah as an earthly king who would put Israel at the center of the world as the everlasting superpower. When the humble King walked the earth, however, many could not put aside their preconceived ideas about who that King was meant to be. Often God acts differently than what His people expect; to believe otherwise is to make our God too small.

LET'S TALK ABOUT IT

1. What does it mean to be part of Jesus' Kingdom on earth?

In every way, Jesus is a King like no other. Because of this, we are to be a people like no other, through the Spirit's empowerment to embody Jesus on this earth until His return. But has the Church become like every other world power, seeking power, advancement, and prestige? Are we more concerned with our congregation's inner workings than with the good of the outsider—the widow, the orphan, the foreigner? Do we feel entitled to treat our enemies as the world treats its enemies and not in love, as we've been taught? God forbid! Following Jesus means following a King whose only earthly crown was mockingly made out of thorns and placed on His already bloody brow. He is a King like no other. Pray to God we would be a people like no other.

THE THIRD DAY

ADULT TOPIC:	BACKGROUND SCRIPTURES:
DELIVERANCE	HOSEA 6:1-3; LUKE 24:1-12

HOSEA 6:1–3; LUKE 24:1-12

King James Version

COME, and let us return unto the LORD: for he hath torn, and he will heal us; he hath smitten, and he will bind us up.

2 After two days will he revive us: in the third day he will raise us up, and we shall live in his sight.

3 Then shall we know, if we follow on to know the LORD: his going forth is prepared as the morning; and he shall come unto us as the rain, as the latter and former rain unto the earth.

• • • Luke 24:1–12 • • •

NOW upon the first day of the week, very early in the morning, they came unto the sepulchre, bringing the spices which they had prepared, and certain others with them.

2 And they found the stone rolled away from the sepulchre.

3 And they entered in, and found not the body of the Lord Jesus.

4 And it came to pass, as they were much perplexed thereabout, behold, two men stood by them in shining garments:

5 And as they were afraid, and bowed down their faces to the earth, they said unto them, Why seek ye the living among the dead?

6 He is not here, but is risen: remember how he spake unto you when he was yet in Galilee,

New Revised Standard Version

"COME, let us return to the LORD; for it is he who has torn, and he will heal us; he has struck down, and he will bind us up.

2 After two days he will revive us; on the third day he will raise us up, that we may live before him.

3 Let us know, let us press on to know the LORD; his appearing is as sure as the dawn; he will come to us like the showers, like the spring rains that water the earth."

• • • Luke 24:1–12 • • •

BUT on the first day of the week, at early dawn, they came to the tomb, taking the spices that they had prepared.

2 They found the stone rolled away from the tomb,

3 but when they went in, they did not find the body.

4 While they were perplexed about this, suddenly two men in dazzling clothes stood beside them.

5 The women were terrified and bowed their faces to the ground, but the men said to them, "Why do you look for the living among the dead? He is not here, but has risen.

6 Remember how he told you, while he was still in Galilee,

MAIN THOUGHT: He is not here, but is risen: remember how he spake unto you when he was yet in Galilee, saying, The Son of man must be delivered into the hands of sinful men, and be crucified, and the third day rise again. (Luke 24:6-7, KJV)

HOSEA 6:1-3; LUKE 24:1-12

King James Version	*New Revised Standard Version*
7 Saying, The Son of man must be delivered into the hands of sinful men, and be crucified, and the third day rise again.	7 that the Son of Man must be handed over to sinners, and be crucified, and on the third day rise again."
8 And they remembered his words,	8 Then they remembered his words,
9 And returned from the sepulchre, and told all these things unto the eleven, and to all the rest.	9 and returning from the tomb, they told all this to the eleven and to all the rest.
10 It was Mary Magdalene and Joanna, and Mary the mother of James, and other women that were with them, which told these things unto the apostles.	10 Now it was Mary Magdalene, Joanna, Mary the mother of James, and the other women with them who told this to the apostles.
11 And their words seemed to them as idle tales, and they believed them not.	11 But these words seemed to them an idle tale, and they did not believe them.
12 Then arose Peter, and ran unto the sepulchre; and stooping down, he beheld the linen clothes laid by themselves, and departed, wondering in himself at that which was come to pass.	12 But Peter got up and ran to the tomb; stooping and looking in, he saw the linen cloths by themselves; then he went home, amazed at what had happened.

LESSON SETTING

Time: 735 B.C. (Hosea);
A.D. 30 (Luke)

Place: Jerusalem

LESSON OUTLINE

I. **The People Turn to God**
(Hosea 6:1-3)

II. **The Women at the Tomb**
(Luke 24:1-9)

III. **Witnesses of the Tomb**
(Luke 24:10-12)

UNIFYING PRINCIPLE

Sometimes people do not recognize the accomplishment of long-held goals because they are achieved in different form from what was expected. What sustains the motivation of people to keep going when victory looks improbable? Jesus' forecast of His resurrection on the third day alluded to the Hebrew scripture theme (tradition) of deliverance in defiance of the horror of the crucifixion.

INTRODUCTION

Hosea was a prophet to the northern kingdom in the eighth century B.C. in the years leading up to its subjugation to Assyria. His prophecies focused primarily on Israel. At that time, Israel was doing quite well economically, and although the country had given up on anointing the kings of God's choosing, they continued to prosper for a time. Hosea's book is best remembered for the extended metaphor in chapters 1—3 of Hosea's marriage to a promiscuous woman, Gomer, and its analogy to God's covenant relationship with Israel. Israel's idolatry is often misunderstood. This was usually no straightforward rejection of God, but rather a syncretism of God and the false gods of the pagan nations. Whereas God was recognized as the greatest warrior (Israel need only look to Joshua, Gideon, David, etc., to see this confirmed), could Israel be sure that He was also good for fertility? Did He control the sea? Thus, Israel tried to appease God with His festivals and sacrifices but added other gods to their worship as well, just to be safe.

One note about the text of Hosea—it can be difficult to sometimes interpret. As will be seen in the exposition, there are times when it is unclear what the relationships between verses and the meanings are.

On the other hand, Luke as a book bears little resemblance to Hosea. Whereas Hosea's poetic book centers on prophecies of judgment and occasional hope, Luke's history in prose focuses on the events of Jesus' life and its importance first within the Jewish faith and then moving out into the Gentile world in Acts. His context is also very different—he is not concerned with the disobedience of a nation but rather with the spread of truth throughout the world. Luke, a doctor and disciple, admits to the use of sources in his writing; the truth of this is clear in the various connections between his Gospel and the other Synoptic Gospels. David E. Garland explains that the dating of the book, while useful for reconstructing Christian history, does very little for interpretation and, thus, the lack of consensus should pose little problem for interpretation (*Luke* [Grand Rapids: Zondervan, 2011], 31). A date between the years A.D. 60-62 is generally accepted.

EXPOSITION

I. THE PEOPLE TURN TO GOD (HOSEA 6:1-3)

In these verses, the people of Israel hold counsel with one another, calling for repentance and reassuring themselves that God's blessing is sure. There is some debate as to whether the people speak sincerely or if perhaps the prophet speaks for them, mocking what they would say. Both Elizabeth Achtemeier and Homer Hailey find this speech to be insincere, albeit for different reasons. Achtemeier regards this as a distinct section of text and does not require a direct relationship to anything surrounding it. She reads these verses as Hosea's mocking quote of the people's repentance, pointing out that they never actually pray to God yet assume that He will do what they need (*Minor Prophets I* [Grand Rapids: Hendrickson, 1996], 50). She goes so far as to suggest that they have confused God with Baal, assuming that He becomes stronger and weaker with the seasons as in the Baal myths (51). Hailey, on the other hand, sees verses 1-3 as closely related to verse four in which the people's affections are likened to "the dew that goes away early" (Hos. 6:4, NRSV), suggesting that the moment they receive what they need from God, they will carry on with life as usual and give Him no more thought. The people believe that they need only go through the motions and then God will heal them, thus betraying "a low estimate of the demands of Jehovah on His people" (*A Commentary on the Minor Prophets* [Grand Rapids: Baker Books House, 1972], 155).

It is not without precedent to regard words said as true and prophetic without fully understanding them. Certainly, John intended this when writing Caiaphas' prophecy that "'it is better for you to have one man die for the people than to have the whole nation destroyed'" (11:50,

NRSV). Caiaphas concerned himself with the state's political standing in the Roman Empire, whereas John intends his readers to understand that God was using even disreputable men to further His Kingdom plans on earth.

Thus, this passage in Hosea and that of John 11 serve as examples of *sensus plenior*—"fuller meaning" indicating that the speaker, for whatever reason, did not understand to the fullest degree how his or her words would be fulfilled. We find that definition at work in many prophetic passages. With this in mind, we can move on to a closer examination of the text itself.

These verses demonstrate parallelism that is typical of Hebrew poetry. The phrase "'he who has torn'" correlates to "'he has struck down'" in the same way that "'he will heal us'" and "'he will bind us up'" do (Hos. 6:1, NRSV). The images are meant to build upon one another, giving a more robust sense of both the distress the people find themselves in (torn up, stricken) and the relief they expect to experience (healing, binding).

The same literary device is employed in verse two: "'After two days *he will revive us*; on the third day *he will raise us up*'" (NRSV, emphasis added). Hebrew writers, rather than repeating a number, often used the formula ($n + 1$) to indicate numerical parallels. Thus, while we can read back into the text and see Christ's resurrection after the requisite three days, this would not have been in view at the original writing of this text.

The first phrase of verse three recalls its counterpart in verse one: "'Come, let us return to the LORD.... Let us know, let us press on to know the LORD'" (Hos. 6:1, 3,

NRSV). *Returning* is language of repentance while *knowing* denotes more than mere intellectual acquiescence. Consider Exodus 6: "'I will take you as my people, and I will be your God. You shall *know* that I am the LORD your God, who has freed you from the burdens of the Egyptians'" (v. 7, NRSV, emphasis added). This knowledge is rehearsed every year at Passover and is meant to change how the people live. Because they were slaves and foreigners, they are to treat slaves and foreigners differently than other nations because of their working knowledge of what God did for them when they were in the same state.

The rest of verse three breaks from the parallelism of verses 1-2 but has much of the same building effect—"he will come to us like the showers, like the spring rains that water the earth" (Hos. 6:3, NRSV). The second clause emphasizes and makes more specific the first, showing the utter confidence of the people. The verse demonstrates a faith that God, like the spring rain which brings the earth back to life, will certainly act on their behalf.

II. THE WOMEN AT THE TOMB (LUKE 24:1-9)

We will now look at the fulfillment of Hosea's prophecy in the Gospel of Luke. Jesus was crucified the day before the Sabbath, so the women, who would have been observing the Sabbath, couldn't go to take care of His body. However, very early the next day, they took their spices and went to the tomb. All this is fairly unremarkable, and Luke relates that the stone was rolled away as though this, too, were unremarkable, when in fact this is the first hint that something may be amiss. Who moved the stone? Could it have been grave robbers? A gardener? The women, too, were mystified, but the story moves on quickly.

"Suddenly two men in dazzling clothes stood beside them" (Luke 24:4, NRSV). Though they are not called angels until Luke 24:23, these two are messengers from God (which is the angelic role), and their "dazzling" clothing suggests again that they are supernatural. The women's reactions of terror further imply that these two "men" are actually angels. It is interesting to note that at least two witnesses were necessary to testify in a court of law (see Deut. 19:15), and God provides two at the empty tomb (Darrell L. Bock, *Luke* [Grand Rapids: Zondervan], 606).

Garland draws two parallels between the accounts of Jesus' birth and His resurrection in the book of Luke: both events are announced by angels, and after each announcement, it is a woman or group of women who believe and act in faith (ibid., 941-942). In this text, the angels, nonplussed by the women's bowing and fear, give a "mild rebuke" (David Lyle Jeffrey, *Luke* [Grand Rapids: Brazos Press, 2012], 282)—"'Why do you look for the living among the dead?... Remember how he told you, while he was still in Galilee, that the Son of Man must be handed over to sinners, and be crucified, and on the third day rise again'" (Luke 24:5-7). Indeed, the women have forgotten, and these words remind them of Jesus' own words. In tandem, the angels' reminder and the empty tomb result in the women's faithfully returning to the Eleven (who were sans Judas) and the other disciples to share the good news they had discovered at the empty tomb.

III. Witnesses of the Tomb (Luke 24:10-12)

Luke emphasizes that the first witnesses to the resurrection are women by naming them—"Mary Magdalene, Joanna, Mary the mother of James, and the other women" (24:10)—and having them repeat their testimony to the disciples. Jeffrey argues that the witness of the women is "one persuasive indicator that we are dealing with facts as they happened [because this was] so unconventional an imagination for this culture" (284). More plainly, "one of the main proofs that the resurrection story is credible is [the] realization that the first-century church would never have created a story whose main first witnesses were women" (Bock, 607).

The Disciples do not believe the women. Although these women studied under Jesus in similar fashion to the men, the disciples cannot believe their words which sounded like "the delirious talk of the very sick" (Garland, 943). Whether they specifically couldn't believe women is debatable, as even a man is unbelievable in a delirium, but the result is a lack of belief.

Peter once again thinks and behaves independently from the other disciples. Perhaps he is beginning to believe that Jesus, the Son of Man, knew what would happen and that perhaps the story isn't over. Peter has learned at least enough from Jesus to be curious and inspect for himself the women's claims, so he "ran to the tomb … [and] saw the linen cloths by themselves" (24:12). "Since the linen cloths would be the only valuable thing to steal, and since it also would be unlikely that anyone would strip the body before stealing it, their presence discredits any suspicion that tomb raiders broke in and stole the body" (Garland, 943). Thus, Luke adds this detail to give further credence to Jesus' resurrection.

This Greek verb *thaumazō* (wondering, marveling) does not definitively indicate that Peter went away believing the tale even after seeing the tomb empty and the linens in place—although he definitely will come to believe it (Bock, 607-608). Presenting Peter as marveling but not necessarily speaking after his own experience at the tomb further highlights the importance of the women's testimony (Garland, 942-943). In the accounts to follow, Jesus Himself will bodily appear and vindicate the women (see Luke 24:13-49).

THE LESSON APPLIED

The Church must keep in mind that it cannot know what God has planned for tomorrow, next year, or even a century from now. God may have planned a blessing, as Israel hoped, or it may be a cursing, which is what Israel ultimately received in the form of its Assyrian exile following Hosea's prophecies. We cannot assume God's blessings, but we must continuously return to the Lord. In the Christ event—Jesus' birth, ministry, death, resurrection, and ascension—we find God's definitive salvific action in the world. Although Israel did not know it, this was the act they were waiting for. Today, it is the source of everlasting hope and comfort for us. Because of Jesus, we can accept either blessing or cursing from God, knowing that He has fulfilled His plan for the nations which is being brought to completion through His Church.

LET'S TALK ABOUT IT

1. Are we listening to "the others" in our churches?

The Disciples did not believe the women's testimony, partially because the story was so fantastic, but also because the witnesses were not considered reliable. By discounting the messengers, the Disciples missed out on the truth and would have been left in the dark had not Jesus bodily visited them. Are we doing the same? Are we discounting the messengers God sends to us?

In our churches, it is important not to judge anyone based on social status, outward appearance, or any other preconceived notions of who can speak the truth, for we know that God judges based on one's heart, not one's gender, race, money, or power. Therefore, let us be intentional about listening to people we might ordinarily discredit for they could be the very ones speaking the words we need to hear.

HOME DAILY DEVOTIONAL READINGS
APRIL 21-27, 2014

MONDAY	TUESDAY	WEDNESDAY	THURSDAY	FRIDAY	SATURDAY	SUNDAY
Seeking the Answer to Suffering	The Completion of God's Plans	A Man of Suffering	Undergoing Great Suffering	Servant of All	We Have Seen His Glory	The Messiah's Necessary Suffering
Job 23:1-7	Job 23:8-14	Isaiah 52:13—53:4	Matthew 16:21-28	Mark 9:30-37	John 1:10-18	Luke 24:25-27, 44-47; Isaiah 53:5–8

FROM SUFFERING TO GLORY

ADULT TOPIC:	BACKGROUND SCRIPTURES:
GREATER UNDERSTANDING	ISAIAH 52:13—53:12; LUKE 24:25-27, 44-50

ISAIAH 53:5-8; LUKE 24:25-27, 44-47

King James Version

BUT he was wounded for our transgressions, he was bruised for our iniquities: the chastisement of our peace was upon him; and with his stripes we are healed.

6 All we like sheep have gone astray; we have turned every one to his own way; and the LORD hath laid on him the iniquity of us all.

7 He was oppressed, and he was afflicted, yet he opened not his mouth: he is brought as a lamb to the slaughter, and as a sheep before her shearers is dumb, so he openeth not his mouth.

8 He was taken from prison and from judgment: and who shall declare his generation? for he was cut off out of the land of the living: for the transgression of my people was he stricken.

• • • Luke 24:25-27, 44-47 • • •

THEN he said unto them, O fools, and slow of heart to believe all that the prophets have spoken:

26 Ought not Christ to have suffered these things, and to enter into his glory?

27 And beginning at Moses and all the prophets, he expounded unto them in all the scriptures the things concerning himself.

• • • • • •

44 And he said unto them, These are the words which I spake unto you, while I was yet with you, that all things must be fulfilled, which were written in the law of Moses, and in the prophets, and in the psalms, concerning me.

New Revised Standard Version

BUT he was wounded for our transgressions, crushed for our iniquities; upon him was the punishment that made us whole, and by his bruises we are healed.

6 All we like sheep have gone astray; we have all turned to our own way, and the LORD has laid on him the iniquity of us all.

7 He was oppressed, and he was afflicted, yet he did not open his mouth; like a lamb that is led to the slaughter, and like a sheep that before its shearers is silent, so he did not open his mouth.

8 By a perversion of justice he was taken away. Who could have imagined his future? For he was cut off from the land of the living, stricken for the transgression of my people.

• • • Luke 24:25-27, 44-47 • • •

THEN he said to them, "Oh, how foolish you are, and how slow of heart to believe all that the prophets have declared!

26 Was it not necessary that the Messiah should suffer these things and then enter into his glory?"

27 Then beginning with Moses and all the prophets, he interpreted to them the things about himself in all the scriptures.

• • • • • •

44 Then he said to them, "These are my words that I spoke to you while I was still with you—that everything written about me in the law of Moses, the prophets, and the psalms must be fulfilled."

MAIN THOUGHT: And beginning at Moses and all the prophets, he expounded unto them in all the scriptures the things concerning himself. (Luke 24:27, KJV)

Isaiah 53:5-8; Luke 24:25-27, 44-47

King James Version

45 Then opened he their understanding, that they might understand the scriptures,

46 And said unto them, Thus it is written, and thus it behoved Christ to suffer, and to rise from the dead the third day:

47 And that repentance and remission of sins should be preached in his name among all nations, beginning at Jerusalem.

New Revised Standard Version

45 Then he opened their minds to understand the scriptures,

46 and he said to them, "Thus it is written, that the Messiah is to suffer and to rise from the dead on the third day,

47 and that repentance and forgiveness of sins is to be proclaimed in his name to all nations, beginning from Jerusalem."

LESSON SETTING

Time: 735 B.C. (Isaiah); A.D. 33 (Luke)

Place: Jerusalem (Isaiah); Emmaus and Jerusalem (Luke)

LESSON OUTLINE

I. The Suffering Servant (Isaiah 53:5-8)

II. Jesus on the Road to Emmaus (Luke 24:25-27)

III. Jesus Appears to His Disciples (Luke 24:44-47)

UNIFYING PRINCIPLE

Confusion, disappointment, and sorrow in life often result from not understanding fully what has happened. How can the true meaning be discovered and understood? After Jesus explained His life, death, and resurrection within the context of Hebrew Scriptures, the two travelers on the road to Emmaus understood better what had happened.

INTRODUCTION

Today's lesson concludes our unit on Jesus' fulfillment of the Old Testament prophecy. Last week's lesson studied how Jesus' resurrection three days after His crucifixion was a fulfillment of Hosea 6:1-3. This week's lesson will study a section from Isaiah 53 and then look at how Jesus explained to various groups of disciples that His death and resurrection were a direct fulfillment of the Old Testament Scriptures.

Isaiah 53 is recognized as the fourth and final Servant Song in the writings of Isaiah. Briley writes, "Throughout the song the hearer should feel the tension between the servant's experience of suffering and the accomplishment of God's powerful purpose through him" (Terry Briley, *Isaiah Volume 2* [Joplin, MO: College Press Publishing Company, 2004], 209). Thus, God's purpose in sending His Son to die is intentionally paralleled with the graphic suffering that He will face. The song is divided into four sections. Verses 1-3 give a description of the Servant; verses 4-6 tell why and how the Servant suffers; verses 7-9 describe the innocence of the Servant; verses 10-12 explain the results of the Servant's death.

The identity of the speaker has long been a subject of debate. Within the song's description of the Messiah, alternating stanzas feature the pronouns *we* and *he*.

The uses of *he* obviously refer to the Servant. John Oswalt recommends that *we* describes Israel and that the speaker has identified himself with Israel (*The Book of Isaiah Chapters 40-66* [Grand Rapids, MI: Eerdmans, 1998], 381). Also, *we* signifies that the people are witnesses to what is happening to the suffering Servant. This parallel will resurface later in Luke 24 where individuals become witnesses of Jesus' resurrection and in the necessity of divine revelation for understanding the Scriptures.

EXPOSITION

I. THE SUFFERING SERVANT (ISAIAH 53:5-8)

Isaiah 53:1-3 gives a general description of the Servant. First, though, verse one expresses the need for divine revelation to understand what has been seen. The "arm of the LORD" (v. 1, NRSV) is a metaphor for the Servant, and it is only after the Servant "has...been [divinely] revealed" to Israel that the witnesses' report will be "believed" (ibid.). The song says the Servant had no noteworthy appearance and men did not esteem Him. He was "despised and rejected of men; a man of sorrows, and acquainted with grief" (v. 3, KJV). Oswalt explains that *despised* (Heb. *nibzeh*) connotes "someone to be worthless, unworthy of attention" (383). Thus, a "hasty dismissal" (ibid.) was given the Servant by His peers. Briley notes that "man of sorrows reflects the Hebrew construct state ('man/woman of...' or 'son/daughter of...') that describes a fundamental characteristic of a person" (212-213). Everything about the Servant suggests pain and grief.

Whereas verses 1-3 of Isaiah 53 describe the nature of the Servant, verses 4-6 explain why He suffered: the Servant suffered to serve as a substitutionary atonement for the sins of Israel. Verse four is significant in that the witnesses realize that the Servant bore their sicknesses even though they had viewed Him as "stricken, struck down by God, and afflicted" (NRSV). Their recognition continues in verse five: the Servant "was wounded for our transgressions, crushed for our iniquities; upon him was the punishment that made us whole, and by his bruises we are healed" (NRSV). The witnesses proclaim that this Servant bore their sins and iniquities and was unjustly given the punishment that they deserved. Oswalt points out that *crushed* is an especially violent word and connotes "breaking into pieces and in some cases even pulverizing" (387). The witnesses also note that, as a result of the Servant's suffering, they attained healing; thus, the Servant served as a substitute for their sins and "made [them] whole" (v. 5, NRSV). Through the Servant's suffering, peace could be restored between God and the witnesses.

Verse six further expresses the guilt felt by the witnesses. The suffering endured by the Servant was in large part the result of their sins. They admit, "like sheep [we] have gone astray; we have all turned to our own way" (NRSV). Thus, the Servant was isolated in His suffering and the ones for whom He accepted the punishment had abandoned Him. While the Servant was isolated, God placed on the Servant "the iniquity" of all the witnesses (ibid.). The witnesses' comparing themselves to sheep emphasizes the substitutionary nature of the Servant's suffering. It recalls Leviticus 16 where a goat was slaughtered by a priest as a sin offering and then another goat was sent out of the camp as a scapegoat for the people's sins (Briley, 214). A point to note, though, is that while the Old Testament teaches of the necessity of animal sacrifices, the concept of human sacrifice was never promoted. Micah 6:6-8 teaches that a sheep or goat cannot serve as the proper atonement for a man's sin. Instead, a perfect man who is also God could serve as the atonement for imperfect men and women (see Heb. 9:11-14).

Verses 7-9 of Isaiah 53 explain how the Servant was innocent and unjustly killed. He is described as "a lamb that is led to the slaughter, and like a sheep that before its shearers is silent, so he did not open his mouth" (v. 7, NRSV). Even though He was innocent, the Servant did not protest His unjust slaughter. According to Oswalt, many commentators believe this verse might have served as the inspiration for John the Baptist's cry, "'Here is the Lamb of God who takes away the sin of the world!'" (John 1:29, NRSV) (385).

Verse eight of Isaiah 53 plainly states that the Servant's death was a "perversion of justice" (NRSV). From beginning to end, the Servant's pain and death were completely unjust. The question "Who shall declare his generation?" (v. 8, KJV) refers to the shame that accompanies one who is "cut off out of the land of the living" (ibid.) before leaving any children behind. Oswalt explains, "The Servant was left without children in a culture where to die childless was to have lived an utterly futile existence" (395). Verse eight concludes with the speaker's recognition

that the Servant died for all the people of Israel. Verse nine describes the ignominious burial afforded the dead Servant, further illustrating the injustice done to Him.

Verses 10-12 conclude the Servant Song by telling of the results of His suffering. While all of the previous suffering has been in past tense, verses 10-12 are in the future tense and tell of the triumphs of the Servant. The speaker clearly states that it was the Lord's will that His Servant should suffer in this way, but through His death "the righteous one, my servant, shall make many righteous, and he shall bear their iniquities" (v. 11, NRSV). Because of the Servant's obedience to God, He will receive "a portion with the great, and he shall divide the spoil with the strong" (v. 12, NRSV). The witnesses recognize that God will bless the Servant for becoming the substitutionary atonement for Israel.

II. JESUS ON THE ROAD TO EMMAUS (LUKE 24:25-27)

As stated in the introduction, today's passages from Luke emphasize that Jesus' death and resurrection were clearly foretold in the Old Testament. Joel Green writes, "From the standpoint of the Lukan narrative, the key to making sense of the death of Jesus lies in construing it within the matrix of the 'scriptures' (vv. 25-27, 32). This draws attention both to Luke's perspective on the prophetic role of the Scriptures and to the necessity of interpreting them faithfully" (*The Gospel of Luke* [Grand Rapids, MI: Eerdmans, 1997], 843). R. Alan Culpepper argues that Luke emphasizes Jesus' life as the fulfillment of Old Testament prophecy more so than any other New Testament writer ("The Gospel of Luke" in *The New Interpreter's Bible*,

Vol. 9 [Nashville: Abingdon Press, 1995], 486). Clearly, Luke wanted his audience to connect the events in Jesus' life with the Old Testament.

As today's text opens, two disciples are walking from Jerusalem to Emmaus, and they encounter Jesus, but "their eyes [are] kept from recognizing him" (Luke 24:16, NRSV). One of the men, Cleopas, recounts to Jesus the events of the past three days. His description of Jesus as "'a prophet mighty in deed and word before God and all the people'" (v. 19, NRSV) is very similar to how Deuteronomy 34:10-12 describes Moses, thus linking Jesus to Israel's greatest prophet (Green, 846). Furthermore, these two disciples had hoped that Jesus would be the one "'to redeem Israel'" (v. 21, NRSV) just like Moses had been the one to redeem the Israelites from Egyptian bondage. Unfortunately, any hopes of this occurrence were dashed when Jesus was crucified and buried.

Then Jesus responds to Cleopas, "'Oh, how foolish you are, and how slow of heart to believe all that the prophets have declared! Was it not necessary that the Messiah should suffer these things and then enter into his glory?'" (vv. 25-26, NRSV). Green explains that "'slow of heart'" (ibid.) "calls attention to their failure to orient themselves fully around Jesus' teaching" (848). What the disciples do not understand is that throughout His ministry and death Jesus was fulfilling the pattern that most prophets experienced in the Old Testament. Green explains, "As God's prophet, Jesus must fulfill the destiny of the prophets: rejection, suffering, and death" (846). Luke then writes, "beginning with Moses and all the prophets, he interpreted to them the things about himself in all the scriptures" (v. 27, NRSV).

Just as divine revelation was necessary for the witnesses in Isaiah 53 to understand the mission of the suffering Servant, the two disciples on the road to Emmaus had to have their eyes opened to the truth of the Scriptures. Jesus explains to them how the books of Moses and the Prophets foretold the events that would take place. Later in the narrative, the two disciples invite Jesus to eat with them, and after Jesus breaks bread, their eyes are fully opened, and they realize they have been made witnesses of Christ's death and resurrection as foretold centuries before (see Luke 24:28-35).

III. JESUS APPEARS TO HIS DISCIPLES (LUKE 24:44-47)

The appearance by Christ on the road to Emmaus differs from the one to His Disciples, whose eyes are not kept from seeing His resurrected body. Upon seeing Jesus, they are terrified. Only after Jesus has eaten some broiled fish are His Disciples convinced that He has been physically resurrected and is not a ghost. Jesus then reminds His Disciples that He had foretold His death and resurrection time and time again (see Luke 9:22, 44; 13:33; 17:25; 18:31-33) (Culpepper, 486). All of these events had been foretold "'in the law of Moses, the prophets, and the psalms'" (Luke 24:44, NRSV). After this, Luke writes that Jesus "[opens] their minds to understand the scriptures" (v. 45, NRSV). Just as the two disciples going to Emmaus had needed divine help to fully comprehend the Scriptures, so do the remaining eleven Disciples who had spent the last three years of their lives traveling with Jesus.

While interpreting the Scriptures, Jesus explains, "'Thus it is written, that the Messiah is to suffer and to rise from the dead on the third day, and that repentance and forgiveness of sins is to be proclaimed in his name to all nations, beginning from Jerusalem'" (vv. 46-47, NRSV). Only after Jesus' death and resurrection are the Disciples able to fully comprehend the events that have taken place. Green writes, "What has happened with Jesus can be understood only in light of the Scriptures, yet the Scriptures themselves can be understood only in light of what has happened with Jesus. These two are mutually informing" (844).

Jesus continues in verse forty-eight by informing His Disciples that they, too, have been made witnesses of the fulfillment of the Old Testament prophecy. After this, He commands them to stay in Jerusalem until they "'have been clothed with power from on high'" (Luke 24:49, NRSV). The last three verses of Luke then tell how the Disciples witness Jesus' ascension to heaven and then joyfully return to Jerusalem.

THE LESSON APPLIED

Today's lesson talked about the importance of divine revelation in understanding the Scriptures. Only after the Lord intervenes are the witnesses in Isaiah 53 and Luke 24 able to fully comprehend what all they have seen. The New Testament speaks about how the natural man is unable to fully understand the Bible. Only after being enlightened with the power of the Holy Spirit are individuals able to fully discern the teachings of the Scriptures (see 1 Cor. 2:6-16). Christians should strive daily to understand the Scriptures to the best of their abilities and ask for God to open their eyes to the truth of His Word.

LET'S TALK ABOUT IT

1. What does this lesson have in common with the parable of the Rich Man and Lazarus?

While suffering in hell, the rich man asks if Lazarus can go back and warn the rich man's five brothers about the torments of hell. Abraham tells him that the brothers have the teachings of Moses and the prophets to warn them. The rich man pleads again and says if Lazarus were resurrected, then they will believe him. Abraham solemnly tells the rich man, "'If they do not listen to Moses and the prophets, neither will they be convinced even if someone rises from the dead'" (Luke 16:31, NRSV). The Old Testament served as God's Word for people then and now.

HOME DAILY DEVOTIONAL READINGS
APRIL 28—MAY 4, 2014

MONDAY	TUESDAY	WEDNESDAY	THURSDAY	FRIDAY	SATURDAY	SUNDAY
Testing What Is in Your Heart	Keep Watching and Praying	Take Care Against Being Tempted	Do Not Lead Us into Temptation	Kept from Trial and Testing	Guarded in All Your Ways	Serve Only God
Deuteronomy 8:1-11	Matthew 26:36-41	Galatians 6:1-5	Matthew 6:9-13	Revelation 3:8-13	Psalm 91:1-12	Deuteronomy 6:13-16; Matthew 4:4-11

JESUS RESISTS TEMPTATION

ADULT TOPIC: BACKGROUND SCRIPTURES:
JUST SAY NO!   DEUTERONOMY 6:13–16; 8:3; PSALM 91:11–12; MATTHEW 4:1–11

DEUTERONOMY 6:13–16; MATTHEW 4:4–11

King James Version

THOU shalt fear the LORD thy God, and serve him, and shalt swear by his name.

14 Ye shall not go after other gods, of the gods of the people which are round about you;
15 (For the LORD thy God is a jealous God among you) lest the anger of the LORD thy God be kindled against thee, and destroy thee from off the face of the earth.

16 Ye shall not tempt the LORD your God, as ye tempted him in Massah.
• • • Matthew 4:4-11 • • •
BUT he answered and said, It is written, Man shall not live by bread alone, but by every word that proceedeth out of the mouth of God.
5 Then the devil taketh him up into the holy city, and setteth him on a pinnacle of the temple,
6 And saith unto him, If thou be the Son of God, cast thyself down: for it is written, He shall give his angels charge concerning thee: and in their hands they shall bear thee up, lest at any time thou dash thy foot against a stone.
7 Jesus said unto him, It is written again, Thou shalt not tempt the Lord thy God.
8 Again, the devil taketh him up into an exceeding high mountain, and sheweth him all the kingdoms of the world, and the glory of them;
9 And saith unto him, All these things will I give thee, if thou wilt fall down and worship me.

New Revised Standard Version

THE LORD your God you shall fear; him you shall serve, and by his name alone you shall swear.

14 Do not follow other gods, any of the gods of the peoples who are all around you,
15 because the LORD your God, who is present with you, is a jealous God. The anger of the LORD your God would be kindled against you and he would destroy you from the face of the earth.

16 Do not put the LORD your God to the test, as you tested him at Massah.
• • • Matthew 4:4-11 • • •
BUT he answered, "It is written, 'One does not live by bread alone, but by every word that comes from the mouth of God.'"
5 Then the devil took him to the holy city and placed him on the pinnacle of the temple,

6 saying to him, "If you are the Son of God, throw yourself down; for it is written, 'He will command his angels concerning you,' and 'On their hands they will bear you up, so that you will not dash your foot against a stone.'"
7 Jesus said to him, "Again it is written, 'Do not put the Lord your God to the test.'"
8 Again, the devil took him to a very high mountain and showed him all the kingdoms of the world and their splendor;

9 and he said to him, "All these I will give you, if you will fall down and worship me."

MAIN THOUGHT: But he answered and said, It is written, Man shall not live by bread alone, but by every word that proceedeth out of the mouth of God. (Matthew 4:4, KJV)

DEUTERONOMY 6:13–16; MATTHEW 4:4–11

King James Version	*New Revised Standard Version*
10 Then saith Jesus unto him, Get thee hence, Satan: for it is written, Thou shalt worship the Lord thy God, and him only shalt thou serve.	10 Jesus said to him, "Away with you, Satan! for it is written, 'Worship the Lord your God, and serve only him.'"
11 Then the devil leaveth him, and, behold, angels came and ministered unto him.	11 Then the devil left him, and suddenly angels came and waited on him.

LESSON SETTING

Time: Mid-1400s B.C. (Deuteronomy); ca. A.D. 30 (Matthew)

Place: Jordan River (Deuteronomy); Wilderness (Matthew)

LESSON OUTLINE

I. Warnings Against Forgetting God's Blessings (Deuteronomy 6:13-16)

II. Jesus Uses the Scriptures While Tested (Matthew 4:4-11)

UNIFYING PRINCIPLE

In a world that offers persons countless ways to satisfy their lusts and appetites, discipline is required to maintain high ethical and moral standards. What helps people stick to their principles when other options tempt them? Jesus' thorough knowledge of Scripture gave Him strength to withstand difficult temptations.

INTRODUCTION

This week's lesson begins a new unit: "Jesus' Use of Scripture." In these lessons, we will see how Jesus uses the Law of Moses, the Prophets, and the Psalms throughout His ministry on earth. For today, we will study some of Moses' farewell address to the Israelites before they crossed the Jordan River and then see how Jesus combated the testing of Satan by quoting Moses' words from Deuteronomy. We will also note several parallels between the Israelites' and Jesus' testing in the wilderness.

EXPOSITION

I. WARNINGS AGAINST FORGETTING GOD'S BLESSINGS (DEUTERONOMY 6:13-16)

Deuteronomy 6 is divided into three sections, which not only detail the blessings that await the Israelites after they enter the Promised Land, but also warn them not to forget God but to devote themselves to worshiping Him only after they enter. Christopher Wright notes, "The overall flavor of the chapter is thus characteristic of the balance of Deuteronomy as a whole: obedience, though sanctioned by the reality of God's wrath, should be primarily motivated by gratitude and love in responding to God's grace" (*Deuteronomy* [Peabody, MA: Hendrickson Publishers, 1996], 101). The first section, comprising verses 1-9, tells how Israel is to relate to Yahweh. The *Shema* comes from verses 4-9 and commands the Israelites to love Yahweh with their whole being. The second section is composed of verses 10-19 and offers three warnings to the Israelites about the dangers of forgetting

God's blessings. Finally, verses 20-24 offer a model to be followed in teaching their children about God's protection over Israel and living a life that pleases Him.

In verses ten and eleven, Moses reminds the people that God has brought them to this land that had been promised centuries earlier to the Jewish patriarchs (see Gen. 12:1-3). The land they will soon be inhabiting is "a land with fine, large cities that you did not build, houses filled with all sorts of goods that you did not fill, hewn cisterns that you did not hew, vineyards and olive groves that you did not plant" (Deut. 6:10-11, NRSV). This land they will be living in will be a stark contrast to the dangers and barrenness of the wilderness. Walter Brueggemann notes that Moses recognizes the land "is ripe for disobedience" (*Deuteronomy* [Nashville: Abingdon Press, 2001], 85) because the Jews will face the temptation to become complacent and to forget the land was a gift from Yahweh.

Thus, Moses warns that after the Israelites feast on the plenteous food found in the land, they must "take care that [they] do not forget the LORD, who brought [them] out of the land of Egypt, out of the house of slavery" (v. 12, NRSV). In their complacency, Moses fears they will forget that God had rescued the Israelites from the bondage of Egypt. According to Wright, the Hebrew words for *slavery* and *serve* are derived from the same root, therefore, "those whom God had emancipated out of slavery to Egypt must live as God's own loyal slaves" (101). God demands total allegiance from His covenant people, so Moses commands the people, "The LORD your God you shall fear; him you shall serve, and by his name alone you shall swear" (v. 13, NRSV). Brueggemann explains, "In Hebrew, the normal word order of the sentence is inverted so that the emphasis falls upon YHWH: *YHWH* you will fear; *him* you will serve; *his name* you will swear by" (86). God is to be the foremost priority in the lives of His covenant people.

Verses fourteen and fifteen give a second warning from Moses: the people are not to forget Yahweh. Nor should they follow any of the other gods in the land. If the people do so, "the anger of the LORD [their] God would be kindled against [them] and he would destroy [them] from the face of the earth" (v. 15, NRSV). When the people take the land, they will be tempted by the numerous idols of the Canaanites, but worshiping anything other than Yahweh will be a direct violation of the covenant He established with Israel. He will have no choice but to punish Israel drastically. Brueggemann points out that Moses does not even name the false gods of the region to show his total disregard of their status and power (86).

Moses' final warning in verse sixteen involves Israel's forgetting Yahweh when difficulties arise. He reminds the Israelites how they tested Yahweh approximately forty years earlier at Massah. Wright explains that testing "does not mean to tempt someone by trying to entice them to do what is wrong, but rather to test or prove whether someone will really do what they say" (102). In Exodus 17:1-7, the account is given of how the people tested the Lord by inquiring whether He was able to supply water for them. Such questioning showed a severe lack of trust in God's faithfulness and ability to provide. Thus, Moses warns the people to learn from the mistakes of their ancestors and not to lose faith in God during difficult days. Instead, they must "diligently keep the commandments of the LORD [their] God, and his decrees, and his statutes that he has commanded" them (Deut. 6:17, NRSV). If the Israelites will remain faithful to God's commands, then it will "go well" (v. 18, NRSV) with them after they enter the Promised Land. Moses then concludes Deuteronomy 6 by telling of the importance of teaching their children about God's protection and provision for those who follow His commands.

II. JESUS USES THE SCRIPTURES WHILE TESTED (MATTHEW 4:4-11)

Several parallels can be found between the Israelites' wilderness wandering and the Matthew 4 account of Jesus' testing. Matthew begins by noting that Jesus was "led up by the Spirit into the wilderness" (v. 1, NRSV). Thus, Jesus shows His obedience to the Father by going into the wilderness. The first parallel can be found in that just as Jesus was led by the Spirit, so were the people led by Moses into the wilderness. In addition, Matthew observes that Jesus came out of Egypt, too, just as the enslaved Israelites did (see Matt. 2:15). While in the wilderness, Jesus fasts for forty days and forty nights, possibly alluding either to Moses' fasting for the same length of time while on Mt. Sinai (see Exod. 34:28) or to the Israelites' wandering in the wilderness for forty years. Throughout the account of Jesus' testing, Israel's past failures in the wilderness are implicitly contrasted to the actions of

Jesus who remains faithful and refuses to disobey the will of His Father. R. T. France writes, "The story of the testing in the wilderness is thus an elaborate typological presentation of Jesus as himself the true Israel, the 'Son of God' through whom God's redemptive purpose for his people is now at last to reach its fulfillment" (*The Gospel of Matthew* [Grand Rapids, MI: Eerdmans, 2007], 128).

Matthew writes that after His fasting, Jesus is "famished" (Matt. 4:2, NRSV) to emphasize the humanity of Christ and show that He will be facing Satan with the same human conditions of any other individual (M. Eugene Boring "The Gospel of Matthew, in The New Interpreter's Bible, Vol. 8 [Nashville: Abingdon Press, 1995], 163). In verse three, Satan knows Jesus is suffering from hunger and sees a prime opportunity to test Him. He tells Jesus, "'If you are the Son of God, command these stones to become loaves of bread'" (NRSV). France points out that the manna provided for the Israelites in the wilderness was picked up "like stones" in Exodus 16:14-16 (130). The qualifier regarding whether or not Jesus truly is the Son of God explains the nature of the testing by Satan. Satan is trying to see the true nature of the Father/Son relationship and how strongly the Son trusts the Father. Also note, the same qualifier will be applied to Jesus during His ultimate test three years later by those who mock Him on the cross (see Matt. 27:40) (France, 127).

So when Satan asks Jesus to turn the stones into bread, he wants to know if Jesus will provide food for Himself or whether He will trust the Father to provide. Jesus responds by referencing Deuteronomy

8:3: "'It is written, "One does not live by bread alone, but by every word that comes from the mouth of God"'" (Matt. 4:4, NRSV). France writes that one should not be surprised to see Jesus combat Satan's testing with Scriptures from the beginning of Deuteronomy because the *Shema* is found there. The *Shema* "[was] precisely that total commitment to God that this wilderness experience is designed to test" (128). If the Israelites had been fully committed to God, then they would not have failed so miserably in the wilderness. By responding to Satan in such a manner, Jesus is illustrating that obedience to the Father is of higher priority than self-gratification. Jesus recognizes that His hunger is a result of the Father's will at this time (France, 131).

Satan then transports Jesus to Jerusalem and perches Him on the pinnacle of the temple. Satan then quotes the Scriptures himself, but he perverts the true meaning of Psalm 91:11-12. He says, "'If you are the Son of God, throw yourself down; for it is written, "He will command his angels concerning you," and "On their hands they will bear you up, so that you will not dash your foot against a stone"'" (Matt. 4:6, NRSV). While the psalm does teach that God will protect His followers from danger, the verse does not insinuate that God's followers should actively seek perilous situations. Boring points out that Matthew "is illustrating that even the well-intentioned theologies and interpretations of Scripture in his own community can become the vehicle of a demonic alternative to the path of obedient suffering that Jesus has chosen as the path of messiahship" (164).

In response to Satan's test, Jesus once more references the words of Moses: "'Again it is written, "Do not put the Lord your God to the test"'" (v. 7, NRSV). This is the same warning Moses gave to the Israelites in Deuteronomy 6:16 when he reminded them how they had tested the Lord at Massah. Satan wants to create a situation where Jesus will force God to intervene and save His Son's life. France explains that doing so would compel the Father to serve the Son rather than for the Son to fulfill His role as a servant to the Father (133).

Next, Satan takes Jesus to "a very high mountain [to show] him all the kingdoms of the world and their splendor" (Matt. 4:8, NRSV). Boring notes that the reference to a mountain parallels Moses' ascending Mt. Sinai (164). Satan tells Jesus he will give Him all of the kingdoms of the world if He will prostrate Himself and worship Satan. Boring writes that "the temptation is for Jesus to rule the kingdoms of the world—i.e., to assume the role presently played by the Roman emperor, and to do it by capitulating to the devil's kingship" (164). Jesus will be publicly pronounced as the ruler of the world if He switches His allegiance from the Father to Satan.

Jesus tells Satan, "'Away with you, Satan! for it is written, "Worship the Lord your God, and serve only him"'" (v. 10, NRSV), quoting the warning of Moses in Deuteronomy 6:13. This is the first time Jesus uses words other than the Scriptures to respond to Satan. France explains that "Away with you" (Grk. *hypage*) is "an imperative occurring many times in Matthew, usually in the quite positive sense of sending someone to undertake a task or sending them away with their request granted" (135). One famous occurrence, though, of the phrase not being used positively is when Jesus responds to Peter's protesting that He will one day suffer and die. Jesus tells Peter, "'Get behind me, Satan!'" (Matt. 16:23, NRSV). The forcefulness of Jesus' words to Satan in Matthew 4 is quite apparent because Satan immediately leaves Him. France says, "Jesus is not just terminating the interview: he is sending his adversary packing" (136).

After Satan vanishes, Jesus' trusting in the Father is rewarded as angels come and bring food to Him. While this account of Satan's testing Jesus ends here, Matthew continues to illustrate the influence of Satan on Jesus' ministry. Boring explains, "In Matthew's theology, Satan, though defeated (12:28-29) continues to tempt Jesus during his ministry (16:23), at the crucifixion, and into the time of the church (13:19, 39); Satan is finally abolished at the end time (25:41)" (163). Also, even though Satan did offer Jesus all the kingdoms of the earth, Matthew records Jesus' words on the Mount of Olives (see Acts 1:12) at the conclusion of His Gospel: "'All authority in heaven and on earth has been given to me'" (Matt. 28:18, NRSV). After Jesus' resurrection, He rightfully accepts the authority over all kingdoms and powers due Him (Boring 164).

THE LESSON APPLIED

Christians ought to respond to temptation as Christ did. Whenever Satan tested Christ, the Son of God retorted with the Scriptures. Such a response showed that Christ was well-versed in the teachings of Moses, the Prophets, and the Psalms. He knew the words and their intent so that they could not be used against Him. Revealed in His knowledge of the Scriptures was Jesus' absolute trust in His Father. Without faith, knowledge does us no more good than Satan's did for him. Christians also need to study the Word daily and commit it to memory. When times of testing come, they can then rely on the Word of God as a viable aid.

LET'S TALK ABOUT IT

1. What does James say about Christians being tested?

James says that Christians should consider it a joyous occasion when they are tested because "the testing of [their] faith produces endurance; and let endurance have its full effect, so that [they] may be mature and complete, lacking in nothing" (James 1:3-4, NRSV). God allows His children to go through times of testing to strengthen their faith. Spiritual maturity comes from having overcome difficult situations and leaning on God.

HOME DAILY DEVOTIONAL READINGS
MAY 5-11, 2014

MONDAY	TUESDAY	WEDNESDAY	THURSDAY	FRIDAY	SATURDAY	SUNDAY
I Came from the Father	I Came to Do God's Will	I Came to Bring Light	I Came to Testify to Truth	I Came to Draw All People	I Came to Give Abundant Life	The Lord's Spirit Is upon Me
John 16:25-33	John 6:35-40	John 12:44-50	John 18:33-38	John 12:27-32	John 10:1-10	Luke 4:14-21

JESUS' MISSION ON EARTH

ADULT TOPIC:	BACKGROUND SCRIPTURES:
A FULFILLING VOCATION	LEVITICUS 25:8-55; ISAIAH 61:1-2; LUKE 4:14-21

LUKE 4:14–21

King James Version	*New Revised Standard Version*
AND Jesus returned in the power of the Spirit into Galilee: and there went out a fame of him through all the region round about.	THEN Jesus, filled with the power of the Spirit, returned to Galilee, and a report about him spread through all the surrounding country.
15 And he taught in their synagogues, being glorified of all.	15 He began to teach in their synagogues and was praised by everyone.
16 And he came to Nazareth, where he had been brought up: and, as his custom was, he went into the synagogue on the sabbath day, and stood up for to read.	16 When he came to Nazareth, where he had been brought up, he went to the synagogue on the sabbath day, as was his custom. He stood up to read,
17 And there was delivered unto him the book of the prophet Esaias. And when he had opened the book, he found the place where it was written,	17 and the scroll of the prophet Isaiah was given to him. He unrolled the scroll and found the place where it was written:
18 The Spirit of the Lord is upon me, because he hath anointed me to preach the gospel to the poor; he hath sent me to heal the broken-hearted, to preach deliverance to the captives, and recovering of sight to the blind, to set at liberty them that are bruised,	18 "The Spirit of the Lord is upon me, because he has anointed me to bring good news to the poor. He has sent me to proclaim release to the captives and recovery of sight to the blind, to let the oppressed go free,
19 To preach the acceptable year of the Lord.	19 to proclaim the year of the Lord's favor."
20 And he closed the book, and he gave it again to the minister, and sat down. And the eyes of all them that were in the synagogue were fastened on him.	20 And he rolled up the scroll, gave it back to the attendant, and sat down. The eyes of all in the synagogue were fixed on him.
21 And he began to say unto them, This day is this scripture fulfilled in your ears.	21 Then he began to say to them, "Today this scripture has been fulfilled in your hearing."

MAIN THOUGHT: And he began to say unto them, This day is this scripture fulfilled in your ears. (Luke 4:21, KJV)

LESSON SETTING
Time: A.D. 30
Place: Nazareth

LESSON OUTLINE
I. Jesus Begins His Ministry in Galilee
(Luke 4:14-15)
II. Jesus in the Synagogue at Nazareth
(Luke 4:16-21)

UNIFYING PRINCIPLE

Many people wrestle with issues around finding or choosing a job. What considerations should drive their decision-making process when it comes to vocation? Jesus Christ's identity and mission was informed by the prophetic tradition of the Hebrew Scriptures.

INTRODUCTION

Last week's lesson covered Jesus' testing in the wilderness by Satan. Satan tested Jesus in an attempt to determine how much the Son of God truly trusted the Father. Each of the three temptations Christ underwent tested this filial relationship. In response to each temptation, Jesus quoted from Deuteronomy 6—8, thereby providing a model for how Christians should respond to temptations today. For this week, we will look at the early days of Jesus' ministry and how He uses the words of Isaiah to proclaim that salvation has come to the world through Him.

EXPOSITION

I. JESUS BEGINS HIS MINISTRY IN GALILEE (LUKE 4:14-15)

Luke 4:14-15 serve as the prologue to the beginning of Jesus' ministry. Immediately after undergoing His wilderness testing, Luke records that Jesus is "filled with the power of the Spirit" (v. 14, NRSV) and returns to Galilee. According to R. Alan Culpepper, Luke wants to emphasize that Jesus' ministry is anointed by the Spirit just as His birth (see Luke 1:35), baptism (see Luke 3:22), and testing in the wilderness (see Luke 4:1) all were ("The Gospel of Luke" in *The New Interpreter's Bible*, Vol. 9 [Nashville: Abingdon Press, 1995], 103). While in Galilee, Jesus begins to teach in the synagogues, and a favorable report about Him begins to spread throughout the region.

Jesus' teaching will be a common theme in Luke's Gospel (see Luke 4:31; 5:3, 17; 6:6) (Culpepper, 103). In his introduction to Jesus' Galilean ministry, Luke emphasizes how Jesus works as a teacher, where He teaches, how the Holy Spirit anoints His teaching, and the results of His teaching. Culpepper summarizes, "This scene, therefore, functions as a keynote to the entire ministry of Jesus, setting forth the perspective from which it is to be understood" (102). This sets the pattern for Jesus to further His ministry: whenever He travels to new locales, He will usually begin by teaching in the synagogue and then ministering to the people.

As a result of Jesus' teaching, people praise the Father. Praising God will be another important theme in Luke. On two other occasions in Galilee alone, people leave Jesus and begin praising God after encountering Him (see Luke 5:25-26; 7:16). Culpepper writes that praising God "is the only appropriate response to God's disclosure of Jesus as the Savior" (103).

II. JESUS IN THE SYNAGOGUE AT NAZARETH (LUKE 4:16-21)

As verse fifteen shared, Jesus was widely appreciated early in His ministry—this will change dramatically after His first appearance in the synagogue at Nazareth. In Luke 4:16-30, several examples of Lukan motifs are found: the anointing of the Holy Spirit on Jesus' ministry, the parallels between Jesus' ministry and those of the Old Testament prophets, the proclamation of the Gospel to the Jews first, acceptance which is then followed by rejection, and the proclamation that the Gospel will also be for the Gentiles (Culpepper, 104). Joel Green points out that this particular account in Luke will be a significant milestone in Jesus' ministry and is later referred to in Luke 7:21-22 and Acts 10:38 (*The Gospel of Luke* [Grand Rapids, MI: Eerdmans, 1997], 207).

In verse sixteen, Jesus arrives in Nazareth, and Luke reminds his readers that this is where Jesus spent His childhood. Most of the people in the town knew who Jesus and His parents were. On the Sabbath, Jesus goes into the synagogue. Not much is concretely known about the order of worship in synagogues at this time. More than likely, the following elements occurred in some fashion: a recitation of the *Shema* and the Decalogue, the giving of eighteen benedictions, a public reading from a particular passage of Scripture, a reading from the Psalms, and a blessing (Culpepper, 105). Various individuals might have been asked to read the Scriptures and lead in prayer.

In verse seventeen, Jesus is given a scroll containing the words of Isaiah to read. He finds the passage He wishes to read and does so while standing. According to Culpepper, Jesus would have read the scroll aloud in Hebrew and then translated and explained the Scriptures in Aramaic. This custom of reading and translating the Scriptures can be traced back as early as Nehemiah 8:8 after the Jews returned from Babylonian captivity (105). After reading the passage He sits down and begins to teach.

The Isaiah passage that Luke records Jesus reading is a redacted combination of Isaiah 58:6 and 61:1-2. Luke purposefully modifies the Scriptures to highlight certain themes. For instance, Luke omits "to bind up the brokenhearted" (NRSV) from Isaiah 61:1, and he changes the conclusion of the passage to read as "'to proclaim the year of the Lord's favor'" (Luke 4:19, NRSV). He also changes the verb in Isaiah 58:6 to an infinitive to set up four infinitive phrases: "'to bring good news ... to proclaim ... to let the oppressed go free ... to proclaim'" (Luke 4:18-19, NRSV). Also, the word *me* appears three times in the passage to emphasize that Jesus is the one who is carrying out God's purpose and salvation can only be found in Him (Green, 214).

In Luke 4:18, Jesus reads that "'The Spirit of the Lord is upon me'" (NRSV). Again, Luke is sure to point out that the Spirit's anointing is on Jesus. Jesus then reads that He has been anointed by the Holy Spirit "'to bring good news to the poor'" (ibid.). These words echo those of Mary in the *Magnificat* (see Luke 1:46-55). Green points out that being poor in the ancient Mediterranean world did not just connote poverty; rather, being poor could also imply having a lack of social status and education (211). The reader of Luke's Gospel will soon realize that Luke stresses the plight of the poor more than any other Gospel writer (Culpepper, 105). For example, only Luke expands Jesus' beatitudes by including an exhortation of the poor and a warning to the rich in Luke 6:20-25, and Luke is the only Gospel writer to include the parable of the rich man and Lazarus (see Luke 16:19-31). Thus, Jesus seeks to empower people of lower social status and not just those who are in extreme poverty.

Jesus continues by saying that the Spirit has anointed Him to "'to proclaim release to the captives'" (Luke 4:18, NRSV). Interestingly, this is the only time in the New Testament that this form of the word *captives* is used (Culpepper, 105). Throughout His ministry, Jesus will free people from various types of bondage, both spiritual and physical. The Greek word for *release* used in Luke's Gospel implies forgiveness of sins. Culpepper writes, "Forgiveness of sin, therefore, can also be seen as a form of release from bondage" (106). When people encounter the Son of God and place their faith in Him, they are set free from sin and guilt.

The Spirit has also anointed Jesus to restore "'sight to the blind'" (v. 18, NRSV). For the Jews, the blind receiving their sight "was closely associated with the prophetic vision of the fulfillment of God's promises to Israel" as seen in the prophecies of Isaiah (Culpepper,106). Isaiah 35:5 states that when God promises that the redeemed will return to Israel from captivity, "the eyes of the blind shall be opened" (NRSV). In Isaiah 42:6-7, the Lord promises to send a Servant who will come to be "a light to the nations, to open the eyes that are blind, to bring out the prisoners from the dungeon, from prison those who sit in darkness" (NRSV). Thus, Jesus is pronouncing that He is the promised "light to the nations" (ibid.) who has come to bring salvation to Israel. Those suffering from spiritual blindness will regain their sight and see clearly after meeting Him.

Jesus concludes by saying that the Spirit has anointed Him "'to let the oppressed go free, to proclaim the year of the Lord's favor'" (vv. 18-19, NRSV). These two phrases evoke language related to teachings on the year of Jubilee from Leviticus 25. Every fiftieth year, the Jews were supposed to forgive their neighbors' debts and give freedom to their slaves. Green notes that both Isaiah 58 and 61 develop these Jubilee themes and describe "the coming redemption from exile and captivity in the eschatological language of jubilary release" (212). Jesus announces that He is bringing the same kind of release from sin.

After Jesus finishes reading, He sits down and "the eyes of all in the synagogue [are] fixed on him" (v. 20, NRSV). He then proclaims, "'Today this scripture has been fulfilled in your hearing'" (v. 21, NRSV), declaring once and for all that He is the one whom the Scriptures described. Green writes that Jesus has informed the crowd that "the long-awaited epoch of salvation had been inaugurated" (214). The crowd is delighted by this news because in their minds Jesus has said that He has come to bless those in Nazareth specifically. Luke describes the people's response: "All spoke well of him and were amazed at the gracious words that came from his mouth" (v. 22, NRSV). The people marvel and ask "'Is not this Joseph's son?'" (ibid.) to show approval of their hometown hero.

Jesus recognizes immediately that the people approve of His message for the wrong reasons and will one day reject Him just as they did the prophets of old. Since the people desire only to see miracles and wonders within a fully restored Israelite nation, they will fail to understand the true purpose of His coming and start to mock Him. They will scornfully tell Him, "'Doctor, cure yourself'" and "'Do here also in your hometown the things that we have heard you did at Capernaum'" (v. 23, NRSV). This is what spurs Jesus to say, "'Truly I tell you, no prophet is accepted in the prophet's hometown'" (v. 24, NRSV).

His ministry will parallel those of the Old Testament prophets who were rejected by their own people. In order to explain that His ministry is for the poor and oppressed everywhere and not just the Jews, Jesus recounts specific stories of Elijah and Elisha when they ministered to Gentiles (see Luke 4:25-27). In 1 Kings 17:8-24, Elijah was sent to minister to a widow at Zarapeth, which was a city in Sidon. There he performed the miracle of providing never-ending oil for the widow as well as raising her son form the dead. In 2 Kings 5:1-19, the story of Elisha's curing of Naaman is found. Naaman was a commander of the Syrian army and suffering from leprosy. He went to Elisha and was healed after following Elisha's commands to wash himself seven times in the Jordan River. Both of these stories showed God's favor on the Gentiles. Upon hearing this, the crowd becomes enraged and tries to throw Jesus off of a cliff (see Luke 4:29-30). Thus, the words of Jesus Christ came true: He was accepted and then rejected by those in His hometown.

THE LESSON APPLIED

Today's lesson stressed the importance of remaining true to one's ministry calling. Jesus knew what His true purpose was for coming to earth. He did not come just to perform miracles and alleviate physical oppression; He came to bring spiritual freedom from sins and usher in God's Kingdom through His life death, and resurrection. He knew that, although He would be popular initially, He would one day be faced with hatred and scorn. He knew that His own people would reject Him. Christians today know they must remain faithful to the ministry God has called them to even if they will be hated and rejected for the Lord's sake.

LET'S TALK ABOUT IT

1. Why did Luke emphasize so much the anointing of the Spirit on Jesus' life and ministry?

Repeatedly throughout his Gospel, Luke stressed the anointing of the Holy Spirit on Jesus. Doing so continued to illustrate to His readers that Jesus was truly the Son of God and His work was done in obedience to the Father's will. Christians today are also anointed by the Holy Spirit. Their bodies are temples in which the Holy Spirit dwells. The Holy Spirit guides and directs Christians just as it did Jesus.

HOME DAILY DEVOTIONAL READINGS
MAY 12-18, 2014

MONDAY	TUESDAY	WEDNESDAY	THURSDAY	FRIDAY	SATURDAY	SUNDAY
Commandments Learned by Rote	Testing and Fear	We Uphold the Law	Fulfilling the Law	But I Say to You	Be Perfect	What Proceeds from the Heart
Isaiah 29:13-19	Exodus 20:12-21	Romans 3:21-31	Matthew 5:14-20	Matthew 5:27-37	Matthew 5:38-48	Matthew 15:1-8

JESUS' TEACHING ON THE LAW

ADULT TOPIC:	BACKGROUND SCRIPTURES:
GET IT RIGHT	EXODUS 20; ISAIAH 29:13-14; MATTHEW 5:17-48; 15:1-19; ROMANS 3:31

MATTHEW 15:1–11, 15–20

King James Version

THEN came to Jesus scribes and Pharisees, which were of Jerusalem, saying,

2 Why do thy disciples transgress the tradition of the elders? for they wash not their hands when they eat bread.

3 But he answered and said unto them, Why do ye also transgress the commandment of God by your tradition?

4 For God commanded, saying, Honour thy father and mother: and, He that curseth father or mother, let him die the death.

5 But ye say, Whosoever shall say to his father or his mother, It is a gift, by whatsoever thou mightest be profited by me;

6 And honour not his father or his mother, he shall be free. Thus have ye made the commandment of God of none effect by your tradition.

7 Ye hypocrites, well did Esaias prophesy of you, saying,

8 This people draweth nigh unto me with their mouth, and honoureth me with their lips; but their heart is far from me.

9 But in vain they do worship me, teaching for doctrines the commandments of men.

10 And he called the multitude, and said unto them, Hear, and understand:

11 Not that which goeth into the mouth defileth a man; but that which cometh out of the mouth, this defileth a man.

• • • • • •

New Revised Standard Version

THEN Pharisees and scribes came to Jesus from Jerusalem and said,

2 "Why do your disciples break the tradition of the elders? For they do not wash their hands before they eat."

3 He answered them, "And why do you break the commandment of God for the sake of your tradition?

4 For God said, 'Honor your father and your mother,' and, 'Whoever speaks evil of father or mother must surely die.'

5 But you say that whoever tells father or mother, 'Whatever support you might have had from me is given to God,' then that person need not honor the father.

6 So, for the sake of your tradition, you make void the word of God.

7 You hypocrites! Isaiah prophesied rightly about you when he said:

8 'This people honors me with their lips, but their hearts are far from me;

9 in vain do they worship me, teaching human precepts as doctrines.'"

10 Then he called the crowd to him and said to them, "Listen and understand:

11 it is not what goes into the mouth that defiles a person, but it is what comes out of the mouth that defiles."

• • • • • •

MAIN THOUGHT: This people draweth nigh unto me with their mouth, and honoureth me with their lips; but their heart is far from me. But in vain they do worship me, teaching for doctrines the commandments of men. (Matthew 15:8–9, KJV)

MATTHEW 15:1-11, 15-20

King James Version	*New Revised Standard Version*
15 Then answered Peter and said unto him, Declare unto us this parable.	15 But Peter said to him, "Explain this parable to us."
16 And Jesus said, Are ye also yet without understanding?	16 Then he said, "Are you also still without understanding?
17 Do not ye yet understand, that whatsoever entereth in at the mouth goeth into the belly, and is cast out into the draught?	17 Do you not see that whatever goes into the mouth enters the stomach, and goes out into the sewer?
18 But those things which proceed out of the mouth come forth from the heart; and they defile the man.	18 But what comes out of the mouth proceeds from the heart, and this is what defiles.
19 For out of the heart proceed evil thoughts, murders, adulteries, fornications, thefts, false witness, blasphemies:	19 For out of the heart come evil intentions, murder, adultery, fornication, theft, false witness, slander.
20 These are the things which defile a man: but to eat with unwashen hands defileth not a man.	20 These are what defile a person, but to eat with unwashed hands does not defile."

LESSON SETTING

Time: ca. A.D. 30
Place: Galilee

LESSON OUTLINE

I. **Jesus Rebukes the Pharisees (Matthew 15:1-9)**
II. **What Defiles a Person (Matthew 15:10-11, 15-20)**

UNIFYING PRINCIPLE

Traditions are powerful guides for determining actions and behavior. How can Christians avoid using traditions to set up the word of the Law against the spirit of the Law? While Jesus was a firm believer in tradition, he warned against a misuse of tradition that makes "'void the word of God'" (Matt. 15:6, NRSV).

INTRODUCTION

The previous week's lesson involved a study of the onset of Jesus' ministry in Galilee. While in his hometown of Nazareth, He spoke at the synagogue and announced that salvation had come through Him. Today, we are going to look at the last major account of Jesus' ministry in Galilee as recorded in Matthew 15:1-20. Jesus teaches that the heart is what determines if a person is clean or unclean—not simply washing hands before a meal.

A brief overview of the Gospel of Matthew is imperative to understand the context in which today's lesson takes place. Matthew was the favorite Gospel of the early Church fathers and was quoted the most in their writings (M. Eugene Boring, "The Gospel of Matthew" in *The New Interpreter's Bible*, Vol. 8 [Nashville: Abingdon Press, 1995], 89). One of the reasons Matthew was a favorite is because the Gospel was written in a way that aided memorization. This is why so many people quote passages such as the Lord's Prayer, the Beatitudes, and Peter's confession from Matthew. Also, until the middle of the nineteenth century, most scholars believed it to be the first written Gospel of the New Testament. This is why the book was placed first in the New Testament canon. Today, against Church tradition, many biblical scholars argue that Mark was written first due to text critical considerations. This argument in no way detracts from Matthew's authority as one of four canonical Gospels.

Most conservative scholars believe Matthew composed his book ca. A.D. 50-60, prior to the destruction of the temple because numerous references to Jerusalem are found in the Gospel as though it were still standing. Matthew's Gospel was written with a Jewish audience in mind, thereby leading many to refer to it as the "Jewish Gospel." Matthew doesn't explain the various Jewish customs that are mentioned in his book as does Mark, who was writing to a Gentile audience. Matthew's purpose in writing his Gospel is to explain to Jews the validity of the claim that Jesus is the Son of God and is bringing a new covenant which is not an abolishment of the Law of Moses but rather its fulfillment. This is why Matthew begins his Gospel with a genealogy "which served the ancient reader as a bridge connecting the Gospel with the story of salvation in the Hebrew Bible" (ibid., 89). Matthew seeks to reveal how Jesus, the promised Messiah, was a direct descendant of Abraham and David.

In addition, Matthew presents Jesus as the King who has begun a new Kingdom on earth which will include both Jews and Gentiles. R. T. France writes, "Matthew portrays a new community which is both faithful to its scriptural heritage and open to the new directions demanded by Jesus' proclamation of the kingdom of heaven, and therefore necessarily expanding beyond the bounds of the Jewish people" (*The Gospel of Matthew* [Grand Rapids: Eerdmans, 2007], 18). Salvation has been made possible for all people, not just the Jews who had always been God's covenant people. Boring also points out that in the Gospel of Matthew, the Kingdom of God is in constant struggle with Satan's worldly kingdom. Jesus struggles throughout the Gospel with Satan, who does not appear only at Jesus' wilderness temptation (see Matt. 4:1-11). For example, references to Beelzebub in Matthew 9:32-34 and 10:25 stress the tension between the two warring kingdoms (117). In the end, though, the Kingdom of God will triumph and Satan will be defeated.

EXPOSITION

I. JESUS REBUKES THE PHARISEES (MATTHEW 15:1-9)

Matthew 15:1-20 is centered on one theme although the audience changes three times throughout the narrative. The first audience present in verses 1-9 is the Pharisees and scribes. Matthew writes that the Pharisees and scribes come from Jerusalem to speak to Jesus. Boring notes that their coming from Jerusalem is "an anticipation of the passion" (331). They ask Jesus, "'Why do your disciples break the tradition of the elders? For they do not wash their hands before they eat'" (Matt. 15:2, NRSV). The issue that the Pharisees and scribes are noting is not simply about cleanliness before a meal; rather, they are asking about ritual purity and being deemed clean before God.

The practice of washing hands for lay-persons is actually not a regulation of the Mosaic Law. The only rules for washing of hands are given for the priests in Exodus 30:17-21 who are commanded to wash their hands and feet prior to performing their duties in the temple (Boring, 332). When the Pharisees cite "'the traditions of the elders'" (Matt. 15:2, NRSV), they are referring to a Pharisaic tradition which they have imposed on the people. The regulations were meant to protect the people from accidentally breaking the law but had themselves become rigid and unforgiving.

Even so, the Pharisees once had good reasoning and intentions for their codes. Boring explains that for the Jews, "what is 'clean' and 'unclean' is a matter of maintaining the holiness to which the people of God are called, and it corresponds to God's own holiness" (331). Since God is holy, He demands that His people be cleansed from sin and be holy and righteous like Him. This is what the Pharisees felt was at stake when their traditions were flouted.

France points out that the issue of purification has already been present in Matthew. In chapters eight and nine alone, Jesus had healed unclean Gentiles, two demon-possessed men in Gadarenes, had been touched by a woman with an issue of blood, and brought a dead girl back to life. For Jesus to have performed these miracles, He would have put Himself at risk of becoming unclean according to the teachings of Moses (575). France continues by saying that Jesus' dealing with unclean individuals goes "to the heart of Jesus' ministry" (ibid.). Another example of Jesus' involvement with unclean people immediately follows today's passage when Jesus encounters a Canaanite woman whose faith He will praise (see 15:21-28). Matthew intends to drive home the principle to His Jewish audience that Jesus came for all people—not just "clean" Jews.

Jesus takes the question asked by the Pharisees and scribes as an opportunity to teach, saying, "'And why do you break the commandment of God for the sake of your tradition?'" (v. 3, NRSV). He then references an obscure but familiar Jewish law. Jesus says that while the Decalogue commands that one honors one's parents, some of the Pharisees were neglecting to honor their parents by citing the law of Corban. Mark 7:1-23 offers a parallel account of Matthew 15:1-20 and explains more fully what Jesus is talking about. If a person presented a piece of property as an offering to the temple, he could say the offering was "Corban" and make a vow that the property could never be taken back. While the property was offered to the temple, it was still technically in the possession of the giver. What the Pharisees and scribes were doing was instead of using their property to help provide for their parents, they were keeping the property for themselves under the guise of offering it to the temple (France, 581). Jesus knows that the Pharisees and scribes were deceitfully disobeying the fifth commandment in the name of making offerings to God and pronounces, "'For the sake of your tradition, you make void the word of God'" (Matt. 15:6, NRSV). He accuses the religious leaders of voiding the Law of its original intent and rendering it useless (France, 581).

Jesus continues His attack on the Pharisees and scribes by calling them hypocrites and quoting from Isaiah 29:13: "'This people honors me with their lips, but their hearts are far from me; in vain do they worship me, teaching human precepts as doctrines'" (Matt. 15:8-9, NRSV). Isaiah had been speaking of the false piety of the Jews in the eighth century B.C., but the words apply perfectly to the Pharisees and scribes' false worship. Their worship means nothing to God because their worship comes from what they have invented rather than what God had instructed. France points out that the mentioning of lips and hearts by Jesus will serve as a prelude to Matthew 15:11 (582).

II. WHAT DEFILES A PERSON (MATTHEW 15:10-11, 15-20)

The audience shifts in verses 10-11 to the crowd around Jesus. Jesus declares publicly, "'Listen and understand: it is not what goes into the mouth that defiles a person, but it is what comes out of the mouth that defiles'" (vv. 10-11, NRSV). With this statement, Jesus has made a radical assertion about the Law. The Jews had always been taught they must avoid any unclean foods in order to retain their purity as a nation (see Lev. 11; 17:10-16). Eating clean foods separated the Jews from the pagan nations surrounding them. Now, Jesus is teaching that impurity comes from the internal rather than the external. Boring writes that Jesus is "declaring the relative importance of the inner commitments of the heart, as they come to expression in the way one speaks and acts, over against the ritual commandments, which are still not abolished" (333).

Jesus is not doing away with the teachings of Moses entirely; instead, He is emphasizing such teachings as Hosea 6:6: "For I desire steadfast love and not sacrifice, the knowledge of God rather than burnt offerings" (NRSV). God desires people's love and dedication more than offerings and sacrifices alone. Boring notes that Matthew quotes Hosea twice in his Gospel (see Matt. 9:13; 12:7), giving credence to subtle echoes of Hosea which can be found in Jesus' words (333).

Beginning in verse twelve, the audience shifts again to a private discussion with the Disciples who tell Jesus that the Pharisees are offended at His words. Jesus then compares the Pharisees to "'blind guides of the blind'" (Matt. 15:14, NRSV), meaning they are dangerously teaching the people the wrong way because they also lack understanding. France writes, "If these leaders of Israel have themselves missed the way in their understanding of what it means to be the people of God (as vv. 7-9 have powerfully alleged), their influence on other Jews can only lead them into the same 'ditch' of distorted religious values" (585). Peter then asks Jesus to explain fully what He told them about defilement. Jesus chastises His Disciples because of their continued lack of understanding and reminds them that what goes into a person is not the issue of concern because it eventually comes out as waste. Instead, the sinful words and thoughts that proceed from a person are what defile because they come from the heart and show the true nature of that person.

Jesus continues by giving a vice catalogue similar to others found in the New Testament (see Rom. 1:29-31; Gal.

5:19-20): "'For out of the heart come evil intentions, murder, adultery, fornication, theft, false witness, slander. These are what defile a person, but to eat with unwashed hands does not defile'" (Matt. 15:19-21, NRSV). The thoughts of the heart are what lead to sinful behavior. Four of the six vices are taken directly from the Decalogue and listed in the same order (France, 586). When Jesus mentions slander and fornication, He is showing that they are branches of the sixth and ninth commandment (ibid.). Jesus ends His teaching by reiterating that the inside of a person is what determines if he or she is clean, not just outward rituals which do not change the heart.

THE LESSON APPLIED

Today's lesson emphasized the importance of following the spirit of the Law as opposed to merely the letter of the Law. The Pharisees and scribes were so determined to follow the Law at all costs that they forgot why they were doing so. Both church leaders and members must be wary of the same temptation. While it is important to keep God's Law, moral and ethical rules are not the goal of a Christian life. Rather, these are tools which help us to bring glory to God and draw outsiders into His family of believers. Law-keeping without love will not result in the Church that God desires or the lives that we desire when we seek His face.

God desires worship that comes from a "broken and contrite heart" (Ps. 51:17, NRSV). In John 4, Jesus tells the Samaritan woman, "'The hour is coming, and is now here, when the true worshipers will worship the Father in spirit and truth, for the Father seeks such as these to worship him. God is spirit, and those who worship him must worship in spirit and truth'" (vv. 23-24, NRSV). Those who worship God must do so with the right motives and pure hearts.

LET'S TALK ABOUT IT

1. **Does the heart only produce evil intents and desires?**

While Jesus does teach that evil intents and desires come from the heart in Matthew 15, the Gospel of Matthew teaches that the heart is capable of being pure and producing good fruits. In Matthew 5:8, Jesus says, "'The pure in heart ... will see God'" (NRSV). Jesus says in Matthew 12:34-35, "'Out of the abundance of the heart the mouth speaks. The good person brings good things out of a good treasure'" (NRSV). Finally, Matthew 22:37 lists the heart as being one of the parts of the body that must fully love the Lord when Jesus names the greatest commandment. A person's heart is capable of producing good and bad fruits; the person must decide which is going to be produced.

HOME DAILY DEVOTIONAL READINGS
MAY 19–25, 2014

MONDAY	TUESDAY	WEDNESDAY	THURSDAY	FRIDAY	SATURDAY	SUNDAY
Love and Commandment Keeping	Serving God with Heart and Soul	Keeping God's Commandments Always	Relating to Your Neighbor	Sin Against a Neighbor or God	They Shall Not Be Moved	Loving God and Neighbor
Deuteronomy 7:7-16	Deuteronomy 10:12-21	Deuteronomy 11:1-7	Leviticus 19:11-17	1 Kings 8:31-36	Psalm 15	Leviticus 19:18; Deut. 6:4-9; Mark 12:28-34

THE GREATEST COMMANDMENT

ADULT TOPIC: BACKGROUND SCRIPTURES:
FIRST THINGS FIRST   LEVITICUS 19:18; DEUTERONOMY 4:35; 6:1-9; MARK 12:28-34

LEVITICUS 19:18; DEUTERONOMY 6:4-9; MARK 12:28-34

King James Version

THOU shalt not avenge, nor bear any grudge against the children of thy people, but thou shalt love thy neighbour as thyself: I am the LORD.

• • • Deuteronomy 6:4-9 • • •

HEAR, O Israel: The LORD our God is one LORD:

5 And thou shalt love the LORD thy God with all thine heart, and with all thy soul, and with all thy might.

6 And these words, which I command thee this day, shall be in thine heart:

7 And thou shalt teach them diligently unto thy children, and shalt talk of them when thou sittest in thine house, and when thou walkest by the way, and when thou liest down, and when thou risest up.

8 And thou shalt bind them for a sign upon thine hand, and they shall be as frontlets between thine eyes.

9 And thou shalt write them upon the posts of thy house, and on thy gates.

• • • Mark 12:28-34 • • •

AND one of the scribes came, and having heard them reasoning together, and perceiving that he had answered them well, asked him, Which is the first commandment of all?

New Revised Standard Version

YOU shall not take vengeance or bear a grudge against any of your people, but you shall love your neighbor as yourself: I am the LORD.

• • • Deuteronomy 6:4-9 • • •

HEAR, O Israel: The LORD is our God, the LORD alone.

5 You shall love the LORD your God with all your heart, and with all your soul, and with all your might.

6 Keep these words that I am commanding you today in your heart.

7 Recite them to your children and talk about them when you are at home and when you are away, when you lie down and when you rise.

8 Bind them as a sign on your hand, fix them as an emblem on your forehead,

9 and write them on the doorposts of your house and on your gates.

• • • Mark 12:28-34 • • •

ONE of the scribes came near and heard them disputing with one another, and seeing that he answered them well, he asked him, "Which commandment is the first of all?"

MAIN THOUGHT: And thou shalt love the Lord thy God with all thy heart, and with all thy soul, and with all thy mind, and with all thy strength: this is the first commandment. And the second is like, namely this, Thou shall love thy neighbour as thyself. There is none other commandment greater than these. (Mark 12:30–31, KJV)

LEVITICUS 19:18; DEUTERONOMY 6:4-9; MARK 12:28-34

King James Version	*New Revised Standard Version*
29 And Jesus answered him, The first of all the commandments is, Hear, O Israel; The Lord our God is one Lord:	29 Jesus answered, "The first is, 'Hear, O Israel: the Lord our God, the Lord is one;
30 And thou shalt love the Lord thy God with all thy heart, and with all thy soul, and with all thy mind, and with all thy strength: this is the first commandment.	30 you shall love the Lord your God with all your heart, and with all your soul, and with all your mind, and with all your strength.'
31 And the second is like, namely this, Thou shall love thy neighbour as thyself. There is none other commandment greater than these.	31 The second is this, 'You shall love your neighbor as yourself.' There is no other commandment greater than these."
32 And the scribe said unto him, Well, Master, thou hast said the truth: for there is one God; and there is none other but he:	32 Then the scribe said to him, "You are right, Teacher; you have truly said that 'he is one, and besides him there is no other';
33 And to love him with all the heart, and with all the understanding, and with all the soul, and with all the strength, and to love his neighbour as himself, is more than all whole burnt offerings and sacrifices.	33 and 'to love him with all the heart, and with all the understanding, and with all the strength,' and 'to love one's neighbor as oneself,'—this is much more important than all whole burnt offerings and sacrifices."
34 And when Jesus saw that he answered discreetly, he said unto him, Thou art not far from the kingdom of God. And no man after that durst ask him any question.	34 When Jesus saw that he answered wisely, he said to him, "You are not far from the kingdom of God." After that no one dared to ask him any question.

LESSON SETTING

> **Time:** circa 1350 B.C.; A.D. 29
>
> **Place:** Mount Sinai; Mount Nebo; Jerusalem

LESSON OUTLINE

I. **The Call to Holiness (Leviticus 19:18)**

II. **Memory and Identity (Deuteronomy 6:4-9)**

III. **The Orienting Commands (Mark 12:28-34)**

UNIFYING PRINCIPLE

In societies that traditionally value individual achievement, it is assumed that people will look out for their best interests before the interests of others. What safeguards exist to counter such narcissistic inclinations? When Jesus quoted Deuteronomy 6:4–5, he reminded the disputants that tradition had already determined which commandment was greatest. In addition, he said that Christians are not far from the Kingdom of God when the highest priority in their lives is to love God and neighbor.

INTRODUCTION

In today's passages, we encounter what Jesus identifies as the first and second commands. The reference to the first and second commands is not a matter of distinguishing importance, but a means of discerning which commands give shape to the rest of the Law. This is an essential question because it is attempting to discover the core of the identity of the

Israelites. Much of the conflict that arises between Jesus and His interlocutors concerns the identity of the Jewish faith (and, by extension, the identity of the Christian faith). Jesus calls His followers to find their identity in the love of God and love of neighbor. Jesus' teaching is that practices and purity are to be directed toward love of neighbor. In directing these towards love of neighbor, they should be further characterized by the love of God. This discussion is concerned with arriving at an understanding of memory and identity that is characterized by the holiness of God and the holiness of God's people.

EXPOSITION

I. THE CALL TO HOLINESS (LEVITICUS 19:18)

The command of Leviticus 19:18 is found in the context of the holiness code of Leviticus 19. *Holiness* is being set apart, but it is being set apart for a reason. "If holiness is about separation, then it is a separation for the sake of granting life and the giving over of oneself as the basis for its very being" (Ephraim Radner, *Leviticus* [Grand Rapids: Brazos Press, 2008], 202). Radner goes on to further describe holiness as "a kind of approach" (ibid., 203). This indicates that holiness may not be so much a quality, but is instead the way one approaches their Christian walk and challenges others in that approach. In the commandment of Leviticus 19:18, "taking vengeance" and "bearing a grudge" become a hindrance to being set apart for the giving of life because these are antithetical to life. They draw one away from the love that binds together the divine life of God in the perfect love of Father, Son,

and Holy Spirit. Yahweh commands the Israelites not only to "not take vengeance" and "not bear a grudge," but He also commands them, "'You shall love your neighbor as yourself'" (Lev. 19:18, NRSV). This command is both outwardly and inwardly focused: to love one's neighbor, one must love one's self. This also means that to be drawn into the life of God—into God's holiness—one must give one's self completely to loving his or her neighbor in a way that is life-giving to the neighbor.

II. MEMORY AND IDENTITY (DEUTERONOMY 6:4-9)

The second passage that we are discussing today comes from a section of Deuteronomy that is referred to as the *Shema*. This name derives from the Hebrew imperative form of *shama'*, which means "hear." This command of Moses to the people of Israel to *hear* serves as a point of orientation. The following command has a certain level of ambiguity due to a lack of verbs in the Hebrew text. Most of the discussion concerns the translation of *Yahweh 'ekhad*. This can be translated either "Yahweh is one" or "Yahweh alone." Both translations affirm certain true elements of the nature of Yahweh. In both, there is an affirmation that Israel's worship should be solely directed to Yahweh. The idea that Yahweh alone is God affirms that the Israelites are called to a singular allegiance, and their identity is found in this allegiance.

As the Israelites are called to worship God, Moses calls the Israelites to love Yahweh their God "with all [their] heart, and with all [their] soul, and with all [their] might" (Deut. 6:5, NRSV). Walter Brueggemann, in agreement with S. Dean

McBride, affirms "that the factoring out of 'heart, mind, soul' as distinctive spheres of commitment or psychological elements is not very helpful…. Rather the effect of the triad is cumulative" (*Deuteronomy* [Nashville: Abingdon Press, 2001], 83). The command to the Israelites is that their worship of Yahweh their God should be embodied in a love that requires the entirety of their being. The love and worship of the Israelites can be directed toward no other.

Now Moses commands the Israelites to remember. The Israelites are commanded to "keep these words … in [their] heart" (Deut. 6:6, NRSV). They are to do this through recitation and discussion at every point in the day. They are also to write the words of the commandments everywhere so that they will be visually reinforced. "Moses proposes 'saturation education' so that a child's imaginative horizon is completely pervaded by signs and reminders of this imperative" (Brueggemann, 85). Moses commands specifically that the Israelites must recite these commandments to their children. This is again to reinforce the importance of memory in the life of Israel. However, this is not a memory that is identified with one generation alone, but this is memory that is passed down from generation to generation. The Israelites, as do Christians, need a constant reminder of who they are and the God they serve. The call to pass this memory down from generation to generation is a call to establish and reinforce a tradition. This tradition then serves the Israelites in reorienting them in their service to Yahweh their God.

III. THE ORIENTING COMMANDS (MARK 12:28-34)

As we enter this final passage, we find Jesus being asked a question by a scribe. Throughout the Gospel of Mark, Jesus has been asked questions by interlocutors who intend to trap Him. In contrast, this scribe is portrayed as asking an honest question "in search of truth" (Morna Hooker, *The Gospel According to Saint Mark* [Peabody: Hendrickson Publishers, 1991], 286). The scribe asks the question because he has heard the dispute between Jesus and the Sadducees concerning the resurrection. Thus the scribe, trusting Jesus' ability to answer questions about the Law well, asks Jesus which commandment is the greatest of all. The scribe is not attempting to trap Jesus as many of His interlocutors have attempted up to this point but is asking an honest question, seeking a truthful reply. The question of which commandment is first is not a question about importance, but is instead a question about which commandment gives shape to the rest of the Law. "The issue was not which of the commandments was the most important (since all were important and must be kept), but whether there was some basic principle from which the whole Law could be derived" (ibid.).

In his response, Jesus identifies the first commandment as the statement of Moses in Deuteronomy 6:4-5. As we have noted above, this commandment is one that concerns the identity and orientation of the people of Israel. This is also a commandment that concerns the God that the Israelites are called to worship. Worship, therefore, serves as an orienting action, shaping the direction of the life of the worshiper. "The

Jewish law begins with worship, with the love of God, because if it's true that we're made in God's image we will find our fullest meaning, our true selves, the more we learn to love and worship the one we are designed to reflect" (Tom Wright, *Mark for Everyone* [Louisville: Westminster John Knox, 2004], 170).

Jesus then moves on to state that the second commandment is the commandment to love neighbor (see Leviticus 19:18). As stated above, this is a commandment that is located in the holiness code of Leviticus 19. Jesus identifies the first two commands as those that form a specific identity in the people of Israel. The commandment to love their neighbor is as much concerned with being drawn into the life of God as is the commandment to worship Yahweh, the one God, alone.

THE LESSON APPLIED

In light of the foregoing discussion of the first and second commandments, it is appropriate to discuss what Jesus means by the Kingdom of God. The *Kingdom of God* is ultimately defined by submitting completely to the will of God. "The Aramaic phrase underlying the Greek *[hē basileia tou Theou]* would perhaps be better translated as 'the kingship of God': the emphasis is on the rule of God, rather than on the territory where this rule is exercised" (Hooker, 55). In drawing upon the first and second commandments, the Kingdom of God can be seen in those who are pursuing a life of holiness so that they can be drawn into the life of God. As we noted above, this holiness is identified by the love of neighbor that is oriented by the love of God. The Kingdom of God is, therefore, an orientation that finds its ultimate meaning in the God who is Father, Son, and Holy Spirit.

LET'S TALK ABOUT IT

1. **How do we become disciples whose identities are formed by the commandments Jesus identifies as first and second?**

As noted above, Walter Brueggemann discusses Moses' program of "saturation education" for the people of Israel in remembering the first commandment. This is a practice that should be extended to the life of the Church. However, this saturation should not come about through the practice of simply teaching facts. This is teaching that needs to be seen and experienced in other ways. In the Bible, this is done through telling the story again and again of the way God has worked on behalf of the Israelites. These commandments can also be taught by the lives of faithful disciples who consistently demonstrate what it means to love God and neighbor.

HOME DAILY DEVOTIONAL READINGS						
MAY 26—JUNE 1, 2014						
MONDAY	**TUESDAY**	**WEDNESDAY**	**THURSDAY**	**FRIDAY**	**SATURDAY**	**SUNDAY**
A House of Prayer	The Fall of Jerusalem	The Temple Destroyed	Given into Enemy Hands	Carried Away into Captivity	Rebuild God's House	God's House Lies in Ruins
Luke 19:41-48	Jeremiah 52:1-9	Jeremiah 52:10-14	2 Chronicles 36:15-21	2 Kings 24:8-17	Ezra 1:1-8	Haggai 1:1-11

FOURTH QUARTER

Lesson material is based on International Sunday School Lessons and International Bible Lessons for Christian Teaching. Copyrighted by the International Council of Religious Education, and is used by its permission.

JUNE, JULY, AUGUST 2014

WRITER: REV. DR. PETER DARE

SUGGESTED OPENING EXERCISES

1. **Usual Signal for Beginning**
2. **Prayer (Closing with the Lord's Prayer)**
3. **Singing (Song to Be Selected)**
4. **Scripture Reading:**
   Haggai 2:6-9 (KJV)

Director: For thus saith the LORD of hosts: Yet once, it is a little while, and I will shake the heavens, and the earth, and the sea, and the dry land;

School: And I will shake all nations, and the desire of all nations shall come: and I will fill this house with glory, saith the LORD of hosts.

Director: The silver is mine, and the gold is mine, saith the LORD of hosts.

All: The glory of this latter house shall be greater than of the former, saith the LORD of hosts: and in this place will I give peace, saith the LORD of hosts.

Recitation in Concert:
2 Corinthians 2:5-8, 10-11 (KJV)

5 But if any have caused grief, he hath not grieved me, but in part: that I may not overcharge you all.

6 Sufficient to such a man is this punishment, which was inflicted of many.

7 So that contrariwise ye ought rather to forgive him, and comfort him, lest perhaps such a one should be swallowed up with overmuch sorrow.

8 Wherefore I beseech you that ye would confirm your love toward him.

10 To whom ye forgive any thing, I forgive also: for if I forgave any thing, to whom I forgave it, for your sakes forgave I it in the person of Christ;

11 Lest Satan should get an advantage of us: for we are not ignorant of his devices.

CLOSING WORK

1. **Singing**
2. **Sentences:**
   Ephesians 4:1-6 (KJV)

1 I therefore, the prisoner of the Lord, beseech you that ye walk worthy of the vocation wherewith ye are called,

2 With all lowliness and meekness, with longsuffering, forbearing one another in love;

3 Endeavouring to keep the unity of the Spirit in the bond of peace.

4 There is one body, and one Spirit, even as ye are called in one hope of your calling;

5 One Lord, one faith, one baptism,

6 One God and Father of all, who is above all, and through all, and in you all.

3. **Dismissal with Prayer**

OBEY THE LORD

ADULT TOPIC:	BACKGROUND SCRIPTURE:
DO WHAT IS REQUIRED	HAGGAI 1:1-11

HAGGAI 1:1-11

King James Version

IN the second year of Darius the king, in the sixth month, in the first day of the month, came the word of the LORD by Haggai the prophet unto Zerubbabel the son of Shealtiel, governor of Judah, and to Joshua the son of Josedech, the high priest, saying,

2 Thus speaketh the LORD of hosts, saying, This people say, The time is not come, the time that the LORD's house should be built.

3 Then came the word of the LORD by Haggai the prophet, saying,

4 Is it time for you, O ye, to dwell in your cieled houses, and this house lie waste?

5 Now therefore thus saith the LORD of hosts; Consider your ways.

6 Ye have sown much, and bring in little; ye eat, but ye have not enough; ye drink, but ye are not filled with drink; ye clothe you, but there is none warm; and he that earneth wages earneth wages to put it into a bag with holes.

7 Thus saith the LORD of hosts; Consider your ways.

8 Go up to the mountain, and bring wood, and build the house; and I will take pleasure in it, and I will be glorified, saith the LORD.

9 Ye looked for much, and, lo it came to little; and when ye brought it home, I did blow upon it. Why? saith the LORD of hosts. Because of mine house that is waste, and ye run every man unto his own house.

10 Therefore the heaven over you is stayed from dew, and the earth is stayed from her fruit.

New Revised Standard Version

IN the second year of King Darius, in the sixth month, on the first day of the month, the word of the Lord came by the prophet Haggai to Zerubbabel son of Shealtiel, governor of Judah, and to Joshua son of Jehozadak, the high priest:

2 Thus says the Lord of hosts: These people say the time has not yet come to rebuild the Lord's house.

3 Then the word of the Lord came by the prophet Haggai, saying:

4 Is it a time for you yourselves to live in your paneled houses, while this house lies in ruins?

5 Now therefore thus says the Lord of hosts: Consider how you have fared.

6 You have sown much, and harvested little; you eat, but you never have enough; you drink, but you never have your fill; you clothe yourselves, but no one is warm; and you that earn wages earn wages to put them into a bag with holes.

7 Thus says the Lord of hosts: Consider how you have fared.

8 Go up to the hills and bring wood and build the house, so that I may take pleasure in it and be honored, says the Lord.

9 You have looked for much, and, lo, it came to little; and when you brought it home, I blew it away. Why? says the Lord of hosts. Because my house lies in ruins, while all of you hurry off to your own houses.

10 Therefore the heavens above you have withheld the dew, and the earth has withheld its produce.

MAIN THOUGHT: Then came the word of the LORD by Haggai the prophet, saying, Is it time for you, O ye, to dwell in your cieled houses, and this house lie waste? (Haggai 1:3-4, KJV)

HAGGAI 1:1-11

King James Version	New Revised Standard Version
11 And I called for a drought upon the land, and upon the mountains, and upon the corn, and upon the new wine, and upon the oil, and upon that which the ground bringeth forth, and upon men, and upon cattle, and upon all the labour of the hands.	11 And I have called for a drought on the land and the hills, on the grain, the new wine, the oil, on what the soil produces, on human beings and animals, and on all their labors.

LESSON SETTING
Time: 520 B.C.
Place: Jerusalem

LESSON OUTLINE
I. **The Lord's House Is in Ruins (Haggai 1:1-6)**
II. **God Commands His People to Rebuild His House (Haggai 1:7-11)**

UNIFYING PRINCIPLE
Sometimes personal needs and desires prevent Christians from giving priority to that which is most important in their lives. How can Christians identify and give priority to what is important? God spoke through Haggai saying that the people's first priority should be rebuilding God's house and not their own houses.

INTRODUCTION
In 586 B.C., King Nebuchadnezzar laid his final siege on Babylon and destroyed Jerusalem and the temple. He also took many of the Jews with him back to Babylon in captivity, where they remained for almost seventy years. In approximately 549 B.C., the Persian leader Cyrus conquered Media and united the Medes and Persians under his control. Ten years later, Cyrus overthrew Babylon, which had fallen prey to weak leadership after Nebuchadnezzar's successful reign; as a result, the Jews found themselves under the control of a new world power (Homer Hailey, *A Commentary on the Minor Prophets* [Grand Rapids: Baker Book House, 1972], 299).

Cyrus had a much different philosophy than the Babylonians and Assyrians before him regarding territorial conquest. Instead of displacing conquered people to different areas, Cyrus believed in allowing people to return home and rebuild their cities and houses of worship. In 538 B.C., Cyrus issued a decree which gave the captives the choice to return home. Two years later, the first remnant of Jewish exiles, led by Sheshbazzar, (see Ezra 1:8, 11) began the journey back to Jerusalem from Babylon. Eventually, Zerubbabel took over as leader of this group. According to Hailey, this act did not mean Cyrus was a devout follower of Jehovah; rather, he merely sought to please the deities of the various captive people groups (299). During the rule of Cyrus, Judah became a province under Persian rule called "Babylon and Beyond the River." Samaria became the most important city in the area, and Tattenai was placed in charge of this particular district (Eugene March, "The Book of Haggai" in *The New Interpreter's Bible*, Vol. 7 [Nashville: Abingdon Press, 1996], 709).

After Cyrus' death, his son Cambyses came to rule in 529 B.C. Cambyses had a violent reign and is remembered most for the murder of his brother Bardiya, who posed a threat to his rule. Following Cambyses' violent rule, chaos broke out within the Persian Empire, and uprisings began. A man by the name of Darius I Hystaspes successfully led men to end these uprisings. Then, at the age of twenty-eight, Darius I became ruler of the Persian Empire in 522 B.C. (ibid.).

This is the world in which the returning Jews found themselves upon their return to Jerusalem. First, we need to go back sixteen years, though, to 536 B.C. when Sheshbazzar led the first remnant, approximately fifty thousand Jews, back to Jerusalem. The land to which they returned was in total disrepair: their houses, the city walls, and the temple were in ruins; the land was uncultivated; and either remaining Jews had claimed sections of the land for themselves or other foreigners now occupied the area. After Sheshbazzar led the Jews in laying the foundation, Zerubbabel led them in building an altar and then gathered supplies to start rebuilding the temple. After two years, work began on the temple (see Ezra 3:1-10), but opposition arose by foreigners in the area and by Tattenai, the Persian governor in the region. The opposition forced construction on the temple to come to a halt for approximately fifteen years by writing to the Persian king and telling him that the Jews were a threat and should not be allowed to rebuild their temple (see Ezra 4).

The book of Haggai opens in 520 B.C. after construction on the temple has ceased. The book is composed of four separate messages by Haggai with the central focus being the prophet's encouragement to the Jews to recommence building the temple. Almost no biographical information is known about the prophet Haggai. March points out that Haggai is similar to other prophets such as Amos, Habakkuk, and Obadiah in that no lineage is mentioned (707). Haggai's name means "festival" (Hailey, 297), and Richard Taylor and Ray Clendenen argue that Haggai's name could have related to his birth on a holy day in Babylonian captivity or his parents' desire to one day see holy days reinstituted (*Haggai and Malachi* in *The New American Commentary* [Nashville: Broadman & Holman, 2004], 44). The only conclusive information about Haggai is he was a prophet with authority, who addressed both the governor and high priest. Also, the book calls him "the prophet" five times (see Hag. 1:1, 3, 12; 2:1, 10; March, 708).

One unique feature of the book of Haggai is its extensive use of dating. Tremper Longman III and Raymond Dillard write "although [...] Ezekiel has a larger number of dates than this short book, of all the prophetic books, Haggai has the greatest 'density' of dated material" (*An Introduction to the Old Testament, Second Edition* [Grand Rapids: Zondervan, 2006], 479). Taylor and Clendenen share why the dating is important: "The specificity with which these dates are given in Haggai serves two purposes. First, it underscores the factuality of the events that are described, situating them within a verifiable historical context. Second, it lends credibility to the predictive portions of the prophet's message, since his accuracy on past allusions can be readily established" (106). More information about the specific dates will come later in this lesson.

EXPOSITION

I. THE LORD'S HOUSE IS IN RUINS (HAGGAI 1:1-6)

The first of four messages by the prophet Haggai comes "In the second year of King Darius, on the first day of the sixth month" (Hag. 1:1, NIV). This date is equivalent to August 29, 520 B.C., on the Gregorian calendar (William Brown, *Obadiah Through Malachi* in *Westminister Bible Companion Series* [Louisville, John Knox Press, 1996], 122). Specifying that this message is given on the first day of the month is significant because this day was usually set aside for sacrifices, but "in the absence of an altar or temple, such special feast days were impossible to observe in a ritually appropriate manner" (March, 715). Thus, Haggai approaches the people knowing that they are unable to make proper sacrifices without the existence of the Lord's temple.

Another point of importance is the mention of Darius. The books of Haggai and Zechariah are unique in that they don't chronicle the events in their books around a king of Judah or Israel since they both take place after the exile. According to Brown, this means Haggai "must be dated in relation to a *foreign* king.... By default, then, the prophetic word is given an international context" (122, emphasis in text). Furthermore, when studying the book as a whole, one notices that although the book opens with Darius on the throne, the book concludes with Zerubbabel being recognized as the one who continues the Davidic lineage in anticipation of the reign of Christ (131).

Also introduced in verse one are two leaders of Judah: "Zerubbabel son of Shealtiel, governor of Judah, and [...] Joshua son of Jehozadak, the high priest" (NIV). Zerubbabel, whose name means "son of Babylon" (Taylor and Clendenen, 108), was more than likely born to parents in captivity. Zerubbabel is a direct descendant of Jehoiachin, who was the king of Judah when Babylon captured the southern kingdom in 597 B.C. (see 2 Kings 24). Zerubbabel's title of governor is better translated from Hebrew as the "lord of a district" (Taylor and Clendenen, 111). Joshua, whose name means "God saves," is the high priest for the returning Jews and leads the people in their corporate worship. He is the grandson of Seraiah, who was the high priest killed by Nebuchadnezzar (see 2 Kings 25:18-21). Haggai addresses his first message to these two men.

Haggai begins by indirectly scolding Zerubbabel and Joshua for their failure to lead the people in finishing the rebuilding of the temple. According to Paul House, the Jews to whom Haggai speaks are confused because they had expected God's blessings upon their return to Jerusalem; instead, they have only faced various trials and struggles (*Old Testament Theology* [Downers Grove: IVP Academic, 1998], 384). A close reading of the text reveals that God says "'these people [have said] "the time has not yet come for the Lord's house to be built"'" (Hag. 1:2, NIV). Such a description of His covenant people may show that God is displeased with His people and "His reluctance to claim them as His own" (Hailey, 304). House builds upon this same argument and writes, "Their delay in building shows that they are hardly purified and obedient servants of God" (384). The people's attitude toward the temple is not acceptable to God, and their lack of progress showcases their thinking.

God continues His chastisement by asking, "'Is it a time for you yourselves to be living in your paneled houses, while this house remains a ruin?'" (v. 4, NIV). According to David Pennant, the use of "'paneled houses'" (v. 4, NIV) by Haggai "implies prosperity and comfort, and that the building of their homes was complete" ("Haggai" in *The New Bible Commentary, 21st Century Edition*, [Downers Grove: IVP Academic, 1994], 859). As mentioned earlier, the houses to which the people returned were in total disrepair; therefore, one should not be surprised that the people had devoted themselves to rebuilding nice houses and land. Unfortunately, they had done this solely and forgotten about the house of the Lord.

Verse five offers a solemn warning by God: "'Give careful thought to your ways'" (NIV). God wants the people to seriously consider what they have done and the results of their failure to act. March explains this phrase is better translated as "set the heart [to your ways]," and "the 'heart' is the organ of thinking and will in Hebrew psychology. The people are enjoined, on the one hand, to reflect, to decide, and then to act in the light of what has and has not been happening to them" (716). As God elaborates in verse six: "'You have planted much, but have harvested little. You eat, but never have enough. You drink, but never have your fill. You put on clothes, but are not warm.

You earn wages, only to put them in a purse with holes in it'" (NIV). While some of the people are living in nice houses, the rest of the community is in shambles. As verse six describes a lack of clothing, food, money, and water is prevalent. Verses ten and eleven divulge that a drought has evidently ravaged the land for an extended period of time. As Brown notes, "Home security is nothing but a façade when the community lies in shambles, whether from rampant crime, economic problems, or ecological disaster" (124). All of these communal problems are a direct result of judgment from God for the people's disobedience by failing to rebuild the temple.

II. God Commands His People to Rebuild His House (Haggai 1:7-11)

Verse seven repeats the warning for the people to reconsider their actions. Then in verse eight, God tells the people to "'Go up into the mountains and bring down timber and build the house, so that I may take pleasure in it and be honored'" (NIV). Elizabeth Achtemeier believes verse eight to be the key verse of the book of Haggai because it illustrates the importance of God's temple as a symbol of God's presence among His chosen people. Achtemeier explains, "When Haggai, 'the messenger of the Lord' (1:13), calls for temple rebuilding, it is therefore an announcement that the Lord of Hosts yearns to give himself again. That is what the Book of Haggai is about—God's yearning to enter into covenant fellowship with his Chosen People once more" (*Nahum—Malachi* in *Interpretation: A Bible Commentary for Teaching and Preaching* [Louisville: John Knox Press, 1986], 97). As mentioned earlier, God had used the phrase "'these people'" (v. 2, NIV) to describe the Jews, but if the temple is rebuilt, then He can claim them once again as His own.

Verses 9-11 continue God's declaration of His curses on the people for their attitude toward His temple. The people had "'expected much'" (v. 9, NIV) but were gravely disappointed by the outcome. The crops that they had managed to produce, the Lord "'blew away'" because His temple "'remains a ruin, while each of [them] is busy with his own house'" (ibid.). Then God says, "'Therefore, because of you the heavens have withheld their dew and the earth its crops. I called for a drought on the fields and the mountains, on the grain, the new wine, the oil and whatever the ground produces, on men and cattle, and on the labor of your hands'" (vv. 10-11, NIV). Pennant writes that rain had always been deemed a blessing from the Lord (see Ps. 65:9-10), thus, "the lack of rain matched the lack of attention paid to God's house" (859). Until the people stopped focusing on themselves instead of on God's house, they would continue to suffer His judgment.

THE LESSON APPLIED

Today's passage in Haggai 1:1-11 said much about the judgment of God on the Jewish people after they had returned from captivity. Even after having gone into Babylonian captivity because of their disobedience, the Jews still managed to anger God shortly after their return by neglecting to rebuild His house. How much do people still receive judgment from Him today because of disobedience? This could be considered from the perspective of a nation as a whole as well as the individual lives of Christians. People should not focus only on the love and mercy of God without recognizing that judgment possibly remains for those who are disobedient to His will.

LET'S TALK ABOUT IT

1. Why is it important for Christians to put God first?

In this first message given to Haggai, the Lord wants believers to know that it is dangerous and destructive to put anything or anyone before the Lord. The Lord might say to believers today, "Why haven't you done My work? Why have you not given to the Church? Have you not taken time to buy your fancy cars and built your fine houses and bought nice clothes?" God is of greater value than anything we do or own. We must be careful not to allow the devil and others to weaken our commitment to Him and the work of the Lord. Only when we are willing to put God first will our priorities in life be properly ordered.

HOME DAILY DEVOTIONAL READINGS
JUNE 2-8, 2014

MONDAY	TUESDAY	WEDNESDAY	THURSDAY	FRIDAY	SATURDAY	SUNDAY
My Spirit Seeks You	The Blessings of Obedience	The Consequences of Disobedience	The Fear of the Lord	I Am with You	Take Courage	Obeying the Voice of God
Isaiah 26:1-13	Leviticus 26:3-13	Leviticus 26:14-26	Deuteronomy 6:17-25	Isaiah 41:1-10	Psalm 27:7-14	Haggai 1:12—2:9

TRUST GOD'S PROMISES

ADULT TOPIC:	BACKGROUND SCRIPTURES:
BUILD FOR THE FUTURE	HAGGAI 1:12—2:9

HAGGAI 1:12; 2:1-9

King James Version

THEN Zerubbabel the son of Shealtiel, and Joshua the son of Josedech, the high priest, with all the remnant of the people, obeyed the voice of the LORD their God, and the words of Haggai the prophet, as the LORD their God had sent him, and the people did fear before the LORD.

• • • 2:1-9 • • •

IN the seventh month, in the one and twentieth day of the month, came the word of the LORD by the prophet Haggai, saying,

2 Speak now to Zerubbabel the son of Shealtiel, governor of Judah, and to Joshua the son of Josedech, the high priest, and to the residue of the people, saying,

3 Who is left among you that saw this house in her first glory? and how do ye see it now? is it not in your eyes in comparison of it as nothing?

4 Yet now be strong, O Zerubbabel, saith the LORD; and be strong, O Joshua, son of Josedech, the high priest; and be strong, all ye people of the land, saith the LORD, and work: for I am with you, saith the LORD of hosts:

5 According to the word that I covenanted with you when ye came out of Egypt, so my spirit remaineth among you: fear ye not.

6 For thus saith the LORD of hosts; Yet once, it is a little while, and I will shake the heavens, and the earth, and the sea, and the dry land;

7 And I will shake all nations, and the desire of all nations shall come: and I will fill this house with glory, saith the LORD of hosts.

New Revised Standard Version

THEN Zerubbabel son of Shealtiel, and Joshua son of Jehozadak, the high priest, with all the remnant of the people, obeyed the voice of the LORD their God, and the words of the prophet Haggai, as the LORD their God had sent him; and the people feared the LORD.

• • • 2:1-9 • • •

IN the second year of King Darius, 1 in the seventh month, on the twenty-first day of the month, the word of the LORD came by the prophet Haggai, saying:

2 Speak now to Zerubbabel son of Shealtiel, governor of Judah, and to Joshua son of Jehozadak, the high priest, and to the remnant of the people, and say,

3 Who is left among you that saw this house in its former glory? How does it look to you now? Is it not in your sight as nothing?

4 Yet now take courage, O Zerubbabel, says the Lord; take courage, O Joshua, son of Jehozadak, the high priest; take courage, all you people of the land, says the LORD; work, for I am with you, says the LORD of hosts,

5 according to the promise that I made you when you came out of Egypt. My spirit abides among you; do not fear.

6 For thus says the LORD of hosts: Once again, in a little while, I will shake the heavens and the earth and the sea and the dry land;

7 and I will shake all the nations, so that the treasure of all nations shall come, and I will fill this house with splendor, says the LORD of hosts.

MAIN THOUGHT: The glory of this latter house shall be greater than of the former, saith the LORD of hosts: and in this place will I give peace, saith the LORD of hosts. (Haggai 2:9, KJV)

King James Version	New Revised Standard Version
8 The silver is mine, and the gold is mine, saith the LORD of hosts.	8 The silver is mine, and the gold is mine, says the Lord of hosts.
9 The glory of this latter house shall be greater than of the former, saith the LORD of hosts: and in this place will I give peace, saith the LORD of hosts.	9 The latter splendor of this house shall be greater than the former, says the Lord of hosts; and in this place I will give prosperity, says the Lord of hosts.

LESSON SETTING
  Time: 520 B.C.
  Place: Jerusalem

LESSON OUTLINE
  I. Obey the Lord
     (Haggai 1:12)
  II. Be Strong
     (Haggai 2:1-5)
  III. Reap God's Blessings
     (Haggai 2:6-9)

UNIFYING PRINCIPLE

Some communities find it difficult to begin a project that will benefit them. What motivates communities to get started on a new project? God promised to be with the people as they completed the task of rebuilding God's temple.

INTRODUCTION

After the people had returned from Babylonian exile in 536 B.C., they laid the foundation of the temple that had been destroyed and began repairing their homes and crops. Political pressure combined with the people's apathetic attitudes toward God's house forced the rebuilding process to cease. Beginning in 520 B.C., the prophet Haggai began preaching to the people to encourage them to get back to work rebuilding God's temple. Haggai 1:2-11 comprises the prophet's first message, asking the people why they had devoted their time to rebuilding their own houses yet had failed to devote the same time and energy to rebuilding God's house. As a result, God had allowed a drought to dry up the land as well as a shortage of drink, clothing, and money to plague the Jews. Until God's house was rebuilt, they would continue to face God's judgment.

EXPOSITION

I. OBEY THE LORD
   (HAGGAI 1:12)

Haggai 1:12 reveals the response of the people to Haggai's first message: "Then Zerubbabel son of Shealtiel, Joshua son of Jehozadak, the high priest, and the whole remnant of the people obeyed the voice of the LORD their God and the message of the prophet Haggai, because the LORD their God had sent him. And the people feared the LORD" (NIV). Over the course of Haggai 1:1-11, Zerubbabel and Joshua were told why the people had faced so many difficulties after their return to Jerusalem and were reminded of why the rebuilding of God's temple was so important. David Pennant summarizes Haggai's first message with this statement: "God's curse is not a sign that God has rejected his people; rather, it shows his love for them. He wants to draw them back to him, and uses disaster to wake them up" ("Haggai" in *The New Bible Commentary*, 21st Century Edition, [Downers Grove:

IVP Academic, 1994], 860). The people now fully understand what God desires, and verse twelve says they respond immediately—quite a different reaction from the response of the Jews to prophets before Haggai. Most of the time, the prophets' warnings were disregarded, and the people continued to turn away from God; as a result, the Assyrian and Babylonian invasions were the pinnacle of God's judgment on His unresponsive people.

Eugene March points out the connection between the people hearing the Word of God, obeying it, and then fearing the Lord; he argues that the people are in awe that God has remained faithful to them even when their ancestors had not ("The Book of Haggai" in *The New Interpreter's Bible*, Vol. 7 [Nashville: Abingdon Press, 1996, 719). He then parallels this passage with Deuteronomy 6:4, where Moses issues the famous Shema prayer, "'Hear, O Israel: The LORD our God, the LORD is one'" (NIV), because this prayer involves hearing the voice of the Lord and then responding (721). March references James 1:22-24 as an example for modern-day Christians to follow in terms of hearing the Word and then acting on it (ibid.).

In Haggai 1:13, God once again tells the people, "'I am with you'" (NIV). William Brown says, "God declares solidarity with the people (see Isa. 41:10; 43:5)" (*Obadiah Through Malachi* in *Westminister Bible Companion Series* [Louisville, John Knox Press, 1996], 125) with these words. As noted last week, God had distanced Himself from His people by using phrases like "'these people'" (Hag. 1:2, NIV), but now God's presence is with the Jews once more. In addition, Haggai 1:14-15 gives greater detail of what the Jews do after hearing Haggai's warning to them: "So the LORD stirred up the spirit of Zerubbabel son of Shealtiel, governor of Judah, and the spirit of Joshua son of Jehozadak, the high priest, and the spirit of the whole remnant of the people. They came and began to work on the house of the LORD Almighty, their God, on the twenty-fourth day of the sixth month in the second year of King Darius" (NIV). The work officially begins on the temple once again on September 21, 520 B.C. According to Brown, the people who were described as "stirred up" is reminiscent of the enthusiasm the Jews had when they first built the tabernacle in the wilderness in Exodus 35:21 (ibid.).

II. BE STRONG (HAGGAI 2:1-5)

Haggai 2 opens with the second message by Haggai to the people. The modern-day calendar date for the prophet's second message is October 17, 520 B.C., almost a month after the first one was given. This date is significant because it is the seventh day of one of Israel's most important festivals: the festival of booths (Brown, 126). This festival closely followed the Day of Atonement (see Lev. 23:39-44). Haggai 2:5 will shed further light on possibly why Haggai received his second message on this particular day.

Haggai 2:2 states this message is for Zerubbabel, Joshua, and the people, whereas the first message had been addressed specifically to just the governor and the high priest. March argues "the remnant of the people" probably refers to those who had not gone into Babylonian captivity but had stayed behind in Jerusalem among the ruins (722). In verse three, the Lord asks several questions: "'Who of you is left who saw this house in its former glory? How does it look to you now? Does it not seem to you like nothing?'" (NIV). Ezra recounts how "many of the older priests and Levites and family heads, who had seen the former temple, wept aloud when they saw the foundation of this temple being laid" (Ezra 3:12, NIV). Haggai captures this same sentiment of those who might have been among the people who would have seen the grandeur of Solomon's original temple and are now working on the rebuilding project.

Homer Hailey explains one of the reasons for the people's weeping is they "realize that the glory of the former had vanished with the glory of the nation, and now they must build anew from the ground up" (*A Commentary on the Minor Prophets* [Grand Rapids: Baker Book House, 1972], 308). The glory that had once been Solomon's temple had been entwined with God's favor on Israel, and now Israel must recapture it. March says God's asking "'Does it not seem to you like nothing?'" (Hag. 2:3, NIV) is meant to encourage the people because "by so doing [Haggai] silenced the complainers and challenged them, along with all the others, to have confidence in what God was about to do" (723). God is about to offer great words of encouragement to the Jews in verse four.

In verse four, God says "'be strong'" (NIV) three times because He wants to emphasize that He is with Zerubbabel, Joshua, and the people and that this should give them courage to overcome all odds. Pennant parallels this repeated command for the returned exiles to be strong with the same words repeated by God to the military leader Joshua before the Jews conquered the land of Canaan after their wandering in the wilderness (see Josh. 1:1-18) (860). Also noted by Pennant is that a leader named Joshua is present in each text—the military leader, Joshua and the high priest, Joshua. Pennant explains: "Both Joshuas acted on the word of the LORD to be strong, and so inherited God's promises" (ibid.).

Haggai 2:5 explains why the Jews should trust God and have strength and courage: "'This is what I covenanted with you when you came out of Egypt. And my Spirit remains among you. Do not fear'" (NIV). God reminds them that He had been with the Jews in the wilderness to guide and protect them until they reached the promised land once again. Brown elaborates, "As God liberated their ancestors from Pharaoh and his army, God will now deliver the community from the enemies of apathy, despair, and fear" (127). The same God who rescued the Jews centuries prior will continue to rescue them now. Also, God's referencing the exodus fits the date of this message well on the seventh day of the feast of booths (March, 722). The feast of booths was established by God in the wilderness (and reinstituted by Ezra in Nehemiah 8) to commemorate God's protection of the children of Israel in the wilderness for forty years. The exodus theme will resurface again in verses six and seven of this same chapter.

III. REAP GOD'S BLESSINGS (HAGGAI 2:6-9)

The interpretation of Haggai 2:6-9 is heavily debated by many biblical scholars.

Depending on how one interprets the original Hebrew, numerous conclusions can be drawn about the meaning of "'the desired of all nations'" (v. 7, NIV) and when the timing of this passage is to be fulfilled. In verses 6-7, the Lord says, "'In a little while I will once more shake the heavens and the earth, the sea and the dry land. I will shake all nations, and the desired of all nations will come, and I will fill this house with glory'" (NIV).

First of all, the allusion to the Exodus journey should be pointed out again: this language is very similar to the description of the earthquake and lightning that surrounded Mt. Sinai at the giving of the Decalogue. March explains, "The imagery used to describe God's action [in Haggai 2:6-7] is reminiscent of the theophanic tradition, [which is] the tradition of God's appearing accompanied by the cataclysmic shaking of the heavens and the earth (Exod. 19:18; Judg. 5:4-5)" (723). In typical "revelation of God" events, the nations and creation usually shook of their own accord at the sight of God, but in Haggai 2:6-7 God says He will do the shaking (ibid.).

March goes on to explain that the word *shake* can have several connotations in the Bible. For instance, in Amos 1:1, an earthquake is referenced, but Haggai 2:6 appears to speak more of the shaking of human institutions as seen in biblical passages such as Isaiah 14:16 and Ezekiel 31:16 (ibid.). Most scholars would agree with March's assertion that this is what Haggai refers to in this verse.

Before returning to Haggai 2:6-7, another biblical allusion should be noted. Hebrews 12 explicitly references the occurrences at Mount Sinai and also quotes Haggai 2:6: "At that time his voice shook the earth, but now he has promised, 'Once more I will shake not only the earth but also the heavens.' The words 'once more' indicate the removing of what can be shaken—that is, created things—so that what cannot be shaken may remain" (Heb. 12:26-27, NIV). The author of Hebrews writes this to encourage the Christians about the coming of a new kingdom at the Lord's return. An understanding of this later allusion in the New Testament will aid in rightly understanding Haggai 2:6-7.

After God shakes the nations, "'the desired of all nations will come'" (Hag. 2:7, NIV). Two points of interpretation should be noted. First, the Hebrew noun used for desire is actually plural. Second, the noun is better translated "splendor" or "treasure" instead of "desire." Thus, scholars such as Pennant suggest the translation is best understood as "the treasures of the nations will come" (861). So after God shakes the human institutions of the world, the treasures of these institutions will come, resulting in God's house (i.e., the temple) being filled with the riches of the world.

In verse eight, God explicitly states that the "'The silver is mine and the gold is mine'" (NIV). Evidently, the treasure at one time belonged to the temple, hinting to the fact that it had been taken away at some point in Israel's past. As a result of this treasure being rightfully restored to the temple, God proclaims, "'The glory of this present house will be greater than the glory of the former house.... And in this place I will grant peace'" (v. 9, NIV). In other words, the rebuilt temple will be far more glorious than the temple built by Solomon centuries prior.

The question is then raised as to what treasures will be restored and when this event will take place. Many scholars say God is referring to restoring the temple's gold and silver that was taken during the Babylonian invasion—and these scholars use verse eight to support this view. Alas, the confusion does not end here. Since scholars today know that the temple rebuilt by Zerubbabel never fully regained the glory of Solomon's temple and the gold and silver had already been returned by kings such as Darius and Artaxerxes (see Ezra 6:6-15; 7:12-26), then a prophecy about a new kingdom of peace being established at the second coming of Christ is very possible (Hailey 311).

The addition of Hebrews 12:26-27 as a reference to a coming kingdom also validates this view. Hailey believes this passage ties in well with Isaiah 65:16-17: "It was this removing of the old order and the founding of a new one that was before Isaiah's mind when he wrote of old things being forgotten and the creation of new heavens and a new earth" (ibid.). In this new peaceful kingdom, the temple will regain all of its glory.

THE LESSON APPLIED

The response of the people to Haggai's message is very applicable to the modern-day Church. Despite earlier reluctance, upon hearing the command of God, the Jews obeyed immediately and began rebuilding the temple. Believers today should seek to have the same quick reaction to God's commands. God's Word can be trusted; therefore, obedience should be swift and deliberate. Only then will we fully experience the blessings of God.

LET'S TALK ABOUT IT

1. What does it mean for a believer to be strong today?

God's words to "'be strong'" (Hag. 2:4) should remain true for Christians today. The exiles faced great hardships in returning to a ravaged land and trying to begin their lives again. They also failed in restoring their covenant relationship with the Lord. As a result, they faced many trials and difficulties.

These trying times are not always the result of God's judgment. The life of a believer today can also be marred by trials and difficult circumstances. The question is how does a Christian handle such situations. A believer should find his or her strength in the Lord and cling to faith in His power and wisdom. As Christians we must trust that God "is able to do immeasurably more than all we ask or imagine" (Eph. 3:20, NIV).

HOME DAILY DEVOTIONAL READINGS
JUNE 9-15, 2014

MONDAY	TUESDAY	WEDNESDAY	THURSDAY	FRIDAY	SATURDAY	SUNDAY
A Highway Called the Holy Way	Established As God's Holy People	You Shall Be Holy	You Have Been Born Anew	You Are God's People	You Are the Temple of God	The Hope for God's Blessing
Isaiah 35	Deuteronomy 28:1-9	1 Peter 1:13-21	1 Peter 1:22—2:3	1 Peter 2:4-10	2 Corinthians 6:14—7:1	Haggai 2:10-19

LIVE PURE LIVES

ADULT TOPIC: LIVE HONORABLE LIVES	BACKGROUND SCRIPTURE: HAGGAI 2:10-19

HAGGAI 2:10-19

King James Version

IN the four and twentieth day of the ninth month, in the second year of Darius, came the word of the LORD by Haggai the prophet, saying,

11 Thus saith the LORD of hosts; Ask now the priests concerning the law, saying,

12 If one bear holy flesh in the skirt of his garment, and with his skirt do touch bread, or pottage, or wine, or oil, or any meat, shall it be holy? And the priests answered and said, No.

13 Then said Haggai, If one that is unclean by a dead body touch any of these, shall it be unclean? And the priests answered and said, It shall be unclean.

14 Then answered Haggai, and said, So is this people, and so is this nation before me, saith the LORD; and so is every work of their hands; and that which they offer there is unclean.

15 And now, I pray you, consider from this day and upward, from before a stone was laid upon a stone in the temple of the LORD:

16 Since those days were, when one came to an heap of twenty measures, there were but ten: when one came to the pressfat for to draw out fifty vessels out of the press, there were but twenty.

17 I smote you with blasting and with mildew and with hail in all the labours of your hands; yet ye turned not to me, saith the LORD.

18 Consider now from this day and upward, from the four and twentieth day of the ninth

New Revised Standard Version

ON the twenty-fourth day of the ninth month, in the second year of Darius, the word of the LORD came to the prophet Haggai:

11 Thus says the LORD of hosts: Ask the priests for a ruling:

12 If one carries consecrated meat in the fold of one's garment, and with the fold touches bread, or stew, or wine, or oil, or any kind of food, does it become holy? The priests answered, "No."

13 Then Haggai said, "If one who is unclean by contact with a dead body touches any of these, does it become unclean?" The priests answered, "Yes, it becomes unclean."

14 Haggai then said, So is it with this people, and with this nation before me, says the LORD; and so with every work of their hands; and what they offer there is unclean.

15 But now, consider what will come to pass from this day on. Before a stone was placed upon a stone in the LORD's temple,

16 how did you fare? When one came to a heap of twenty measures, there were but ten; when one came to the wine vat to draw fifty measures, there were but twenty.

17 I struck you and all the products of your toil with blight and mildew and hail; yet you did not return to me, says the LORD.

18 Consider from this day on, from the twenty-fourth day of the ninth month. Since the day

MAIN THOUGHT: Is the seed yet in the barn? yea, as yet the vine, and the fig tree, and the pomegranate, and the olive tree, hath not brought forth: from this day will I bless you. (Haggai 2:19, KJV)

King James Version

month, even from the day that the foundation of the LORD's temple was laid, consider it.
19 Is the seed yet in the barn? yea, as yet the vine, and the fig tree, and the pomegranate, and the olive tree, hath not brought forth: from this day will I bless you.

New Revised Standard Version

that the foundation of the LORD's temple was laid, consider:
19 Is there any seed left in the barn? Do the vine, the fig tree, the pomegranate, and the olive tree still yield nothing? From this day on I will bless you.

LESSON SETTING
Time: 520 B.C.
Place: Jerusalem

LESSON OUTLINE
I. Contagious Ungodliness (Haggai 2:10-14)
II. A New Day of Blessing (Haggai 2:15-19)

UNIFYING PRINCIPLE

Almost everyone wants to belong to something that will make a difference in the world. What or who could help Christians feel that sense of belonging? God rewards and blesses the community of believers that lives in righteousness and fear of God.

INTRODUCTION

Last week's lesson covered a very difficult passage for biblical scholars to interpret. First, we talked about God's words of encouragement to Zerubbabel, Joshua, and the people to "'be strong'" (Hag. 2:4, NIV) in spite of the many difficulties they have faced and will face in the future. Just as God had been with the Jews in the wilderness, He would remain with His chosen people in their present circumstances. Then, we looked at Haggai's words in Haggai 2:6-9. While many scholars interpret the words at face value to foretell the birth of Christ, a closer study of the Hebrew text lends

itself to a different interpretation. Since the noun typically translated into English as "desire" (Hag. 2:7, KJV) is plural in the Hebrew, a better understanding is that the passage refers to wealth or splendor being restored to the temple of God in the future. Finally, an attempt was made to place this restoration in a proper time frame. Because Hebrews 12:26-27 references Haggai 2:6-7 in anticipation of the second coming of Christ, one can argue that Haggai is speaking about God's establishing His perfect Kingdom on earth. Today, the focus shifts to the third message delivered by Haggai in 2:10-19.

EXPOSITION

I. CONTAGIOUS UNGODLINESS (HAGGAI 2:10-14)

Haggai's third message comes on "the twenty-fourth day of the ninth month, in the second year of Darius," (Hag. 2:10, NIV) which is the equivalent of December 18, 520 B.C., on the Gregorian calendar (William P. Brown, *Obadiah Through Malachi* in *Westminister Bible Companion Series* [Louisville, John Knox Press, 1996], 128). As verse eighteen will share, this is also the day the foundation of the temple is laid and a new day of blessing comes to Israel. Tremper Longman III and Raymond Dillard explain that "December was the middle of the growing season, and the prophet assures the people that time away from farm work to work on the temple would not mean poor harvests, but to the contrary, a great harvest was ahead" (*An Introduction to the Old Testament*, Second Edition [Grand Rapids: Zondervan, 2006], 482). Finally, instead of addressing Zerubbabel or Joshua as he did in the first two messages, Haggai speaks solely to the priests.

The summative thought behind the next few verses of Haggai is the people's failure to purify themselves. The Lord commands Haggai to ask the priests: "'If a person carries consecrated meat in the fold of his garment, and that fold touches some bread or stew, some wine, oil or other food, does it become consecrated?'" (v. 12, NIV). The priests respond to Haggai's question in verse twelve by answering no. Homer Hailey points out the reason the Lord speaks directly to the priests is because their duty is to teach the people what is clean and what is unclean (*A Commentary on the Minor Prophets* [Grand Rapids: Baker Book House, 1972], 312.).

Food that has been consecrated is food that has been dedicated to God. Now, if food that had been sanctified touched other food or objects in the temple, on very rare instances, these other objects could become holy, too. This would have been known to the priests based on their knowledge of the Law: "'The priest who offers [the sin offering] shall eat it; it is to be eaten in a holy place, in the courtyard of the Tent of Meeting. Whatever touches any of the flesh will become holy, and if any of the blood is spattered on a garment, you must wash it in a holy place'" (Lev. 6:26-27, NIV). On the other hand, in almost all cases, an unclean object would make a clean object unholy. Haggai elaborates by saying if the food was removed from the temple and taken home, the consecrated food would not transfer holiness to the unconsecrated food; instead, consecrated food would become unconsecrated.

Haggai then asks another question: "'If a person defiled by contact with a dead body touches one of these things, does it become defiled?'" (Hag. 2:13, NIV). The priests affirm that such an object would become defiled because of what the Law teaches about coming in contact with corpses: "'Whoever touches the dead body of any-one will be unclean for seven days'" (Num. 19:11, NIV) as well as "'Anything that an unclean person touches becomes unclean'" (v. 22, NIV). Such people had to be cer-emonially purified to be deemed clean once again (see Num. 19:12-13).

Haggai then drives home the words of the Lord: "'So it is with this people and this nation in my sight…. Whatever they do and whatever they offer there is defiled'" (Hag. 2:14, NIV). Haggai condemns the people because the sacrifices they have been making to the Lord are impure. They should not think that they became holy because they were working on the temple. According to Eugene March, when the Babylonians destroyed Jerusalem in 587 B.C., they had destroyed the temple and at least defiled, if not destroyed, the altar upon which sacrifices were made. Furthermore, March points out that the prophet Ezekiel writes in Ezekiel 8:5-18 that the Babylonians had defiled the temple so greatly that God's presence left ("The Book of Haggai" in *The New Interpreter's Bible*, Vol. 7 [Nashville: Abingdon Press, 1996], 727). God had no choice but to leave His people because of their impure practices. Until they purified themselves, they could not ask for God's blessings (Hailey, 313).

March also notes that God has once again used "'this people' and 'this nation'" to describe His people (Hag. 2:14, NIV) (727). As in previous instances in the book of Haggai, such phrasing shows a distancing between God and His people. Since they have been using a defiled temple and altar to offer sacrifices, God cannot have the intimate relationship He desires with His covenant people. This is perhaps the saddest aspect of the message Haggai brings to the returned exiles. Such a truth should drive the priests and the people to rebuild a pure temple and altar in order to offer the proper sacrifices to the Lord and restore their relationship with God.

II. A New Day of Blessing (Haggai 2:15-19)

Whereas Haggai 2:10-14 focused on God's chastising His people for their impure practices, the remaining verses in Haggai's third message tell of the forthcoming blessings of God on Israel. As stated at the beginning of the lesson, this day in Israel's history is significant because the temple's foundation is officially laid. While work on the temple foundation had been taking place prior to this date, "the actual setting of the foundation stone and rededication of the Temple, including its cleansing from defilement, took place on December 18" (March, 728).

Beginning in verse fifteen, God repeats the command from Haggai 1:5 for the people to consider their ways: "'Now give careful thought to this from this day on—consider how things were before one stone was laid on another in the Lord's temple'" (NIV). Before looking at what the people are to consider, a point should be made about the construction of the temple inferred from verse fifteen. March explains, "According to custom, a stone from the previous Temple was put in place as part of the foundation of the new structure, thereby assuring continuity with the past as the community moves toward the future" (728). This moving towards the future ties perfectly with the blessings that God promises at the end of verse nineteen. Also, March reiterates how the cornerstone has implications of Christ's being the cornerstone of the New Testament Church in which the glory of God dwells (729).

Since the people have returned from the Babylonian exile, they have endured an agricultural nightmare. In Haggai 2, God tells the people to again remember all they have endured agriculturally: "'When anyone came to a heap of twenty measures, there were only ten. When anyone went to a wine vat to draw fifty measures, there were only twenty'" (v. 16, NIV). God reminds the people that they have been enjoying only half of His blessings since their return from Babylon. Yet, God does not stop here. He tells the people how He had cursed them in hopes of turning their hearts back to Him: "'I struck all the work of your hands with blight, mildew and hail, yet you did not turn to me'" (v. 17, NIV). God's use of such punishment is an attempt to drive the people to repentance. Brown states: "God is the expressed agent behind such calamities, whose purpose is to bring about repentance, […] but without success" (129).

God then asks a question related to the Jews' current status: "'Is there yet any seed left in the barn? Until now, the vine and the fig tree, the pomegranate and the olive tree have not borne fruit'" (v. 19, NIV). As a result of the people's refusal to rebuild the temple, the barns are empty and the trees are barren. Brown argues that God's mentioning of the fruit trees and seed paves the way for the era of blessing that is promised at the conclusion of verse nineteen. For Brown, these objects are "natural, simple signs of new life" (129). The olive trees will produce oil to be used for cooking and lighting, and the pomegranate and figs can be used to make wine (ibid.).

Finally, God tells His people the result of their rebuilding the temple foundation: "'From this day on I will bless you'" (v. 19, NIV). That day marks the beginning of a new era for the returned exiles. Since the Jews have done their part in beginning the restoration of their covenant relationship with God, the people can now expect and enjoy the blessings of God. The presence of God can now abide once more among His chosen people. Brown states, "Small and gradual at first, blessing follows the completion of the temple's foundation, a turning point for the community. Haggai depicts this event as the axis upon which defilement is displaced by holiness, and judgment gradually makes way for grace" (130). The Jews can now expect God's favor to shine upon them once more.

THE LESSON APPLIED

What was the problem with the Jews and ritual purity? God wanted the people of Israel to see their life through the Lord's lens of holiness based on the Law. Often, believers look at their lives in comparison to others. Holiness and righteous living cannot be achieved by examining how fellow believers live their lives. Godliness is the result of walking in obedience with God. The rewards are blessings that are in direct proportion to God's grace, love and mercy.

LET'S TALK ABOUT IT

1. How can believers protect themselves from unclean things in today's sinful world?

Christians today are surrounded by sinful forces in the world. A believer cannot walk out the front door (or even look in a mirror) without seeing the effects of sin in the lives of everyday people. How can a Christian maintain a positive impact in the world without allowing the world to have too large of an impact him or her? During Paul's day, the believers in Corinth, struggled with the same issue. He advised them to remain strong in the face of temptation and sin and God would help them to escape (see 1 Cor. 10:13). By praying and asking for guidance from the Holy Spirit, Christians can better determine how to deal with and be victorious in the midst of worldly situations.

HOME DAILY DEVOTIONAL READINGS
JUNE 16-22, 2014

MONDAY	TUESDAY	WEDNESDAY	THURSDAY	FRIDAY	SATURDAY	SUNDAY
What Hope for the Godless?	Hope in God	Hope in God's Steadfast Love	In Hope We Were Saved	Accounting for the Hope in You	The Confession of Our Hope	I Have Chosen You
Job 27:8-12	Psalm 43	Psalm 33:13-22	Romans 8:18-25	1 Peter 3:13-17	Hebrews 10:19-24	Haggai 2:23; Zechariah 4:1-3, 6-14

HOPE FOR A NEW DAY

ADULT TOPIC:	BACKGROUND SCRIPTURES:
EXPECT SUCCESS	NEHEMIAH 7:1-7; HAGGAI 2:20-23; ZECHARIAH 4

HAGGAI 2:20-23; ZECHARIAH 4:5-14

King James Version	*New Revised Standard Version*
AND again the word of the LORD came unto Haggai in the four and twentieth day of the month, saying,	THE word of the LORD came a second time to Haggai on the twenty-fourth day of the month:
21 Speak to Zerubbabel, governor of Judah, saying, I will shake the heavens and the earth;	21 Speak to Zerubbabel, governor of Judah, saying, I am about to shake the heavens and the earth,
22 And I will overthrow the throne of kingdoms, and I will destroy the strength of the kingdoms of the heathen; and I will overthrow the chariots, and those that ride in them; and the horses and their riders shall come down, every one by the sword of his brother.	22 and to overthrow the throne of kingdoms; I am about to destroy the strength of the kingdoms of the nations, and overthrow the chariots and their riders; and the horses and their riders shall fall, every one by the sword of a comrade.
23 In that day, saith the LORD of hosts, will I take thee, O Zerubbabel, my servant, the son of Shealtiel, saith the LORD, and will make thee as a signet: for I have chosen thee, saith the LORD of hosts.	23 On that day, says the LORD of hosts, I will take you, O Zerubbabel my servant, son of Shealtiel, says the LORD, and make you like a signet ring; for I have chosen you, says the LORD of hosts.
• • • Zechariah 4:5-14 • • •	• • • Zechariah 4:5-14 • • •
THEN the angel that talked with me answered and said unto me, Knowest thou not what these be? And I said, No, my lord.	THEN the angel who talked with me answered me, "Do you not know what these are?" I said, "No, my lord."
6 Then he answered and spake unto me, saying, This is the word of the LORD unto Zerubbabel, saying, Not by might, nor by power, but by my spirit, saith the LORD of hosts.	6 He said to me, "This is the word of the LORD to Zerubbabel: Not by might, nor by power, but by my spirit, says the LORD of hosts.
7 Who art thou, O great mountain? before Zerubbabel thou shalt become a plain: and he shall bring forth the headstone thereof with shoutings, crying, Grace, grace unto it.	7 What are you, O great mountain? Before Zerubbabel you shall become a plain; and he shall bring out the top stone amid shouts of 'Grace, grace to it!'"
8 Moreover the word of the LORD came unto me, saying,	8 Moreover the word of the LORD came to me, saying,
9 The hands of Zerubbabel have laid the foundation of this house; his hands shall also	9 "The hands of Zerubbabel have laid the foundation of this house; his hands shall also

MAIN THOUGHT: Then he answered and spake unto me, saying, This is the word of the LORD unto Zerubbabel, saying, Not by might, nor by power, but by my spirit, saith the LORD of hosts. (Zechariah 4:6, KJV)

HAGGAI 2:20-23; ZECHARIAH 4:5-14

King James Version	New Revised Standard Version
finish it; and thou shalt know that the LORD of hosts hath sent me unto you.	complete it. Then you will know that the LORD of hosts has sent me to you.
10 For who hath despised the day of small things? for they shall rejoice, and shall see the plummet in the hand of Zerubbabel with those seven; they are the eyes of the LORD, which run to and fro through the whole earth.	10 For whoever has despised the day of small things shall rejoice, and shall see the plummet in the hand of Zerubbabel. These seven are the eyes of the LORD, which range through the whole earth."
11 Then answered I, and said unto him, What are these two olive trees upon the right side of the candlestick and upon the left side thereof?	11 Then I said to him, "What are these two olive trees on the right and the left of the lampstand?"
12 And I answered again, and said unto him, What be these two olive branches which through the two golden pipes empty the golden oil out of themselves?	12 And a second time I said to him, "What are these two branches of the olive trees, which pour out the oil through the two golden pipes?"
13 And he answered me and said, Knowest thou not what these be? And I said, No, my Lord.	13 He said to me, "Do you not know what these are?" I said, "No, my lord."
14 Then said he, These are the two anointed ones, that stand by the Lord of the whole earth.	14 Then he said, "These are the two anointed ones who stand by the Lord of the whole earth."

LESSON SETTING
   Time: 520 B.C.
   Place: Jerusalem

LESSON OUTLINE
   I. God's Signet Ring
      (Haggai 2:20-23)
   II. Zechariah's Vision
      (Zechariah 4:5-14)

UNIFYING PRINCIPLE

Communities need capable leadership to stay motivated through a project's completion. Where can Christian communities find this kind of leadership? God speaks through the prophets to affirm that the temple will be completed under Zerubbabel—not by human might or power, but by the Spirit of the Lord.

INTRODUCTION

Today's lesson covers two passages and emphasizes the importance of Zerubbabel's role in establishing God's kingdom on earth. The first passage concludes the study of Haggai and elevates Zerubbabel to be the one through whom the Davidic covenant is restored. The second passage comes from Zechariah 4 where a vision offers encouragement for Zerubbabel and shows a divine anointing on this great servant of God.

EXPOSITION

I. GOD'S SIGNET RING (HAGGAI 2:20-23)

Haggai's fourth and final message comes on the same day the third message was delivered. The temple's foundation had been laid, and God had promised to bless Israel and dwell among His covenant people once more. This message is directed solely to the leader of the Jews: "'Tell Zerubbabel governor of Judah that I will shake the heavens and the earth. I will overturn royal thrones and shatter the power of the foreign kingdoms. I will overthrow chariots and their drivers; horses and their riders will fall, each by the sword of his brother'" (v. 22, NIV). The language of "shaking" appears once more in Haggai's prophecy, just as it did in Haggai 2:6. Again, just as its usage earlier in the chapter, the meaning of political upheaval is intended; the only question is why and when this political upheaval will occur. William Brown notes the difference between the two passages: "Whereas the cosmic shake-up in 2:6 meant wealth for the temple, this quake spells disaster for all oppressive military powers" (*Obadiah Through Malachi* in *Westminister Bible Companion Series* [Louisville, John Knox Press, 1996], 130). In verses 21-22, Haggai is referring to a time in the future when all military superpowers will be overthrown and a reign of peace will ensue. Such an interpretation further builds upon the argument that Haggai 2:6-7 is not a messianic prophecy of Christ's birth but one that alludes to the establishing of Christ's eternal Kingdom on earth.

Possibly in the back of some of the returned Jews' minds is the remembrance of the promise made to David in 2 Samuel 7 that his kingdom would be an eternal one. In Haggai 2:23, God reaffirms His promise: "'On that day ... I will take you, my servant Zerubbabel son of Shealtiel ... and I will make you like my signet ring, for I have chosen you'" (NIV). Zerubbabel is the grandson of Jehoiachin, the last king of Judah who was taken into captivity by King Nebuchadnezzar of Babylon (see 2 Kings 24:12-17). God's disdain for Jehoiachin was so great that He said: "'Even if you, Jehoiachin son of Jehoiakim king of Judah, were a signet ring on my right hand, I would still pull you off'" (Jer. 22:24, NIV). God's words to Zerubbabel, though, show His unending favor on this man: He is reestablishing the promise of David's eternal reign through the person of Zerubbabel.

God's use of "signet ring" (Hag. 2:23, NIV) is significant and carries much meaning. In Persian culture, signet rings were used to make impressions on clay tablets or wax. The rings were closely attached to their owners and usually remained around their necks or on their fingers. They were also used to bind Persian laws, which when sealed, could never be revoked (see Dan. 6:17). Yet, God's calling Zerubbabel His signet ring is an obvious reversal of the judgment on Jehoiachin (David F. Pennant, "Haggai" in *The New Bible Commentary*, 21st Century Edition [Downers Grove: IVP Academic, 1994], 862). According to Eugene March, with this ring, God designates Zerubbabel as the agent "authorized to act on behalf of [Him] in rebuilding the Temple and, perhaps, in accomplishing even greater things in the days ahead" ("The Book of Haggai" in *The New Interpreter's Bible*, Vol. 7 [Nashville: Abingdon Press, 1996, 731). Great honor and responsibility have been placed on Zerubbabel's shoulders, and he is the man who is to carry out God's divine purposes for Israel.

Thus, the book of Haggai ends with the promise of a new kingdom that will be ushered in through Zerubbabel. The Davidic covenant has been restored and will reach its fulfillment in the person of Jesus Christ. As mentioned in the first week of the study of the book of Haggai, the prophet frames the events of his book around a foreign king—Darius I. However, for the conclusion of the book, Haggai sets the stage for a new kingdom which will be centered on Jewish lineage and Jesus Christ.

II. ZECHARIAH'S VISION (ZECHARIAH 4:5-14)

In the fourth chapter of the book of Zechariah, Zerubbabel is also featured prominently. Zechariah, which means "whom Jehovah remembers," was a common name throughout the Old Testament—at least twenty-seven other individuals have the same name (Homer Hailey, *A Commentary on the Minor Prophets* [Grand Rapids: Baker Book House, 1972], 316). More biographical information is known about the prophet Zechariah than the prophet Haggai. In Zechariah 1:1, the prophet states he is the son of Berechiah and the grandson of Iddo. In Nehemiah 12:12-16, Iddo is described as being from a priestly family (Brown, 135). More than likely, Zechariah accompanied Zerubbabel back from Babylon with the returning captives.

Much debate rages over the dates for the composition of the book of Zechariah, but not enough space is present here to discuss such matters. What remains pertinent to today's study is knowing the book takes place at the same time as the ministry of Haggai, of whom Zechariah was a contemporary. The prophecies of Zechariah began two months after Haggai's preaching and the work on the rebuilding of the temple had initiated. The prophecies concluded in the ninth month of Darius' fourth year on the throne. Hailey summarizes the chief aim of Zechariah's book: "Zechariah looks beyond the immediate temple to the Messiah and the spiritual temple of God, and to the final consummation of God's purpose in the glory of the Messiah and His rule" (317). Hailey recognizes how prevalent eschatology and messianic prophecies are within the book. He also explains how the book differs from the other minor prophets in three ways. First, a strong emphasis on divine revelation coming through visions is present. Second, the use of angels serving as mediators is also found in the book. Finally, much of the book is characterized by symbols of the apocalypse (319).

The book of Zechariah shares eight night visions in total that the prophet receives. The fourth chapter details his fifth vision, which Brown notes, "constitutes nothing less than the centerpiece of Zechariah's message" (149). In verses 1-2, an angel awakens Zechariah from his sleep and asks him to describe what he sees. Brown says this awakening by the angel signifies that "the backdrop to this vision is one of utter darkness, in the middle of the night, as it were, a time of potentially horrific proportions" (150). Responding to the angel, Zechariah says, "'I see a solid gold lampstand with a bowl at the top and seven lights on it, with seven channels to the lights. Also there are two olive trees by it, one on the right of the bowl and the other on its left'" (vv. 2-3, NIV).

The lampstand described is different from the one used in the tabernacle or the traditional menorah. Hailey explains that much debate over the translation of verse two results in differing images: the KJV says the lampstand has "seven pipes to the seven lamps," and the ASV says "seven pipes to each of the [seven] lamps" (339). The differing translations result in either seven pipes or forty-nine pipes being present.

Zechariah asks the angel twice to explain the meaning of what he sees before him. The angel basically brushes off the prophet's question and gives a message that is intended for Zerubbabel: "'This is the word of the LORD to Zerubbabel: "Not by might nor by power, but by my Spirit," says the Lord Almighty.'" (v. 6, NIV). Elizabeth Achtemeier writes that verse six is the key verse to the entire chapter (*Nahum—Malachi*, Interpretation: A Bible Commentary for Teaching and Preaching [Louisville: John Knox Press, 1986], 123). She explains that the word *might* (v. 6, NIV) refers to army forces or great wealth: "It has to do with human resources, the provisions we use to fight our battles" (124). She then explains that the word *power* (ibid.) denotes "purposeful force, dynamic strength, and resoluteness" (125). Thus, the message for Zerubbabel is that he will not rebuild the temple with human strength but only by being empowered by God's Spirit.

Zechariah 4:7 continues the message for Zerubbabel: "'What are you, O mighty mountain? Before Zerubbabel you will become level ground. Then he will bring out the capstone to shouts of "God bless it! God bless it!"'" (NIV). Brown and Hailey have differing interpretations of this verse. Brown sees the words as very literal: "That mountain is no doubt the massive ruins of the former temple complex that must be cleared from the temple mount" (150). Hailey believes the mountain refers to any kind of obstacles that stand in the way of the rebuilding project: "whether the power of world kingdom, or the obstacles within Judah, or both; but most probably the world's power that always stood in opposition to God's work is emphasized" (340). Both authors also disagree on the meaning of *capstone*. Brown believes the stone to be the cornerstone which is placed with great celebration (151). Hailey argues the cornerstone would have already been laid by this point; instead, the stone refers to the finishing stone which is placed on the temple construction to complete the project (340).

In verse nine, the Lord reiterates that Zerubbabel has laid the temple's foundation, and "'his hands will also complete it'" (NIV). In Ezra 5:16, Sheshbazzar is credited with laying the foundation. Therefore, it can be surmised that Zerubbabel finished it. The question "'Who despises the day of small things?'" (Zech. 4:10, NIV) is a reference to those who remember Solomon's temple in its glory and think the new temple is smaller in comparison. God wants to emphasize that nothing He does is without meaning and purpose (Hailey, 341). The Lord continues by saying, "'Men will rejoice when they see the plumb line in the hand of Zerubbabel'" (v. 10, NIV). A plumb line was a tool used to make sure the stones were aligned correctly in the construction of a building. Therefore, when the Jews see the tool in Zerubbabel's hand, they will know the completion of the temple is near.

Also in verse ten, the angel finally tells Zechariah what the lampstand and two olive trees represent—the angel says to Zechariah, "'These seven are the eyes of the LORD, which range throughout the earth'" (NIV). This answer describes the lampstand with the seven lamps. Achtemeier explains that the lampstand represents the Jews who are to shine the light of God to a dark world. Furthermore, the lamps are called "'eyes'" (ibid.) because the eyes are considered the source of light for the human body (see Matt. 6:22; Achtemeier 124). Then Zechariah asks the angel to explain the "'two olive trees on the right and the left of the lampstand'" (Zech. 4:11, NIV). The angel explains, "'These are the two who are anointed to serve the Lord of all the earth'" (v. 14, NIV). Brown says "two who are anointed" (ibid.). literally translates to read as "'sons of oil'" (152). In addition, "the particular Hebrew word here denotes fresh, unprocessed oil, as opposed to the traditional oil of anointment, whose detailed recipe can be found in Exodus 30:22-33" (ibid.). Such an understanding alludes to a new work in effect.

Most scholars believe the two anointed individuals are Joshua the high priest and Zerubbabel the governor. Brown writes: "Equal and symmetric in their relationship to each other, these two figures stand by God's side in a doubled form of messiahship. Rather than the old order of royal dominance over the priesthood, a new model of governance has emerged: Royal and priestly figures are set on the same footing" (152). Furthermore, both Zerubbabel (the picture of Davidic kingship) and Joshua (the picture of the sacrificial system) prefigure the coming of the ultimate High Priest and King: Jesus Christ (Hailey, 343). Thus, the symbolism is complete: the two olive trees (Zerubbabel and Joshua) provide the oil necessary for the lamps (Jews) to shine—and the Spirit of God is the motivating force behind this process.

THE LESSON APPLIED

In today's lesson, although the people had been lazy, they began to rebuild God's house. God has assured them that since they are working, they are once again ready for God to bless them. First, when believers are obedient and worship the Lord in spirit and truth, God's blessings are unlimited. Second, when believers rely on the Spirit of God to accomplish even the most unbelievable, it can and will happen if they take God at His word. As the Lord said to Zechariah, "'Not by might nor by power, but by my Spirit'" (Zech. 4:6, NIV). All things are possible with God.

LET'S TALK ABOUT IT

1. **What happens when men and women rely on their strength instead of God's?**

God tells Zerubbabel that human strength is not what will complete the building of the temple; rather, the Spirit of God will be what empowers him. When men and women rely on their own devices, they will usually fail. Recall when the Jews were in the wilderness and tried to conquer enemies without the help of God—the Jews were defeated (see Josh. 7). Physical strength can only get people so far; they need the power and strength that only God provides.

HOME DAILY DEVOTIONAL READINGS
JUNE 23-29, 2014

MONDAY	TUESDAY	WEDNESDAY	THURSDAY	FRIDAY	SATURDAY	SUNDAY
Being of the Same Mind	Empowered by the Same Spirit	Maintaining the Unity of the Spirit	Many Members in One Body	No Dissension Within the Body	Members of the Body of Christ	Agreement Without Divisions
Philippians 4:1-7	1 Corinthians 12:4-11	Ephesians 4:1-6	1 Corinthians 12:12-20	1 Corinthians 12:21-26	1 Corinthians 12:27-31	1 Corinthians 1:10-17

A CALL TO UNITY

1 CORINTHIANS 1:10-17

King James Version

NOW I beseech you, brethren, by the name of our Lord Jesus Christ, that ye all speak the same thing, and that there be no divisions among you; but that ye be perfectly joined together in the same mind and in the same judgment.

11 For it hath been declared unto me of you, my brethren, by them which are of the house of Chloe, that there are contentions among you.

12 Now this I say, that every one of you saith, I am of Paul; and I of Apollos; and I of Cephas; and I of Christ.

13 Is Christ divided? was Paul crucified for you? or were ye baptized in the name of Paul?

14 I thank God that I baptized none of you, but Crispus and Gaius;

15 Lest any should say that I had baptized in mine own name.

16 And I baptized also the household of Stephanas: besides, I know not whether I baptized any other.

17 For Christ sent me not to baptize, but to preach the gospel: not with wisdom of words, lest the cross of Christ should be made of none effect.

New Revised Standard Version

NOW I appeal to you, brothers and sisters, by the name of our Lord Jesus Christ, that all of you be in agreement and that there be no divisions among you, but that you be united in the same mind and the same purpose.

11 For it has been reported to me by Chloe's people that there are quarrels among you, my brothers and sisters.

12 What I mean is that each of you says, "I belong to Paul," or "I belong to Apollos," or "I belong to Cephas," or "I belong to Christ."

13 Has Christ been divided? Was Paul crucified for you? Or were you baptized in the name of Paul?

14 I thank God that I baptized none of you except Crispus and Gaius,

15 so that no one can say that you were baptized in my name.

16 (I did baptize also the household of Stephanas; beyond that, I do not know whether I baptized anyone else.)

17 For Christ did not send me to baptize but to proclaim the gospel, and not with eloquent wisdom, so that the cross of Christ might not be emptied of its power.

MAIN THOUGHT: Now I beseech you, brethren, by the name of our Lord Jesus Christ, that ye all speak the same thing, and that there be no divisions among you; but that ye be perfectly joined together in the same mind and in the same judgment. (1 Corinthians 1:10, KJV)

LESSON SETTING

    Time: A.D. 50
    Place: Corinth

LESSON OUTLINE

  I. **Paul Calls for Unity in the Church (1 Corinthians 1:10-13)**
  II. **Paul's True Mission As an Apostle (1 Corinthians 1:14-17)**

UNIFYING PRINCIPLE

Disagreements in a community may cause division. How can community disagreements be resolved? Paul called the disputing people to find common ground by taking on the mind of Christ.

INTRODUCTION

The next several lessons will focus on one of Paul's letters to the Corinthian church. The book of 1 Corinthians is more than likely a second letter written to the church by Paul. The first one was probably lost (see 1 Cor. 5:9-111; J. Paul Sampley, "The First Letter to the Corinthians" in *The New Interpreter's Bible*, Vol. 10 [Nashville: Abingdon Press, 2002], 777). The church at Corinth was established by Paul in approximately A.D. 50 (ibid.). Acts 18:1-18 provides the narrative account of Paul in Corinth. During that time he planted the church, befriended Aquila and Priscilla, and worked as both a tentmaker and an evangelist for eighteen months. From Corinth, he sailed to Ephesus, where scholars believe Paul wrote the letter now designated as the book of 1 Corinthians (see 1 Cor. 16:8).

Corinth was an important commercial city in the ancient world. The city was located forty miles southwest of Athens on the Isthmus of Corinth. Its two port cities, Lechaeum and Cenchreae, were part of a major trade route between the Aegean and Ionian seas (Richard Hays, *First Corinthians* in *Interpretation: A Bible Commentary for Teaching and Preaching* [Louisville: John Knox Press, 1997], 3). This ideal location led to many merchants and sailors bringing various goods as well as their religious beliefs to the city (Sampley, 773). Although Corinth had been destroyed in 146 B.C., Julius Caesar rebuilt the city in 44 B.C. as a Roman colony and populated it with freed slaves and other individuals who sought new opportunities in the restored city (Hays, 3). Many Jews also settled in the area after being banished from Rome by the emperors Tiberius and Claudius; Sampley argues that Aquila and Priscilla could have possibly been part of these Jews (774). He also tells how much Rome depended on Corinth: "the senate looked to Corinth even more than to Athens as the lead city of the Roman province of Achaia, and Corinth paid taxes directly to Rome well into the second century" (ibid.). Such wealth and esteem led to even Cicero's proclaiming Corinth to be "the light of all Greece" (qtd. in Raymond Brown, *An Introduction to the New Testament* [New York: Doubleday, 1997], 512).

Of course, one cannot talk about Corinth without mentioning its notorious reputation as a city of promiscuity. Sampley writes, "The transitory nature of ancient commerce, with sailors relishing life in a city and then moving along, contributed to Corinth's becoming known as 'Sin City'" (775). Michael Gorman says the sex trade industry was very strong and possibly associated with the worship of Aphrodite

(*Apostle of the Crucified Lord* [Grand Rapids: Eerdmans Publishing, 2004], 228). Gorman also notes how the word *Corinth* was even made into a verb. To say something had become *corinthianized* was to imply that it had become "thoroughly immoral and materialistic" (ibid.). Amidst this sinful city, the Corinthian church found itself striving to be an effective agent of change for the Gospel.

When Paul initially departed from Corinth, the church was thriving and harmonious, but since then he had received word that quarrels were breaking out within the body of believers. From their reading, scholars have detected some of the issues facing the church. The church in Corinth was comprised of mostly Gentile believers (see 1 Cor. 12:2) and some Jewish Christians. Hays writes, "Paul was faced with a major task of reshaping the thinking of his Corinthian converts into the symbolic world of Judaism and the emergent Christian movement, in which one God alone was to be worshiped" (4). In addition, a strong divide existed between the rich and the poor in the congregation, possibly leading to some of the numerous divisions that were occurring within the church. Some of the believers also claimed to have more spiritual insight or maturity than others, and this was leading to strife. Gorman explains, "The situation at Corinth was a complex set of interrelated social, sexual, and spiritual problems that frequently pitted the supposedly enlightened or elite against the supposedly unenlightened or nonelite" (236). As chapter one will illustrate, many of the believers began breaking off into factions claiming to follow different leaders of the early

Church. As a result, Paul writes this letter in order to stress the importance of unity in the body of Christ.

Paul's letter opens with the typical salutation of his other epistles; the book also closes with his usual greetings and benediction. What is unique about 1 Corinthians is that the primary appeal of the letter comes at the beginning (see 1 Cor. 1:10), instead of a building up to an appeal as a conclusion (see Rom. 12:1; Phil. 4:2; Sampley, 779). Also, no other Pauline epistles are centered on answering questions from a church. The church had written to Paul asking about how to deal with certain matters (see 1 Cor. 8:1; 12:1; 16:1) (ibid.). Some scholars think the relationship between the Corinthian believers and Paul is strained and others think Paul and the believers are on good terms. On the other hand, an obvious falling out had occurred between the two parties by the time 2 Corinthians was composed.

EXPOSITION

I. PAUL CALLS FOR UNITY IN THE CHURCH
(1 CORINTHIANS 1:10-13)

After his usual method of opening a letter, Paul immediately makes known his primary concern for the Corinthian church in verse ten: it needs to be unified as one body. The whole of the book hinges on these words: "I appeal to you, brothers, in the name of our Lord Jesus Christ, that all of you agree with one another so that there may be no divisions among you and that you may be perfectly united in mind and thought" (1 Cor. 1:10, NIV). First, Paul says the believers should be in agreement with each other. Doing so will keep divisions from springing up among them. As a result, they will be "perfectly united in mind and thought" (v. 10, NIV). The word *united* (Grk. *katartizo*) is the same verb form that appears in Mark 1:19 and Matthew 4:21 to describe the mending of fish nets (Hays, 21). Paul perhaps intends to "carry the connotation of restoration to a prior condition, the putting in order of something that has fallen into disarray" (ibid.). Thus, Paul says these divisions that have been created need to dissolve and the believers need to have the same mind. Sampley points out that Paul does not mean all the believers need to be uniform in thought and have the same opinions about everything; rather, "the unity that believers experience in Christ is supposed to be so profound and so encompassing that they share the demeanor, the outlooks, and the goals that really matter" (807). Being unified will bring the church together and allow it to better fulfill its goals and missions for the kingdom of God.

Paul then addresses the factions that are forming within the church: "One of you says, 'I follow Paul'; another, 'I follow Apollos'; another, 'I follow Cephas'; still another, 'I follow Christ'" (1 Cor. 1:12, NIV). All of those could be seen as slogans of each party. According to Robert Picirilli, those who claim to follow Paul are probably some of his earliest converts in the church. Those who adhere to the teachings of Apollos could be impressed with his reputation as an eloquent speaker and are probably Greek converts. The followers of Cephas are perhaps Judaizers who are strong opponents to Paul's ministry (*The Randall House Bible Commentary: 1, 2 Corinthians* [Nashville: Randall House Publications, 1987], 17). And what is wrong with some saying they solely follow Christ? More than likely, these individuals are saying they are the only true followers of Christ and they are placing their faith on a pedestal (Hays, 23).

Verse thirteen utilizes the use of rhetorical questions, which would have appealed greatly to the Greek converts since rhetoric was so highly esteemed in that day: "Is Christ divided? Was Paul crucified for you? Were you baptized into the name of Paul?" (NIV). Paul literally asks the Corinthians if Christ had been cut up and dispensed among each of the divisions that had formed. Do they believe Christ is a commodity meant to be divided and sold? (Hays, 23). Also, Paul seeks here to lessen the importance of his role in the Corinthian believers' conversion. Paul points out that Christ was the one crucified on the cross and Christ is the one in whose name they were baptized. Paul had done nothing to earn the believers their salvation; therefore, why should they devote themselves solely to his teachings? Everything was accomplished by the work of Christ on the cross.

II. PAUL'S TRUE MISSION AS AN APOSTLE (1 CORINTHIANS 1:14-17)

Some people misinterpret Paul's next few words: "I am thankful that I did not baptize any of you except Crispus and Gaius, so no one can say that you were baptized into my name. (Yes, I also baptized the household of Stephanas; beyond that, I don't remember if I baptized anyone else)" (vv. 14-16). Such interpreters believe that Paul is downplaying the importance of baptism—nothing could be further from the truth. All Paul seeks to do in these verses is to downplay his role in baptism because he wants to emphasize that all believers are baptized into Christ and nothing is truly important about who baptizes whom. The men Paul lists are just those who come to his mind offhand.

Finally, in verse seventeen, Paul explains his true mission as an apostle: "For Christ did not send me to baptize, but to preach the gospel—not with words of human wisdom, lest the cross of Christ be emptied of its power" (NIV). Yes, baptism is important, but Paul's chief mission is not to be one who baptizes but one who wins souls for Christ by the preaching of the Word. The latter half of this verse also lays the groundwork for Paul's argument in 1:18—2:16. Following this passage, Paul will contrast human wisdom with the power of the cross. The wisdom of the world is full of eloquent speech told by great philosophers; the cross is simple and not much to behold yet more powerful than any words espoused by Plato or Socrates. Sampley explains further: "Here 'cross' stands for, signifies, a much larger, pivotal cluster of events so central to Paul's proclamation: the death and resurrection of Jesus Christ. For Paul, the cross, planted squarely in history, stands for the whole story of Christ's death and resurrection as a sign of God's grace and caring for human beings" (808). While the teachings of sages and philosophers might be important to history, their accomplishments are nothing compared to Christ's work on the cross. Paul wants unity in the Corinthian church because a church divided risks voiding the cross of its meaning and power.

THE LESSON APPLIED

The body of Christ is one unified body. This theme will appear repeatedly in the book of 1 Corinthians. In chapters twelve and fourteen, Paul talks about how each member of the church body has a specific role to fulfill, yet the body remains intact. He also writes that if one member of the body suffers, then the entire body suffers. All of the parts must be functioning together in order for the church to maximize its full potential for the Kingdom.

LET'S TALK ABOUT IT

1. What is the importance of baptism?

According to traditional Baptist teachings, baptism is the sign of the new covenant for believers. Just as circumcision was the mark used by those who adhered to the Law of Moses in the Old Testament, baptism incorporates believers into the community of faith. Some denominations believe that baptism is necessary for salvation, but Baptist groups believe salvation only comes through faith in Christ; therefore, baptism is merely showing the world one has placed his or her faith in Christ.

HOME DAILY DEVOTIONAL READINGS
JUNE 30—JULY 6, 2014

MONDAY	TUESDAY	WEDNESDAY	THURSDAY	FRIDAY	SATURDAY	SUNDAY
Building Up the Body of Christ	Building Up the Beloved	Sincerity and Truth in the Body	Dissociating from Immorality in the Body	Washed, Sanctified, and Justified	A Particular Gift from God	Glorify God in Your Body
Ephesians 4:7-16	2 Corinthians 12:14-21	1 Corinthians 5:1-8	1 Corinthians 5:9-13	1 Corinthians 6:1-11	1 Corinthians 7:1-9	1 Corinthians 6:12-20

GLORIFY GOD WITH YOUR BODY

ADULT TOPIC:	BACKGROUND SCRIPTURES:
DO NO HARM	1 CORINTHIANS 6:12—7:9

1 CORINTHIANS 6:12–20

King James Version

ALL things are lawful unto me, but all things are not expedient: all things are lawful for me, but I will not be brought under the power of any.

13 Meats for the belly, and the belly for meats: but God shall destroy both it and them. Now the body is not for fornication, but for the Lord; and the Lord for the body.

14 And God hath both raised up the Lord, and will also raise up us by his own power.

15 Know ye not that your bodies are the members of Christ? shall I then take the members of Christ, and make them the members of an harlot? God forbid.

16 What? know ye not that he which is joined to an harlot is one body? for two, saith he, shall be one flesh.

17 But he that is joined unto the Lord is one spirit.

18 Flee fornication. Every sin that a man doeth is without the body; but he that committeth fornication sinneth against his own body.

19 What? know ye not that your body is the temple of the Holy Ghost which is in you, which ye have of God, and ye are not your own?

20 For ye are bought with a price: therefore glorify God in your body, and in your spirit, which are God's.

New Revised Standard Version

"ALL things are lawful for me," but not all things are beneficial. "All things are lawful for me," but I will not be dominated by anything.

13 "Food is meant for the stomach and the stomach for food," and God will destroy both one and the other. The body is meant not for fornication but for the Lord, and the Lord for the body.

14 And God raised the Lord and will also raise us by his power.

15 Do you not know that your bodies are members of Christ? Should I therefore take the members of Christ and make them members of a prostitute? Never!

16 Do you not know that whoever is united to a prostitute becomes one body with her? For it is said, "The two shall be one flesh."

17 But anyone united to the Lord becomes one spirit with him.

18 Shun fornication! Every sin that a person commits is outside the body; but the fornicator sins against the body itself.

19 Or do you not know that your body is a temple of the Holy Spirit within you, which you have from God, and that you are not your own?

20 For you were bought with a price; therefore glorify God in your body.

MAIN THOUGHT: What? know ye not that your body is the temple of the Holy Ghost which is in you, which ye have of God, and ye are not your own? (1 Corinthians 6:19, KJV)

LESSON OUTLINE
> I. **Not Everything Is Beneficial**
>   **(1 Corinthians 6:12-14)**
> II. **Flee Sexual Immorality**
>   **(1 Corinthians 6:15-18)**
> III. **Your Body Is a Temple**
>   **(1 Corinthians 6:19-20)**

UNIFYING PRINCIPLE

Personal, moral, and physical purity are beneficial to the community. How does the behavior of one person affect the whole community? Paul said that because Christians are all one within the body of Christ, what harms one will harm other members, and what benefits one will benefit all.

INTRODUCTION

Today's passage does not focus on unity but does emphasize how sexual immorality negatively affects not just the transgressor but the church community as a whole. Before studying 1 Corinthians 6:12-20, one must understand how Paul frames some of his arguments throughout 1 Corinthians. Often, Paul will present an argument by first quoting a popular Corinthian maxim. These maxims were "characteristic of Greco-Roman education and culture . . . [and] considered epitomes of truth, of commonly shared convictions or perceptions" (J. Paul Sampley, "The First Letter to the Corinthians" in *The New Interpreter's Bible*, Vol. 10 [Nashville: Abingdon Press, 2002], 860). A maxim was never disputed outright; if someone disagreed with a maxim, then this individual would offer another one to be considered in its place (ibid.). This was the method Paul used when encountering the Corinthian maxims.

EXPOSITION

I. NOT EVERYTHING IS BENEFICIAL (1 CORINTHIANS 6:12-14)

Paul begins by quoting a Corinthian maxim: "'Everything is permissible for me'" (v. 12, NIV). More than likely, many of the Corinthian believers were using this maxim to emphasize their Christian liberty. Unfortunately, some were abusing this liberty. Sampley argues this could have been the case with the Christian brother in 1 Corinthians 5:1 who was openly involved in an incestuous relationship with his step-mother (861). Also, seeing that Paul will focus on the topic of prostitution, perhaps some of the believers were engaging in sexual solicitation because in Corinthian culture "prostitution was not only legal; it was a widely accepted social convention" (Richard Hays, "First Corinthians" in *Interpretation: A Bible Commentary for Teaching and Preaching* [Louisville: John Knox Press, 1997], 102). Most citizens saw nothing wrong with prostitution at this time.

Paul first responds to the Corinthians' maxim by giving his own qualifier: "but not everything is beneficial" (1 Cor. 1:12, NIV). While certain actions might, indeed, be permissible for someone to commit, this does not mean all actions offer optimal results for the individual or for the community. Continuing his discussion, Paul quotes the Corinthian maxim again, and then offers another maxim to be considered in its place: "I will not be mastered by anything" (ibid.). This maxim sounds possibly Stoic in origin because Paul says he will not allow his passions and desires to enslave him: he will always be in control of his body. Essentially, Christians are to only be mastered by Christ and no one else (Sampley, 862).

Paul then lists another Corinthian maxim: "'Food for the stomach and the stomach for food'" (v. 13, NIV). The Corinthians believed bodies were inconsequential; thus, any actions one committed with his or her body had no lasting importance. If someone desired to eat, then he or she should; if someone desired the company of a prostitute, then what was the concern if no long-term effects remained (Hays, 103)? Paul responds to this idea by stating, "God will destroy them both" the stomach and food (v. 13, NIV). Furthermore, "the body is not meant for sexual immorality, but for the Lord, and the Lord for the body" (ibid.). Paul opposes the notion entirely that the body is insignificant because it belongs to the Creator.

In verse fourteen, Paul expresses the importance of the body in light of the Christian's hope of a resurrection: "By his power God raised the Lord from the dead, and he will raise us also" (NIV). Just as Christ's body was physically raised from the dead, so will believers' bodies be raised, too. Paul will expound upon this topic in greater detail later in the fifteenth chapter of 1 Corinthians.

II. FLEE SEXUAL IMMORALITY (1 CORINTHIANS 6:15-18)

In verses 15-18, Paul creates a powerful analogy of the spiritual union between a believer and Christ to that of the physical union between a believer and a prostitute. Paul raises two questions: "Do you not know that your bodies are members of Christ himself? Shall I then take the members of Christ and unite them with a prostitute?" (v. 15, NIV). Paul could be doing a play on words with this verse. First, he points out that all Christians are members of the body of Christ. Second, Paul's use of the word *members* could have an intended sexual connotation in reference to being joined together with a prostitute.

Verse sixteen continues the analogy: "Do you not know that he who unites himself with a prostitute is one with her in body? For it is said, 'The two will become one flesh.'" (NIV). Paul now emphasizes the gravity of the sexual union between a man and a woman. Hays explains that sex is not an act of instant gratification. Instead, "it creates a mysterious but real and enduring union between man and woman" (105). The passage Paul references to support his argument is found in Genesis 2:24: "For this reason a man will leave his father and mother and be united to his wife, and they will become one flesh" (NIV). When God instituted marriage in the Garden of Eden, He intended for sexual relations to only occur within the confines of wedlock because of the man and woman's becoming "one flesh" (ibid.).

In the same way, when an individual converts to Christianity, he or she becomes "one flesh" with Jesus Christ: "He who unites himself with the Lord is one with him in spirit" (1 Cor. 6:17, NIV). Just as husband and wives' bodies belong to each other, the believer's body belongs to Christ. The book of Ephesians further explains this mystical union between Christ and believers (see Eph. 5:22-32), and Revelation presents a picture of Christ as the Bridegroom and the Church as His Bride (see Rev. 19:7; 21:2, 9-10). Therefore, Paul is telling the Corinthians that "the man who has sexual intercourse with a prostitute is therefore not only committing an act of infidelity to Christ but also taking something that belongs to Christ (his own body) and linking it to the sphere of the unholy" (Hays, 104). The believer must keep herself pure and undefiled for the Bridegroom.

Another point that should be made is that sexual immorality does not only affect the individual who commits the sin. Instead, the entire Christian community is negatively affected because all members of the body are joined together in the body of Christ. An extreme example of this has already been seen in the unrepentant member in 1 Corinthians 5:1 who was openly involved with his father's wife. Paul commanded that such an individual be expelled from the community of faith until he had repented because of the influence such a person continued to have with the other believers. When one part of the body suffers, the whole body suffers; therefore, sin must be kept from infecting the entire body. With this in mind, Paul commands all members of the church body to "Flee from sexual immorality" (6:18, NIV) so they can avoid the disastrous consequences of sexual immorality.

Paul's next statement, "All other sins a man commits are outside his body, but he who sins sexually sins against his own body" (ibid.), has been a cause of debate among scholars and can be interpreted in two different ways. First, Paul could be implying that fornication is a greater sin than other sins because of its personal effects on the individual's body. An alternate and more likely interpretation is to understand "All other sins a man commit are outside his body" (ibid.) as a Corinthian maxim to which Paul retorts with "but he who sins sexually sins against his own body" (ibid.; Hays, 105). Such a Corinthian maxim correlates well with the earlier assertion that the Corinthians believed nothing a person did with his or her body had any lasting significance. Paul is then making the claim once again that how a person conducts his or her body is of great importance because the body belongs to God.

III. YOUR BODY IS A TEMPLE (1 CORINTHIANS 6:19-20)

In verse eighteen, Paul again stressed the importance of the body and explains why in verses nineteen and twenty: "Do you not know that your body is a temple of the Holy Spirit, who is in you, whom you have received from God? You are not your own; you were bought at a price" (NIV). The believer's body is significant because it is a consecrated vessel for the spirit of the living God. In the same way that the Jews honored and maintained the temple that housed God's presence, so should believers honor and maintain their vessels in which the Holy Spirit resides.

Also, Paul reminds the believers that their bodies are not their own because of the price Christ paid for them with His blood. The picture Paul evokes is that of a slave market where Christ purchases (or redeems) the believer (Sampley, 864). Such imagery is found earlier in the Bible when Hosea bought Gomer back after she had abandoned him and become the property of another man (see Hos. 3:2). The book of Hosea parallels the prophet's buying back Gomer to that of God's buying back Israel after she prostituted herself to idolatry. Of further interest is that Hosea bought back Gomer for the equivalent of thirty pieces of silver—the same amount of the blood money Judas was paid to deliver Christ to the Pharisees (Homer Hailey, *A Commentary on the Minor Prophets* [Grand Rapids: Baker Book House, 1972], 145).

Since Christ has paid such an exorbitant price for the believers, Paul commands them to "honor God with [their] body" (1 Cor. 6:20, NIV). Every action believers commit should strive to bring honor to God. Sampley explains that glorifying God with their bodies "will at once mean (1) that individuals exercise stewardship of their own bodies, their very selves, and (2) that collectively the believers live lovingly and in an edifying fashion with each other as members of the one body that is Christ's" (866). Like a marriage relationship in which each spouse seeks to bring honor to the other, so should believers seek to maintain and purify their bodies for the honor of God.

THE LESSON APPLIED

Sex outside of marriage infects the believer's relationship with God. It also damages the individual, and it affects the community. When a church is aware of these intentional acts and does not address them, it is like having an infectious virus that goes unattended. The viral effect starts small and spreads outward from the individual, to the family, to the community, and to the country. But when believers appreciate the gift of the Holy Spirit, who dwells within them, they will bring honor and respect to God and to themselves.

LET'S TALK ABOUT IT

1. What does Paul mean when he says "your body is a temple of the Holy Spirit" (v. 19, NIV)?

When Paul speaks of the body as the temple where the Holy Spirit resides, he is mindful of the importance of the temple in Jewish heritage. The temple was the center of sacrificial activity—where prayers, praises, sacrifices, and ritual ceremonies were done on behalf of God and His people. Great care was given in the construction and maintenance of the Hebrew temple. When people receive Christ as their Lord and Savior, the Holy Spirit indwells them. In the same way as a temple, the believer's body is a sacred vessel and should receive the utmost care and respect. It should not be defiled by sin.

LOVE BUILDS UP

ADULT TOPIC: LOVE BUILDS UP	BACKGROUND SCRIPTURE: 1 CORINTHIANS 8

1 CORINTHIANS 8

King James Version

NOW as touching things offered unto idols, we know that we all have knowledge. Knowledge puffeth up, but charity edifieth.

2 And if any man think that he knoweth any thing, he knoweth nothing yet as he ought to know.

3 But if any man love God, the same is known of him.

4 As concerning therefore the eating of those things that are offered in sacrifice unto idols, we know that an idol is nothing in the world, and that there is none other God but one.

5 For though there be that are called gods, whether in heaven or in earth, (as there be gods many, and lords many,)

6 But to us there is but one God, the Father, of whom are all things, and we in him; and one Lord Jesus Christ, by whom are all things, and we by him.

7 Howbeit there is not in every man that knowledge: for some with conscience of the idol unto this hour eat it as a thing offered unto an idol; and their conscience being weak is defiled.

8 But meat commendeth us not to God: for neither, if we eat, are we the better; neither, if we eat not, are we the worse.

9 But take heed lest by any means this liberty of yours become a stumblingblock to them that are weak.

10 For if any man see thee which hast knowledge sit at meat in the idol's temple, shall not the conscience of him which is weak be

New Revised Standard Version

NOW concerning food sacrificed to idols: we know that "all of us possess knowledge." Knowledge puffs up, but love builds up.

2 Anyone who claims to know something does not yet have the necessary knowledge;

3 but anyone who loves God is known by him.

4 Hence, as to the eating of food offered to idols, we know that "no idol in the world really exists," and that "there is no God but one."

5 Indeed, even though there may be so-called gods in heaven or on earth—as in fact there are many gods and many lords—

6 yet for us there is one God, the Father, from whom are all things and for whom we exist, and one Lord, Jesus Christ, through whom are all things and through whom we exist.

7 It is not everyone, however, who has this knowledge. Since some have become so accustomed to idols until now, they still think of the food they eat as food offered to an idol; and their conscience, being weak, is defiled.

8 "Food will not bring us close to God." We are no worse off if we do not eat, and no better off if we do.

9 But take care that this liberty of yours does not somehow become a stumbling block to the weak.

10 For if others see you, who possess knowledge, eating in the temple of an idol, might they not, since their conscience is weak, be

MAIN THOUGHT: But take heed lest by any means this liberty of yours become a stumblingblock to them that are weak. (1 Corinthians 8:9, KJV)

1 CORINTHIANS 8

King James Version

New Revised Standard Version

King James Version

emboldened to eat those things which are offered to idols;

11 And through thy knowledge shall the weak brother perish, for whom Christ died?

12 But when ye sin so against the brethren, and wound their weak conscience, ye sin against Christ.

13 Wherefore, if meat make my brother to offend, I will eat no flesh while the world standeth, lest I make my brother to offend.

New Revised Standard Version

encouraged to the point of eating food sacrificed to idols?

11 So by your knowledge those weak believers for whom Christ died are destroyed.

12 But when you thus sin against members of your family, and wound their conscience when it is weak, you sin against Christ.

13 Therefore, if food is a cause of their falling, I will never eat meat, so that I may not cause one of them to fall.

LESSON SETTING
Time: A.D. 55
Place: Corinth

LESSON OUTLINE
I. **Love Trumps Knowledge (1 Corinthians 8:1-3)**
II. **Do Not Cause Your Brother to Fall (1 Corinthians 8:4-13)**

UNIFYING PRINCIPLE

What may be right for some members of a community may not be right for others. How are community members to hold one another accountable? Paul cautioned the faithful to behave in ways that would not cause others to falter in their faith.

INTRODUCTION

Last week's lesson covered Paul's warning against sexual immorality in 1 Corinthians 6:12-20. He reminded the believers that their bodies housed the Holy Spirit; therefore, they should seek to honor God with the way they used their bodies—especially in regards to sexual immorality. Following this discussion, Paul talks about principles regarding Christian marriage. For example, he answered questions regarding whether widows should remarry or what to do if a spouse becomes a believer while the other does not (see 1 Cor. 7:8-16). For today's lesson, Paul's attention shifts to how the Corinthian believers should respond when other issues arise regarding Christian liberty.

Paul's next discussion essentially spans 1 Corinthians 8:1—11:1. The main principle Paul seeks to impart to his readers is that a love for others should be elevated over one's personal knowledge and freedom. Apparently the question has been raised regarding whether or not believers could partake of food that had already been offered in sacrifice to idols. The common practice of that day was for animals to be sacrificed to some deity with some of the flesh being burned on the altar while the rest of the meat was either eaten at a celebration or sold in the marketplace (J. Paul Sampley, "The First Letter to the Corinthians" in *The New Interpreter's Bible,* Vol. 10 [Nashville: Abingdon Press, 2002], 893).

Richard Hays argues that more than likely the wealthier converts would have had much more contact with meat being offered to idols because poor people couldn't afford such a meal; rather, consecrated meat would have only been dispensed publicly during a religious festival of some kind. He explains, "For example, the sanctuary of Asclepius in Corinth comprised both an area for cultic sacrifice and several dining rooms that opened onto a pleasant public courtyard. The wealthier Corinthians would have been invited to meals in such places as a regular part of their social life, to celebrate birthdays, weddings, healings attributed to the god, or other important occasions" ("First Corinthians" in *Interpretation: A Bible Commentary for Teaching and Preaching* [Louisville: John Knox Press, 1997], 137). Thus, Hays sees this discussion possibly having issues relating to social classes where the richer Christians would not have seen anything wrong with eating such meat because it was a part of their daily lives.

EXPOSITION

I. LOVE TRUMPS KNOWLEDGE
(1 CORINTHIANS 8:1-3)

Paul begins his response to the Corinthians' question by quoting a common Corinthian saying of the day: "We know that we all possess knowledge" (v. 1, NIV). Paul does not see anything wrong with knowledge because truth comes from God. Even so, he recognizes that some of the Corinthian believers are flawed in their thinking because they have equated having knowledge with having total freedom to do what they wish at the expense of others. This is why Paul gives his own maxim in response to the Corinthians': "Knowledge puffs up, but love builds up" (ibid.). Knowledge can lead to pride and

the tearing down of others, whereas love can only edify and strengthen the body of Christ. Also, as verse three explains, being known by God and one's love for God are both more valuable than any knowledge men and women can attain hope to attain. As Sampley explains, "When one knows oneself to be known by God, then love falls into place and knowing is placed in perspective" (896). The Corinthians need to have their priorities in proper order.

II. DO NOT CAUSE YOUR BROTHER TO FALL
(1 CORINTHIANS 8:4-13)

Paul agrees that eating meat offered to idols is fundamentally harmless because "an idol is nothing at all in the world and that there is no God but one" (v. 4, NIV). What harm can come from eating something that has been offered to a lifeless statue? Both the Corinthians and Paul know that all life derives from "Jesus Christ, through whom all things came and through whom we live" (v. 6, NIV). Thus, eating meat that has been offered to a deity that does not exist should not affect one's relationship with God.

Even if eating meat sacrificed to idols is harmless, Paul says "not everyone knows this" because some believers have a weaker "conscience" (v. 7, NIV). Paul exhorts the mature believers not to allow their freedom to become "a stumbling block to the weak" (v. 9, NIV). He warns that such an exercise of Christian liberty can lead to severely damaging effects. For example, if a newer convert who had practiced pagan worship and eaten meat offered to idols saw one of the other Corinthian believers engaging in the same meal, how would he or she respond? Paul asks, "Won't he be emboldened to eat what has been sacrificed to idols?" (v. 10, NIV). This convert could be encouraged to return to his or her former lifestyle and forsake the truth. As a result, Paul warns that this newer convert is "destroyed by your knowledge" (v. 11, NIV). Knowledge in this instance has led to the destruction of a believer.

Furthermore, even more egregious than possibly destroying the faith of a new convert is the fact that such behavior causes a mature Christian to "sin against Christ" (v. 12, NIV). As a result, Paul proclaims, "if what I eat causes my brother to fall into sin, I will never eat meat again, so that I will not cause him to fall" (v. 13, NIV). Hays points out that the Greek rendering of *meat* in this verse refers to meat generically and not just the meat offered to idols (142); thus, Paul is speaking hyperbolically in saying that he will never eat any kind of meat again if it was causing tension in the Christian community. Exercising his Christian liberty simply isn't worth the trouble of causing another believer to stumble.

Paul wants the Corinthians to ponder one question: are one's eating habits really worth causing strife in the body of Christ? He argues that a concern for others should always be at the forefront of a Christian's mind in order to unify both weak and strong Christians in the body of Christ. Hays concludes: "Thus 1 Corinthians 8 must be read as a compelling invitation to the 'strong' Corinthians to come over and join Paul at table with the weak. This invitation is far more urgent than any invitation to savor meat with their rich friends in the respectable world of Corinthian society" (142-143).

THE LESSON APPLIED

According to the Apostle Paul, each believer comes to Christ as a babe, or child in the faith. "Brothers, I could not address you as spiritual but as worldly—mere infants in Christ. I gave you milk, not solid food, for you were not yet ready for it. Indeed, you are still not ready" (1 Cor. 3:1-2, NIV). As there are various levels to one's physical maturation, there are also various levels to the maturity of a believer's faith. As Paul writes to the church in Corinth, he is mindful of the differences between mature Christians and young Christians. He reminds the church that some weak believers might be sensitive to perceived issues of morality; therefore, spiritually mature believers should abstain, even when they are free to indulge, for the sake of new believers.

Actions without love can affect others in negative ways. We must be careful not to offend or cause others to sin by our actions. Believers should be aware of the different levels of Christian spiritual maturity. Being mature in the faith is not based on the number of years a believer has been a Christian as much as the believer's relationship with God. Spiritual maturity is determined by the degree of knowledge that the believer has concerning the Word of God and that person's willingness to obey the Word in love.

LET'S TALK ABOUT IT

1. What does "knowledge puffs up, but love builds up" (v. 1, NIV) mean?

Paul understood that too much knowledge can open the door for arrogance or being "puffed up" (v. 1, NIV). It's not that learning is wrong or should not be undertaken as a goal. The Bible supports learning. Proverbs 1:7 reads, "The fear of the LORD is the beginning of knowledge, but fools despise wisdom and discipline" (NIV). The problem arises when Christians are not using their knowledge to build up one another. When knowledge is not coupled with love, it needs correction. Christians are encouraged to grow in both knowledge *and* love.

Knowledge without love runs the risk of being puffed up. This kind of thinking does not benefit or lift up others because of the excessive focus on the needs, desires, and wants of one's self. Many people with this type of attitude are unwilling to learn or listen to others or even to God. They are (ironically) unteachable. Love on the other hand does not need to be puffed up. It simply exists as it is. Christians should exhibit the kind of love that has the ability to love in spite of all opposition. Paul says this kind of love seeks to edify rather than tear down. Knowledge and love must be properly balanced.

2. What are some other areas in which believers may cause others to stumble in their faith?

Paul touched on a common infringement of Christian liberty during his day—eating food offered to idols. In America there aren't really concerns about eating food offered in this way; however, there are other areas in which mature believers indulge that may cause new or weak Christians to stumble. For example, weaker Christians may be offended if they witness the actions of some Christians at parties. Attendance at the party may not be the offense but what is done while there may cause alarm. Some Christians indulge in drinking, smoking, playing cards, and so forth. While perhaps not wrong in and of themselves, these actions may be confusing to new Christians who turned away from activities of this nature when they came to Christ.

Because of the freedoms in our culture, we must carefully evaluate standards that may be offensive to a weaker brother or sister in Christ. From the clothes we wear, to the foods we eat, to the places we go, to the things we say, we must question their potential to cause others to stumble. In Romans 14:13, Paul says we should, "make up [our] mind[s] not to put any stumbling block or obstacle in [our] brother's way." Our chief aim should be to always show love and concern for all the Christians around us. Our Christian liberty should be something we use only when it benefits the entire Christian community and does not cause anyone to stumble.

HOME DAILY DEVOTIONAL READINGS
JULY 14-20, 2014

MONDAY	TUESDAY	WEDNESDAY	THURSDAY	FRIDAY	SATURDAY	SUNDAY
Turning Aside from God's Commands	Turning Away from Following God	Putting the Lord to the Test	Search with Heart and Soul	Holding Firm to the End	Examples That Deter from Evil	God's Faithfulness in Our Testing
Exodus 32:1-10	Deuteronomy 7:1-6	Acts 5:1-11	Deuteronomy 4:25-31	Hebrews 3:7-14	1 Corinthians 10:1-8	1 Corinthians 10:9-21

OVERCOMING TEMPTATION

ADULT TOPIC: STRENGTH TO MEET TEMPTATION	BACKGROUND SCRIPTURE: 1 CORINTHIANS 10:1-22

1 CORINTHIANS 10:12–22

King James Version	*New Revised Standard Version*
WHEREFORE let him that thinketh he standeth take heed lest he fall.	SO if you think you are standing, watch out that you do not fall.
13 There hath no temptation taken you but such as is common to man: but God is faithful, who will not suffer you to be tempted above that ye are able; but will with the temptation also make a way to escape, that ye may be able to bear it.	13 No testing has overtaken you that is not common to everyone. God is faithful, and he will not let you be tested beyond your strength, but with the testing he will also provide the way out so that you may be able to endure it.
14 Wherefore, my dearly beloved, flee from idolatry.	14 Therefore, my dear friends, flee from the worship of idols.
15 I speak as to wise men; judge ye what I say.	15 I speak as to sensible people; judge for yourselves what I say.
16 The cup of blessing which we bless, is it not the communion of the blood of Christ? The bread which we break, is it not the communion of the body of Christ?	16 The cup of blessing that we bless, is it not a sharing in the blood of Christ? The bread that we break, is it not a sharing in the body of Christ?
17 For we being many are one bread, and one body: for we are all partakers of that one bread.	17 Because there is one bread, we who are many are one body, for we all partake of the one bread.
18 Behold Israel after the flesh: are not they which eat of the sacrifices partakers of the altar?	18 Consider the people of Israel; are not those who eat the sacrifices partners in the altar?
19 What say I then? that the idol is any thing, or that which is offered in sacrifice to idols is any thing?	19 What do I imply then? That food sacrificed to idols is anything, or that an idol is anything?
20 But I say, that the things which the Gentiles sacrifice, they sacrifice to devils, and not to God: and I would not that ye should have fellowship with devils.	20 No, I imply that what pagans sacrifice, they sacrifice to demons and not to God. I do not want you to be partners with demons.
21 Ye cannot drink the cup of the Lord, and the cup of devils: ye cannot be partakers of the Lord's table, and of the table of devils.	21 You cannot drink the cup of the Lord and the cup of demons. You cannot partake of the table of the Lord and the table of demons.

MAIN THOUGHT: There hath no temptation taken you but such as is common to man: but God is faithful, who will not suffer you to be tempted above that ye are able; but will with the temptation also make a way to escape, that ye may be able to bear it. (1 Corinthians 10:13, KJV)

1 CORINTHIANS 10:12-22

King James Version	*New Revised Standard Version*
22 Do we provoke the Lord to jealousy? are we stronger than he?	22 Or are we provoking the Lord to jealousy? Are we stronger than he?

LESSON SETTING
   Time: A.D. 55
   Place: Corinth

LESSON OUTLINE
   I. **How to Overcome Temptation (1 Corinthians 10:12-13)**
   II. **Idol Worship and the Lord's Supper (1 Corinthians 10:14-22)**

UNIFYING PRINCIPLE
The pride of individual persons and communities can lead them to act in destructive and harmful ways. How can communities resist the desire to move in harmful directions? Paul reminded the Corinthians that all believers are tempted but God will not let them be tested beyond their strength—God will provide the way out.

INTRODUCTION
Before beginning a study of today's passage from 1 Corinthians 10, one needs to understand the concept of Gentiles being grafted into the Jewish tradition and heritage upon converting to Christianity. The congregation in Corinth is composed of mostly Gentile converts to Christianity, so one could be puzzled by Paul's using such references "our forefathers" (1 Cor. 10:1) to describe the events in Jewish history. Romans 11:11-24 details how the Gentiles are grafted into the same plan of salvation that had once been only available to Jews under the Old Testament covenant. Thus, references to Moses and Abraham that had

only pertained to the Israelites could now be applied to Gentiles who had partaken of the New Testament covenant that was instituted after the universal sacrifice of Christ on the cross.

On a side note, while today's lesson is titled "Overcoming Temptation," this title actually relates much better to 1 Corinthians 10:1-13. Verses 14-22, the bulk of today's Scripture passage, cover another topic altogether about idol worship and the Lord's Supper. Thus, this commentary will be divided into two sections.

EXPOSITION

I. HOW TO OVERCOME TEMPTATION (1 CORINTHIANS 10:12-13)
A full understanding of verses 12-13 cannot occur without looking at what Paul covers in the eleven verses prior. As mentioned in the introduction, Paul speaks with the understanding that the Gentiles have been grafted into Christianity and are now under the umbrella of Jewish heritage. Thus, it is appropriate that Paul begins chapter ten by giving examples from Israel's history to warn against immorality and idolatry. He writes that after the Exodus, their ancestors (i.e., the Israelites) were "under the cloud and that they all passed through the sea. They were all baptized into Moses in the cloud and in the sea. They all ate the same spiritual food and drank the same spiritual drink;

for they drank from the spiritual rock that accompanied them, and that rock was Christ" (1 Cor. 10:1-4, NIV). In short, Paul explains how Moses safely led the people through the Red Sea and forty years of wandering in the wilderness. They also ate the manna from heaven and drank water from the rock which Moses struck instead of speaking to it (see Num. 20:1-13). J. Paul Sampley explains that Paul's referencing the events in Israel's past "highlights the connections of his readers by retrofitting baptism and Lord's supper motifs onto the old story" ("The First Letter to the Corinthians" in *The New Interpreter's Bible*, Vol. 10 [Nashville: Abingdon Press, 2002], 914). Paul has been able to incorporate Christian imagery into Jewish tradition to relate the events to the Corinthians.

Paul doesn't stop here—he then tells of the horrific punishments the people faced as a result of their sexual immorality, complaining, and idolatry: "Do not be idolaters, as some of them were; as it is written: 'The people sat down to eat and drink and got up to indulge in pagan revelry.' We should not commit sexual immorality, as some of them did—and in one day twenty-three thousand of them died. We should not test the Lord, as some of them did—and were killed by snakes. And do not grumble, as some of them did—and were killed by the destroying angel" (1 Cor. 10:7-10, NIV). The specific incidents Paul references are when the Israelites worshiped the golden calf and were punished (see Exod. 32); when Israelites committed sexual immorality with the people of Moab and were killed by a plague (see Num. 25); and when the people complained and God sent venomous snakes which could only be combated by looking at the bronze snake Moses constructed (see Num. 21:4-9). Hay posits that the incident of grumbling may refer to the people speaking against Moses and Aaron while in the wilderness (see Num. 14).

Paul explains solemnly to the Corinthians, "These things happened to them as examples and were written down as warnings for us, on whom the fulfillment of the ages has come" (1 Cor. 10:11, NIV). Thus, the Corinthians who have been grafted into the Jewish tradition can look at these past events and take heed. Those in the church who are tempted by sexual immorality or idolatry should remember how God punished earlier transgressors. This is why Paul says in verse twelve "So, if you think you are standing firm, be careful that you don't fall!" (NIV). The Jews in the wilderness had also benefited from the Lord's protection and provisions in the wilderness. They became overly confident in their abilities to withstand temptations and paid dearly for their sin. Paul wants the Corinthians to avoid the same judgment.

He further says, "no temptation has seized you except what is common to man" (v. 13, NIV). Paul wants his readers to know that if temptations are not handled properly the results can be devastating in that the Corinthian believers will end up being punished just as their ancestors were in the wilderness. But if they look to God, recognizing that He is faithful, they can be successful in overcoming any temptation they may face.

Furthermore, it might give his readers hope, then and now, that these are not new temptations—God has been dealing with people for many years who have faced similar tests. Jesus Himself was tested in the desert and so shares intimate knowledge of both our side and God's side of temptation (see Matt. 4:1-11).

Therefore, believers should seek God's care during trying times. They know that God, who is faithful, will not allow more to be placed on them (as an animal carrying a heavy load) then they can handle. Sampley says this "way out" for believers is like a second exodus (915). He will also provide a way out. In any case, believers are not on their own.

II. Idol Worship and the Lord's Supper

(1 Corinthians 10:14-22)

Paul has just provided examples on how to be successful when facing temptation, and he explained how idolatry, sexually immoral acts, and grumbling and complaining could lead to a downfall. Armed with Paul's advice and now this imperative, believers should be on guard against idolatry, or as Paul says: "Therefore, my dear friends, flee from idolatry" (1 Cor. 10:14, NIV).

Verses 14-22 will detail how the Corinthians are to separate themselves from the idol feasts that were prevalent during that day. Evidently, some of the Corinthian believers were taking part in both the Lord's Supper as well as the meals dedicated to pagan worship. Paul must explain why these two actions are incompatible. As Sampley explains, "Prior to their conversion, most of the Corinthian believers would have been participants in the cultic festivals—which usually included a festal meal as a high social and

religious event—so it is reasonable for them to wonder whether they can continue to take part in the festivals with their unbelieving friends" (917).

This passage should not be understood in the same context of Paul's teaching in 1 Corinthians 8 regarding eating meat offered to idols. The openly active participation of the Corinthians in pagan festivals differed greatly from the issue of whether or not they could eat meat that had been previously offered to an idol in a pagan festival. Partaking in festivals that celebrated pagan deities exceeded any questions about the limitations of Christian liberty.

Paul refers to the Corinthian believers as "sensible people" (1 Cor. 10:15, NIV). He is confident that they have the wisdom to understand and receive what he is sharing. Paul also invites them to judge for themselves. He knows the Christians in Corinth can understand that Christ's desire for their lives is not the same as that of a pagan lifestyle. Believers in America today are faced with similar decisions. They may not have to deal with the worship of golden calves or carved wooden images, but they contend with the worship of material goods and that which brings only temporary pleasure. Any object that gets in the way of our relationship with God is an idol.

Paul admonishes the believers in Corinth to remember what the blood of Christ and the bread of Christ means to the believer and the body of Christ. The Gospel of Mark reminds believers that Jesus took a cup and gave thanks and told the Disciples that this cup was the "new testament," a new covenant between them and Jesus Christ (Mark 14:24, KJV). The bread serves as a reminder of the body of Christ. Partaking in the Lord's Supper is a commemoration of the death of Christ and His work of salvation.

Paul refers to the bread as "one loaf" (1 Cor. 10:17, NIV) and explains what this means. One loaf of bread was used in the early Church to partake of the Lord's Supper. Paul stresses that many people eating from one loaf symbolizes their unity in Christ. (He more fully develops the idea of the unity of the body in 1 Corinthians 12:14-27.) The emphasis in this verse is on the unity that binds all believers in the body of Christ.

Paul next admonishes the Corinthian believers to carefully consider their actions. He returns to the sacrifice given by the Israelites, comparing it to the sacrifice offered in pagan worship. Paul asks a rhetorical question, and then subsequently answers his own question: "Do I mean then that a sacrifice offered to an idol is anything, or that an idol is anything? No, but the sacrifices of pagans are offered to demons, not to God, and I do not want you to be participants with demons" (1 Cor. 10:19-20, NIV). Even though sacrifices to idols accomplished nothing, they still had the same significance for the pagans as the sacrifices made by the Jews in the Old Testament sacrificial system.

The Corinthian believers must decide whose side they are on. Will they participate in pagan sacrifice and worship false gods, or will they eat the bread and drink the wine in recognition of the body and blood of Jesus Christ? With which would they choose to associate? Participation in the Lord's Supper is fellowshiping with believers, while participation in idol worship means having fellowship with pagans and demons. Paul encourages them to choose one or the other; they cannot participate in both.

Paul then declares, "You cannot have a part in both the Lord's table and the table of demons" (v. 21, NIV). This statement implies that there must be total allegiance to the Father, the Son, and the Holy Spirit for a Christian believer. This means the Corinthian believers must hold to the principles of God's Word. There may have been some believers in Corinth who thought there was no harm in attending the pagan festivals, but Paul is clear in the difference it makes. In the Old Testament, Joshua had to challenge the Israelites to make a similar decision. He said, "But if serving the LORD seems undesirable to you, then choose for yourselves this day whom you will serve, whether the gods your forefathers served beyond the River, or the gods of the Amorites, in whose land you are living. But as for me and my household, we will serve the LORD" (Josh. 24:15, NIV). The Corinthian believers have to make the same commitment to serve only the Lord and forsake the worship of idols.

THE LESSON APPLIED

Today's lesson covered the first twenty verses of chapter ten. Verses 1-12 are one elaborate explanation by Paul about why the Corinthian believers should heed the warnings of what happened to the Israelites who were wandering in the wilderness. They had fallen into temptation and turned from God to worship false idols, sexual immorality, and complain extensively about their circumstances. As a result, they faced the harsh judgment of God. Believers today should be wary of temptation of these and any other kinds. They must not allow their pride to allow themselves to think they are impervious to certain kinds of sin. And when tempted, believers should trust that God is with them and has provided a way to escape.

The second half of today's lesson involved Paul's condemning the Corinthian believers who were partaking in both the Lord's supper and festivals for pagans. Paul says they must choose either to wholly follow God or the false deities. Believers today face the same temptation to follow false teachings. They must choose whom they will serve will their whole hearts.

LET'S TALK ABOUT IT

1. How dangerous is it to not be fully committed to Christ?

The Bible presents several warnings to Christians about the gravity of not being fully committed to Him. It is a very serious offense to God. In Matthew 6:24, Jesus says, "No man can serve two masters: for either he will hate the one, and love the other; or else he will hold to the one, and despise the other. Ye cannot serve God and mammon" (KJV). Often, the desire for material possessions or the desire for pleasure causes believers to compromise their relationship with Christ. This in turn causes the believer to turn a deaf ear to the truth of God's Word.

In our lesson today, Paul provided a similar warning to the church in Corinth. He tells them of the danger of worshiping Christ halfheartedly and warns that compromising leads to a halfhearted devotion to God. The danger is that a Christian doesn't know how far he or she can fall.

2. What does Paul means when he says "flee from idolatry" (v. 14, NIV)?

In a nutshell, being an idolator means being unfaithful to God. For the Israelites, idolatry was in the form of statues and idols that were worshiped. For today's Christian, idolatry can be cell phones, designer clothes, pickup trucks, or other material possessions that supplant affection that should be focused toward God. When we are faced with choosing between these things and God, we can be sure that Satan will tempt us to make the wrong choice. With God's help, we can be effective against the temptations of Satan that leads to idolatry. James writes in his epistle, "Submit yourselves therefore to God. Resist the devil, and he will flee from you" (James 4:7, KJV). If we yield to the authority of God, Satan will flee.

HOME DAILY DEVOTIONAL READINGS
JULY 21-27, 2014

MONDAY	TUESDAY	WEDNESDAY	THURSDAY	FRIDAY	SATURDAY	SUNDAY
Imitate What Is Good	Doing the Right Thing	Complete in Everything Good	Devoted to Good Works	So All Learn and Are Encouraged	All Done Decently and in Order	Praying with Spirit and Mind
3 John 2-12	James 4:13-17	Hebrews 13:16-21	Titus 3:8-14	1 Corinthians 14:27-33	1 Corinthians 14:37-40	1 Corinthians 14:13-26

SEEK THE GOOD OF OTHERS

ADULT TOPIC: BUILD UP YOUR NEIGHBOR	BACKGROUND SCRIPTURE: 1 CORINTHIANS 14:13-26

1 CORINTHIANS 14:13-26

King James Version

WHEREFORE let him that speaketh in an unknown tongue pray that he may interpret.

14 For if I pray in an unknown tongue, my spirit prayeth, but my understanding is unfruitful.

15 What is it then? I will pray with the spirit, and I will pray with the understanding also: I will sing with the spirit, and I will sing with the understanding also.

16 Else when thou shalt bless with the spirit, how shall he that occupieth the room of the unlearned say Amen at thy giving of thanks, seeing he understandeth not what thou sayest?

17 For thou verily givest thanks well, but the other is not edified.

18 I thank my God, I speak with tongues more than ye all:

19 Yet in the church I had rather speak five words with my understanding, that by my voice I might teach others also, than ten thousand words in an unknown tongue.

20 Brethren, be not children in understanding: howbeit in malice be ye children, but in understanding be men.

21 In the law it is written, With men of other tongues and other lips will I speak unto this people; and yet for all that will they not hear me, saith the Lord.

22 Wherefore tongues are for a sign, not to them that believe, but to them that believe not: but prophesying serveth not for them that believe not, but for them which believe.

New Revised Standard Version

THEREFORE, one who speaks in a tongue should pray for the power to interpret.

14 For if I pray in a tongue, my spirit prays but my mind is unproductive.

15 What should I do then? I will pray with the spirit, but I will pray with the mind also; I will sing praise with the spirit, but I will sing praise with the mind also.

16 Otherwise, if you say a blessing with the spirit, how can anyone in the position of an outsider say the "Amen" to your thanksgiving, since the outsider does not know what you are saying?

17 For you may give thanks well enough, but the other person is not built up.

18 I thank God that I speak in tongues more than all of you;

19 nevertheless, in church I would rather speak five words with my mind, in order to instruct others also, than ten thousand words in a tongue.

20 Brothers and sisters, do not be children in your thinking; rather, be infants in evil, but in thinking be adults.

21 In the law it is written, "By people of strange tongues and by the lips of foreigners I will speak to this people; yet even then they will not listen to me," says the Lord.

22 Tongues, then, are a sign not for believers but for unbelievers, while prophecy is not for unbelievers but for believers.

MAIN THOUGHT: How is it then, brethren? when ye come together, every one of you hath a psalm, hath a doctrine, hath a tongue, hath a revelation, hath an interpretation. Let all things be done unto edifying. (1 Corinthians 14:26, KJV)

1 CORINTHIANS 14:13–26

King James Version

23 If therefore the whole church be come together into one place, and all speak with tongues, and there come in those that are unlearned, or unbelievers, will they not say that ye are mad?

24 But if all prophesy, and there come in one that believeth not, or one unlearned, he is convinced of all, he is judged of all:

25 And thus are the secrets of his heart made manifest; and so falling down on his face he will worship God, and report that God is in you of a truth.

26 How is it then, brethren? when ye come together, every one of you hath a psalm, hath a doctrine, hath a tongue, hath a revelation, hath an interpretation. Let all things be done unto edifying.

New Revised Standard Version

23 If, therefore, the whole church comes together and all speak in tongues, and outsiders or unbelievers enter, will they not say that you are out of your mind?

24 But if all prophesy, an unbeliever or outsider who enters is reproved by all and called to account by all.

25 After the secrets of the unbeliever's heart are disclosed, that person will bow down before God and worship him, declaring, "God is really among you."

26 What should be done then, my friends? When you come together, each one has a hymn, a lesson, a revelation, a tongue, or an interpretation. Let all things be done for building up.

LESSON SETTING
Time: A.D. 55
Place: Corinth

LESSON OUTLINE
I. Use Spiritual Gifts to Edify
(1 Corinthians 14:13-17)
II. Self-Discipline in Worship
(1 Corinthians 14:18-19)
III. Speaking in Tongues Can Cause Confusion for Unbelievers
(1 Corinthians 14:20-26)

UNIFYING PRINCIPLE

Communities function best when the members can articulate a shared system of values. How do community members communicate their beliefs to one another? When communicating in a community, it's important to show respect by ensuring that one is understood. Paul exhorted the Corinthians to speak plainly so that both believers and unbelievers could benefit from the leading of the Holy Spirit.

INTRODUCTION

Paul continues to deal with issues in the Corinthian church. Following are a few issues that he addressed in 1 Corinthians 11—13: He spoke about proper attire and behavior for men and women in the worship service (see 11:2-16); he addressed proper conduct during the Lord's Supper (see 11:17-34); in chapter twelve, Paul talked about the importance of spiritual gifts in the church; in chapter thirteen, Paul dealt with the permanency and the presence of love, calling it the greatest of all of the spiritual gifts.

Paul begins chapter fourteen by exhorting his readers to desire the spiritual gift of prophecy over all others. Prophecy is more desirable than speaking in tongues because it edifies the church: "Everyone who prophesies speaks to men for their strengthening, encouragement and comfort" (1 Cor. 14:3, NIV). Whereas speaking in tongues edifies only the speaker if no interpreter is present, prophesying edifies the entire church body. Another point of significance is that Paul does not think of prophecy as merely telling of future events; rather, "its purpose is to address the hearts of the hearers and to encourage them in the faith" (Richard Hays, ("First Corinthians" in *Interpretation: A Bible Commentary for Teaching and Preaching* [Louisville: John Knox Press, 1997], 235). As a result, Paul proclaims, "He who prophesies is greater than one who speaks in tongues" (v. 5, NIV). The duration of chapter fourteen will emphasize why prophecy is the most desirable gift.

In 1 Corinthians 14:13-26 Paul warns the church about being sure to use spiritual gifts in a beneficial way. Primarily, he deals with the gift of speaking in tongues during worship. If a believer is blessed with this gift, Paul instructs him or her to use the gift to edify the body of Christ or to instruct believers and thereby bring glory to God in worship. If using the gift of speaking of tongues does not benefit or edify the body of Christ, then the believer should be silent until God sends an interpreter. If gifts are used in any other manner, with any other motive, then Paul says they are useless because they benefit no one.

EXPOSITION

I. USE SPIRITUAL GIFTS TO EDIFY (1 CORINTHIANS 14:13-17)

Generally speaking, Paul advises the Corinthian church to seek spiritual gifts that build up the church. The purpose of these gifts is to benefit the body of Christ. In 14:13-26, he narrows the focus to deal specifically with the gift of tongues, saying, "Wherefore let him that speaketh in an unknown tongue pray that he may interpret" (v. 13, KJV). Paul understands that praying in another tongue without an interpreter means no one will understand except God. Therefore, no one will be edified or built up. In Acts 2:1-13, when the Holy Spirit descended upon the disciples, they began speaking in known languages. Everyone in the crowd could understand what each disciple was saying in his or her own native tongue. But when one speaks in tongues without an interpreter, no one understands the message being preached. Using the gift of tongues without an interpreter means the words spoken will be useless and the mind will not benefit because the language is not understood.

Paul addresses using the gift of tongues in a public setting, though his advice may also benefit private use (see 1 Cor. 14:16). Praying or giving thanks is beneficial for an individual, but it becomes more beneficial in the assembled church when other believers can join in. Paul says being a part of worship can become confusing if believers cannot understand the prayers of those who speak in tongues. Corporate worship should be the joint effort of a congregation whose members join together to give glory to God.

However, the intent of worship would be wasted if spoken in an unknown tongue. Worshipers may pray, sing, bless the name of God, and give thanks very well, but if listeners do not understand, they are not being edified. This means they have not learned anything that will increase their knowledge or improve their spiritual lives. Paul wants the entire corporate body to be edified and not just specific individuals.

II. Self-Discipline in Worship (1 Corinthians 14:18-19)

Paul is not bragging in verse eighteen when he says that he speaks "in tongues more than all of you [Corinthian believers]" (NIV). Instead, he is reminding them of the importance of practicing self-discipline in worship for the benefit of the whole body. Paul is grateful to God for giving him the gift to speak in tongues, but this is not his biggest concern. He says he would rather speak five words of an intelligible language to instruct others. This is more effective than someone speaking ten thousand words with little or no comprehension. Intelligible words are beneficial, while words without meaning offer no edification.

Paul raises an important point. Even though he has been blessed with the gift of speaking in tongues and can do it better than any of the Corinthian believers, he does not wish to abuse it. He recognizes that speaking in tongues only utilizes the spirit and emotions of an individual and not the mind. He would rather control his emotional responses in the worship service and be fully alert and mentally engaged with the proceedings. What is truly accomplished if the mind is not stimulated in a worship service? Emotional responses can only take an individual so far. There must be more substance to one's worship experience, and this substance is found when the mind is instructed by the preaching of the Word.

III. Speaking in Tongues Can Cause Confusion for Unbelievers (1 Corinthians 14:20-26)

Now Paul begins to warn about the impact speaking in tongues might have on unbelievers who have joined a worship service. In verse twenty, Paul basically tells the Corinthians to grow up and consider a more mature perspective (Hays, 238). He next quotes Isaiah 28:11, which has confused many biblical scholars because of its obscurity. Hays explains Paul's referencing this passage from the Old Testament: "The point of Isaiah 28:11-13 is that because the scoffing rulers have refused to listen to the prophetic promise of rest, but have instead tried to create security for themselves by making an alliance with Egypt, the word of God will henceforth be to them gibberish spoken in an alien tongue. Thus, the 'sign' of unintelligible speech is a prophetic sign of judgment" (240). Therefore, when Paul says, "Tongues, then, are a sign, not for believers but for unbelievers" (1 Cor. 14:22, NIV), he means that speaking in tongues will be understood as a sign of judgment and condemnation by unbelievers because they cannot understand the divine revelation of God (Hays, 240).

Some readers might be confused by an apparent contradiction by Paul in verses 22-24. In verse twenty-two, Paul says, "prophecy, however, is for believers, not for unbelievers" (NIV). Then in verses 24-25, Paul describes how prophecy is able to convict the unbeliever and prove the presence of God. Paul's words should be understood to mean that prophecy is primarily intended for believers because Christians are better receptive to divine revelation. The unbeliever can only understand so much of the Word of God.

Paul continues to explain in verse twenty-three why prophecy is preferred to speaking in tongues. The unbeliever who comes into a worship service and hears tongues will be confused and find the service of no benefit. Hays states that the unbelievers will think the believers are "caught up in a fit of religious ecstasy, a common phenomenon in that culture" (238). Conversely, if prophecy is taking place, then the unbeliever "will be convinced by all that he is a sinner and will be judged by all, and the secrets of his heart will be laid bare" (vv. 24-25, NIV). The unbeliever will recognize he or she is in the presence of God. This is why Paul argues that prophecy is much more desirable than speaking in tongues. Thus, Paul concludes in verse twenty-six by saying that whatever takes place in a worship service should be done for the edification of all who attend.

THE LESSON APPLIED

Paul provides guidance about using spiritual gifts, in particular the gift of speaking in tongues within a church service. The tendency to "show off" describes some believers in worship. It's a natural tendency because of our selfish natures. The process of spiritual growth and maturity progressively reduces this characteristic. However, when it dominates and drives the use of spiritual gifts, then worship will not benefit anyone. People who attend a worship service should consider themselves to be participants and use love as the chief motivator for their actions.

All of the spiritual gifts are given to edify and build up the body of Christ. When believers within a worship service have the gift of speaking in tongues, they should use them unselfishly, seeking God's guidance through prayer. They should also ask themselves whether their actions will bring glory to God or create a distraction within the worship service.

LET'S TALK ABOUT IT

1. Is speaking in tongues an indication of a believer's spiritual maturity?

The giving of spiritual gifts is God's choice and based on His desire for all believers. We should not conclude that only spiritually mature believers receive spiritual gifts. There are other characteristics that define spiritual maturity. Paul calls the marks of spiritual maturity the "fruit of the Spirit" (Gal. 5:22, NIV). Spiritual gifts are another matter. Romans 12:3-8 makes it clear that every believer is given a spiritual gift by God. Remember, it is God's desire for people to be saved and become His children. He has gifted believers with the means to impact the world for Christ, whether through the gifts of evangelism, teaching, preaching, or even speaking in tongues. All spiritual gifts are empowerments given by God so that the Kingdom of God can impact and reach the world with the love of God.

HOME DAILY DEVOTIONAL READINGS
JULY 28—AUGUST 3, 2014

MONDAY	TUESDAY	WEDNESDAY	THURSDAY	FRIDAY	SATURDAY	SUNDAY
Our Refuge and Strength	The Shield of Your Help	O Lord, We Rely on You	Support the Weak	Admonish, Encourage, Help, and Do Good	A Cause for Giving Thanks	The God Who Consoles Us
Psalm 46	Deuteronomy 33:24-29	2 Chronicles 14:1-12	Acts 20:28-35	1 Thessalonians 5:12-22	Philemon 3-7	2 Corinthians 1:3-11

CONSOLATION GRANTED THROUGH PRAYER

ADULT TOPIC: BACKGROUND SCRIPTURE:
DOES ANYONE CARE?   2 CORINTHIANS 1:3-11

2 CORINTHIANS 1:3-11

King James Version

BLESSED be God, even the Father of our Lord Jesus Christ, the Father of mercies, and the God of all comfort;

4 Who comforteth us in all our tribulation, that we may be able to comfort them which are in any trouble, by the comfort wherewith we ourselves are comforted of God.

5 For as the sufferings of Christ abound in us, so our consolation also aboundeth by Christ.

6 And whether we be afflicted, it is for your consolation and salvation, which is effectual in the enduring of the same sufferings which we also suffer: or whether we be comforted, it is for your consolation and salvation.

7 And our hope of you is stedfast, knowing, that as ye are partakers of the sufferings, so shall ye be also of the consolation.

8 For we would not, brethren, have you ignorant of our trouble which came to us in Asia, that we were pressed out of measure, above strength, insomuch that we despaired even of life:

9 But we had the sentence of death in ourselves, that we should not trust in ourselves, but in God which raiseth the dead:

10 Who delivered us from so great a death, and doth deliver: in whom we trust that he will yet deliver us;

11 Ye also helping together by prayer for us, that for the gift bestowed upon us by the means of many persons thanks may be given by many on our behalf.

New Revised Standard Version

BLESSED be the God and Father of our Lord Jesus Christ, the Father of mercies and the God of all consolation,

4 who consoles us in all our affliction, so that we may be able to console those who are in any affliction with the consolation with which we ourselves are consoled by God.

5 For just as the sufferings of Christ are abundant for us, so also our consolation is abundant through Christ.

6 If we are being afflicted, it is for your consolation and salvation; if we are being consoled, it is for your consolation, which you experience when you patiently endure the same sufferings that we are also suffering.

7 Our hope for you is unshaken; for we know that as you share in our sufferings, so also you share in our consolation.

8 We do not want you to be unaware, brothers and sisters, of the affliction we experienced in Asia; for we were so utterly, unbearably crushed that we despaired of life itself.

9 Indeed, we felt that we had received the sentence of death so that we would rely not on ourselves but on God who raises the dead.

10 He who rescued us from so deadly a peril will continue to rescue us; on him we have set our hope that he will rescue us again,

11 as you also join in helping us by your prayers, so that many will give thanks on our behalf for the blessing granted us through the prayers of many.

MAIN THOUGHT: And our hope of you is stedfast, knowing, that as ye are partakers of the sufferings, so shall ye be also of the consolation. (2 Corinthians 1:7, KJV)

LESSON SETTING
    Time: A.D. 55-57
    Place: Corinth

LESSON OUTLINE
  I. God Comforts Us
    (2 Corinthians 1:3-5)
 II. We Suffer for You
    (2 Corinthians 1:6-7)
III. God Delivers Us
    (2 Corinthians 1:8-11)

UNIFYING PRINCIPLE

In times of trouble, communities may seek consolation and protection from some power or force beyond themselves. What consolation do Christians receive when seeking assistance from a higher power? Paul gave testimony of God's consolation in times of hardship and gave thanks for the mutual consolation that comes from praying for one another.

INTRODUCTION

Today, we begin five lessons on 2 Corinthians. Second Corinthians was written from Macedonia by the Apostle Paul and co-authored by Timothy circa A.D. 55-57. According to Acts 18:1, Paul founded the church at Corinth while he was on his second missionary journey. While in Corinth, Paul preached in the synagogue, teaching that Jesus was the Messiah. Some "Jews opposed Paul and became abusive" (Acts 18:6, NIV). Paul "left the synagogue and went next door to the house of Titius Justus, a worshiper of God" (v. 7, NIV). There he preached and converted the synagogue ruler, his household, and many other Corinthians.

Scholars differ in their opinions about the composition of 2 Corinthians, ranging from believing there are five fragments of letters to believing it is one unified whole.

J. Paul Sampley helps us to understand the difficulty of resolving this issue. He writes, "Absolutely no textual variations or manuscript evidence supports any of the partition theories. The lack of such evidence, however, does not necessarily argue against partition; it could simply be that the editing together of available fragments was done before the oldest extant manuscripts were written" ("The Second Letter to the Corinthians," in *The New Interpreter's Bible*, Vol. 11 [Nashville: Abingdon Press, 2000], 5). However, it is not our purpose to try to resolve this debate.

The relationship between Paul and the church in Corinth was strained. After Paul sent 1 Corinthians, he visited the church in Corinth. "During that visit, one of the Corinthian believers made a verbal attack on Paul, and, to his chagrin, no one came to his defense" (ibid.). He left abruptly, but had planned on returning. However, he decided to send a letter to address the issue, and this letter was filled with "rather harsh frank speech" (ibid.). This letter did cause some tension in the congregation, but also served to help the congregation address the issue (see 2 Cor. 7:5-13).

Paul begins this letter with a traditional salutation and greeting commonly used in epistles. As with his other epistles, Paul identifies himself as an apostle of Christ Jesus. His apostleship is not of his own choosing. Rather, he is an apostle because it is God's will. The letter is addressed to the church in Corinth as well as the "saints throughout Achaia" (1:1, NIV). Achaia is the Roman province that includes Corinth.

The salutation continues with Paul's blessing upon the church. He wishes them grace and peace "from God our Father and the Lord Jesus Christ" (v. 2, NIV). God's grace and peace bring about the restoration of the relationship between God and humanity. Those who have peace with God are able to have peace with one another. Although this salutation and greeting is common in Paul's letters, we will see that it has special significance here in light of the conflict between Paul and the Corinthian church.

EXPOSITION

I. GOD COMFORTS US
(2 CORINTHIANS 1:3-5)

After the greeting and salutation, Paul begins by praising God the Father and Jesus Christ. Sampley writes: "Throughout the literature of Israel and of the early churches the 'blessed be' formula is used only of God.... [It] is a thankful appreciation of *God's faithfulness*, of God's steadfastness in making good on what God has promised" (40, italics in text). Paul knows that it is only through the faithfulness of God that the church in Corinth—and all disciples—can be faithful. Thus, Paul is thankful that God is "the Father of compassion and the God of all comfort" (v. 3, NIV). Paul has in mind the sufferings that those who belong to God can expect to face. We shall return to the sufferings Paul has in mind.

The God whom Paul blesses is "even the Father of our Lord Jesus Christ" (v. 3, KJV). In his salutations Paul identifies the One who authorizes him to speak. He does not speak his own words. Paul is an ambassador of Jesus Christ who is his Lord (see 2 Cor. 5:20; Eph. 6:20). Paul is commissioned to speak by the power of God—Father, Son, and Holy Spirit. This ability to speak authoritatively comes about through Paul's embodying in faithful discipleship the Gospel he proclaims.

In verse four, Paul describes the comfort God gives—He "comforts us in all our troubles" (NIV). When we think of comfort, we often think of cessation of the stimuli that cause us pain. However, the word *comfort* is better understood by the NRSV's rendering *consolation* (the KJV renders the same Greek word *comfort* in verse four and *consolation* in verses 5-8). It is not that the burdens and troubles will be removed, but that God will console those who are facing suffering. In this consolation, God gives his faithful ones the strength to endure. Paul himself is facing trouble from two different directions. The first is the affliction he and his companions endured in Asia. The second is his ongoing, contentious relationship with the Corinthian church. However, in spite of his afflictions, Paul knows that God gives him consolation in all circumstances. With this in mind, Paul wants to comfort the church with the comfort that he receives from God.

In verse five, Paul reminds the church that its members are not alone in their suffering. Indeed, we all suffer just as Christ suffered because we are aligned with Him. At the same time, Christ, who suffered for us, gives us His consolation. Sampley explains how we are consoled in our afflictions: "God's comfort and compassion are not given to believers as a personal possession. Recipients of God's merciful encouragement become the channels through whom God's comfort is made available to others who are themselves 'in any affliction' (v. 4).... Those who experience the abundance of Christ's sufferings by their exposure to affliction in this world experience a corresponding abundance of comfort (v. 5)" (41).

II. WE SUFFER FOR YOU
(2 CORINTHIANS 1:6-7)

The comfort that Paul and his co-laborers receive from Christ is offered by them to the church. Paul writes that he and his associates are "being afflicted" on the Corinthians' behalf—"it is for [their] consolation and salvation" (v. 6, NRSV). At the same time that they are being afflicted, they are also being consoled so they can console the church. The church is consoled when it "patiently [endures] the same sufferings that [Paul and his associates] are also suffering" (v. 6, NRSV). Paul is concerned here with the formation of the character of the Corinthian church. Paul, in fact, agrees with James who writes, "Whenever you face trials of any kind, consider it nothing but joy, because you know that the testing of your faith produces endurance; and let endurance have its full effect, so that you may be mature and complete, lacking in nothing" (1:2-4, NRSV).

Paul wants the church members to know that he is aware that they are suffering just as he and his associates are suffering. In identifying his sufferings with their sufferings, Paul aligns himself with the Corinthian church. This will serve the purpose of further connecting Paul to the church in the later discussion of the conflict. Here, though, Paul describes the suffering he endures on behalf of the faith and identifies the Corinthian church as sharing in that suffering.

III. GOD DELIVERS US
(2 CORINTHIANS 1:8-11)

In this section, Paul tells the Corinthians of the suffering he has experienced. While discussing the suffering he and his companions endured in Asia, he addresses the Corinthian church members as "brothers and sisters" (v. 8, NRSV). This serves to further reinforce Paul's identification with the Corinthian church to show how the suffering of one affects the other.

Paul does not tell the specifics of what caused their afflictions while in Asia. But Paul does want the church to know that the pressure was so great that he and his companions were unable to endure it—"we despaired even of life ... in our hearts we felt the sentence of death" (vv. 8-9, NIV). Paul further explains: "This happened that we might not rely on ourselves but on God, who raises the dead" (v. 9, NIV). Paul thus draws a connection between God's ability to console us in life with His power to raise us from the dead. Sampley writes that Paul could not rely on his own power in his distress. "In his overwhelming distress, Paul relied upon the truth encapsulated in a christological dictum: In raising Christ from the dead, God showed power over death. Paul, despairing of life itself, counted on God, on God's power, a power demonstrated and warranted in Christ's having been raised" (42). The cross and resurrection of Jesus Christ shape Paul's appeal and defense of his ministry throughout 2 Corinthians.

Paul experiences God's deliverance in the face of death. He is confident that God will deliver him regardless of the situations in which he finds himself. Since the church shares in his afflictions and consolation, its members can help him with their prayers. Paul expresses what he believes will be the results of the church's prayers. "Then many will give thanks on our behalf for the gracious favor granted us in answer to the prayers of many" (v. 11, NIV). Paul ends this section the way he began this letter. All things are possible because of God's grace.

THE LESSON APPLIED

In today's passage, we are introduced to some themes about the nature of Christ that will shape Paul's message throughout 2 Corinthians. The first is that in Christ there is a common experience of suffering. As disciples of Christ, the Corinthians will share in the sufferings of Jesus (see Matt. 10:16-25). This suffering, however, is not the last word. Through Jesus' resurrection, God demonstrated His victory over death. In the sufferings of the body of Christ, God is able to give consolation because His victory is sure. This indicates that, in the incarnation of the Second Person of the Trinity, God began a new work. In this new work and new age, suffering and death are no longer seen as ultimate powers. They are taken up in the collective witness of the body of Christ and shown to be powerless in the body that endures.

LET'S TALK ABOUT IT

1. How can the church in America align itself with the suffering of others?

Paul writes concerning the trouble he experienced and how it was on behalf of the church. An important theme throughout the Scriptures is that when one part of the body suffers, the entire body suffers. We know that persecution of Christians happens throughout the world. There are places where Christianity is illegal and conversion to Christianity could cost a convert at the very least the support of family and friends. Christians in these places have churches that are akin to those of Smyrna and Philadelphia (see Rev. 2:8-11; 3:7-13). In the American context, however, the situation is different. Persecution is not necessary because the church has become comfortable in its situation. The church in America espouses and endorses the same views of America to some degree. In this, the American church is like the church in Laodicea: "'For you say, "I am rich, I have prospered, and I need nothing." You do not realize that you are wretched, pitiable, poor, blind, and naked'" (Rev. 3:17, NRSV). We stand oblivious to the needs of others because we have become comfortable. In this, we are in a prison that locks us away from the true life of the church. We need to speak clearly about God's expectations for His Church, and we need to live more faithfully in our discipleship. We need to see the suffering of our fellow believers (and any who suffer) throughout the world and align ourselves with them more clearly.

HOME DAILY DEVOTIONAL READINGS
AUGUST 4-10, 2014

MONDAY	TUESDAY	WEDNESDAY	THURSDAY	FRIDAY	SATURDAY	SUNDAY
Sin and Forgiveness	Confession and Forgiveness	Repentance and Forgiveness	Redemption and Forgiveness	Grace and Justification	Speaking As Persons of Sincerity	Forgiving and Consoling
Acts 13:36-41	1 John 1:5-10	Luke 17:1-6	Ephesians 1:3-10	Romans 5:15-21	2 Corinthians 2:12-17	2 Corinthians 1:23—2:11

A COMMUNITY FORGIVES

ADULT TOPIC:	BACKGROUND SCRIPTURES:
RESTORED RELATIONSHIPS	2 CORINTHIANS 1:23—2:17

2 CORINTHIANS 1:23—2:11

King James Version

MOREOVER I call God for a record upon my soul, that to spare you I came not as yet unto Corinth.

24 Not for that we have dominion over your faith, but are helpers of your joy: for by faith ye stand.

• • • 2:1-11 • • •

BUT I determined this with myself, that I would not come again to you in heaviness.

2 For if I make you sorry, who is he then that maketh me glad, but the same which is made sorry by me?

3 And I wrote this same unto you, lest, when I came, I should have sorrow from them of whom I ought to rejoice; having confidence in you all, that my joy is the joy of you all.

4 For out of much affliction and anguish of heart I wrote unto you with many tears; not that ye should be grieved, but that ye might know the love which I have more abundantly unto you.

5 But if any have caused grief, he hath not grieved me, but in part: that I may not overcharge you all.

6 Sufficient to such a man is this punishment, which was inflicted of many.

7 So that contrariwise ye ought rather to forgive him, and comfort him, lest perhaps such a one should be swallowed up with overmuch sorrow.

8 Wherefore I beseech you that ye would confirm your love toward him.

9 For to this end also did I write, that I might know the proof of you, whether ye be obedient in all things.

New Revised Standard Version

BUT I call on God as witness against me: it was to spare you that I did not come again to Corinth.

24 I do not mean to imply that we lord it over your faith; rather, we are workers with you for your joy, because you stand firm in the faith.

• • • 2:1-11 • • •

SO I made up my mind not to make you another painful visit.

2 For if I cause you pain, who is there to make me glad but the one whom I have pained?

3 And I wrote as I did, so that when I came, I might not suffer pain from those who should have made me rejoice; for I am confident about all of you, that my joy would be the joy of all of you.

4 For I wrote you out of much distress and anguish of heart and with many tears, not to cause you pain, but to let you know the abundant love that I have for you.

5 But if anyone has caused pain, he has caused it not to me, but to some extent—not to exaggerate it—to all of you.

6 This punishment by the majority is enough for such a person;

7 so now instead you should forgive and console him, so that he may not be overwhelmed by excessive sorrow.

8 So I urge you to reaffirm your love for him.

9 I wrote for this reason: to test you and to know whether you are obedient in everything.

MAIN THOUGHT: To whom ye forgive any thing, I forgive also: for if I forgave any thing, to whom I forgave it, for your sakes forgave I it in the person of Christ. (2 Corinthians 2:10, KJV)

2 Corinthians 1:23—2:11

King James Version

10 To whom ye forgive any thing, I forgive also: for if I forgave any thing, to whom I forgave it, for your sakes forgave I it in the person of Christ;

11 Lest Satan should get an advantage of us: for we are not ignorant of his devices.

New Revised Standard Version

10 Anyone whom you forgive, I also forgive. What I have forgiven, if I have forgiven anything, has been for your sake in the presence of Christ.

11 And we do this so that we may not be outwitted by Satan; for we are not ignorant of his designs.

LESSON SETTING
    Time: A.D. 53-54
    Place: Corinth

LESSON OUTLINE
  I. **Paul Expresses His Sorrow (2 Corinthians 1:23—2:4)**
  II. **Forgive and Comfort (2 Corinthians 2:5-8)**
  III. **A Test of Obedience (2 Corinthians 2:9-11)**

UNIFYING PRINCIPLE

When a person violates the code of conduct of a community, he or she may be ostracized or rejected. How can the offender be restored to wholeness within the community? Paul told the Corinthians to forgive the one who had caused them grief in order that the entire community could be made well again.

INTRODUCTION

In last week's lesson, we discussed the shared experience of suffering and consolation in the life of Paul and the Corinthian church. Paul aligned himself with the Corinthian church by explaining that when he suffered and was consoled, he experienced this on behalf of the church. This connection with the Corinthian church gives context for the tension Paul is currently experiencing with them. It allows him to address the conflict with his brothers and sisters in Christ.

In this section, Paul seeks to clarify the reasons he did not visit the Corinthians as he promised. Paul had planned to visit Corinth twice: on his way to Macedonia and on his way back. He wants to assure the Corinthians that he did not make his plans lightly and was truthful in his interactions with them. For Paul, the certainty of his word in this matter is connected to the certainty of his teachings concerning the nature of Jesus Christ. Paul wants the Corinthians to see him as trustworthy in all he says, so he is clear that his intentions were to visit the Corinthian church twice. However, due to the conflict with one of the believers and the painful letter he sent regarding that incident, he decided not to return. In stating his intentions and the issues that caused his change of plans, Paul is attempting to vindicate his actions before the Corinthian church. He makes the appeal that he had submitted himself to God and would not cause greater strife in the Corinthian church by visiting at that time. Paul's appeal to God as a witness is where today's lesson text begins.

EXPOSITION

I. PAUL EXPRESSES HIS SORROW (2 CORINTHIANS 1:23—2:4)

In an effort to demonstrate the seriousness with which he makes his promises,

Paul calls on God as a witness to his intentions. "But I call on God as witness against me: it was to spare you that I did not come again to Corinth" (1:23, NRSV). To call on God as a witness is to call on the One who has power over life and death. In calling God as a witness, Paul is staking his life on the truthfulness of his claim. He cannot afford for this to be an empty gesture. Paul decided not to make the second visit to Corinth out of humility. Scott Hafemann writes: "His decision not to come to Corinth a second time was an act of humble restraint in which he refused to exercise his authority toward them, even when it would have meant his own vindication" (*2 Corinthians* in The NIV Application Commentary [Grand Rapids: Zondervan, 2000], 87).

Instead of visiting again immediately after the conflict, Paul wrote a letter (which is neither 1 nor 2 Corinthians but written during the time between these two) that expresses his disappointment in the congregation for not backing him up when one of the believers questioned his authority. Paul again makes it clear that this was not an attempt to increase pain, but instead his effort was to correct in a way that would eventually lead to rejoicing. The act of writing the letter itself was an act rooted in humility. Paul was allowing the Corinthians time to address the offender internally and give them a chance to restore faithfulness in the church.

When Paul "made up [his] mind not to make [them] another painful visit" (2:1, NRSV), he made a decision that would allow time for healing to take place. Another visit at this time would have caused more pain to the church that already had a strained relationship with him. Paul continues to look for ways to improve the relationship between him and the church. He does not want to cause the Corinthians to grieve because he depends on them to make him glad. While Paul's other letter was harsh in tone, he noted that he had confidence in the ability of the Corinthians to resolve this issue. Paul's confidence in this ability was vindicated, but he needed to send another corrective in 2 Corinthians to remind the church that discipline is not an end in itself but a means of restoration.

II. FORGIVE AND COMFORT (2 CORINTHIANS 2:5-8)

Paul then turns his attention to the man who questioned his authority in the Corinthian church. The man's behavior not only caused Paul grief—it caused grief for the whole church. Paul seems to believe that the church suffered more than he did. "If anyone has caused grief, he has not so much grieved me as he has grieved all of you" (v. 5, NIV).

The man that is mentioned here is frequently confused with the adulterous man mentioned in 1 Corinthians 5:1-8. However, this connection is unlikely. First, the man who committed adultery with his father's wife was unknown to Paul. Paul received a report about the adulterer and wrote to the church. Second, the account of the adulterer is in 1 Corinthians. The man that Paul refers to in 2 Corinthians 2:5-8 had a face-to-face confrontation with Paul during his short painful visit to Corinth—a visit Paul made after he wrote 1 Corinthians.

The majority of the church responded to Paul's letter by punishing the man in question. This was likely done "by excluding him from the fellowship of the Christian community in accordance with the precedent set in 1 Corinthians 5:2, 5, 13" (Hafemann, 88). Paul wants the Corinthians to move to the restoration of this man to the community. He does not want the man to become "overwhelmed by excessive sorrow" (v. 7, NIV). In addition, Paul writes, "I urge you, therefore, to reaffirm your love for him" (v. 8, NIV). By forgiving the man and reaffirming their love for him, the believers are restoring their relationship with him. J. Paul Sampley writes, "In pardoning one whom they have censured, the believers reflect their God, who, as Paul has already written eloquently in chap. 1, comforts and consoles those who suffer." ("The Second Letter to the Corinthians" in *The New Interpreter's Bible*, Vol. 11 [Nashville: Abingdon Press, 2000], 53).

III. A TEST OF OBEDIENCE (2 CORINTHIANS 2:9-11)

In verse nine, Paul writes, "The reason I wrote you was to see if you would stand the test and be obedient in everything" (NIV). When Paul wrote the other letter, he did not know how the church would respond. He could make another painful visit, but he decided that writing a letter was the better choice. The Corinthians responded in a way that was appropriate for addressing the conflict, but now they need further direction. He had not written the letter to simply vent his feelings about the confrontation with the man. As stated earlier, Paul was disappointed that the believers did not support him. However, Paul is more concerned about the effects on the church than he is about his personal feelings. Regardless of all the hurt feelings

that might have arisen due to Paul's letter, he was encouraged by the response that the church made to his letter. The church was improving.

After Paul expresses his pleasure in how they have responded to his letter, he returns to the matter of forgiving the man who has caused the church to grieve. Paul encourages the church to forgive the man, and he shows his solidarity with the church members by telling them that he forgives the man also. His statement, "I have forgiven in the sight of Christ" (v. 10, NIV), has been interpreted differently among scholars. Suffice it to say that Paul is confident that Christ knows that Paul's willingness to forgive the man is sincere. If he does what is right in the eyes of Christ, the church will benefit because all parties agree with Jesus' command that we forgive each other (see Matt. 6:12-15).

THE LESSON APPLIED

Division can easily creep into the life of a congregation through conflict and sin when these things are ignored. It is the responsibility of the church—the community of faith—to address sin and conflict when it arises in the life of the congregation. In *Life Together*, Dietrich Bonhoeffer addresses the obligation of one Christian to another in the community to address sin. "When another Christian falls into obvious sin, an admonition is imperative, because God's Word demands it" (Dietrich Bonhoeffer, *Life Together*, Daniel Bloesch and James Burtness, trans. [Minneapolis: Fortress, 2005], 105). This was the problem that arose in the Corinthian church. We have seen before that the Corinthians failed to address sin when it came into their midst (see 1 Cor. 5:1-8). They also failed to address conflict by not coming to Paul's defense when another man verbally assaulted him. In a later letter, Paul then asked them to address this situation, and they responded by disciplining the man. "The practice of discipline in the community of faith begins with friends who are close to one another. Words of admonition and reproach must be risked when a lapse from God's Word in doctrine or life endangers a community that lives together, and with it the whole community of faith" (Bonhoeffer, 105). What was at stake if the Corinthians had not responded appropriately to this situation was the continuing life of the community. In disciplining the man and restoring him, the Corinthians practice community discipline in a way that sustains the life of the church.

The members' love for each other was threatened in the church in Corinth. We learn that love can be secured if the church is willing to address the wrong. The church must be obedient to Christ in all things. This means that the church must be willing to discipline wrongdoers when needed. The goal of church discipline is not to destroy someone; rather, it is to help the offender correct his or her wrong. The church must be willing to forgive and restore the guilty party to the fellowship. If the church is unwilling to discipline, forgive, and restore, it leaves open a door of opportunity for Satan to divide the church.

LET'S TALK ABOUT IT

1. What is meant by forgiveness, and what is its purpose?

Forgiveness is a difficult practice to address. It is often confused by the proverb "Forgive and forget." This proverb, however, has no root in Christian thinking. Forgiveness has nothing to do with forgetting because forgetting fails to address that a wrong has been done. In Christian thought, the proverb could be "Forgive and restore," or "Forgive and reconcile." In forgiveness between individuals, both the offender and the offended are transformed (forgiveness does not transform God because being forgiving is part of the nature of God). God's grace enters the act of forgiveness. The offended forgives and remembers that he or she has been shown the grace of God's forgiveness from the beginning. The offender receives forgiveness, and the burden is lifted from him or her. In forgiving, the disciple of Christ does not forget but remembers the gift of grace in God's forgiveness.

HOME DAILY DEVOTIONAL READINGS
AUGUST 11-17, 2014

MONDAY	TUESDAY	WEDNESDAY	THURSDAY	FRIDAY	SATURDAY	SUNDAY
Enduring Troubles and Calamities	Finding Grace in the Wilderness	Sharing Christ's Sufferings and Glory	Standing Fast in God's True Grace	Walking in Truth and Love	Waiting for the Lord's Mercy	Proclaiming Jesus Christ As Lord
Psalm 71:17-24	Jeremiah 31:1-6	1 Peter 4:12-19	1 Peter 5:8-14	2 John 1-9	Jude 17-25	2 Corinthians 4:2-15

TREASURE IN CLAY JARS

ADULT TOPIC: BACKGROUND SCRIPTURE:
DOWN BUT NOT OUT   2 CORINTHIANS 4:2-15

2 CORINTHIANS 4:2-15

King James Version

BUT have renounced the hidden things of dishonesty, not walking in craftiness, nor handling the word of God deceitfully; but by manifestation of the truth commending ourselves to every man's conscience in the sight of God.

3 But if our gospel be hid, it is hid to them that are lost:

4 In whom the god of this world hath blinded the minds of them which believe not, lest the light of the glorious gospel of Christ, who is the image of God, should shine unto them.

5 For we preach not ourselves, but Christ Jesus the Lord; and ourselves your servants for Jesus' sake.

6 For God, who commanded the light to shine out of darkness, hath shined in our hearts, to give the light of the knowledge of the glory of God in the face of Jesus Christ.

7 But we have this treasure in earthen vessels, that the excellency of the power may be of God, and not of us.

8 We are troubled on every side, yet not distressed; we are perplexed, but not in despair;

9 Persecuted, but not forsaken; cast down, but not destroyed;

10 Always bearing about in the body the dying of the Lord Jesus, that the life also of Jesus might be made manifest in our body.

11 For we which live are always delivered unto death for Jesus' sake, that the life also of Jesus might be made manifest in our mortal flesh.

12 So then death worketh in us, but life in you.

New Revised Standard Version

WE have renounced the shameful things that one hides; we refuse to practice cunning or to falsify God's word; but by the open statement of the truth we commend ourselves to the conscience of everyone in the sight of God.

3 And even if our gospel is veiled, it is veiled to those who are perishing.

4 In their case the god of this world has blinded the minds of the unbelievers, to keep them from seeing the light of the gospel of the glory of Christ, who is the image of God.

5 For we do not proclaim ourselves; we proclaim Jesus Christ as Lord and ourselves as your slaves for Jesus' sake.

6 For it is the God who said, "Let light shine out of darkness," who has shone in our hearts to give the light of the knowledge of the glory of God in the face of Jesus Christ.

7 But we have this treasure in clay jars, so that it may be made clear that this extraordinary power belongs to God and does not come from us.

8 We are afflicted in every way, but not crushed; perplexed, but not driven to despair;

9 persecuted, but not forsaken; struck down, but not destroyed;

10 always carrying in the body the death of Jesus, so that the life of Jesus may also be made visible in our bodies.

11 For while we live, we are always being given up to death for Jesus' sake, so that the life of Jesus may be made visible in our mortal flesh.

12 So death is at work in us, but life in you.

MAIN THOUGHT: We are troubled on every side, yet not distressed; we are perplexed, but not in despair; persecuted, but not forsaken; cast down, but not destroyed. (2 Corinthians 4:8-9, KJV)

2 CORINTHIANS 4:2-15

King James Version

13 We having the same spirit of faith, according as it is written, I believed, and therefore have I spoken; we also believe, and therefore speak;

14 Knowing that he which raised up the Lord Jesus shall raise up us also by Jesus, and shall present us with you.

15 For all things are for your sakes, that the abundant grace might through the thanksgiving of many redound to the glory of God.

New Revised Standard Version

13 But just as we have the same spirit of faith that is in accordance with scripture—"I believed, and so I spoke"—we also believe, and so we speak,

14 because we know that the one who raised the Lord Jesus will raise us also with Jesus, and will bring us with you into his presence.

15 Yes, everything is for your sake, so that grace, as it extends to more and more people, may increase thanksgiving, to the glory of God.

LESSON SETTING

Time: A.D. 55-57
Place: Corinth

LESSON OUTLINE

I. **The Integrity in Paul's Preaching (2 Corinthians 4:2-6)**
II. **The Power in Paul's Preaching (2 Corinthians 4:7-12)**
III. **The Faith in Paul's Preaching (2 Corinthians 4:13-15)**

UNIFYING PRINCIPLE

People in communities rely on one another for protection and continuity of life. Where does the ability to protect and continue the community come from? Paul reminded the Corinthians that the extraordinary power to proclaim Jesus in the face of adversity is a treasure that comes from God through Jesus Christ.

INTRODUCTION

After discussing the one who confronted him in Corinth and the need for him to be restored, Paul briefly discusses his trip "to Troas to proclaim the good news of Christ" (2 Cor. 2:12, NRSV). There was an opportunity for Paul's work to continue, but he was anxious because Titus was not there. This anxiety was likely due to the fact that it was Titus who had delivered the "painful letter" to the Corinthians, and Paul was waiting to hear a report on the situation from him. Thus, he left Troas and went on to Macedonia. Paul discusses the report from Titus in 2 Corinthians 7:2-15.

In chapter three, Paul is making two parallel arguments. The first concerns how Paul vindicates himself before others. Instead of relying on a letter of recommendation to or from the Corinthians, Paul argues that the Corinthians are his letter of recommendation, "written not with ink but with the Spirit of the living God, not on tablets of stone but on tablets of human hearts" (2 Cor. 3:3, NRSV). The letter of recommendation the Corinthians embody is that of a faithful life in Christ.

Paul goes on to contrast living by the dead letter of stone to the living letter animated by the Spirit—"Now if the ministry of death, chiseled in letters on stone tablets, came in glory so that the people of Israel could not gaze at Moses' face because of the glory of his face, a glory now set aside, how much more will the ministry of the Spirit come in glory?" (vv. 7-8, NRSV). Too often, readers address this text and see Paul's setting in opposition the Law of the Old Testament and the New Covenant in Jesus Christ. While there is some element of that present here, the key argument Paul is making concerns what drives the heart of the faithful. Paul is arguing that those who only look to the letter of the Law fail to see the glory and true potential of the Law when it is written on hearts and animated by the Spirit. Paul is not trying to argue for less than the Law but a life that goes beyond the Law in living faithfully by the Spirit of the Lord. This is why the Corinthian church is a living letter of recommendation for Paul. The people are seeking to live in a way that embodies faithfulness to the Spirit of God.

EXPOSITION

I. THE INTEGRITY IN PAUL'S PREACHING
(2 CORINTHIANS 4:2-6)

Paul begins chapter four thankful for the ministry shared by him and his companions. They have this ministry because they have received it from God. Thus, Paul is blessed to preach the Gospel, not because he earned the right, but because God granted him the opportunity by calling him and commissioning him (see Acts 9:15). Paul is confident that God called him to preach, and it is for this reason that he does not lose heart. In spite of his afflictions, he continues for Christ's sake. He is not deterred even if he is accepted by some and rejected by others.

In verse two, Paul alludes to those whom he mentioned before who "peddle the word of God for profit" (2:17, NIV). He claims that his preaching has integrity by saying "we have renounced secret and shameful ways; we do not use deception, nor do we distort the word of God" (4:2, NIV). Paul's claim is that the integrity of his and his companions' ministry requires them to be true to the Word of God. There is no need to distort or use deceptive or cunning ways as those who follow after "the god of this age" (v. 4, NIV).

Paul and his companions are open in their approach to the Corinthian believers and do not dress the Gospel they have been given in fancy clothes that distort its true meaning. They do not hide behind clever turns of phrase, but speak truthfully concerning the nature of the Gospel. This sets them in contrast to the false teachers in Corinth who teach out of selfish ambition. The goal of Paul's preaching is to commend himself to "every man's conscience in the sight of God" (v. 2, NIV). "Conscience and mind are the human capacities that people must use in moral reasoning as they deliberate how they should live their lives, and in this case as they weigh out how, as Paul hopes for it, they ought to reaffirm their relation to him as the one who has faithfully and truthfully brought them the gospel" (J. Paul Sampley, "The Second Letter to the Corinthians," in *The New Interpreter's Bible*, Vol. 11 [Nashville: Abingdon Press, 2000], 74).

Paul understands that in Corinth some are disappointed in him. They do not understand his message that Jesus Christ is the Messiah. Paul admits that the Gospel is being hidden from some who hear it. Their inability to understand the message is not due to a lack of mental ability; instead, "the god of this age has blinded the minds of unbelievers, so that they cannot see the light of the gospel of the glory of Christ, who is the image of God" (v. 4, NIV). Sampley writes: "Whatever is at the center of our lives, whatever governs our decisions and bears on all our actions—that is our god, our true lord [i.e., the god of this age].... Modern gods/lords that bid for our fealty are legion: job, status, money, happiness, acceptance, and you fill in the blank. Even good things, when our desire for them gets out of proportion, can assume lordship over us and become a 'god of this age'" (79).

Paul writes with the awareness that his motives are being questioned by some in the church. He wants them to know that the Gospel that he preaches is not about what is beneficial to him. The Gospel that he preaches is about Jesus Christ who is our Lord. Paul understands that he is a servant of the church. He preaches the Gospel for the sake of the church, not his own glory.

In verse six, Paul speaks about Jesus Christ being the light of God. The word *light* is used as a metaphor for knowledge. He refers to the creation narrative to say that the God who created the world by saying, "'Let light shine out of darkness,'" saved them and called them to preach by "[making] his light shine in [their] hearts to give [them] the light of the knowledge of the glory of God in the face of Christ" (NIV). Light enters darkness and transforms it. The true life that is embodied in the Gospel of Jesus Christ can be seen clearly as the light of Jesus Christ entering the world and reveals that the world is not as it seems. Something new is coming into

being. This new thing gives hope for the life of the world embodied in the incarnation of Jesus Christ.

II. THE POWER IN PAUL'S PREACHING (2 CORINTHIANS 4:7-12)

Paul is working against notions that the Gospel finds its power in the hands of humans. Paul has already noted that he and has companions will not resort to cunning to teach the Gospel, but that the Gospel has power because it is true and it comes from God. "Paul and his team have 'this treasure' (4:7), the 'gospel of the glory of Christ' (4:4), in the fragile pottery of human lives that display weakness (4:7). This reality, described with uncommon eloquence in 4:8-12, makes it plain that the 'extraordinary power' (4:7) of the gospel among the Corinthians and others has its source in God, not in any humans" (Michael Gorman, *Apostle of the Crucified Lord* [Grand Rapids: Eerdmans, 2004], 302). Paul does not want people to judge him based on human characteristics such as speaking ability or personality traits. The people are thinking that human characteristics are determining factors of whether or not one is an authentic apostle of Jesus Christ. For Paul, none of these things matter because all are perishing. Paul does not want the people to focus on the perishable container, the "jar of clay." They are to focus on the priceless content of the Gospel. It is the Gospel that saves humanity. Paul does not want his strained relationship with the Corinthians to hinder their belief in the Gospel.

Paul describes the treasure as having a power that is more excellent than any other power. The weakness of the perishing vessel cannot hold back the power of the Gospel. In fact, contrary to what is said about Paul and his companions, and regardless of what the false teachers are saying about Jesus, the power of the Gospel remains effective in salvation.

In verses 8-9, Paul describes the physical and psychological afflictions that he suffers as an apostle of Jesus Christ. He highlights human helplessness on the one hand with divine enablement on the other. Sampley writes, "The 'A not B' form (4:8-9) is designed to paint a picture of considerable, but not totally overwhelming, hardship. The ready conclusion is that the aforementioned 'power of God' (4:7) is what has kept the difficulties from being overwhelming so that Paul does not 'lose heart' or 'despair'" (81). Paul is not broken by the hardships that he endures because God intervenes and encourages him through all his afflictions. Paul is saying that although the believer may experience affliction, it is not as bad as it seems. Even death is not victorious over the life of the believer because Christ has overcome death.

In verses 10-11, the believers live constantly carrying life's challenges. Paul reminds the Corinthians in these two verses that they ought to live constantly reflecting upon their Christian calling. They are to be mindful of the great sacrifice Jesus made in His death for all. Paul wants them to know that his suffering is connected with the crucifixion of Jesus: "We always carry around in our body the death of Jesus, so that the life of Jesus may also be revealed in our body. For we who are alive are always being given over to death for Jesus' sake, so that his life may be revealed in our mortal body"

(vv. 10-11, NIV). Jesus died so that we might live. Paul preaches on Christ's behalf for the sake of those who hear and believe the Gospel. The suffering of those who carry the message of the Gospel reveals Jesus Christ to the world. In the same way that death could not contain Jesus, the afflictions Paul and his companions suffer cannot contain the message of Jesus.

III. THE FAITH IN PAUL'S PREACHING (2 CORINTHIANS 4:13-15)

Paul centers verse thirteen around words written by the psalmist. These can be rendered "'I believed, therefore I spoke'" (116:10). In their original context, the psalmist recounts what he said: "I believed, therefore I said 'I am greatly afflicted'" (Ps. 116:10, NIV=Ps. 115:1 LXX). Notice, though, that Paul was probably referring not to the middle of a psalm but to the first words of Psalm 115 (LXX). The quoted phrase *"episteusa, dio elalēsai"* stands at the head of a psalm, not in the middle, and is thus thematically key to it (Murray J. Harris, *The Second Epistle to the Corinthians: A Commentary on the Greek Text* [Grand Rapids: Eerdmans, 2005], 352). It seems most likely that Paul intends only for the reader to see the connection between himself and the psalmist—both believed, and therefore both spoke (ibid.).

The faith that Paul mentions leads one to act on what he or she has said. Thus, Paul's faith moves him to preach that Jesus Christ is the Messiah, God's only Son. God loves the Son, therefore, God raised Him from the dead and the grave, and those who believe this confess with their mouth and believe in their hearts that they will also be raised to be with Christ (see Rom. 10:9-10). Paul endures suffering because he is called to carry the Gospel message to all people, especially Gentiles. He also suffers on behalf of the saints in Corinth. Again, Paul seeks reconciliation and solidarity with the Corinthians because of their strained relationship.

The phrase "all this is for your benefit" (2 Cor. 4:15, NIV) could refer to God's acts of grace in salvation. It could also indicate the afflictions that Paul endures to preach the Gospel, especially to the Corinthians. Either reading is acceptable since the *telos* is "so that the grace that is reaching more and more people may cause thanksgiving to overflow to the glory of God" (v. 15, NIV). God extends grace, and human life is changed. The transformation of human life leads to the glorification of God.

THE LESSON APPLIED

It was God who took the initiative to save human beings. God sent His Son in the form of human flesh. Jesus is the light that gives us knowledge of God's love, demonstrated in His grace and mercy. The light shines in the darkness of our lives so that we become aware of the evil and sin in our lives.

This lesson also reminds us that the Christian's journey is accompanied by suffering. Sometimes, suffering is caused by conflicts that exist among believers. Paul teaches us that conflicts among Christians cannot prevent the spread of the Gospel. We are reminded that God's grace moves us to forgiveness and reconciliation.

In their suffering, believers bear the marks of the crucified Jesus (see Paul's experience in particular in Gal. 6:17). This bears not simply a verbal witness, but a visual witness to the risen Savior. Throughout the centuries, Christians have been willing to suffer and die for the faith because of the hope they have in God's glorious future.

LET'S TALK ABOUT IT

1. **Who is "the god of this age" (v. 4, NIV)?**

The god of this age is not readily recognized. In the American church, Christians have often become acculturated to the ways of the nation so thoroughly that we are not able to see how the god of this age has ensnared us. Churches have often accepted the tenets of American civil religion in a way that compromises the ability to faithfully witness to our Lord Jesus Christ. Instead, we conflate American values with Christian teaching in a way that inhibits our ability to speak truthfully concerning the nature of Christian discipleship.

HOME DAILY DEVOTIONAL READINGS
AUGUST 18-24, 2014

MONDAY	TUESDAY	WEDNESDAY	THURSDAY	FRIDAY	SATURDAY	SUNDAY
A Failed Attempt at Reconciliation	Reconciled to God Through Christ	Making Peace Through the Cross	The Ministry and Message of Reconciliation	A Harvest of Righteousness	First Be Reconciled	Open Wide Your Hearts
Acts 7:23-28	Romans 5:6-11	Colossians 1:15-23	2 Corinthians 5:16-21	James 3:13-18	Matthew 5:21-26	2 Corinthians 6:1-13; 7:2-4

AN APPEAL FOR RECONCILIATION

ADULT TOPIC: ADDRESSING TENSIONS	BACKGROUND SCRIPTURES: 2 CORINTHIANS 6:1—7:4

2 CORINTHIANS 6:1-13; 7:2-4

King James Version	*New Revised Standard Version*
WE then, as workers together with him, beseech you also that ye receive not the grace of God in vain.	AS we work together with him, we urge you also not to accept the grace of God in vain.
2 (For he saith, I have heard thee in a time accepted, and in the day of salvation have I succoured thee: behold, now is the accepted time; behold, now is the day of salvation.)	2 For he says, "At an acceptable time I have listened to you, and on a day of salvation I have helped you." See, now is the acceptable time; see, now is the day of salvation!
3 Giving no offence in any thing, that the ministry be not blamed:	3 We are putting no obstacle in anyone's way, so that no fault may be found with our ministry,
4 But in all things approving ourselves as the ministers of God, in much patience, in afflictions, in necessities, in distresses,	4 but as servants of God we have commended ourselves in every way: through great endurance, in afflictions, hardships, calamities,
5 In stripes, in imprisonments, in tumults, in labours, in watchings, in fastings;	5 beatings, imprisonments, riots, labors, sleepless nights, hunger;
6 By pureness, by knowledge, by longsuffering, by kindness, by the Holy Ghost, by love unfeigned,	6 by purity, knowledge, patience, kindness, holiness of spirit, genuine love,
7 By the word of truth, by the power of God, by the armour of righteousness on the right hand and on the left,	7 truthful speech, and the power of God; with the weapons of righteousness for the right hand and for the left;
8 By honour and dishonour, by evil report and good report: as deceivers, and yet true;	8 in honor and dishonor, in ill repute and good repute. We are treated as impostors, and yet are true;
9 As unknown, and yet well known; as dying, and, behold, we live; as chastened, and not killed;	9 as unknown, and yet are well known; as dying, and see—we are alive; as punished, and yet not killed;
10 As sorrowful, yet alway rejoicing; as poor, yet making many rich; as having nothing, and yet possessing all things.	10 as sorrowful, yet always rejoicing; as poor, yet making many rich; as having nothing, and yet possessing everything.
11 O ye Corinthians, our mouth is open unto you, our heart is enlarged.	11 We have spoken frankly to you Corinthians; our heart is wide open to you.
12 Ye are not straitened in us, but ye are straitened in your own bowels.	12 There is no restriction in our affections, but only in yours.

MAIN THOUGHT: Receive us; we have wronged no man, we have corrupted no man, we have defrauded no man. (2 Corinthians 7:2, KJV)

2 CORINTHIANS 6:1-13; 7:2-4

King James Version

13 Now for a recompence in the same, (I speak as unto my children,) be ye also enlarged.

• • • 7:2-4 • • •

RECEIVE us; we have wronged no man, we have corrupted no man, we have defrauded no man.

3 I speak not this to condemn you: for I have said before, that ye are in our hearts to die and live with you.

4 Great is my boldness of speech toward you, great is my glorying of you: I am filled with comfort, I am exceeding joyful in all our tribulation.

New Revised Standard Version

13 In return—I speak as to children—open wide your hearts also.

• • • 7:2-4 • • •

MAKE room in your hearts for us; we have wronged no one, we have corrupted no one, we have taken advantage of no one.

3 I do not say this to condemn you, for I said before that you are in our hearts, to die together and to live together.

4 I often boast about you; I have great pride in you; I am filled with consolation; I am overjoyed in all our affliction.

LESSON SETTING
Time: A.D. 55-57
Place: Corinth

LESSON OUTLINE
I. No Cheap Grace
   (2 Corinthians 6:1-2)
II. A Cruciform Witness
   (2 Corinthians 6:3-10)
III. Paul Desires Reconciliation
   (2 Corinthians 6:11-13, 7:2-4)

UNIFYING PRINCIPLE

Sometimes the community may ignore the good done by a great leader and may become estranged from the leader. What must be done to end separation of a community from its leaders? Paul reminded the Corinthians of all he had done for the sake of Jesus Christ, and, based on that testimony, he asks that they be reconciled to him.

INTRODUCTION

Paul is in the midst of an extended discourse in which he defends his ministry, and part of his defense is rooted in the suffering he has endured. There are times in 2 Corinthians 4:16—5:21 when some see Paul writing as if he is setting up (or assuming) a body versus spirit dichotomy. However, this is not the case. Paul writes: "For while we are still in this tent, we groan under our burden, because we wish not to be unclothed but to be further clothed, so that what is mortal may be swallowed up by life" (2 Cor. 5:4, NRSV). Paul is contrasting the body marked by death and the resurrection body marked by life. "In biblical thought … the body is never considered evil. Paul looks forward to dismantling this tent only so that he can assume the **building** from God, the new body" (James Thompson, *The Second Letter of Paul to The Corinthians* [Austin: R.B. Sweet Co., 1970], 72, emphasis in original). The frailty of the body marked by death is its susceptibility to persecution, but this does not deter Paul. He lives and ministers in anticipation of the resurrection body. This will be important to consider as we discuss 2 Corinthians 6:3-10. Paul's defense of his ministry will be rooted in a grace that demands a faithful life.

EXPOSITION

I. NO CHEAP GRACE
(2 CORINTHIANS 6:1-2)

Paul begins chapter six by acknowledging he is not alone in the ministry. The KJV and the NRSV add "with him" to their translations. Although "with him" is not present in the original Greek, it is an appropriate emendation here as Paul is explaining that his ministry comes from Christ. "Paul has said that he was God's ambassador and that God was making his appeal through him. Because Paul is **working together** with God, he can make the exhortations which follow" (Thompson, 84). It also follows logically that Paul would consider the Corinthian church his fellow workers, although the context indicates Paul is referring here to working together with God. Paul has written throughout the letter in such a way as to demonstrate to the Corinthians that they share in his trials, consolation, and ministry.

Paul urges them not to receive God's grace in vain. "Although grace is free and salvation cannot be earned, there is always the response to God's **grace** which is important. It is possible that one who is saved by **grace** will see the abundance of God's **grace** and therefore conclude that grace is cheap" (Thompson, 84). When the grace of God is taken in vain, it cheapens the gift of life given by Jesus Christ in His incarnation, crucifixion, and resurrection. Dietrich Bonhoeffer wrote on the differences between "cheap grace" and "costly grace": "Cheap grace is the preaching of forgiveness without requiring repentance, baptism without church discipline, Communion without confession, absolution without personal confession. Cheap grace is grace without discipleship, grace without the cross, grace without Jesus Christ, living and incarnate" (*The Cost of Discipleship*, R. H. Fuller, trans. [New York: Touchstone, 1995], 44-45). Cheap grace—grace taken in vain—is grace that does not see that it costs something to follow Jesus. Paul wants the Corinthians to know the gift of grace given through the life and death of Jesus will cost them something. We will see below that this grace is costly for Paul. Bonhoeffer writes further on costly grace: "Above all, it is *costly* because it cost God the life of his Son: 'ye were bought at a price,' and what has cost God much cannot be cheap for us. Above all, it is *grace* because God did not reckon his Son too dear a price to pay for our life, but delivered him up for us. Costly grace is the Incarnation of God" (45; emphasis in original).

II. A CRUCIFORM WITNESS
(2 CORINTHIANS 6:3-10)

Paul now moves to a clear attempt to vindicate his ministry before the Corinthians. "Paul and his coworkers are once again 'commending' themselves only insofar as they are cruciform slaves of God in Christ for the sake of others" (Michael Gorman, *Apostle of the Crucified Lord* [Grand Rapids: Eerdmans, 2004], 308). Paul can commend his ministry because it embodies what he proclaims. Paul's vindication of his ministry is not rooted in clever speech or meaningless sophistry. It is instead rooted in a life that endures on behalf of and through the power of the Gospel. So Paul uses three categories that he has used throughout the letter to bolster his claims: "cruciformity (being afflicted), integrity (not peddling the word of God), and paradox (life in death)" (ibid.).

He begins his list by first describing the hardships he and his companions have endured for the sake of the Gospel. This is what Gorman describes as cruciformity in Paul's letters. For Paul, cruciformity—which "literally means 'in the shape of a cross,' but it can be used metaphorically" (Gorman, 118-119)—reveals the nature of God. "We learn from Paul that the cross of Christ is not only *initiated* by God, it *reveals* God. Christ crucified is the power and wisdom of God" (ibid., emphasis in original; see also 1 Cor. 1:18-25). This nature of God revealed in Christ reveals also the shape of the community God desires. The community will be shaped not only by the words spoken of the Gospel, but by the lives of those who proclaim the Gospel. This is why Paul points to his cruciform life as a defense of the Gospel he proclaims. In a life that is willing to accept both blessing and persecution, the Gospel of the crucified and risen Savior can be proclaimed faithfully. The clever words of Paul's opponents and the easy life they describe bears no resemblance to the Gospel proclaimed in the life and death of Jesus Christ.

He then moves on to describe the virtues that commend him and his companions and allow them to endure various hardships in defense of the Gospel. It is worth noting that what defines how Paul and his coworkers respond to the persecution they have endured is not that they respond in kind, nor do they complain. They respond "by purity, knowledge, patience, kindness, holiness of spirit, genuine love, truthful speech, and the power of God" (2 Cor. 6:6-7, NRSV). Paul describes these as "the weapons of righteousness" which they use to respond to those who afflict them (v. 7, NRSV). These are not what the world would see as weapons, and they are not means of violence. Responding to persecution with violence would run counter to Paul's claim of cruciformity demonstrated through the various persecutions he has endured. In responding to persecution and affliction in unexpected ways, Paul embodies the Gospel Christ proclaims through His life and, particularly, through His crucifixion. Through imitation of the life of Christ, Paul demonstrates that God reveals the various persecutions to be powerless. These persecutions will ultimately be defeated by the world that is coming into existence through the life, death, and resurrection of Jesus Christ.

In verses 8-10, Paul lists nine pairs of paradoxes that are identified by their contrasting responses. He wants the Corinthians to know that the world is not as it appears. He begins by identifying two contrasting ways that others view his ministry—in "honor and dishonor" (v. 8, NRSV)—and he ends this series with the paradox "as having nothing, and yet possessing everything" (v. 10, NRSV). The last two paradoxes are worth noting as they foreshadow the appeal Paul will make concerning the collection, which is rooted in the example of the Macedonians—"as poor, yet making many rich; as having nothing, and yet possessing everything" (v. 10, NRSV). Paul's appeal to the Corinthians to give is at work behind the scenes throughout much of this letter, but he does not want them to give simply for the sake of giving (the explicit appeal to give will be discussed in the next lesson). Paul is hoping for reconciliation before any type of giving takes place. "Paul hopes the Corinthians will not only embrace him fully for embracing this way of life, but also that they, too, will embrace this life for themselves by giving generously to the collection for Jerusalem. Such generosity would be a symbolic gesture of many things, including the Corinthians' reconciliation with Paul and his ministry" (Gorman 308).

III. PAUL DESIRES RECONCILIATION (2 CORINTHIANS 6:11-13; 7:2-4)

Gorman notes that throughout 2 Corinthians Paul uses images creatively, and in this section, Paul uses bodily imagery: "three body parts are mentioned in these verses: mouth, heart, and bowels (*ta splanchna*, one of the sources of affection in antiquity), each referred to as either 'open' or 'constricted'" (Gorman, 309). English translations often fail to capture these images, preferring to give a sense of the words rather than a more literal rendering. For instance, in 2 Corinthians 6:11, the NRSV translates "open mouths" as "spoken frankly" while maintaining the translation of "open heart" in "our heart is wide open to you." By contrast, the KJV maintains the bodily imagery throughout 6:11-13, saying "our mouth is open … our heart is enlarged … but ye are straitened in your own bowels" (vv. 11-12), which gives a clearer view of what Paul is doing in this passage.

The final image, that of the bowels, is the most striking. "As for the Corinthians, however, Paul finds them constricted in the bowels (6:12b; NRSV's bland rendering is 'but [there is restriction] only in yours'— i.e., in your affection). The Corinthians have emotional cramps, and it is time for them to 'open up' (6:13; the word 'hearts' that appears in NRSV and NIV is absent from the Greek)" (Gorman, 309). Paul uses this vivid imagery to move the Corinthians away from being closed off from Paul. Paul believes this restriction in their bowels, this restriction in their affection, is harmful to them, and they must move beyond it in order to survive.

A brief word should be said about 2 Corinthians 6:14—7:1. Though some would argue that these verses are interlopers, either from a Pauline letter we do not have or from another writer entirely, "a growing number of interpreters find that this text is thoroughly Pauline, that it has a rhetorical function within the letter as a whole, and that the text belongs where it is because Paul put it there" (310). The verses describe people who would oppose righteousness and light (see 6:14) and could thus be labeled false teachers. As such, this text clarifies the kind of people Paul claims he and his fellow ministers are not (see 7:2). These false teachers have consistently undermined Paul's relationship with the Corinthian church, so he now requests that the Corinthians no longer share in fellowship with them. This allows Paul to return to his plea for the Corinthians to be open in their affections with him.

This interpretation of 2 Corinthians 6:14—7:1 helps in interpreting 7:2-4 by suggesting that it may be the false teachers who prevent the Corinthians from sharing in fellowship with Paul and his coworkers. These false teachers create barriers and cause the Corinthians to stray from their commitment to the Gospel. On the other hand, Paul and his coworkers "have wronged no one … have corrupted no one … [and] have taken advantage of no one" (7:2, NRSV). "The conclusion of the appeal for reconciliation exudes Paul's consolation and confidence regarding the Corinthians. Inviting them to 'make room' for himself and his coworkers (7:2), Paul stresses once again his integrity, his love for the Corinthians, and his pride in them (7:2-4)" (Gorman, 311). Paul demonstrates his certainty that the Corinthians will respond favorably to his exhortations. He does not condemn them but is confident in their ability to live faithfully. He will see this embodied in how the Corinthians receive Titus, and this will make him certain that his appeal for them to give will bear fruit.

THE LESSON APPLIED

Paul often suffers at the hands of interpreters and translators. There are several examples of this in today's passage. The first instance is seen in the attempt to soften Paul's use of bodily imagery. While the KJV maintains the bodily imagery, the modern translations have often translated in such a way as to make it, as Gorman says above, bland. This does not mean that these translations have altered the meaning of Paul, but they have diminished his effect. The second instance comes about through trying to parse Paul's letters so narrowly—as seen in the questions

concerning 2 Corinthians 6:14—7:1—that the overall effect of Paul's rhetorical style is missed. Paul demands a higher standard of his audience because he is committed to a life of cruciform discipleship before Christ. In order to elicit a faithful response from his readers, he will use strong visual imagery and will make radical demands.

LET'S TALK ABOUT IT

1. How do we avoid making grace cheap?

The Apostle Paul urges the believers living in Corinth "not to accept the grace of God in vain" (2 Cor. 6:1, NRSV). Throughout the following defense of his ministry, Paul demonstrates what it means not to cheapen the grace of God. The acceptance of God's grace allows His grace to make certain demands of us. Having the grace of God means that we will not be left alone when trying to live up to those demands. The life we are called to in the grace of God is a life of faithful discipleship. This means that we are called to risk everything for the sake of God. This can only be embodied in a community which is willing to question the world as it is and live in the way God created the world to be. This is seen in the self-emptying love of Jesus' incarnation and crucifixion, and this is continued in the witnesses who have borne the marks of Jesus' suffering throughout the centuries.

HOME DAILY DEVOTIONAL READINGS
AUGUST 25-31, 2014

MONDAY	TUESDAY	WEDNESDAY	THURSDAY	FRIDAY	SATURDAY	SUNDAY
Treasure in Heaven	The Measure of Your Gift	Giving in Love	Show Proof of Your Love	Sowing and Reaping Bountifully	God Loves a Cheerful Giver	A Wealth of Generosity
Mark 10:17-27	Luke 6:34-38	1 Corinthians 13:1-7	2 Corinthians 8:16-24	2 Corinthians 9:1-6	2 Corinthians 9:7-15	2 Corinthians 8:1-14

A COMMUNITY SHARES ITS RESOURCES

ADULT TOPIC: GIVING TO OTHERS	BACKGROUND SCRIPTURES: 2 CORINTHIANS 8—9

2 CORINTHIANS 8:1-14

King James Version

MOREOVER, brethren, we do you to wit of the grace of God bestowed on the churches of Macedonia;

2 How that in a great trial of affliction the abundance of their joy and their deep poverty abounded unto the riches of their liberality.

3 For to their power, I bear record, yea, and beyond their power they were willing of themselves;

4 Praying us with much intreaty that we would receive the gift, and take upon us the fellowship of the ministering to the saints.

5 And this they did, not as we hoped, but first gave their own selves to the Lord, and unto us by the will of God.

6 Insomuch that we desired Titus, that as he had begun, so he would also finish in you the same grace also.

7 Therefore, as ye abound in every thing, in faith, and utterance, and knowledge, and in all diligence, and in your love to us, see that ye abound in this grace also.

8 I speak not by commandment, but by occasion of the forwardness of others, and to prove the sincerity of your love.

9 For ye know the grace of our Lord Jesus Christ, that, though he was rich, yet for your sakes he became poor, that ye through his poverty might be rich.

10 And herein I give my advice: for this is expedient for you, who have begun before, not only to do, but also to be forward a year ago.

New Revised Standard Version

WE want you to know, brothers and sisters, about the grace of God that has been granted to the churches of Macedonia;

2 for during a severe ordeal of affliction, their abundant joy and their extreme poverty have overflowed in a wealth of generosity on their part.

3 For, as I can testify, they voluntarily gave according to their means, and even beyond their means,

4 begging us earnestly for the privilege of sharing in this ministry to the saints—

5 and this, not merely as we expected; they gave themselves first to the Lord and, by the will of God, to us,

6 so that we might urge Titus that, as he had already made a beginning, so he should also complete this generous undertaking among you.

7 Now as you excel in everything—in faith, in speech, in knowledge, in utmost eagerness, and in our love for you—so we want you to excel also in this generous undertaking.

8 I do not say this as a command, but I am testing the genuineness of your love against the earnestness of others.

9 For you know the generous act of our Lord Jesus Christ, that though he was rich, yet for your sakes he became poor, so that by his poverty you might become rich.

10 And in this matter I am giving my advice: it is appropriate for you who began last year not only to do something but even to desire to do something—

MAIN THOUGHT: Therefore, as ye abound in every thing, in faith, and utterance, and knowledge, and in all diligence, and in your love to us, see that ye abound in this grace also. (2 Corinthians 8:7, KJV)

2 Corinthians 8:1-14

King James Version	*New Revised Standard Version*
11 Now therefore perform the doing of it; that as there was a readiness to will, so there may be a performance also out of that which ye have.	11 now finish doing it, so that your eagerness may be matched by completing it according to your means.
12 For if there be first a willing mind, it is accepted according to that a man hath, and not according to that he hath not.	12 For if the eagerness is there, the gift is acceptable according to what one has—not according to what one does not have.
13 For I mean not that other men be eased, and ye burdened:	13 I do not mean that there should be relief for others and pressure on you, but it is a question of a fair balance between
14 But by an equality, that now at this time your abundance may be a supply for their want, that their abundance also may be a supply for your want: that there may be equality.	14 your present abundance and their need, so that their abundance may be for your need, in order that there may be a fair balance.

LESSON SETTING
Time: A.D. 55-57
Place: Corinth

LESSON OUTLINE
I. The Macedonians' Generosity
   (2 Corinthians 8:1-7)
II. The Character of Giving
    (2 Corinthians 8:8-14)

UNIFYING PRINCIPLE

A small community that possesses much may be part of a larger community that has little and needs the smaller community's assistance. How are members of a community to support one another? Paul reminds the Corinthians that they are part of a larger faith community and that as others have been generous to them, they should repay with equal generosity.

INTRODUCTION

In 2 Corinthians 7, Paul tells how Titus came to Macedonia and reported to Paul that the church in Corinth was doing well. Paul and his companions had anxiously awaited Titus' report and were consoled by his arrival. Paul demonstrates his love and care for the Corinthian congregation throughout his description of Titus' arrival and report. Paul discloses that he both does and does not regret the letter he sent earlier to the Corinthians. He does not regret the letter because it has led to the Corinthians' repentance. But he also regrets the letter because it grieved them. Knowing that this grief has brought the Corinthians to repentance, however, has put Paul's mind at ease. Paul also shares that he is joyful about the way Titus was received by the Corinthians because it confirms Paul's "boasting" about them (v. 14, NRSV). Paul now turns to his request for the Corinthians to give.

EXPOSITION

I. THE MACEDONIANS' GENEROSITY (2 CORINTHIANS 8:1-7)

Paul writes of "the grace of God that has been granted to the churches of Macedonia" (2 Cor. 8:1, NRSV). The contrast Paul sets forth in this section furthers his discussion of the relationship between his ministry and suffering. He is also building on the encouragement he has given to the Corinthians in attempting to elicit the response of giving from the Corinthians. In order to encourage the practice of giving in the Corinthian church, Paul draws on the experience of the Macedonian churches. Paul describes through contrasting language the nature of the grace the Macedonians have received: "During a severe ordeal of affliction, their abundant joy and their extreme poverty have overflowed in a wealth of generosity on their part" (v. 2, NRSV). There are two pairs that Paul uses here that seemingly do not fit. The first is that in their "affliction" the Macedonians have "abundant joy." The second is that through their abundant joy and in "their extreme poverty" their giving "overflowed in a wealth of generosity." Paul uses extreme opposites to demonstrate it is through God's grace that the Macedonians are able to respond in ways that seem to run counter to their situation.

The Macedonians' ability to respond in this way also demonstrates the idea that holds together the entirety of this letter to the Corinthians. "The letter is bound together by what could be called 'apocalyptic discourse'" (Edith Humphrey, "2 Corinthians, Book of" in *Dictionary for Theological Interpretation of the Bible*, Kevin Vanhoozer, ed. [Grand Rapids: Baker, 2005], 139). Apocalyptic literature reveals to the audience that the world as it appears is not the real world. Paul desires to make it clear that in Jesus a new reality has entered the world (or, the world is becoming what God created it to be). So, for Paul, he and the Macedonian churches can be afflicted and persecuted, but he knows that these persecutors will not have the last word. The Macedonians can give abundantly, even in their poverty, because whatever they have is a gift of God and God will continue to provide. Further, for the Macedonians, this is not some health-and-wealth Gospel where they believe they will attain some great material wealth through giving. They are a people who give themselves completely to God—"they voluntarily gave according to their means, and even beyond their means, begging us earnestly for the privilege of sharing in this ministry to the saints—and this, not merely as we expected; they gave themselves first to the Lord and, by the will of God, to us" (2 Cor. 8:3-5, NRSV). The Macedonian churches are, therefore, defined by the reality that is coming into being through the life, death, and resurrection of Jesus Christ.

So now, following up on the work of Titus, Paul makes an appeal to the Corinthian church concerning giving. He builds on the foundation of what has happened in the Macedonian churches and goes on to note that the Corinthians "excel in everything—in faith, in speech, in knowledge, in utmost eagerness, and in our love for you—so we want you to excel also in this generous undertaking" (8:7, NRSV). This builds on Paul's earlier boast to Titus concerning the Corinthians' hospitality and ultimately goes back to the theme of apocalyptic discourse. Paul can make this appeal because the world has changed in Jesus Christ's incarnation, crucifixion, and resurrection. "Hence, knowledge, austerity of life, sacrifice, charitable giving, authority, and even special revelation are not ends in themselves. All are of value because of Jesus, in whom the new creation has been established so that his body grows from glory to glory (3:18)" (Humphrey, 139).

A brief note is needed about the phrase the NRSV translates "in our love for you" (v. 7). It is a difficult phrase in the Greek, and the NRSV further confuses the translation because it does not make sense to say that the Corinthians excel in Paul's love for them. James Thompson helps to clarify this awkward phrase: "[Paul] says, 'the love in you which is from us,' i.e., the love which is in you which we inspired in you by our concern for you" (*The Second Letter of Paul to The Corinthians* [Austin: R. B. Sweet, 1970], 113). Paul will appeal to this loving nature and the other virtues of the Corinthian church in making his plea for them to give.

II. THE CHARACTER OF GIVING (2 CORINTHIANS 8:8-14)

In Paul's plea for the Corinthians, he does not command them to give. Instead, he builds upon the experience of the Macedonians and the hospitable nature of the Corinthians in making his plea—"I do not say this as a command, but I am testing the genuineness of your love against the earnestness of others" (v. 8, NRSV). If we look back to the beginning of this epistle, we can see that Paul has been testing the Corinthians in their faithfulness. He was testing them in their ability to address the one who was causing strife in the church (see 2 Cor. 2:5-11) and now he is testing their love in the matter of giving. This should not be understood as an attempt by Paul to manipulate in a sinister way the life of the Corinthian church. Paul is instead at work to help form their character. He is working to form their character in their ability to address conflicts in the church in a way that builds the church up instead of destroying it. Likewise, he is at work here to form their character into a giving congregation motivated by their love for the Church universal.

Paul contextualizes this notion of giving motivated by love by pointing to Jesus. As Michael Gorman notes, "The brief narrative of Christ's love (8:9) echoes the famous hymn of Christ in Philippians 2:6-11" (*Apostle of the Crucified Lord* [Grand Rapids: Eerdmans, 2004], 315). Gorman goes on to explain the connection between Philippians and 2 Corinthians in Paul's explanation of the kenotic (self-emptying) nature of Christ's love. In Philippians 2, Paul makes his appeal to the Philippians: "Let the same mind be in you that was in Christ Jesus" (v. 5, NRSV). Paul further fleshes this out by explaining that Jesus gave up His equality with God to become human and to further humble Himself to the point of His death on the cross. In 2 Corinthians, Paul uses the same narrative, but transforms it by setting it in economic terms. This is appropriate because Paul is building on the example of the Macedonians—and in doing so, connecting the kenosis of Christ Jesus to the self-giving of the Macedonians—in making his appeal for the Corinthians to give financially (Gorman, 315).

Paul now makes it clear that he is not commanding the Corinthians to give, but exhorting them to reclaim their previous desire to give—"it is appropriate for you who began last year not only to do something but even to desire to do something—now finish doing it, so that your eagerness may be matched by completing it according to your means" (2 Cor. 8:10-11, NRSV). The conflicts that have arisen seem to have distracted the Corinthians away from their promise and desire to give. Paul is using the examples of the Macedonians and Jesus to motivate the Corinthians in the desires they once had.

At the close of today's passage, Paul makes it clear that he does not desire giving to become a burden for the Corinthians. He desires that they should give according to their means. "He is not asking them to bankrupt themselves or to give what they do not have, but merely to give to the needy out of their (relative) abundance, in order that something of a just economic equality might obtain within the churches" (Gorman, 316). Paul sees and wants the Corinthians to see that while a congregation has a responsibility to those in the congregation and the immediate locality, the congregation also has a responsibility to attend to the material and spiritual needs of those in the Church universal.

THE LESSON APPLIED

Throughout 2 Corinthians, Paul is at work to develop the character of the Corinthian church. He does this by pointing to their previous good works and desires. Paul knows that there is within the Corinthian church the ability to live communally in a life of faithful discipleship. This ability, of course, does not come from the Corinthians, but from the grace of God. In his appeal to the story of the Macedonians, Paul describes a people who are living in a way that runs counter to their circumstances. He describes this as grace as well. Far too often, grace is only thought about in terms of justification. Paul, however, is discussing grace as something that forms character. God meets His disciples in their actions with His grace to form them to be the people He intends for the life of the world.

LET'S TALK ABOUT IT

1. Is giving a means of grace?

It may be difficult to see giving as grace because it requires something of us. It also involves something as common as money. God, however, works through the common or mundane to show His grace. The Lord bestows His grace through the bread and the cup of the Lord's Supper and through the water of baptism. The Lord bestows His grace through the gathering of His people and the reading of Scripture. In giving, we give back from that with which God has blessed us. In giving, we also learn to give ourselves to the Lord. Through giving, the Lord reshapes us through His grace to fully be His people.

HOME DAILY DEVOTIONAL READINGS
SEPTEMBER 1-7, 2014

MONDAY	TUESDAY	WEDNESDAY	THURSDAY	FRIDAY	SATURDAY	SUNDAY
Act with Justice and Righteousness	Hear the Words of This Covenant	Only the Lord Will Be Exalted	Turn from Your Evil Ways	A Future with Hope	Hope for Israel's Neighbors	The Days Are Surely Coming
Jeremiah 22:1–9	Jeremiah 11:1–10	Isaiah 2:10–19	Jeremiah 18:1–10	Jeremiah 29:10–14	Jeremiah 12:14–17	Jeremiah 30:1–3, 18–22